CHINESE TRADITIONS & PRACTICES

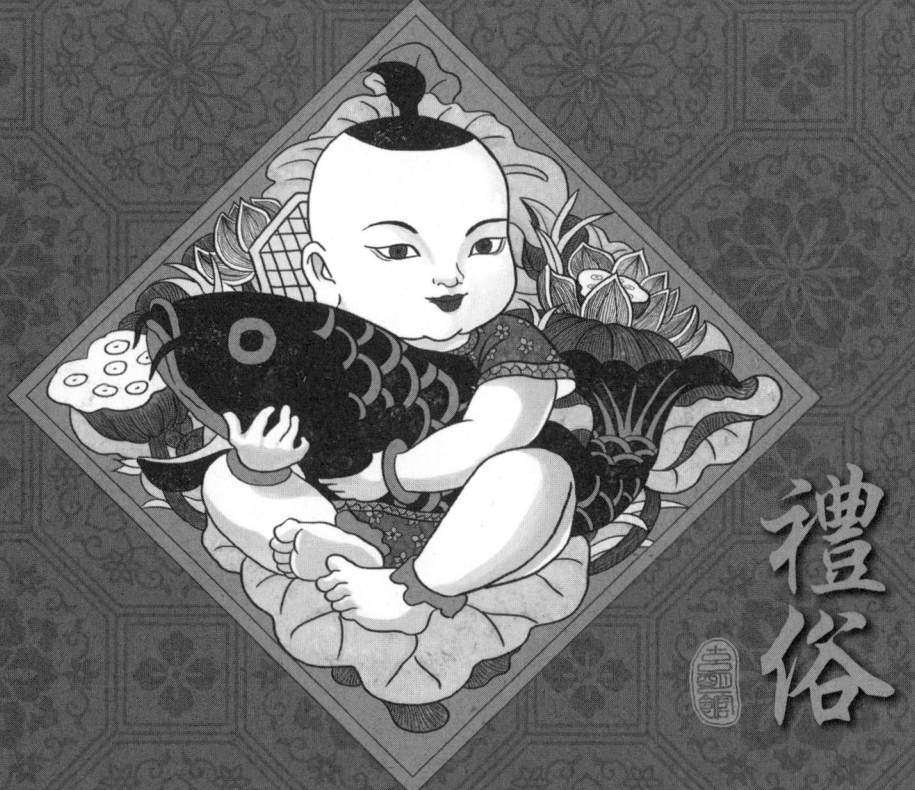

禮俗

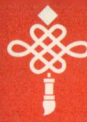

Joey Yap's
Chinese Traditions & Practices

All intellectual property rights including copyright in relation to this book belong to Joey Yap Research Group Sdn. Bhd.

No part of this book may be copied, used, subsumed, or exploited in fact, field of thought or general idea, by any other authors or persons, or be stored in a retrieval system, transmitted or reproduced in any way, including but not limited to digital copying and printing in any form whatsoever worldwide without the prior agreement and written permission of the copyright owner. Permission to use the content of this book or any part thereof must be obtained from the copyright owner. For more details, please contact:

JOEY YAP RESEARCH GROUP SDN BHD (944330-D)
19-3, The Boulevard, Mid Valley City,
59200 Kuala Lumpur, Malaysia.
Tel   : +603-2284 8080
Fax   : +603-2284 1218
Email   : info@masteryacademy.com
Website : www.masteryacademy.com

Copyright © 2017 by Joey Yap Research Group Sdn. Bhd.
All rights reserved.
First Edition October 2017

DISCLAIMER:

The author, copyright owner, and the publishers respectively have made their best efforts to produce this high quality, informative and helpful book. They have verified the technical accuracy of the information and contents of this book. However, the information contained in this book cannot replace or substitute for the services of trained professionals in any field, including, but not limited to, mental, financial, medical, psychological, or legal fields. They do not offer any professional, personal, medical, financial or legal advice and none of the information contained in the book should be confused as such advice. Any information pertaining to the events, occurrences, dates and other details relating to the person or persons, dead or alive, and to the companies have been verified to the best of their abilities based on information obtained or extracted from various websites, newspaper clippings and other public media. However, they make no representation or warranties of any kind with regard to the contents of this book and accept no liability of any kind for any losses or damages caused or alleged to be caused directly or indirectly from using the information contained herein.

INDEX

Preface 4

Introduction 7

Chapter 1:... 19
Chinese Weddings

Chapter 2:... 63
The Miracle of Conceiving A Child

Chapter 3:... 119
The Joy of Adolescence and the Rites of Adulthood

Chapter 4:... 135
Grand Banquets

Chapter 5:... 183
Houses and Homes

Chapter 6:... 217
Funeral Customs

Chapter 7:... 269
The Traditional Chinese Way of Doing Business

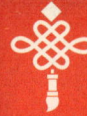

Preface

In my career as a Feng Shui practitioner, I've helped countless clients move house, plan weddings, organize funerals and more. Many of my Feng Shui clients also have an interest in Chinese history and culture at large. They often ask me questions about the customs and traditions associated with Chinese weddings, funerals, moving house and so on while consulting me on matters of Feng Shui.

Most people assume that because I know lots about Feng Shui, I know lots about Chinese cultural practices, too! This, despite the fact that Feng Shui and Chinese customs are completely different areas of study!

The questions I get are as varied as my client's needs.

Among those who need help selecting good moving dates and directions, many want to know how they can perform traditional moving rites. Clients who come to me for help choosing suitable Yin House Feng Shui for a funeral want to know about traditional funeral protocols instead.

Couples who need help choosing the right date for their wedding often ask about wedding rites so that they can incorporate traditional elements into their big day. In the same way, expectant couples who need help choosing a good date for a cesarean often want to know more about the customs of childbirth and confinement.

Of course, there is a noticeable surge of questions as Chinese New Year approaches. People are curious about its history and want to know how to celebrate it in accordance with tradition.

To address these kind of questions and offer extra value to my clients, I have spent a lot of time over the years studying Chinese traditions and cultural practices. I now know the stories behind many cultural practices, and the do's and don'ts associated with them. This gives me the confidence to answer many of my client's questions on the subject. Recently, I had the idea of organizing and compiling my knowledge into this series of books so that I could share what I have learned with a much wider audience and play a part in keeping Chinese traditions alive.

Contrary to popular belief, Feng Shui has very little to do with any Chinese customs. Ignoring them has no impact on one's Feng Shui compliance. In the final analysis, Feng Shui is the science of Qi (energy) management in the environment. Customs merely help one live in a certain way and as such they have no impact on Qi Flow. You can observe customs and tradition without any thought for its impact on your Feng Shui.

With all that being said, customs and traditions are the true bedrock of a country's culture. Learning about Chinese culture will enrich your understanding and give you plenty to talk about during family gatherings. It also makes for fascinating reading matter!

It is my hope that this book will finally give my Feng Shui students and clients the answers to their many questions about Chinese customs and cultural practices and provide you, the reader, with a compelling and educational read.

Warmest Regards,

Dato' Joey Yap
New York, October 2017

Connect with us:

www.joeyyap.com   JOEYYAP TV www.joeyyap.tv

@DatoJoeyYap   @DJoeyYap   @JoeyYap

Academy website:
www.masteryacademy.com | jya.masteryacademy.com | www.baziprofiling.com

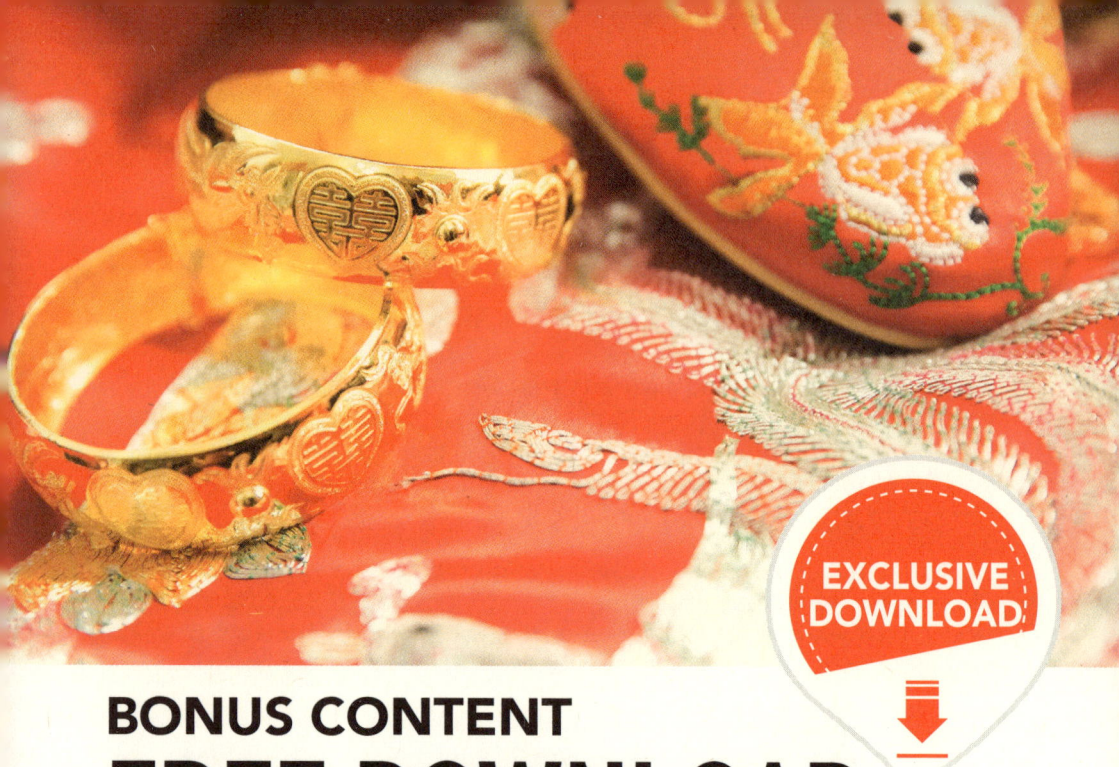

BONUS CONTENT
FREE DOWNLOAD

Exclusive content available for download with your purchase of the The Chinese Traditions & Practices book.

Gain immediate access to Bonus content from Dato' Joey Yap by claiming your FREE ONLINE ACCESS now at:

www.masteryacademy.com/bookbonus2018

CTP18BC5

Introduction

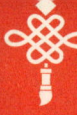

As home to one of the world's first civilisations, China has a long and rich history spanning over 4,000 years. Chinese customs and practices are much easier to understand if one has a general sense of where they came from and the history of Chinese culture.

Chinese culture has constantly evolved over the centuries. One catalyst for change has been technology. The advent of paper and pottery gave the ancient Chinese new ways to develop ideas, create traditions and showcase their identity and beliefs.

Several ideas and concepts have long been a fundamental part of Chinese culture. One of them is the concept of Nature (*Zi Ran* 自然), attributed to the Daoist philosopher *Lao Tzu* (老子). The concept of Nature is the very embodiment of the *Dao* (道) itself.

In ancient China in particular, social standing was immensely important. The need to create social order led to the inception of the feudal class system which later became the imperial class system that is known today. The ideology behind the system is aligned with the teachings of Confucius, who championed obedience and filial piety.

Ancient Chinese culture was Sino-centric. The ancient Chinese believed that their culture was superior to others, particularly that of nomadic tribes. This belief was fuelled by the idea that Confucian rites (*Li* 禮) were the most valid way to differentiate between those who were civilised and those who were not. It was widely understood that an outside person could become Chinese by adopting the Chinese way of life. This opened the door for the integration of other cultures and religions into mainstream Chinese culture, provided that they fulfilled the right criteria. This, in turn, led to the rise of Chinese Buddhism.

History

China's history can be roughly divided into several stages from a literary perspective.

Very little about the time from the Palaeolithic era to the reign of the Xia dynasty (c. 2070 – c. 1600 BC) is known certainty: there is scant archaeological evidence from early China. Indeed, the best evidence for the existence of the Xia dynasty is a handful of literary works written centuries later during the reign of the Han dynasty (206 BC – 220 AD).

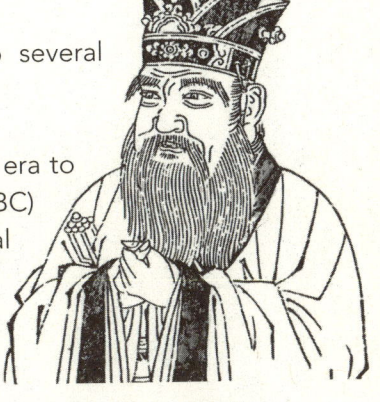
Confucius 孔夫子

Many stories about early Chinese civilization are most likely fictional and cannot be taken at face value. That said, they most likely contain a kernel of truth and depict a time of nomadic hunter-gathering, where food was scarce. Eventually the early Chinese settled into a more stable agrarian lifestyle.

Historians call the period between the birth of the Shang dynasty (c. 1600 – 1046 BC) and the end of the Warring States (*Zhan Guo* 戰國) period (475 – 221 BC) the feudal agrarian stage. This was a pivotal time in Chinese history, as it was during this period that the concept of social stratification was introduced. Many of country's most famous intellectuals including Confucius, *Lao Tzu*, *Han Fei* and *Sun Tzu* became well known during the feudal agrarian period, too. Their philosophies helped bring order to the lives of Chinese people. Eventually, they became pillars of Chinese culture.

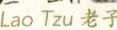
Lao Tzu 老子

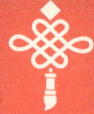

The next stage in Chinese history began with the Qin dynasty (221 – 206 BC) and lasted until the end of the Qing dynasty (1644 – 1912). Historian call it the imperial stage, when China ceased to be a collection of states and became a unified country under one emperor, with a government founded on bureaucracy. Its workings inspired key parts of Chinese mythology like the Jade Emperor (*Yu Huang Da Di* 玉皇大帝) and his divine court.

During the imperial stage, the social stratification practised by the Chinese evolved into the social system that most know today. The social classes introduced in this system assigned different standing to the emperor, local authorities, common people and intellectuals like counsellors or officers. Respect for those with power was mandatory under this system, even within common families. Average citizens were expected to put family first and honour and respect their elders. Many misogynistic ideas and practices gained traction during this period, too – becoming widespread during the Ming dynasty (1368 – 1644) in particular.

The end of the Qing dynasty marked the beginning of what the Chinese call the post-imperial stage, which concluded with the Chinese Civil War. With the rise of Western powers and the expansion of colonialism, the Chinese were forced to adapt to a new world. In the ensuing turmoil, the notion of Chinese supremacy was vigorously challenged and many customs and practices were abolished in the process.

In modern times, China has risen to become an industrial power with a distinct identity. Much of the culture that was lost during the civil war has been restored and adapted for modern society. A good example of this is the way that the traditional funeral customs have been simplified in modern times.

Chinese Metaphysics regained its popularity, with understandable changes. Modern Feng Shui principles are tailored to suit apartments instead of mansions and traditional Chinese medicine is integrated with modern medical knowledge. Even Chinese cooking. techniques and recipes have evolved to take advantage of modern nutritional information and new cooking equipment.

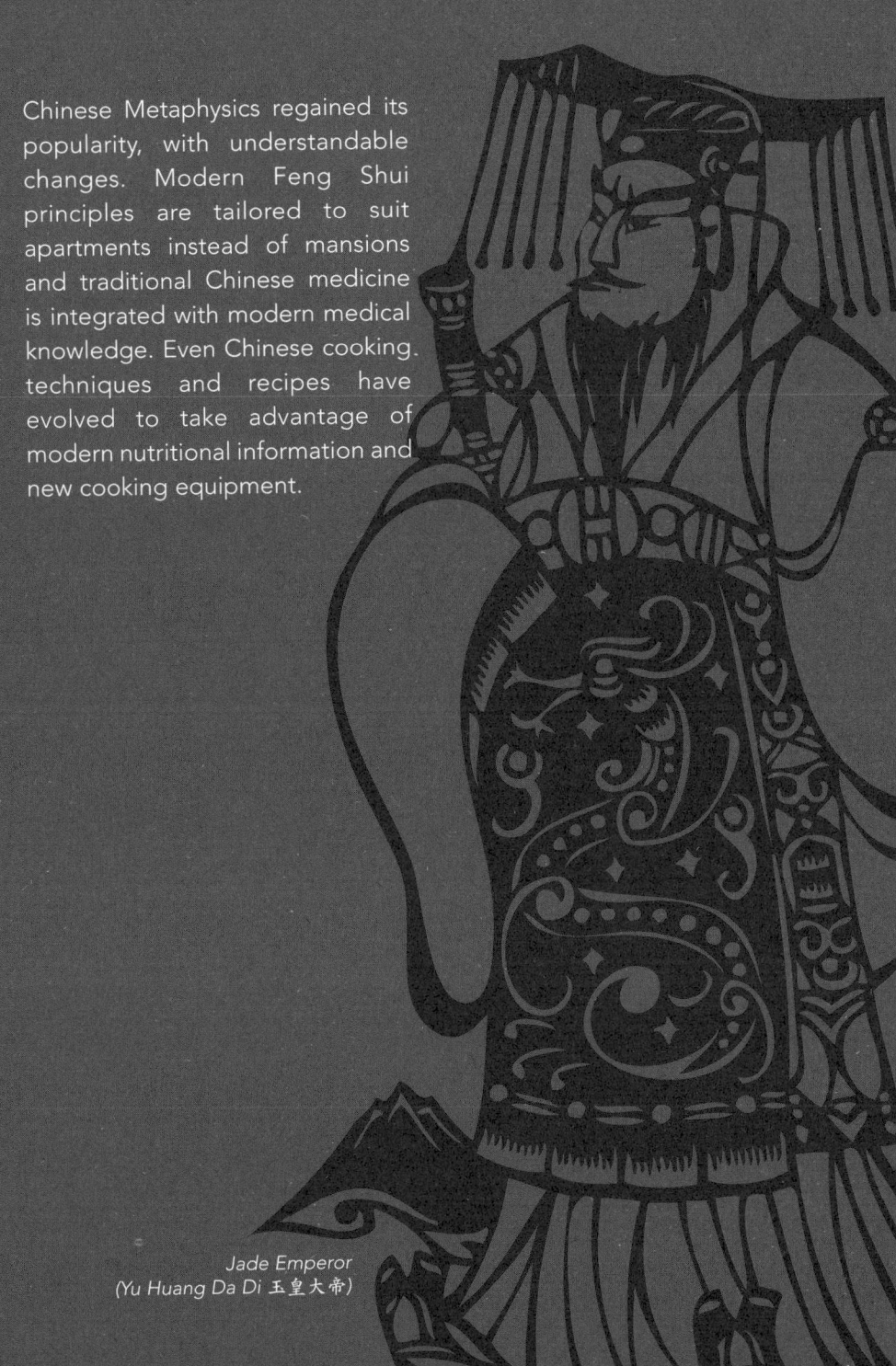

Jade Emperor
(Yu Huang Da Di 玉皇大帝)

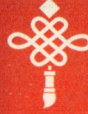

Nature (*Zi Ran* 自然)

The idea of Nature in the context of Chinese culture is slightly hard to pin down in English but it refers to more than the physical natural world. It is embodied by the phrase "It is so by virtue of its own". It can be used as a noun or an adjective depending on context.

The Daoist definition of Nature can be found in Chapter 25 of the Daoist classic *Dao De Jing* (道德經), as follows: "Humans take their law from the Earth; the Earth takes its law from Heaven; Heaven takes its law from the Dao. The law of the *Dao* is its being what it is." (*Ren Fa Di, Di Fa Tian, Tian Fa Dao, Dao Fa Zi Ran.* 人法地，地法天，天法道，道法自然。) In the very same chapter, there is the line "There was something undefined and complete, coming into existence before Heaven and Earth." The "something" mentioned here refers to the *Dao*: the force that makes up all things and the law behind all things. The *Dao* is seen as something fluid, greater than any human or deity. It is the law not in the prohibitive sense but rather in the sense that it was how things simply are. No one was prohibited from going against it, but there was no point in doing so as it was simply illogical and absurd.

The relationship between humans and Nature was the subject of fierce debate between Daoists and the followers of Confucius during the feudal agrarian stage of ancient China. While Daoist teachings focused more on Nature, Confucius' teachings focused more on human and social concerns. Nevertheless, both agreed that humans are subservient to Nature, Nature being the creator of humans. Furthermore, Daoists and Confucian followers agreed that humans and Nature were co-dependant.

Building on this common ground, the idea that things are interdependent became widespread in China. The notion that the physical and metaphysical worlds were intertwined meant that a person's failure to accomplish something was usually the result of a violation of some natural universal law. As such, it was seen as best that humans take the path of least resistance in life and avoid going against Nature. Rather than trying to overcome something with brute force, the best course of action is to find its weak point and attack it there. "Go with the flow", perhaps.

In 1889, the definition of Nature was standardised to better reflect its Western meaning as part of China's attempts to embrace modernisation. However, the original idea which it describes is still important in China today.

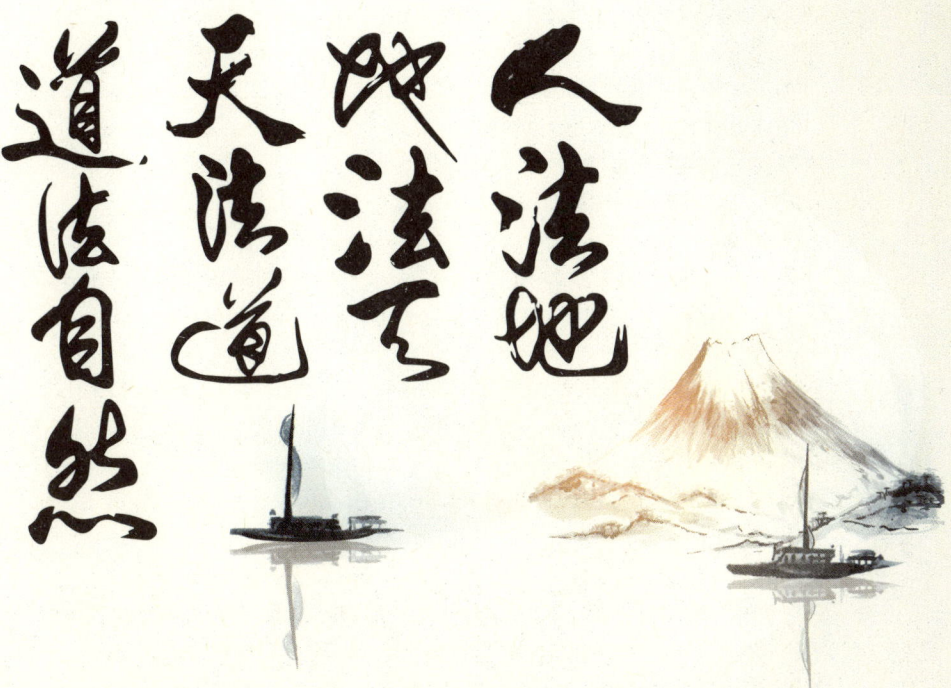

The law of the Dao is its being what it is." (Ren Fa Di, Di Fa Tian, Tian Fa Dao, Dao Fa Zi Ran. 人法地，地法天，天法道，道法自然。) In the very same chapter, there is the line "There was something undefined and complete, coming into existence before Heaven and Earth."

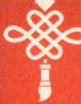

Social Stratification

While every civilization has its own social order, China was one of the earliest to develop a formal social structure. With it, the ancient Chinese created the concept of social stratification. Everyone's place in society was dictated by their contributions to the kingdom overall. The first implementation of this system was the feudal class system. It was eventually replaced with the better-known imperial class system during the Western Zhou dynasty (1046 – 771 BC). The imperial class system placed the emperor at the top of the social hierarchy.

The imperial class system was refined into the version that is known today during the Qin dynasty (221 – 206 BC). Five distinct classes were created. In descending order, people were classified as being the Emperor, the lords (*Zhu Hou* 諸侯), the counsellors (*Qing* 卿), the officers or intellectuals (*Shi* 士) and the commoners. This structure was supported by a centralised government system known as the Chinese bureaucracy which had different branches and departments for various matters, much like modern governments do.

In the first imperial class system, officials were elected by the local community that they would eventually govern. Unfortunately, corruption eventually reared its ugly head as the person with the most power, wealth or admirers was usually chosen instead of the one who was most qualified for the job. This led to the formation of an early version of National Examinations during the short-lived Sui Dynasty (581- 618 CE) which tested candidates to see if they were capable of holding a position.

The National Examinations system was more formally introduced and improved during the Tang dynasty (618 -907 CE). A significant difference between them and their original incarnation was that they were open to all intellectuals instead of the select few from each community. As a result, people could ascend to power regardless of their social class if they proved themselves worthy.

All in all, the system described above played a crucial role in shaping Chinese culture in that it rewarded order in everyday life. This, in turn, cultivated a sense of obedience and made people acknowledge and respect status. Even today, obedience is seen as a virtue in Chinese society. This is best represented by a story in Chapter 12, Verse 11 of the Analects (*Lun Yu* 論語) written by Confucius which goes:

"Duke Jing of Qi asked Confucius about government. Confucius replied, "Let the ruler be a ruler, the minister be a minister, the father be a father and the son be a son." (*Jun Jun, Chen Chen, Fu Fu, Zi Zi.* 君君，臣臣，父父，子子.)"

Confucius regarded the social stratification system of the Western Zhou dynasty to be the best, even though he himself lived during the Spring and Autumn Period (*Chun Qiu* 春秋) which was several centuries afterwards. In his eyes, rites were the ideal social institutions. This led him to promote a respect for the old way of doing things, seeing it as the right way to run the country. As a result, many Chinese customs focus on respecting people in power such as the emperor and intellectuals. Later, this expanded to include parents, the elderly and – in modern times – one's superior at work or in society.

Respect for the Chinese bureaucracy as a whole also became part of the country's mythology and religious views. For example, many Chinese deities such as the City God (*Cheng Huang* 城隍) are actually divine representations of the city's authority.

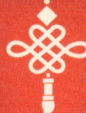

Sino-centrism

The Sino-centric views that the ancient Chinese held allowed for the integration of other cultural beliefs, provided only that they adhered to Confucian principles. This allowed Buddhism to spread across the country, albeit in an amended form better suited to China. The resulting Chinese Buddhism combined the religion of Buddhism with Daoist cosmology and Confucian ethics.

The road towards Chinese Buddhism was not a smooth one. When Buddhism first gained prominence in ancient China, its incompatibility with many of Confucius' principles was glaring. For example, Buddhist monks abstained from earthly pleasures like sex, but Confucius taught that one was obligated to ensure the survival of their family by procreating with a focus on having male children if possible. Having a son was seen as a demonstration of filial piety.

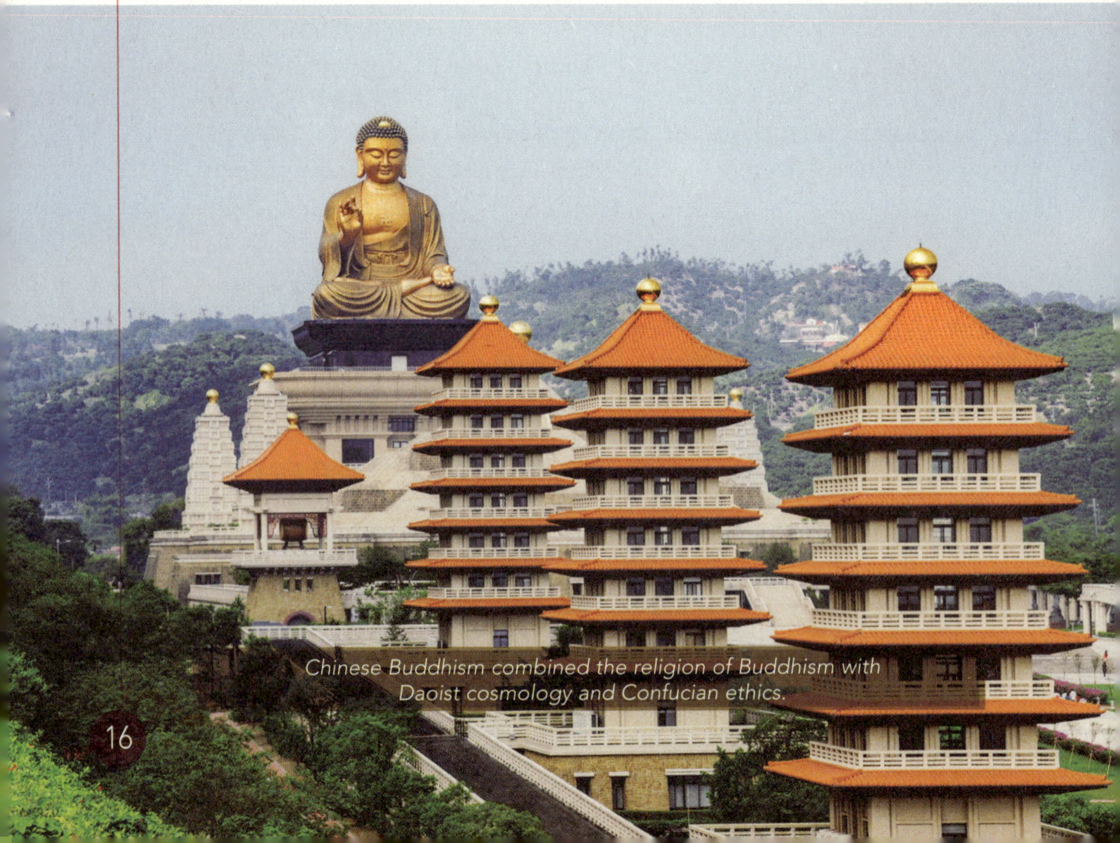

Chinese Buddhism combined the religion of Buddhism with Daoist cosmology and Confucian ethics.

In order to solve this problem, the famous monk Qi Song (契嵩) provided a stellar argument: "A Buddhist does not kill and that matches Confucius' idea of compassion (*Ren* 仁). A Buddhist does not steal and that is similar to Confucius' idea of righteousness (*Yi* 義). A Buddhist [monk] does not have sexual intercourse and that is in line with Confucius' idea of rites (*Li* 禮). A Buddhist does not drink alcohol and that can be seen as being wise (*Zhi* 智). Finally, a Buddhist does not tell lies and that makes him truthful (*Xin* 信)."

The karmic element of Buddhism was eventually integrated with the Confucius idea of filial piety, too. This had consequences for Chinese funeral rites. Many rituals were added to help increase a dead person's chances of being reincarnated as a human and living a noble new life.

On a side note, the initial incompatibility of Buddhism did not bother practitioners of Daoism in the slightest. This was largely because Daoism and Confucianism had a fierce rivalry going on between them and there were many similarities between the cosmology of Buddhism and Daoism. As a result, the integration of Buddhism into Daoism was much simpler than the integration of Buddhism and Confucianism. In fact, it can be said that Buddhism eventually emerged as the more influential force in this new relationship instead of Daoism.

It should be noted that Buddhism introduced the concept of Hell (*Di Yu* 地獄) or the Underworld into Chinese culture. It was eventually described in the context of a Chinese bureaucracy where Hell was governed by the Yama Kings (*Yan Luo Wang* 閻羅王) and served as the initial place where souls went after they left their bodies. These Yama Kings were described using terms for officers in the imperial government. As a result, funeral ceremonies where families attempted to garner the favour of the Yama Kings on their relatives behalf were created.

On a Personal Note…

I would like to take this opportunity to mention that throughout my many years as a Feng Shui practitioner, I have been asked many questions about the matters written in this book.

Before you go any further, I wish to stress the fact that a large majority of the information you will find in the following chapters are simply myths, legends and old customs. They have no basis in real Feng Shui because Feng Shui is a study of Qi, time, space and natural environmental energies. What you will be reading about are practices rooted in culture and mythology. Although undoubtedly interesting, they have no connection to the effectiveness of real Feng Shui. As such, following them or ignoring them will have no real Feng Shui impact.

Chapter 1

Chinese Weddings

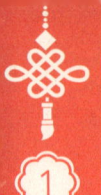

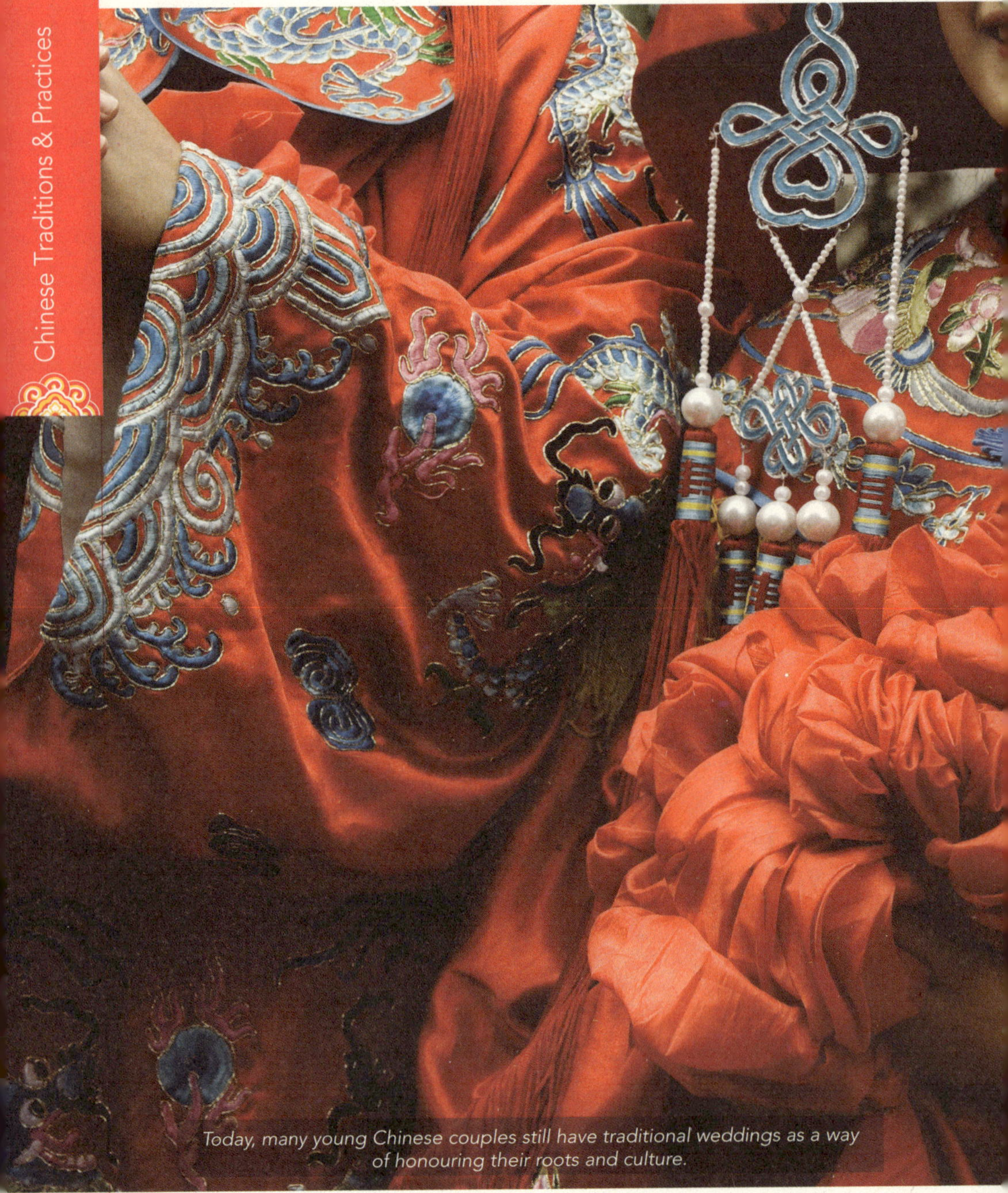

Chinese Traditions & Practices

Today, many young Chinese couples still have traditional weddings as a way of honouring their roots and culture.

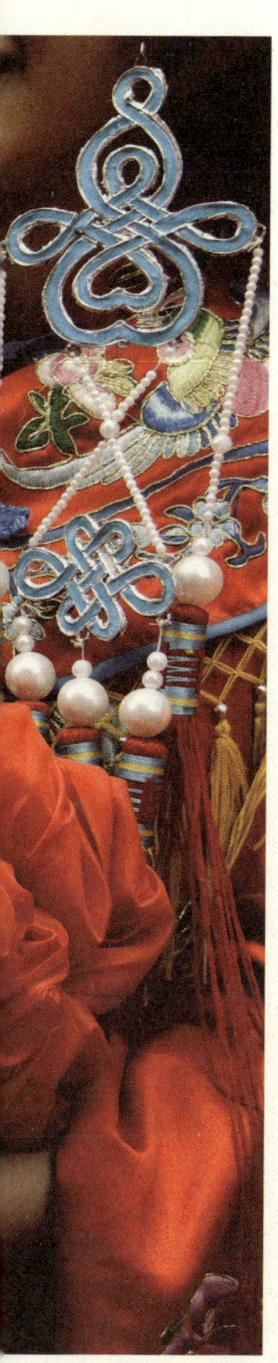

In ancient China, people believed that the three most joyful events a person could experience in life were succeeding in imperial examinations, getting married and having a son.

Of course, things have changed since then - imperial examinations are a thing of the past for example. Getting married, however, remains a highlight of many people's lives.

Many of the traditions associated with Chinese weddings are rooted in Confucianism. At first, they were only practised by China's intellectual class. During the Zhou Dynasty (1046 BC – 256 BC), they were adapted and adopted by commoners. These patriarchal customs - which emphasise the importance of family - have survived to the present day.

For the longest time, Chinese marriages were arranged. Marriages based on romantic love were not openly allowed until the late 1920s. The details of arranged marriages were negotiated by families on behalf of the children they were trying to wed. Family members sometimes prayed to their ancestors for advice on how best to approach the complex issue.

The fact is that women held a lower social status than men in China until the recent past. This meant that a groom's needs were put first and it was understood that a groom's family should benefit most from an arranged union. Aside from a dowry, it was thought that a new bride would "belong" to a groom's family once she got married. The exception to this rule was when a woman was able to marry into a family of lower social status than hers, but this was a rare event.

A complete traditional Chinese wedding can be divided into three broad stages. The first pre-wedding stage has several components. It begins with a proposal (*Na Cai* 納采) which is followed by a negotiation (*Wen Ming* 問名) and tea ceremony (*Feng Cha* 奉茶). Next comes the engagement (*Na Ji* 納吉), Dowry Exchange (*Na Zheng* 納徵) and Date Selection (*Qing Qi* 請期).

The second stage - known as the wedding stage – includes the big day itself where three rituals are observed. The first is called Welcoming the Bride (*Qin Yin* 親迎), the second is called Worshipping Heaven and Earth (*Bai Tian Di* 拜天地) and the third consists of a wedding banquet which is itself accompanied by several customs.

The third stage of a Chinese wedding is the post-wedding stage. This is the shortest stage. It consists of a ritual called Returning to the Household (*Fan Jia* 返家) followed by a tea ceremony (*Chi Cha* 喫茶).

Another set of wedding customs are known collectively as the Three Letters and Six Etiquettes (*San Shu Liu Li* 三書六禮), which draw upon the Book of Rites (*Li Ji* 禮記), the Book of Etiquettes and Ceremonials (*Yi Li* 儀禮) and the Virtuous Discussions of the White Tiger Hall (*Bai Hu Tong De Lun* 白虎通德論). The first two stages involve six "etiquettes" or rituals, where three specific letters are given to the bride's family.

In practice, the average citizen of the Han dynasty (206BC – 220 AD), rarely adhered to every custom outlined above because it was simply too expensive. It was only later, during the Tang Dynasty (618 – 907 CE), that the wedding process was simplified and standardised according to imperial decree. The date selection and negotiation steps were largely discarded. During the Ming dynasty (1368–1644 AD), things were simplified further so that only the proposal, engagement, dowry exchange and actual wedding ceremony remained. This caught on popularly with commoners. The aristocrats of the Qing dynasty (1644–1912 AD) went in the opposite direction and expanded upon the original steps so that there were nine customs in total. The new customs extended the pre-wedding stage and created a new and separate proposal process.

Contemporary Chinese wedding ceremonies are a far cry from their complex counterparts of the past, but they are conducted in the same spirit, and many of their traditions live on. Thus, a valuable part of China's long and illustrious history lives on.

On a Personal Note…

I understandably came to learn about many of these customs when it was my turn to get married. Prior to that point in my life, my knowledge of the subject was cursory at best. Looking back, I can say that I knew very little about the subject.

Needless to say, when the time came I did an extensive amount of research into the matter. In the process, I found countless stories and accounts of traditional weddings written by historians as well as studies written by scholars. It is my hope that you can make use of the information I found and have a classic Chinese wedding, too!

The Proposal

The first step on the road to a traditional Chinese wedding was the proposal (*Na Cai* 納采). This was typically initiated by matchmakers (*Mei Ren* 媒人) who were also called "marriage introducers". Their role in bringing together unmarried men and women was considered so crucial that an official matchmaker post was created during the Zhou dynasty. The post involved supervised matchmaking sessions and promoted the idea of marriage to young people, widows and widowers of appropriate age.

By Confucius' standards, men who were between 20 and 30 were best matched with girls between 15 and 20 years old. Once someone in a particular community reached the right age, a matchmaker was informed and got to work.

The need for matchmakers stemmed from the strict gender segregation rules in ancient China's society. Middle-class women in ancient China grew up and lived entirely in the confines of their home to preserve their modesty. Lower-class women who worked out in the fields were seen as unrefined. Modesty was taken so seriously that a meeting between any middle-class woman and a stranger outside her household – even by accident – was called Unveiling the Appearance (*Pao Tou Lu Mian* 拋頭露面). It was believed that such an event could irreparably tarnish a woman's modesty.

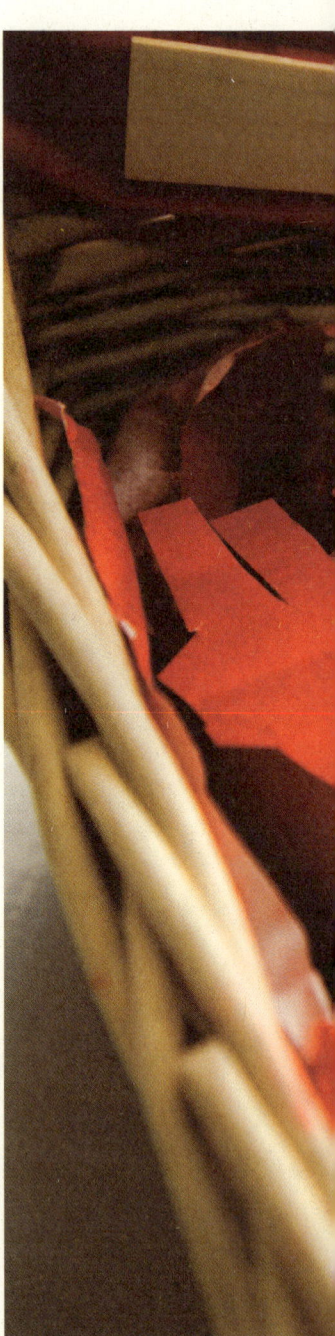

禮俗

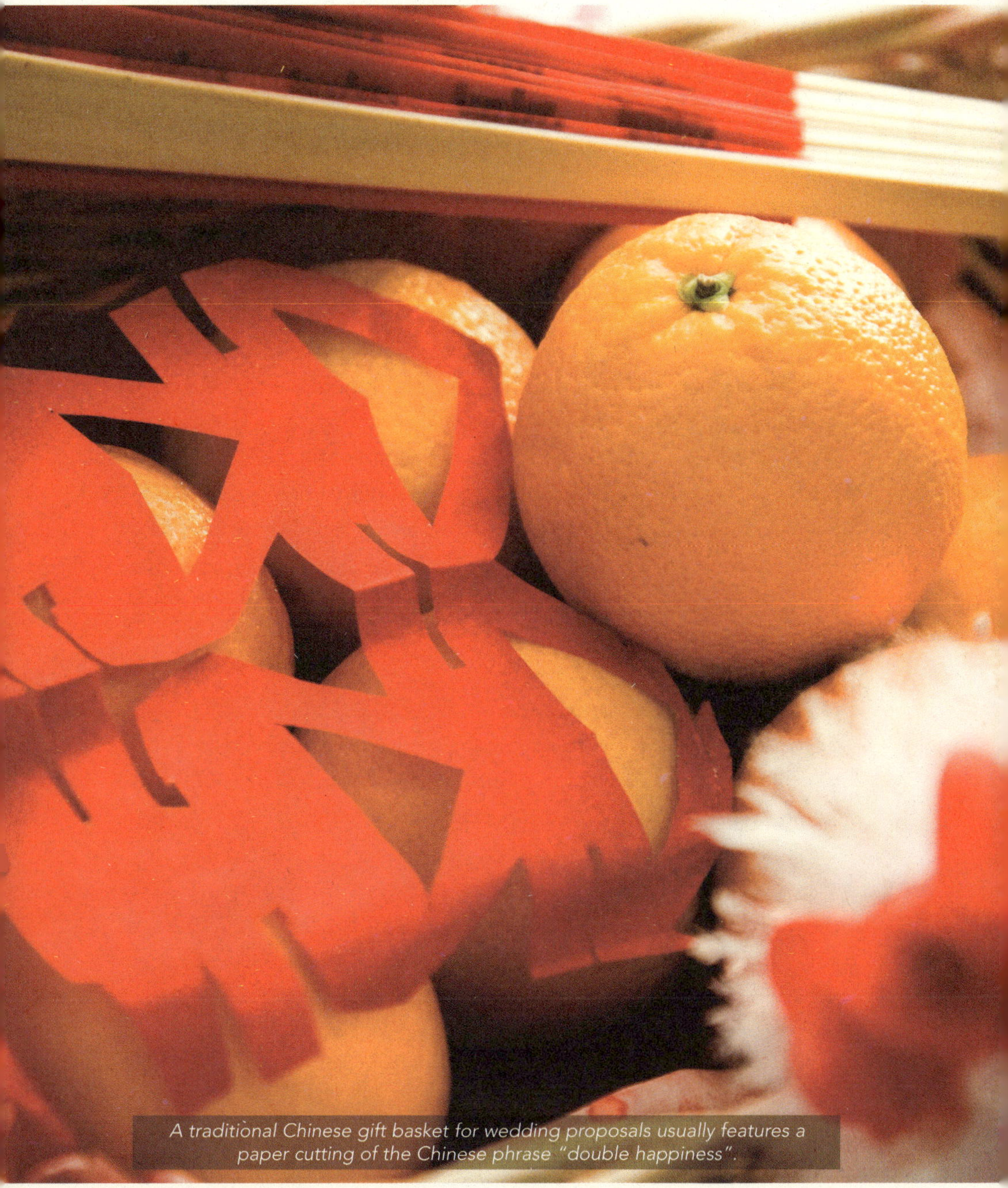

A traditional Chinese gift basket for wedding proposals usually features a paper cutting of the Chinese phrase "double happiness".

The Matchmaking Process

A matchmaker had to consider many factors in the course of their work. First and foremost, they had to ensure that a man and woman had similar social status. Next, they considered family size, properties, reputation, lineage, character and health. To do this, they had to study a potential couple's families.

Although it was possible to marry above or below one's social rank, the practice was heavily frowned upon – especially when it was the woman who came from a less wealthy or powerful family. If a man married a woman of lesser standing then he would tarnish his family name, so such proposals were usually turned down. Ideally, a wealthy man would marry a woman from a rich family and a scholar would get engaged to a girl from an intellectual family and so on. This concept is called Matching Doorposts and Door Sills (*Men Dang Hu Dui* 門當戶對) and it has survived to the present day.

Once a matchmaker had found an appropriate match, a member of the man's family would go to the woman's household bearing gifts to propose marriage. This official proposal marked the beginning of the long wedding process.

The gifts that were chosen were done so with great care as they represented the expectations that a man's family had for the marriage. The most well-known and desirable gift was a live wild goose. It was believed that the animal had Yang energy and that it symbolised a submissive wife. Only those belonging to the Counsellor (*Qing Dai Fu* 卿大夫) social class were allowed to use a live wild goose however so commoners gave live pheasants instead.

Other common proposal gifts included rice wine representing fortune, reeds which were associated with Yin energy due to their flexibility and thus submission and sewn clothes which were associated with longevity and a lasting marital bond. Birds other than those mentioned above were also popular as they were associated with filial piety and a wife's willingness to serve her in-laws.

By accepting whatever gift was offered, a woman's family informally agreed to the proposal that went with it. With that, everyone could move on to the next to the next stage of the process.

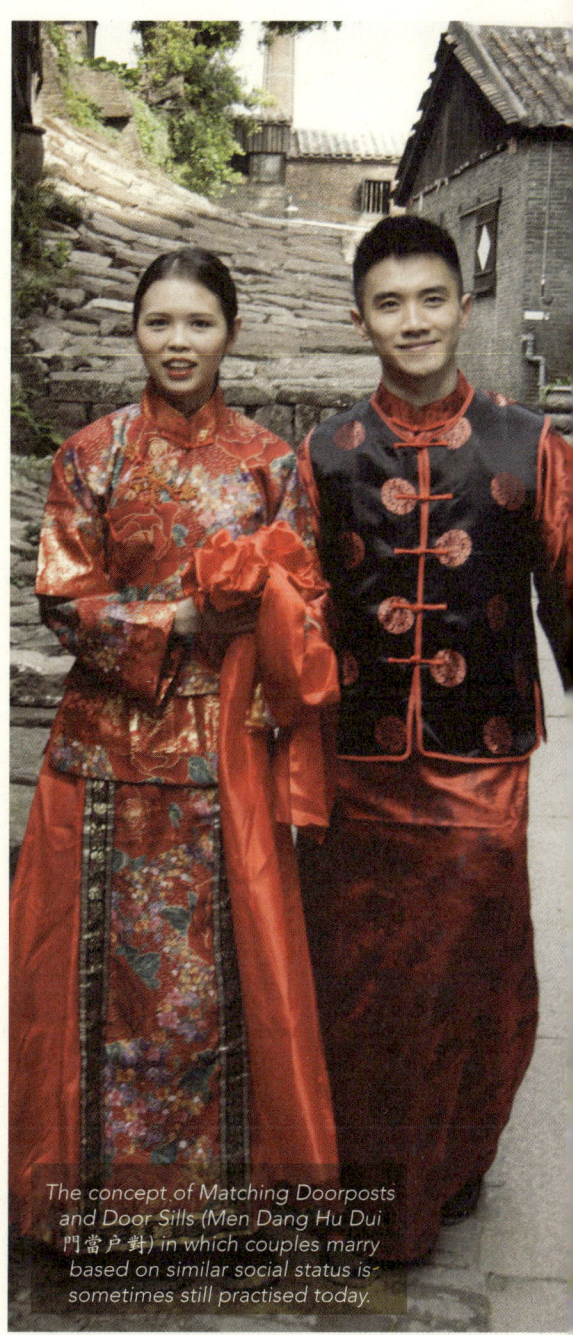

The concept of Matching Doorposts and Door Sills (Men Dang Hu Dui 門當戶對) in which couples marry based on similar social status is sometimes still practised today.

The Negotiation

After a successful proposal, both families began the negotiation (*Wen Ming* 問名) stage, literally called the "name-asking" stage. Both families exchanged .items which helped determine if a union was tenable. The two most common items exchanged for this purpose were a potential couple's BaZi charts and pedigree charts (*Geng Pu* 庚譜). If both families agreed to the match, an engagement letter (Pin Shu 聘書) would be written and sent to put things down in writing.

The BaZi Charts

In order to understand the purpose of this stage, one must remember that ancient China was a patriarchal society and divorce was frowned upon. The fact that women grew up in the confines of their home and were forbidden from interacting with any men outside their families made it very difficult for potential couples to find out if they were compatible for marriage.

This limitation created the need for a tool that could describe a person's character without their input. As such, the information that one could glean from a person's BaZi chart was extremely valuable because it was a chart derived from a person's birth details that could yield a clear picture of an individual's personality. To prevent deceit and ensure accuracy, BaZi charts could be vetted by a Chinese Metaphysics practitioner. If the practitioner determined that a couples' BaZi charts "clashed" or were incompatible then a wedding would be called off.

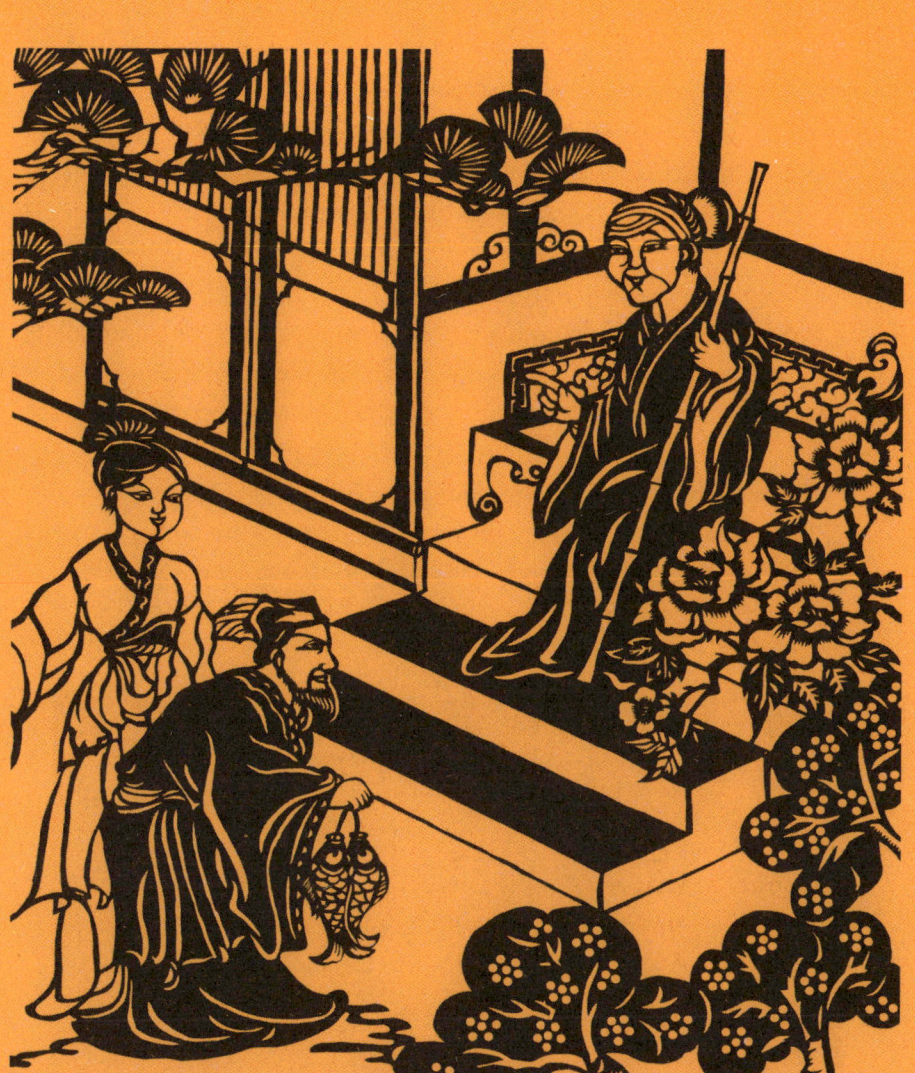

Chinese Metaphysics practitioners were consulted when families wished to determine if the couple's BaZi charts were compatible or not.

The Pedigree Charts (*Geng Pu* 庚譜)

After a couple's BaZi charts had been examined, their pedigree charts were scrutinized. This let both families study the other's ancestry and identify any famous or infamous individuals in their family tree. Having a lineage which featured reputable individuals, like an intellectual, was immensely desirable. A good family tree could go a long way towards landing an agreement.

Although a proposal had not been formally accepted by this point, a couple was generally considered engaged the moment that pedigree charts exchanged hands. Mere possession of pedigree charts could be used as proof of engagement.

Some families presented the pedigree chart of their future in-laws to their ancestors. Offering prayers as they did so, the family asked their ancestors to give a sign passing judgement on the potential new member of the family.

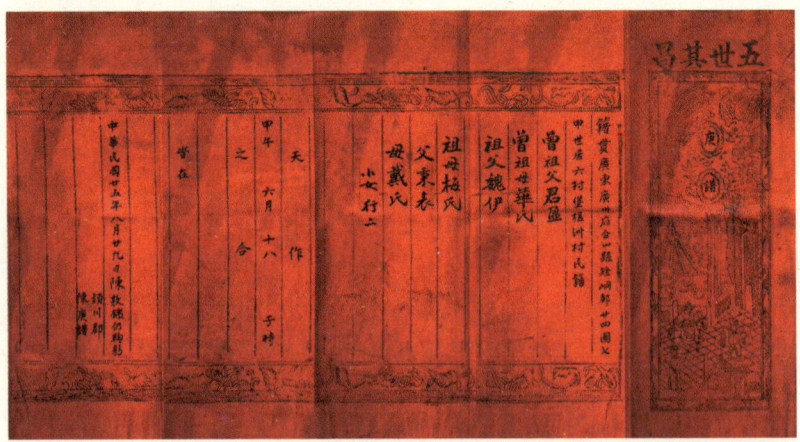

The pedigree charts (Geng Pu 庚譜) were used to see if there were any famous or infamous people in a family tree.

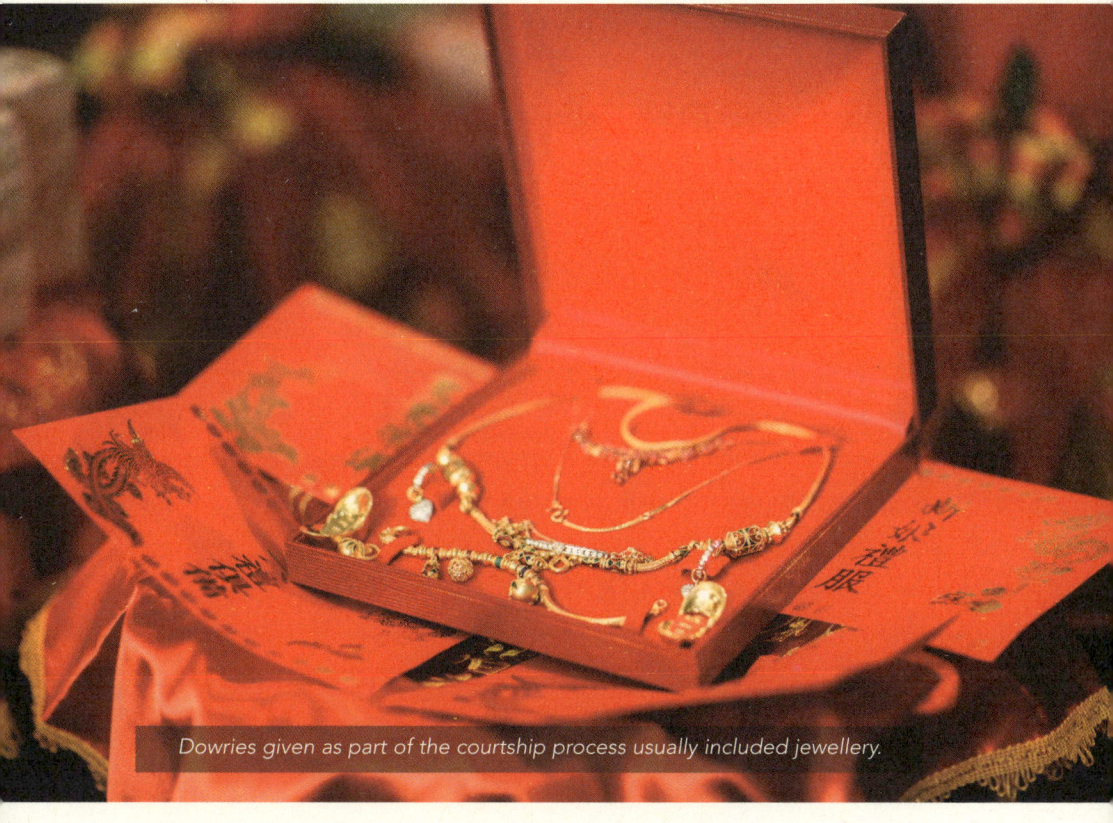
Dowries given as part of the courtship process usually included jewellery.

The Engagement Letter (*Pin Shu* 聘書)

In order to officially confirm the engagement, the future groom or a representative of his family gave an engagement letter to his potential wife's family. This was the first letter sent as part of the Three Letters and Six Etiquettes (*San Shu Liu Li* 三書六禮) tradition mentioned before. This step was essential because it communicated a man's sincere desire to wed a woman. The letter also contained the vows and future undertakings of both parties in their marriage.

The Dowry Exchange

Once negotiations had ended and an engagement letter had been sent, a Dowry Exchange (*Na Zheng* 納徵) took place. As one would imagine, this involved giving a potential bride's family a dowry for her.

The practice of offering dowry was based largely on the notion that women were property and that they had to be "bought" from their birth family. As soon as a woman's family accepted a dowry, the exchange was considered irreversible. Up until this moment, a woman's family reserved the right to call things off and return a man's pedigree chart.

As an aside, dowries typically cost a fair amount of money and were occasionally referred to as the Coin-collecting Ceremony (*Na Bi* 納幣).

Over the centuries, people began to suspect that women might be human beings rather than objects to be bought. Eventually, the Dowry Exchange was replaced by the civil engagement (*Wen Ding* 文定) custom which is described below. A groom's family would still offer a potential bride's family gifts, but without any misogynistic implications.

In any case, the dowry was accompanied by the first of two tea ceremonies (*Feng Cha* 奉茶) and the second of three gift letters (*Li Shu* 禮書) that are sent during the Chinese wedding process.

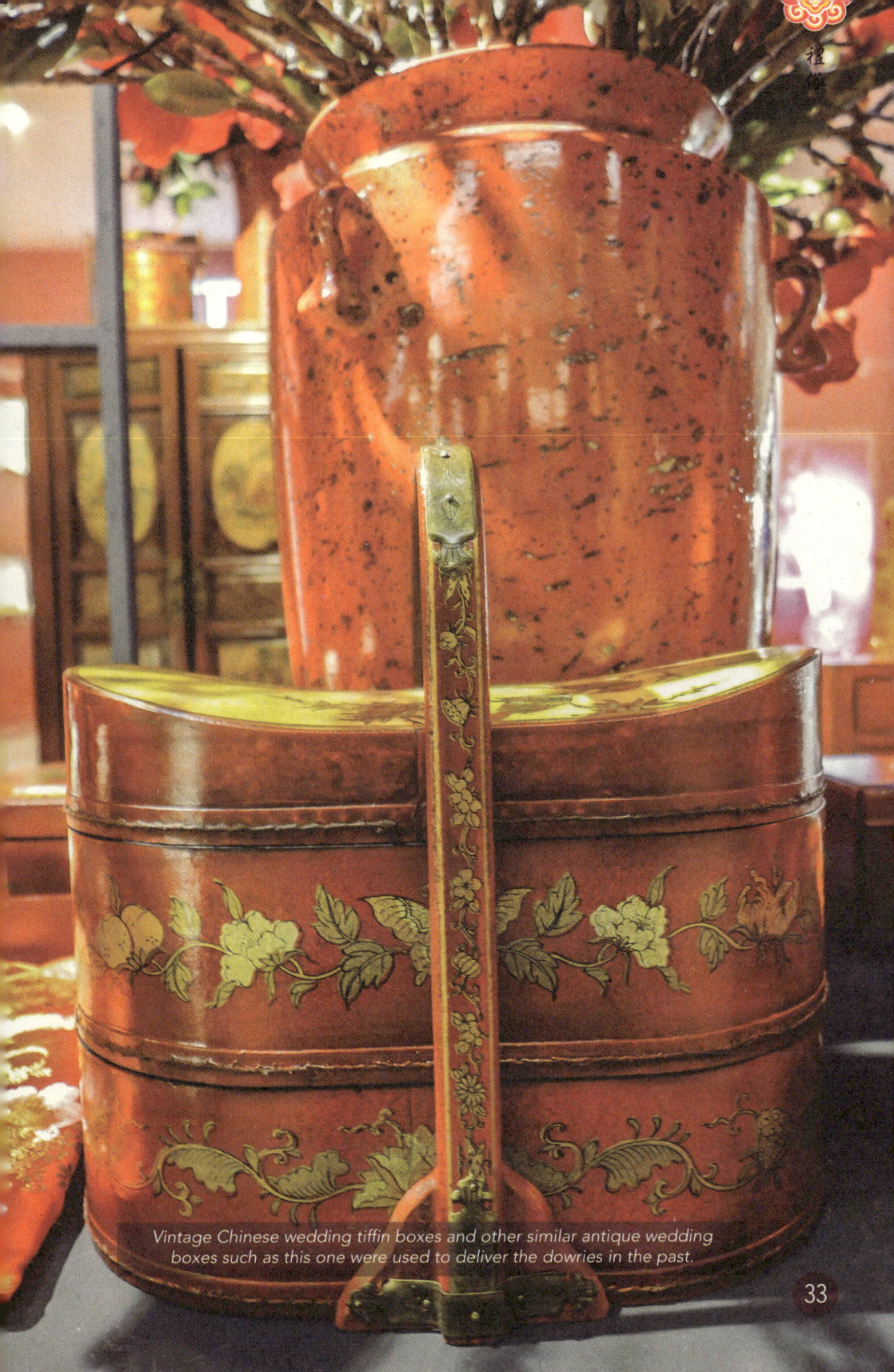

Vintage Chinese wedding tiffin boxes and other similar antique wedding boxes such as this one were used to deliver the dowries in the past.

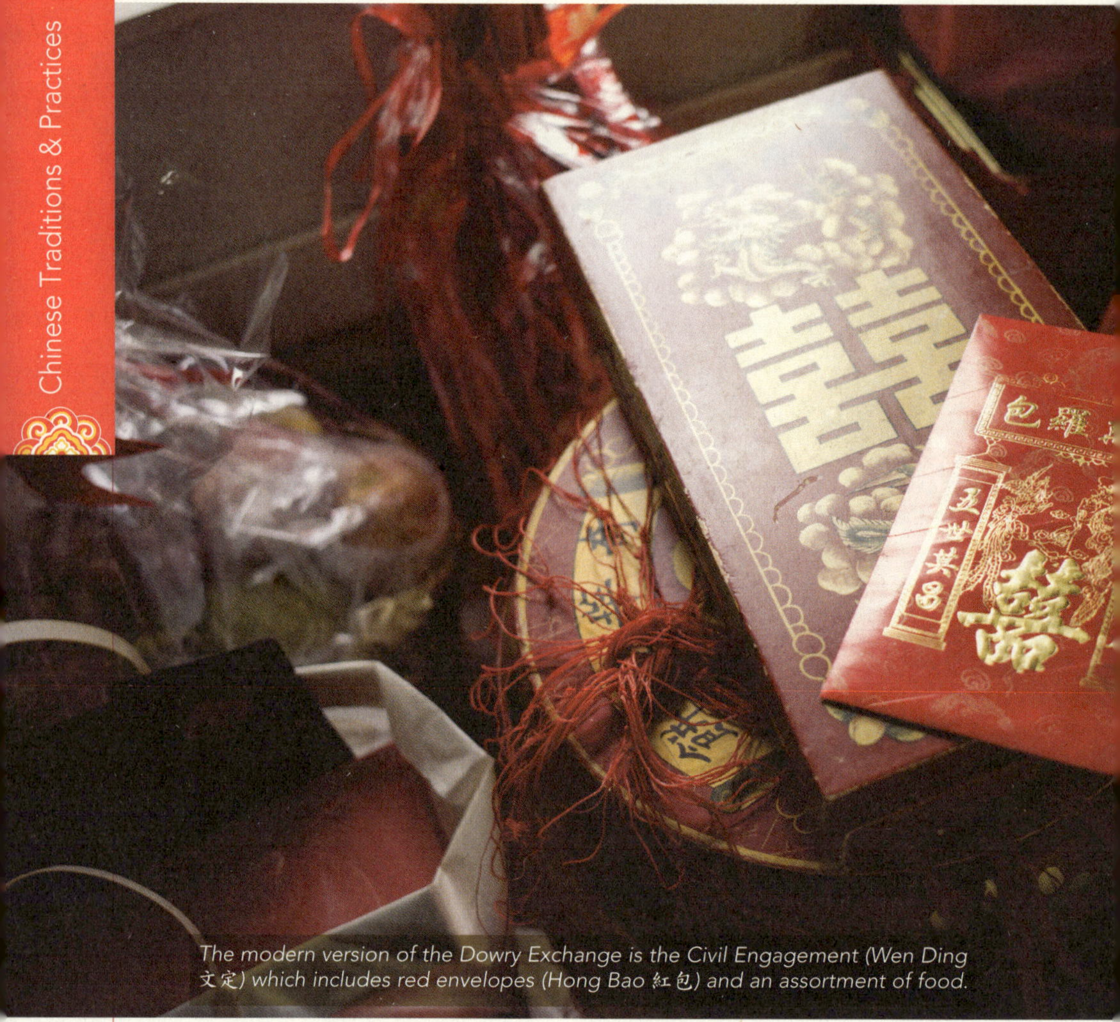

The modern version of the Dowry Exchange is the Civil Engagement (Wen Ding 文定) which includes red envelopes (Hong Bao 红包) and an assortment of food.

The Civil Engagement (*Wen Ding* 文定)

The Civil Engagement custom is the modern incarnation of the Dowry Exchange. A man's family offers a woman's family 12 specific gifts which are symbolic in Chinese culture.

The 12 symbolic gifts given are:

- Flatbread, which symbolises prosperity and a constant supply of food

- Seafood which is associated with the accumulation of wealth

- Poultry which embodies the bond between a couple

- Coconuts which represent the chance of a producing a son

- Red envelopes (*Hong Bao* 红包) or gold jewellery which denote good fortune

- Cookies which also represent prosperity and a steady supply of food

- Chinese wine which represents intense love

- Sticky rice balls which are a representation of binding happiness

- Tea or sesame which is associated with a lasting marriage

- Pork which is an expression of abundance

- Four-coloured candies which symbolise lasting happiness

- Fruits which represent vitality and to boost the chance of producing a son

In modern times, some families only give six of the twelve gifts listed above as part of their dowry: the flatbread, red envelopes or gold jewellery, seafood, coconuts, poultry and cookies.

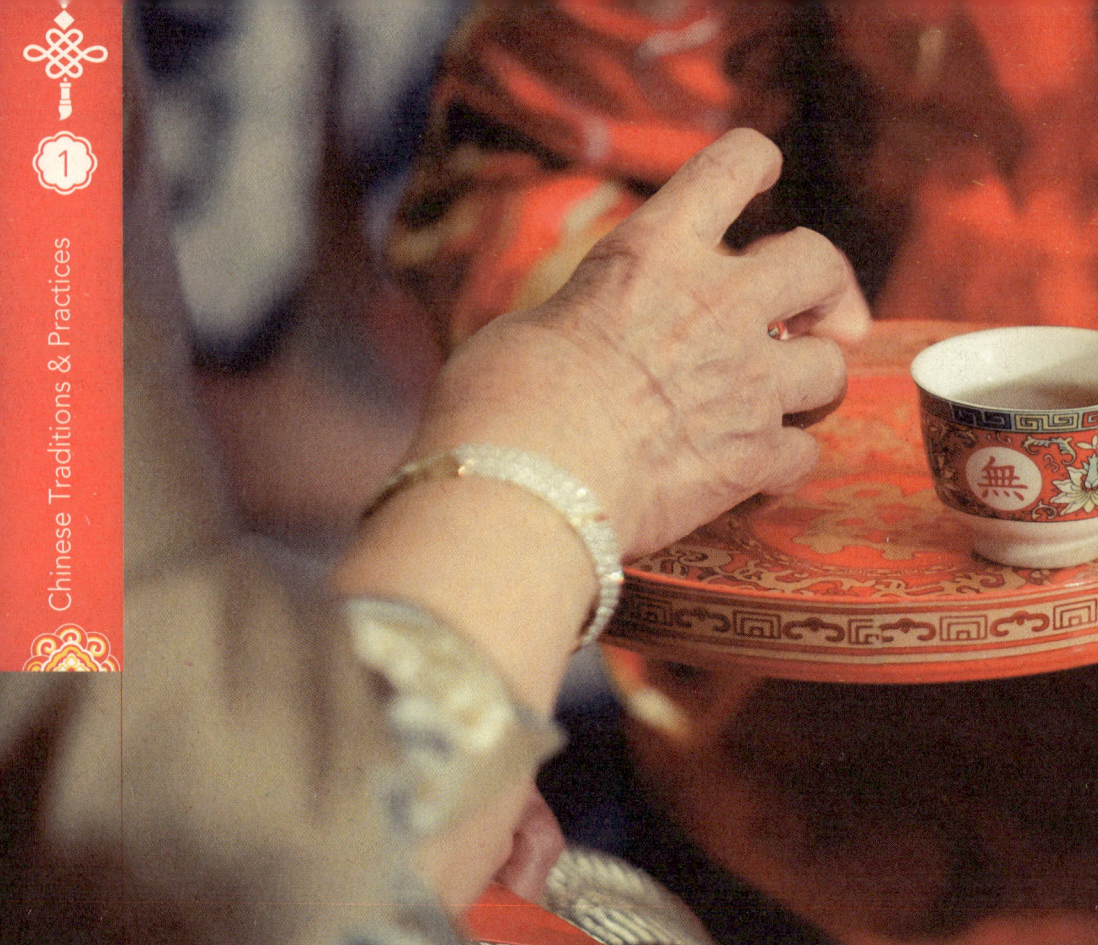

The Gift Letter (*Li Shu* 禮書)

According to tradition, the gift letter was simply a detailed list of the dowry's contents. The acceptance of the gift letter by a woman's family was yet another formal recognition of the wedding. Its acceptance marked the conclusion of this stage of proceedings.

In modern times, the gift letter serves a very different purpose. It lists the gifts that a couple would like to receive on their wedding day. It is sent to relatives on both sides once a marriage has been officially recognised to help them buy appropriate gifts. Western couples often send their wedding guests a similar "wish list".

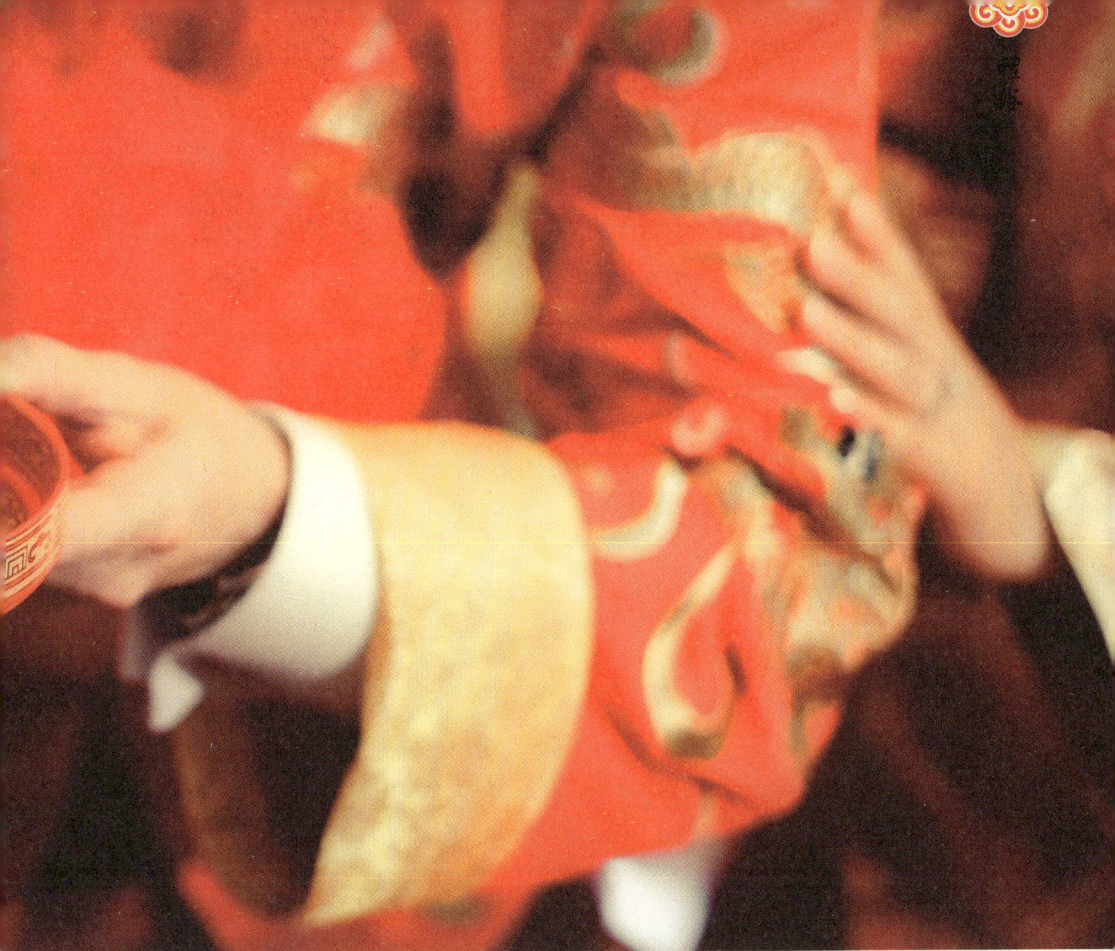

The Tea Ceremony (*Feng Cha* 奉茶)

The tea ceremony is perhaps one of the most well-known Chinese wedding customs. The tea ceremony need not be carried out during the Civil Engagement stage. A couple may choose to conduct several tea ceremonies in between the discussions of the negotiation stage.

This type of tea ceremony is rooted in the ancient tradition which forbade unwed women from leaving the confines of their home, making it necessary for a representative of a man's family to go to her house and handle wedding negotiations. Because the representative usually had to travel a long way, a tea ceremony was held for them out of courtesy.

Subsequent rounds of tea were used to break up the long negotiation process. They were also used to help gauge a woman's patience, mannerisms and carefulness under pressure.

When cultural changes freed up women from the aforementioned restrictions, it was no longer necessary for a representative of the man's family to travel and negotiate things. Couples developed more autonomy and families usually met each other before any proposal was made. All of this meant that the tea ceremony become a ceremonial rather than practical custom when it was officially integrated into the Civil Engagement stage.

In its updated form, a man and five of his relatives would visit a woman's family home where they would be directed to specific seats. The potential bride would then greet them and offer them sweat tea (usually red date and longan tea) while accompanied by an older woman whose husband, parents and in-laws were still alive. The potential bride served her guests from eldest and most powerful first (usually her potential husband's parents) and her potential husband last.

Once everyone had finished their tea, the woman was to collect their cups on a tray in the same order. Throughout this process, each relative was expected to observe a ritual called Pressuring the Cup (*Ya Cha Zhen* 壓茶甄), returning their cup with a red envelope placed underneath it. This officially concluded the tea ceremony. At this point, a woman could reciprocate by offering a gift of some kind as a sign of her gratitude if she wished.

The Planning Stage

Although there are many things which need to be organised in order for a wedding to proceed smoothly, the formal planning stage of a traditional Chinese wedding is limited to choosing a wedding date. This was done through a marital Date Selection method also known as a Date Proposition (*Qing Qi* 請期). The groom's family hired a Chinese Metaphysics practitioner who was skilled at the Art of Date Selection to determine an auspicious day for the wedding.

Once the expert had done his or her job, the man's family would then present the suggested date to the bride's family who would make a show of refusing the proposition. This was done intentionally so that the man's family could choose a wedding date. When the man's family suggested a new date, the woman's family accepted. This interaction was culturally significant in the sense that it represented the ideal Yin-Yang relationship, where Yang is active and Ying is passive. In fact, people referred to this custom as The Yang Proposes and the Yin Gives Her Consent (*Yang Chang Yin He* 陽倡陰和).

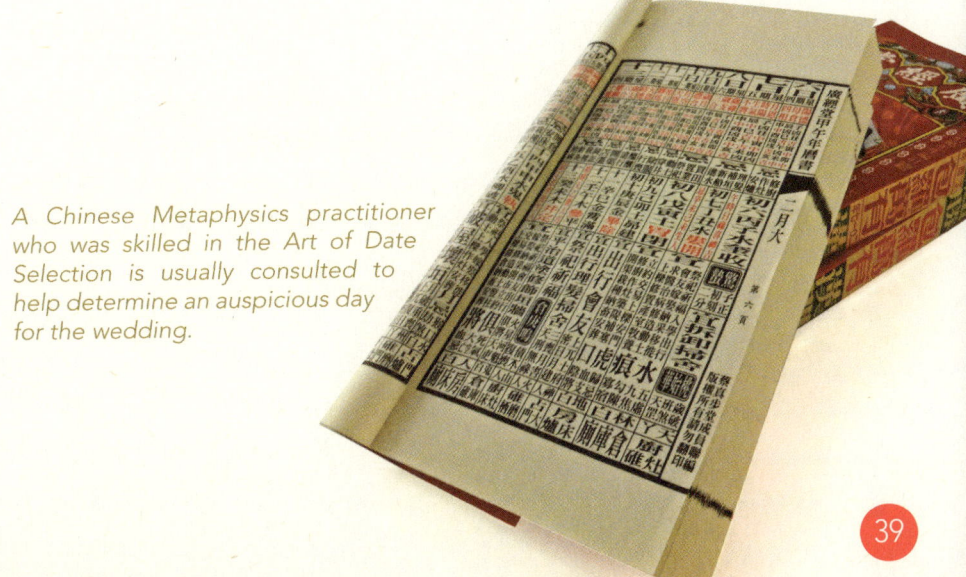

A Chinese Metaphysics practitioner who was skilled in the Art of Date Selection is usually consulted to help determine an auspicious day for the wedding.

The History

The Chinese have used the Art of Date Selection for centuries to identify the perfect time to conduct important events in one's life.

Interestingly, some scholars assert that Date Selection was first used to choose a good wedding day. This is supported by a quote in the Book of Rites (*Li Ji* 禮記) which states:

"Male and female, without the intervention of the matchmaker, do not know each other's name. Unless the marriage presents have been received, there should be neither communication nor affection between them. Following this, the day and month (of the marriage) should be announced to the ruler."

As the "day and month" mentioned refer to the auspicious date for the wedding, this marks the first recorded account of marital Date Selection.

Inspired by this event, Chinese Metaphysics practitioners went on to establish various other Date Selection techniques. Naturally, conflicts arose between different schools of thought. It is said that these disagreements became so volatile that some had to be settled before a court. A good example of this confusion and the eventual resolution of this situation is written in the Records of the Grand Historian (*Shi Ji* 史記). The story goes that Emperor Wu of Han (*Han Wu Di* 漢武帝) asked his consultants to look into the matter and they brought him as many as seven contradicting theories. The Emperor was forced to make a decisive ruling, so he declared the Five Elements (*Yin Yang Wu Xing* 陰陽五行) theory to be official and valid.

禮記 Book of Rites:
博學之，審問之，慎思之，明辨之，篤行之。

Learn extensively, inquire carefully, think deeply, differentiate clearly and practice faithfully.

The Process

In marital Date Selection, Chinese Metaphysics practitioners focus more on the date than the year. They also place less emphasis on choosing the most auspicious month and hour as one is too general and one is too specific to be of much practical use. In any case, the ideal wedding date is usually chosen based on information from a man and woman's BaZi charts.

Overall, the general laymen back in ancient times considered the Year of the Dragon to be the best year for marriage and childbirth. This was because a first born who is born during the Year of the Dragon will have the distinction of being a "Dragon child". For the same reason, getting married in the Year of the Rabbit was also desirable as it is followed by the Year of the Dragon. In practical terms, this meant it was likely that a couple would have a "Dragon child". In contrast, the Years of the Rat, Ox and Tiger were viewed less favourably, although this was because of false facts and misinformation. Any Chinese Metaphysics practitioner worth his or her salt will be able to select a good wedding date, no matter what year it is. Fear not!

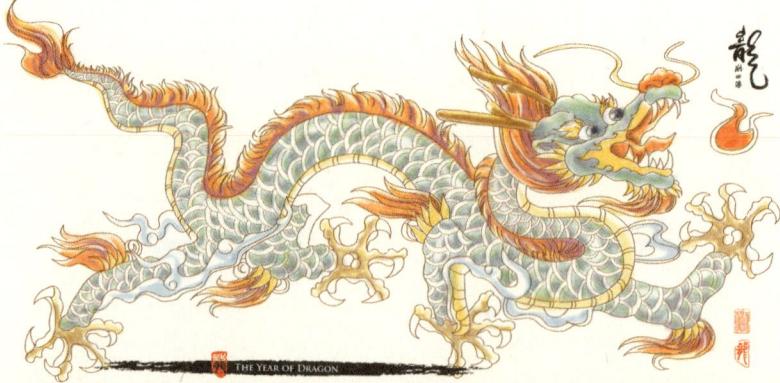

In the olden days, couples would try to have their weddings during the Year of the Dragon as it was considered incredibly auspicious.

The Restrictions

Although a wedding date was usually chosen based on the recommendations of a Chinese Metaphysics practitioner, families had to be aware of a number of restrictions. If for whatever reason they could not contact a Chinese Metaphysics practitioner in a timely manner then they would have to keep them in mind when choosing a date. Commoners who could not afford a consultation adhered to superstitious restrictions, too.

Firstly, it was believed that a wedding should never take place during a mourning period or mourning year (*Xiao Nian* 孝年): the time after a direct member had passed away. Some couples postponed their wedding until 100 days after a relative had passed. Others waited between as little as one and as long as three years as a matter of respect for the dead. It was believed that getting married despite a recent loss would bring bad luck to a family and reduce a couple's fertility.

Couples tried to avoid getting married during certain months, like the fourth Lunar month. Its name sounds like "death month" (*Si Yue* 死月) in Chinese, which ties into a broader Chinese classic avoidance of the number four.

Chinese elders believed that getting married during the sixth Lunar month was inauspicious, too. They believed that "being a bride during the sixth lunar month" (*Liu Yue Xin Niang* 六月新娘) would lead to a higher chance of divorce.

Finally, couples were dissuaded from holding their wedding during the seventh Lunar month, when the Hungry Ghost Festival (*Yu Lan Jie* 孟蘭節) is held. This was based on the notion that holding a happy occasion in the same month as such an "inauspicious" event was unwise.

Of course, it should be reiterated that these are the beliefs held by the general laymen of bygone days who did not have the benefit of the knowledge possessed by qualified Metaphysics and Date Selection masters. In reality, every month of every year has its share of good and suitable dates. What is important here is the BaZi charts of the couple in question. A good practitioner will always be able to find a suitable date which will support the couple's charts or compensate for the weaknesses found in them.

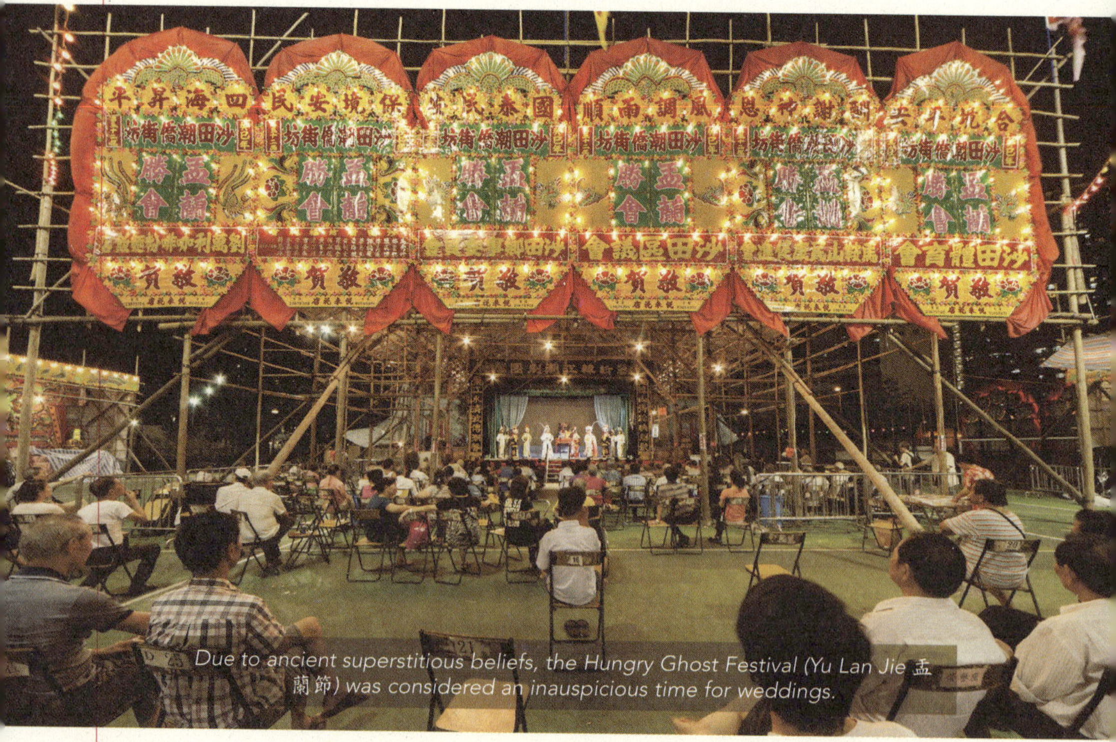

Due to ancient superstitious beliefs, the Hungry Ghost Festival (Yu Lan Jie 孟蘭節) was considered an inauspicious time for weddings.

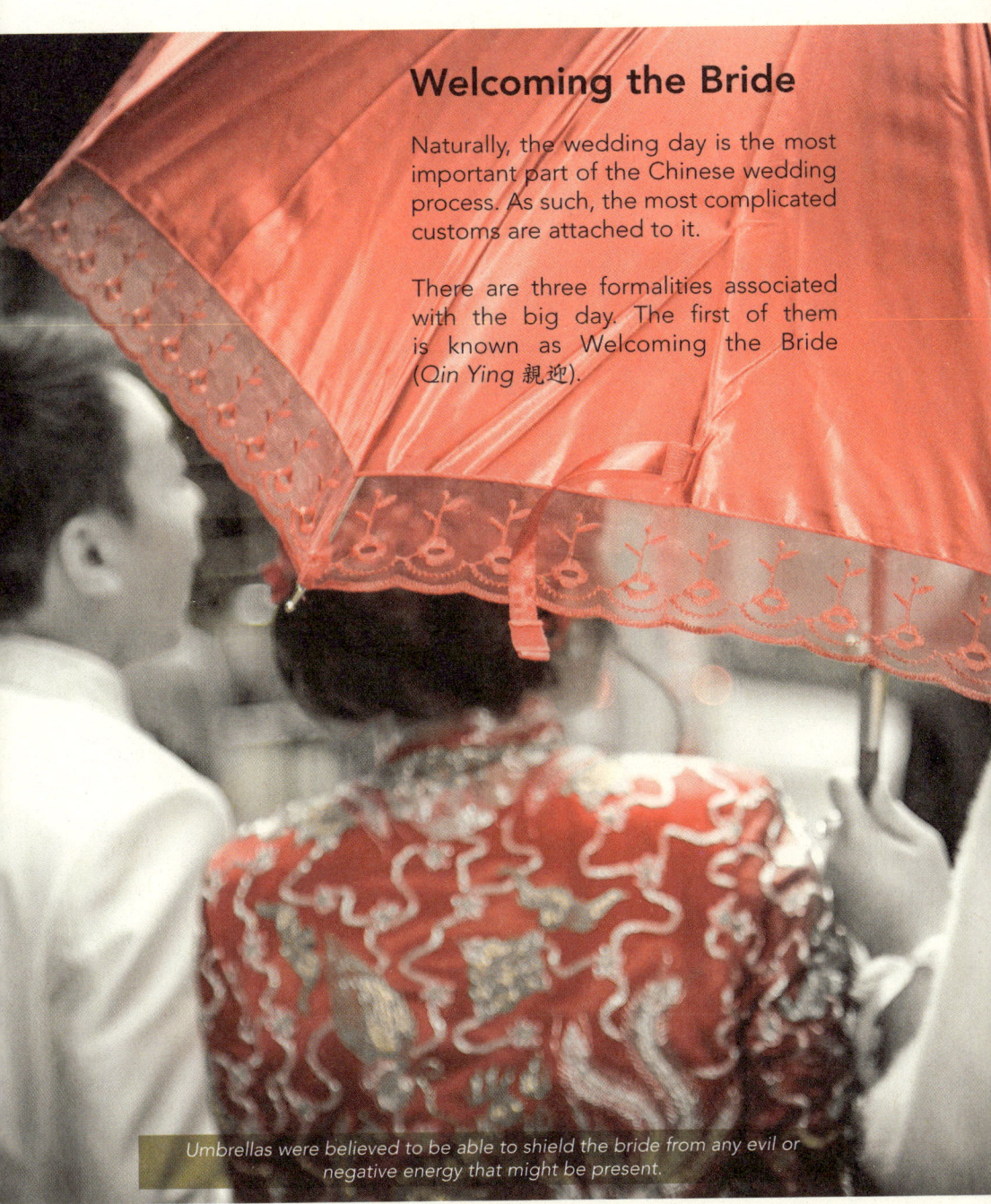

Welcoming the Bride

Naturally, the wedding day is the most important part of the Chinese wedding process. As such, the most complicated customs are attached to it.

There are three formalities associated with the big day. The first of them is known as Welcoming the Bride (*Qin Ying* 親迎).

Umbrellas were believed to be able to shield the bride from any evil or negative energy that might be present.

The Process

The process of Welcoming the Bride (*Qin Ying* 親迎) began on the morning of the wedding, when the groom sat down in the sedan chair that would deliver him to the bride's home.

The groom was to carry eight culturally significant and symbolic gifts with him, all of which he had prepared beforehand;

- Sticky rice balls which represented happiness and completeness
- Pork hocks with a red string tied to them which represented a lasting union
- A black umbrella or rice filter to symbolically protect against evil
- Two oranges which signified good luck
- Red dates and longan tea representing the chance of having a son
- Sweet sticky rice balls representing completeness
- Red envelopes (*Hong Bao* 紅包) or gold jewellery representing good fortune
- Whole bamboo with pork representing chastity and auspiciousness

When the groom arrived at his destination, the bride was expected to be ready to leave. By leaving her home – an action known as Exiting the Pavilion (*Chu Ge* 出閣) – she effectively left her birth family and joined her future husband's household. In accordance with tradition, she was carried out of her house by an old woman whose husband, parents and in-laws were still alive.

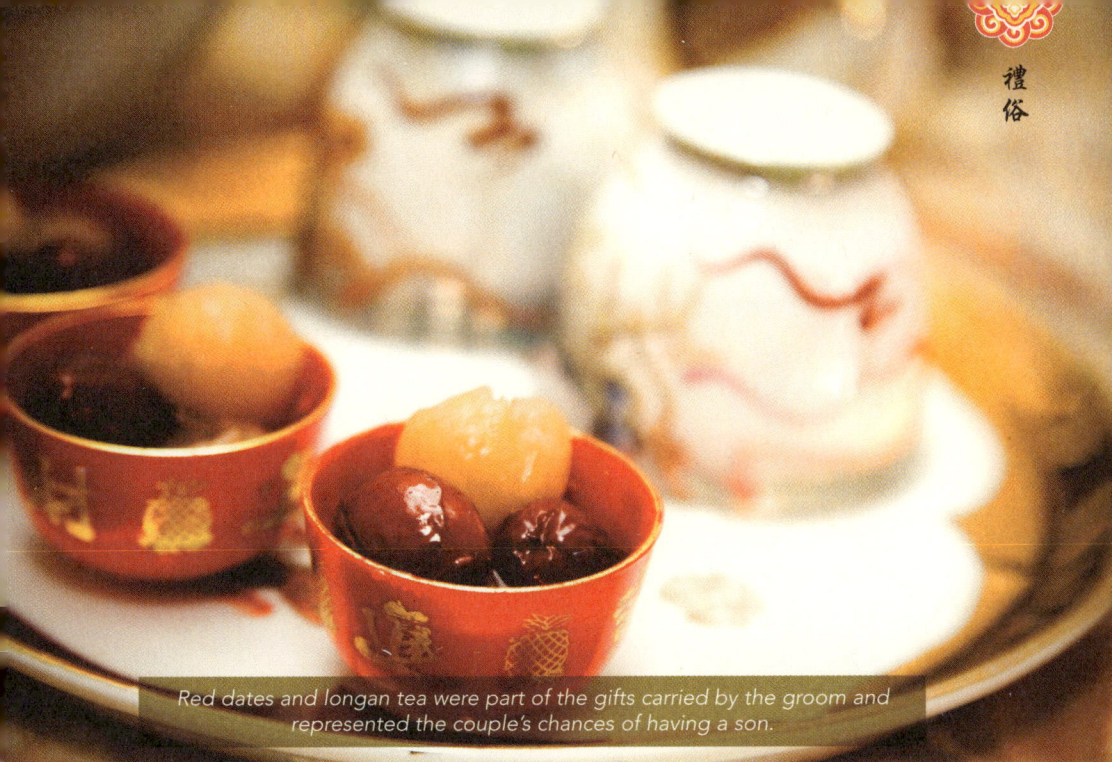

Red dates and longan tea were part of the gifts carried by the groom and represented the couple's chances of having a son.

Before doing this, the old woman opened a black umbrella in order to repel any negative energy that was present. In addition, the bride's face was covered so that her beauty would not incite feelings of jealousy in any spiteful spirits that were nearby.

The moment the bride arrived at the groom's house and stepped out of the sedan chair, the groom's family was expected to be ready with bowls of rice, salt or wine to scatter in her direction. This rite was called Getting Off the Sedan Chair (*Xia Jiao* 下轎) and also helped fend off negative energy and attract auspicious energy in its place.

After the bride had left her sedan chair, the groom would follow suit and stand by her side. His family took this as their cue to literally roll out a red carpet for the couple to walk on as they entered the house. As they passed through the main door, the couple would step over a pot of fire and on some clay prepared beforehand. This ritual was referred to as Entering the Doors (*Ru Men* 入門) and symbolised a fresh start.

Precautions

Over time, guidelines were introduced to ensure that the positive atmosphere of the union was not disrupted. For one thing, a bride's aunts were not invited. If a bride had an older brother who was married, his wife also forbidden from attending. This is because the Chinese words for "aunt" (*Gu* 姑) and "elder brother's wife" (*Sao* 嫂) are phonetically identical to "lonely" (*Gu* 孤) and "sweep" (*Sao* 掃) respectively.

Pregnant women were also barred from attending as it was believed that bad luck would befall the couple if one witnessed the event. Furthermore, pregnant women were discouraged from coming into physical contact with the bodies or clothes of newlyweds. This restriction which is no longer observed today may have been enforced out of concern for pregnant women. There might have been a fear that these expectant mothers might somehow get into an accident and consequently suffer a miscarriage which would have been potentially deadly due to the limited access to medical assistance in that era.

People whose animal birth signs or BaZi charts clashed with the wedding day were also kept off the special guest list for wedding day activities. They were also forbidden from taking up significant positions in a wedding (bridesmaid, best man etc). Fortunately, they were still allowed to attend the wedding banquet.

The sedan responsible for carrying the bride to the groom's house was also bound by its own restriction: under no circumstances should it crash into another sedan during its journey. The belief was that when two sedans collided, a situation referred to as the Clashing of Auspiciousness (*Xi Chong Xi* 喜沖喜) would occur, bringing a couple bad luck.

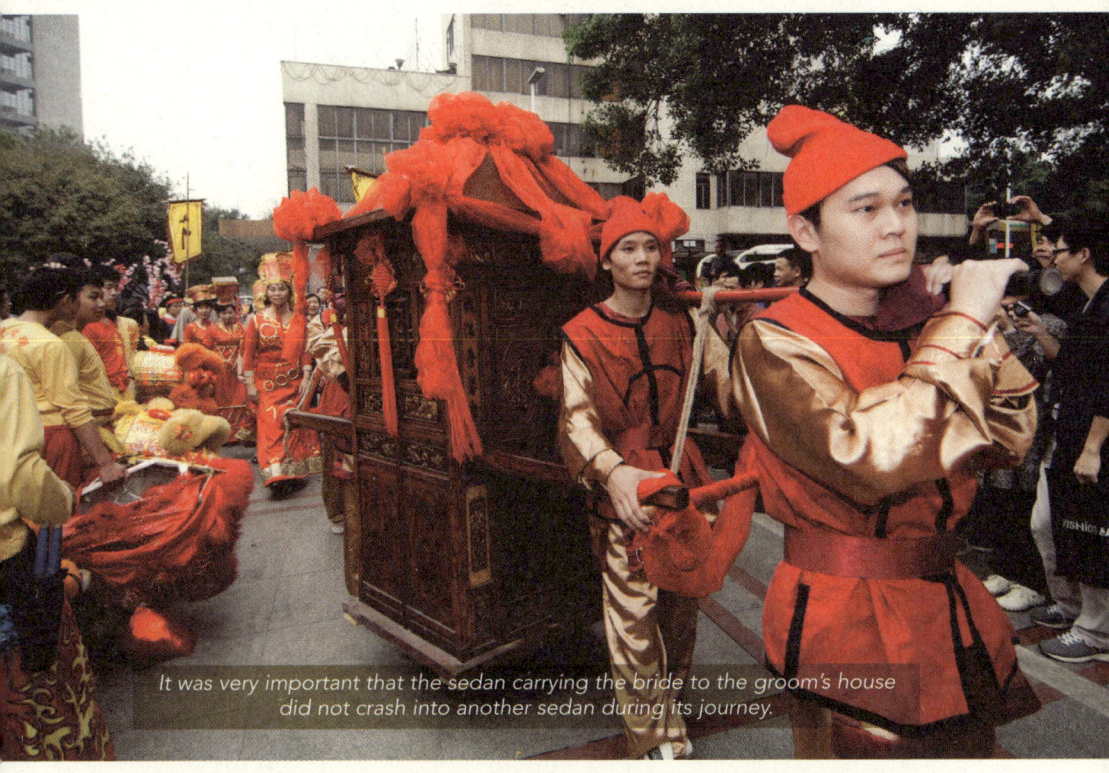

It was very important that the sedan carrying the bride to the groom's house did not crash into another sedan during its journey.

For her part, a bride to be was expected to be composed when she arrived at the groom's house. Although it was natural for women to feel sad when leaving their parents' house, they were discouraged from crying, especially once they reached their destination. It was believed that by showing negative emotions she would bring bad energy or Bad Qi to the groom's parents.

Last but not least, everyone present at the groom's house was expected to hide themselves to avoid the bride when she arrived with the groom. This was done presumably to ensure that they did not disrupt her energy field in any way. They were only allowed to return to the living room after the couple had entered the bridal room.

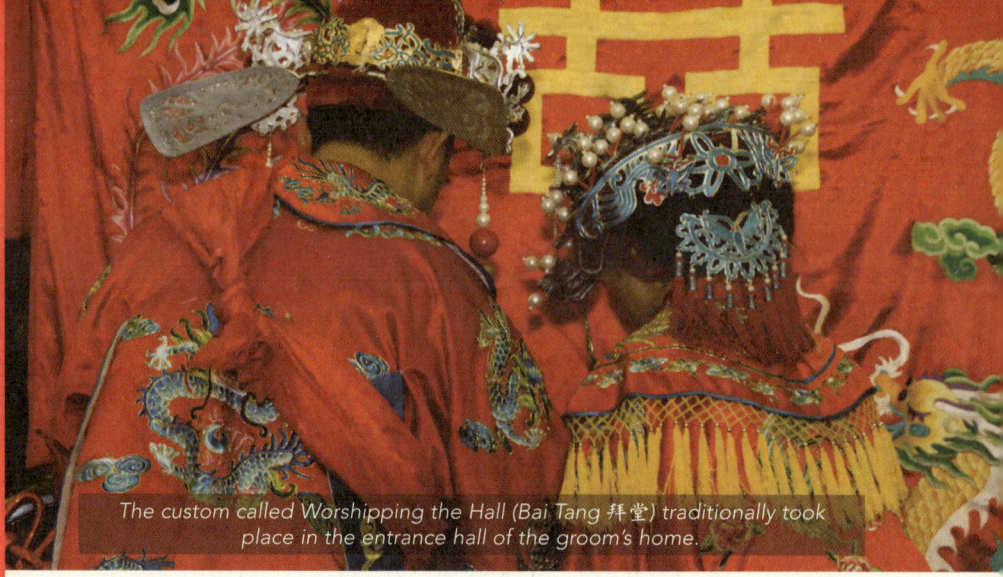

The custom called Worshipping the Hall (Bai Tang 拜堂) traditionally took place in the entrance hall of the groom's home.

Worshipping Heaven and Earth

After a couple had stepped over the fire and onto the clay at the end of the Entering the Doors (*Ru Men* 入門) phase of the Welcoming the Bride (*Qin Ying* 親迎) custom, the Worshipping Heaven and Earth (*Bai Tian Di* 拜天地) ritual would begin.

This traditionally took place in the entrance hall of the groom's home and was originally called Worshipping the Hall (*Bai Tang* 拜堂). Worshipping Heaven and Earth was a colloquial name for the ritual which seceded its original name at some point.

The original version of this custom was developed during the Jin dynasty (265-420 AD) and reflected the sexist culture of the time. It was less about worshipping Heaven and Earth and more about women being submissive towards men. A bride to be would bow to her future husband who would then reciprocate, prompting her to bow again in gratitude. This would be repeated a short while later, so that the woman had bowed four times and the man had bowed twice.

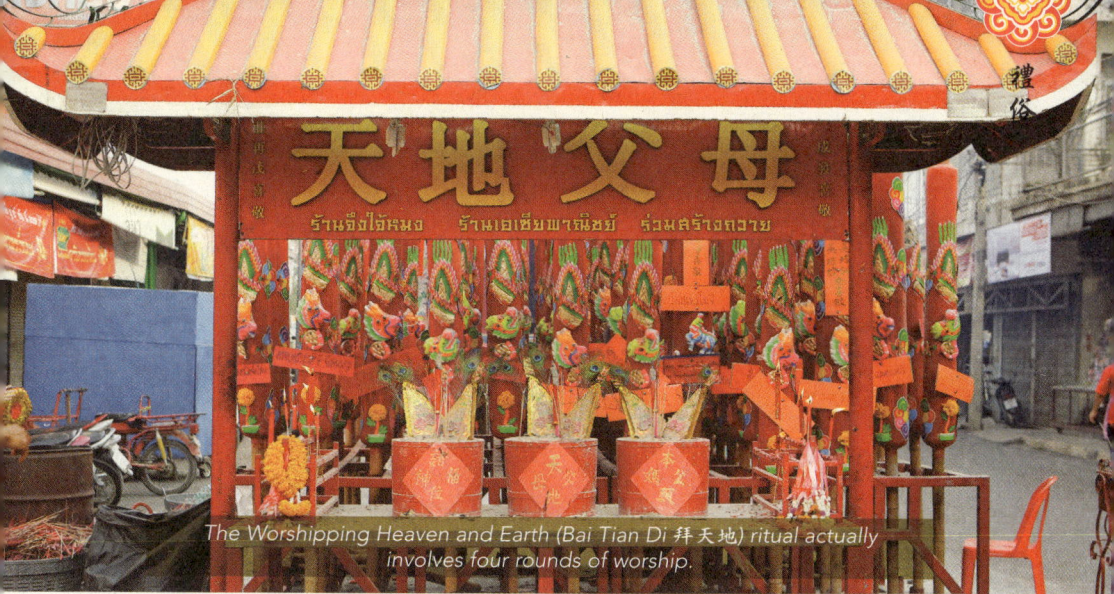

The Worshipping Heaven and Earth (Bai Tian Di 拜天地) ritual actually involves four rounds of worship.

During the Yuan dynasty (1271-1368), this custom was replaced with the one described below.

Worshipping Heaven and Earth (*Bai Tian Di* 拜天地)

The name of this ritual suggests that it involves prayer to divine forces, but it has many beneficiaries. It consists of four rounds of worship. First, a couple worshipped the groom's ancestors. In doing so, they formally informed them that the woman had joined the man's family.

Next, the second round of prayer and the ritual's namesake began. The bride and groom bowed three times and kowtowed nine times in the honour of Heaven and Earth. As the union between Heaven and Earth reflected the union between Yin and Yang, worshipping them was an appropriate way for a Yin husband and Yang wife to pay their respects.

Finally, a couple would bow to the groom's parents as an expression of filial piety. They then faced each other and bowed in a show of mutual respect for one another that would last for the rest of their lives together.

The Wedding Banquet

Sometimes called the Joyful Wine (*Xi Jiu* 喜酒), the wedding banquet is considered by some as more important than the wedding itself! They allow a new couple and their parents to share their happiness with other loved ones and express their gratitude to everyone who set aside time to celebrate the occasion.

Wedding banquets are almost identical to regular banquets. The same decorations and food are used for both. The main difference is that the main table at a wedding banquet is reserved for newlyweds, their parents and grandparents. Other guests are seated based on their relationship to the couple.

In ancient China, wedding banquets were held with an acute awareness of what marriage entailed. This lead to the creation of the development of Pranks on the Bride (*Nao Dong Fang* 鬧洞房) which came to make light of what followed it: Consummation of the Marriage (*Dong Fang* 洞房).

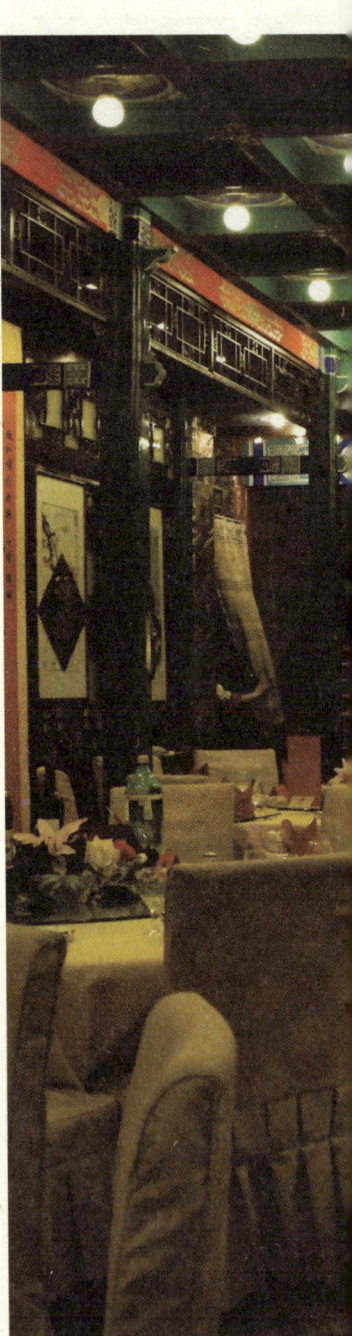

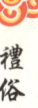
禮俗

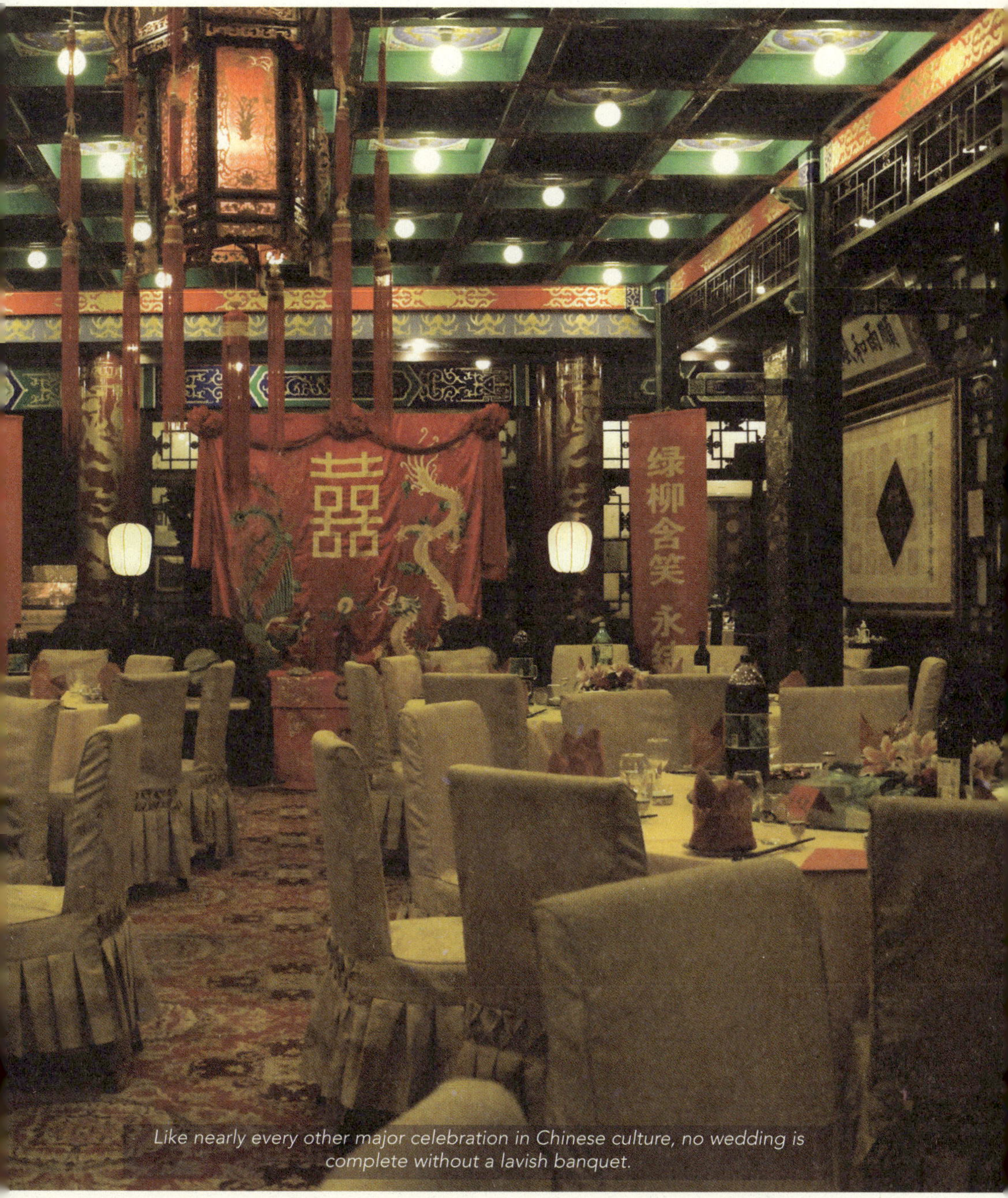

Like nearly every other major celebration in Chinese culture, no wedding is complete without a lavish banquet.

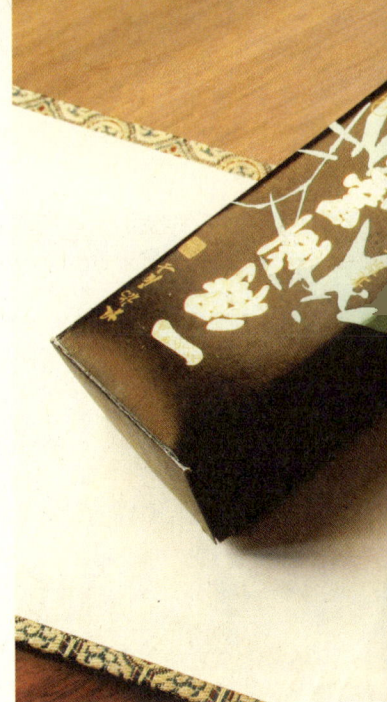

Restrictions

Wedding banquets are differentiated from regular banquets by their additional restrictions. These restrictions are rooted in the belief that certain actions can bring a couple bad vibes in the future. Many were created to help prevent divorce or bad energies which could lead to unhappiness in the marriage.

For their part, guests must take care not to break any kitchenware used for the banquet, the belief being that this suggests that a couple will separate in the future. Guests are also discouraged from stacking their bowls and plates when they finish eating as doing so is associated with remarriage (and the prerequisite separation).

In terms of seating, guests invited by the bride should not be seated with the guests invited by the groom apart from mutual friends. Pains were taken to provide the bride's guest with exemplary service or else it was believed the couple would have an undesirable outlook in regard to their married life.

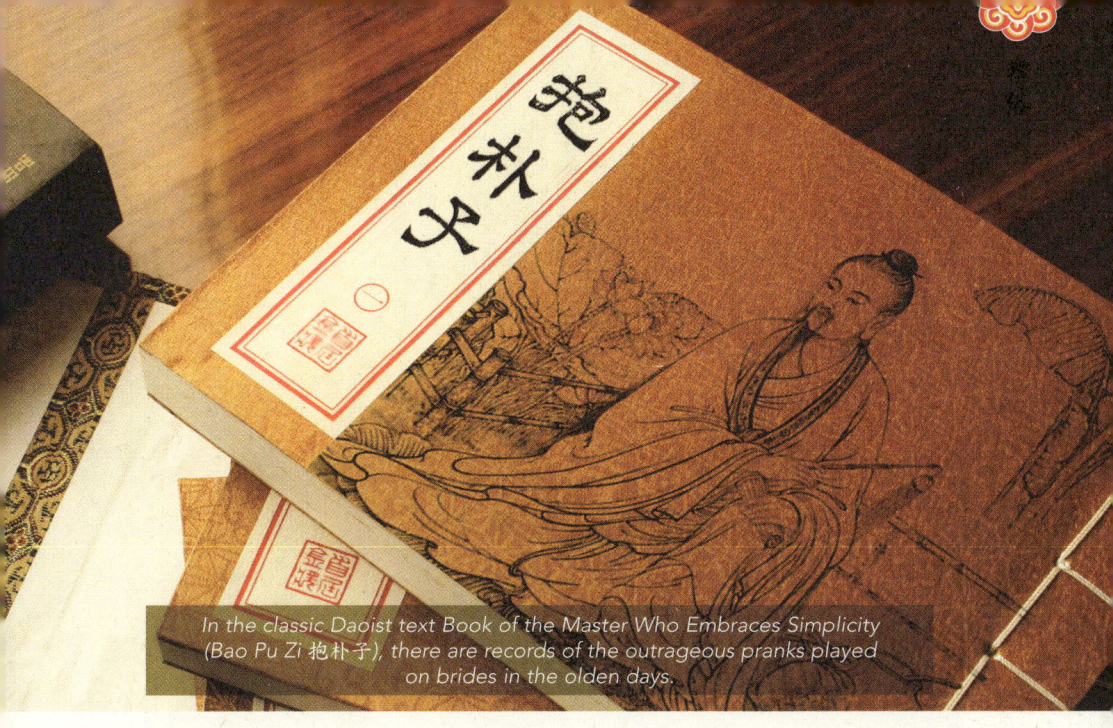

In the classic Daoist text Book of the Master Who Embraces Simplicity (Bao Pu Zi 抱朴子), there are records of the outrageous pranks played on brides in the olden days.

Pranks on the Bride (*Nao Dong Fang* 鬧洞房)

Despite the innocent-sounding name, the Pranks on the Bride tradition has a dark history. It was created during the Han dynasty between 206 BC and 220 AD when a bride was abducted and forced to provide sexual favours to her new husband and his friends.

After the fall of the Han dynasty, the practice lost its sexual component. Instead of sexually coercing a bride, people played pranks on her. The classic Daoist text Book of the Master Who Embraces Simplicity (*Bao Pu Zi* 抱朴子) notes that these pranks were often extreme in and of themselves. In one example, a bride is hung upside down from a tree.

Pranks remained humiliating in nature until the Ming dynasty. By the time the Qing dynasty came to power, wedding guests were limited to making jokes at a bride's expense. In time, brides were spared and the groom became the victim of pranks instead. Since these pranks were carried out during the wedding banquet, they usually involved subjecting the groom to a lot of alcohol.

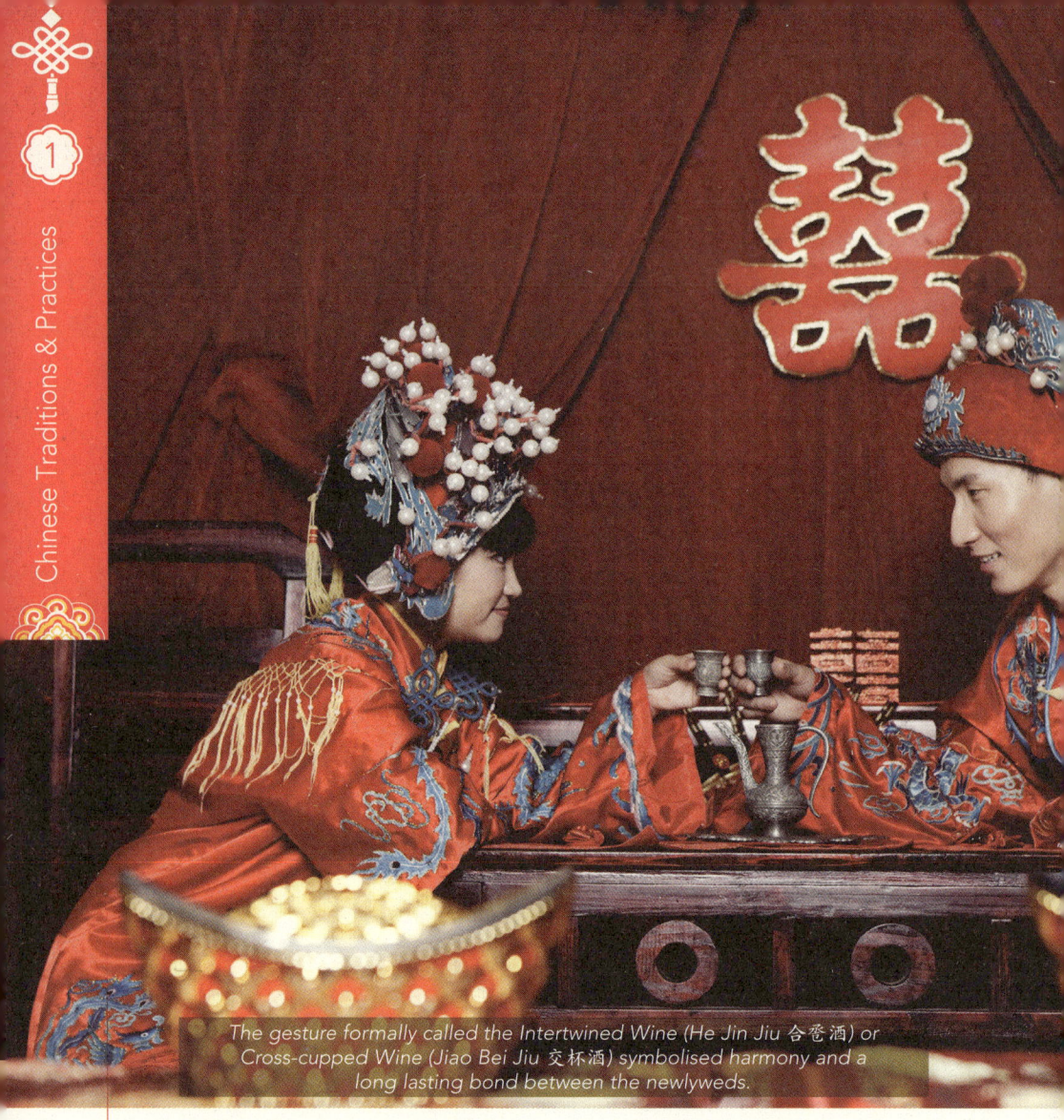

The gesture formally called the Intertwined Wine (He Jin Jiu 合卺酒) or Cross-cupped Wine (Jiao Bei Jiu 交杯酒) symbolised harmony and a long lasting bond between the newlyweds.

Consummation of the Marriage (*Dong Fang* 洞房)

Once the pranks had ended and the banquet was over, it was time for the Consummation of the Marriage to take place! The Chinese name can be dissected to reveal its original meanings which are "a secluded room in the mansion" and a "room deep in the cave" indicating that this is the first time the newlyweds will make love.

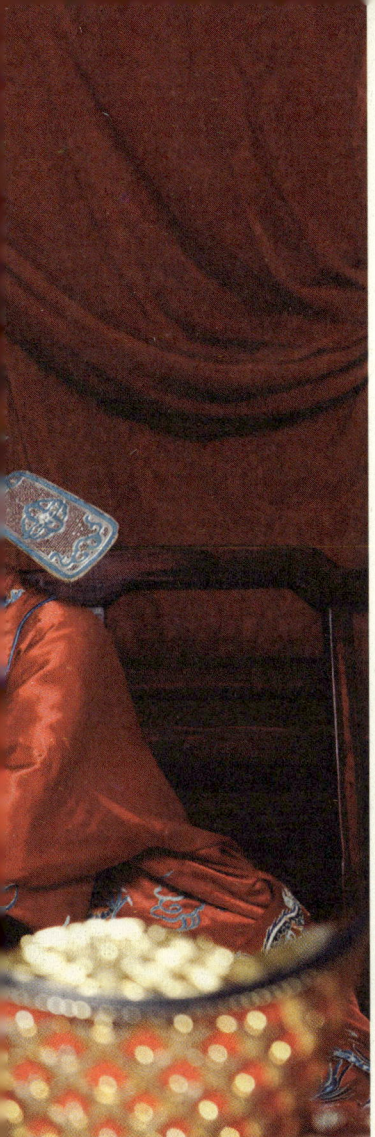

In rural parts of ancient China, wedding guests occasionally gathered outside the newlywed's bedroom door to listen in on what was happening inside. It should be noted that this was done in keeping with the tradition of playing Pranks on the Bride.

Brides from upper-class families were subject to far more considerate behaviour in recognition of their social status. In addition, a well-to-do bride could wear a red veil over her face so that she would feel less self-conscious and more relaxed about everything. One must remember that this would be the first encounter that most women have ever had with a man from outside their family, so nerves may have been the norm!

Before consummating their marriage, a couple first shared a drink with their arms interlocked. This gesture symbolised harmony and a long lasting bond between the newlyweds and it was formally called the Intertwined Wine (*He Jin Jiu* 合巹酒) or Cross-cupped Wine (*Jiao Bei Jiu* 交杯酒). A drinking utensil made out of a dried gourd was split in two to make a pair of nuptial wine cups (Jin 巹) for the custom. The tip of each half was tied to the other with a length of red string. Once a couple had finished their share of the wine, they were formally "tied" to each other.

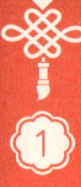

The Post Wedding Ceremonies

After the big day was over, a traditional Chinese wedding was largely finished but not entirely. A few ceremonies had to be performed on the day after the wedding. These formalities helped cement the new union.

The first of these customs was the second tea ceremony (*Chi Cha* 喫茶). This was followed by the Returning to the Household (*Gui Ning* 歸寧) ceremony which brought the overall wedding to an end.

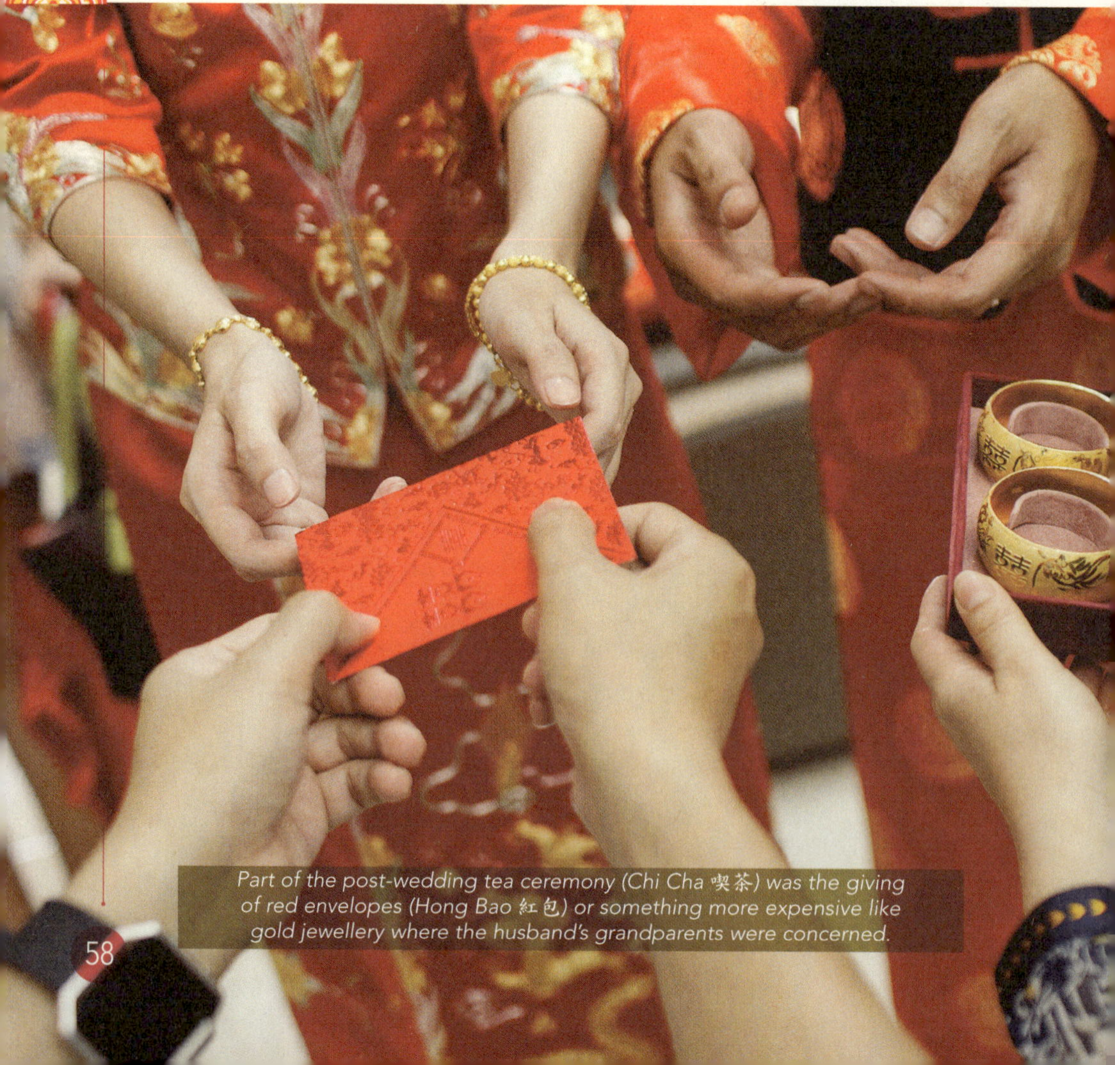

Part of the post-wedding tea ceremony (Chi Cha 喫茶) was the giving of red envelopes (Hong Bao 紅包) or something more expensive like gold jewellery where the husband's grandparents were concerned.

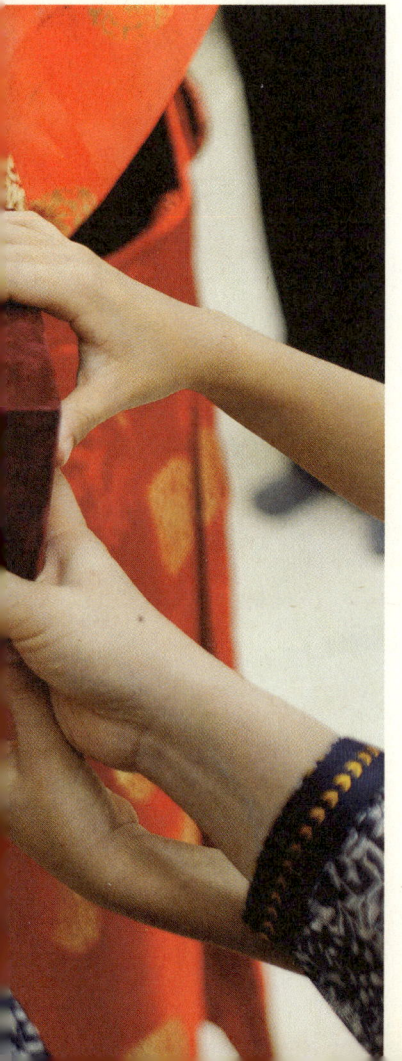

The Tea Ceremony
(*Chi Cha* 喫茶)

This tea ceremony differs from the one held during the Civil Engagement (*Wen Ding* 文定) as it is more formal. Translated literally its name means "drinking tea" rather than "serving tea".

The tea ceremony gave a woman the chance to meet her new husband's family. As such, the majority of his relatives would attend. As in the earlier tea ceremony (*Feng Cha* 奉茶), the woman was expected to serve tea, six cups at a time. She had to do this several times, depending on how many people were in attendance. As she served tea, she would greet and address her husband's family as if they were her own. For example, she would call her father-in-law "father". She would then continue doing this for the duration of her married life.

For their part, her husband's relatives would offer red envelopes (*Hong Bao* 紅包) containing an even sum of money of their choosing. A husband's grandparents were obligated to offer a more expensive gift. Gold jewellery was the most popular choice for this purpose.

Returning to the Household (*Gui Ning* 歸寧)

This gynocentric ritual concluded a Chinese wedding. During the Returning to the Household, a couple would return to the wife's household to greet her birth family. This was usually done three days after the big day as the husband was usually hungover on the first day and the tea ceremony with the husband's family took place on the second day.

On the day, the wife's mother would prepare pastries and two kinds of cookies to welcome the newlyweds in the morning. Although she could cook whatever cookies she wishes, they were referred to as Cookies of Two Colours (*Shuang Se Bing* 雙色餅). The ceremony itself consisted of the couple having lunch with the wife's parents and little more.

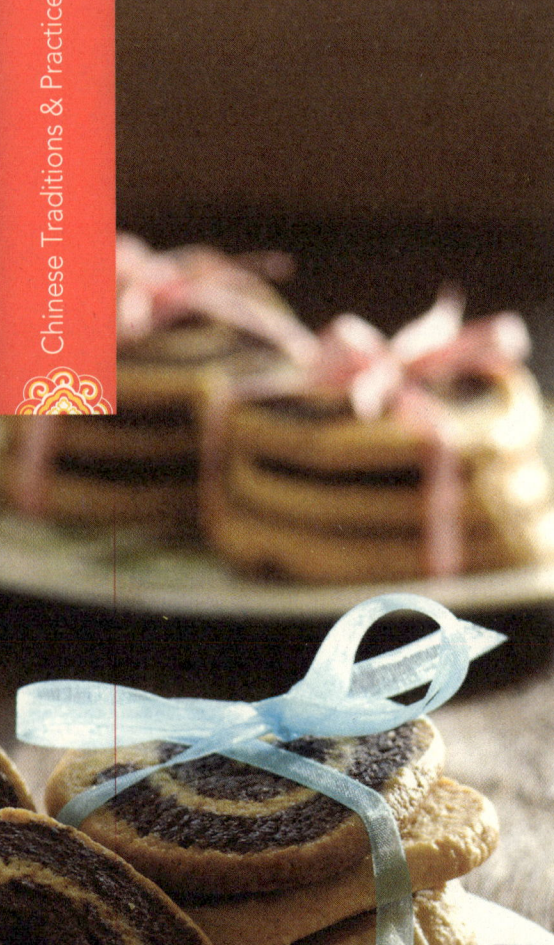

Cookies of Two Colours (*Shuang Se Bing* 雙色餅) awaited the newlyweds upon returning to the wife's household.

When the meal was over and the newlyweds were ready to return to the husband's home, the wife's mother would offer her new son-in-law and his family a gift. Once again, she had free reign but two popular choices were sugarcane and a pair of "leading chickens" (*Dai Lu Ji* 帶路雞). Like all gifts in Chinese customs, these two items held cultural and symbolic significance. The sugarcane's length was meant to represent the duration of the marriage and its sweetness represented joy, making it an apt symbol of marital harmony. This sentiment is embodied in the old saying "sweetness from the tip to the end" (*You Tou Tian Dao Wei* 由頭甜到尾).

Meanwhile, "leading chickens" was the name given to a live rooster and hen symbolizing fertility (hens can produce many eggs in a short period of time). Their name stems from the idea that they would lead the way back to the husband's home. Despite the name, they were actually placed in a basket and it was believed that a couple's first child would be a boy if the rooster was the first of the two to come out.

Some mothers-in-law gave as many as six "leading chickens" along with six eggs. The modern version of this custom substitutes the chickens for more eggs. Today, this entire gift giving process has evolved and a wide variety of gifts are given. Many people simply give red envelopes to avoid the hassle of choosing an appropriate gift.

Gifts aside, it was considered imperative that the couple return to the husband's home before dinnertime as the agrarian-based mindset of ancient China dictated that all productive activity was to cease by nightfall. Additionally, people in ancient China believed that the chances of conception increased at night, so newlyweds were encouraged to return home quickly and begin their attempts to produce a family!

Chapter 2

The Miracle of Conceiving A Child

Throughout human history, civilisations developed their own ever-evolving ideas about human reproduction. The people of ancient China were no exception.

One concept they had about the matter was destiny which refers to the belief that things such as a person's chances of having a child were beyond their control. This idea that things were set in stone was particularly prevalent when it came to the possibility of having a son instead of children in general as people back then vastly valued sons over daughters. To try and predict the gender of a child, families used various metaphysical tools like *Purple Star Astrology* (*Zi Wei Dou Shu* 紫微斗數), *Qi Men Dun Jia* 奇門遁甲, *BaZi* 八字 and *Ghost Valley Divination* (*Gui Gu Zi Zhan Bu* 鬼谷子占卜).

Aside from that, there are the concepts of naturalism and symbolism which assert that human and non-human affairs are shaped and affected by natural forces like causality, the influence of the cosmos and deities. Naturalism led to the development of customs and rituals which were believed to be able to circumvent or manipulate these forces and tilt a couple's odds in favour of producing a son. For example, a woman who desires to be with child may be forbidden from carrying out certain actions or activities for fear of these activities reducing her chances of bearing her husband a son. Her parents-in-law would also worship certain deities hoping for a grandson.

Meanwhile, the concept of spiritual symbolism gave rise to customs which embody the balance of nature or the mutually complementary nature of the existence of men and women.

Modern readers may find the emphasis on producing male children offensive. It is worth noting that the concepts of male supremacy and filial piety were by no means unique to ancient

Chinese culture. Historically, most societies have held a patriarchal belief system wherein sons were seen as the legitimate heirs to prestige and property. In ancient China, only men were able to pass on the family name. Male offspring were therefore essential for preserving a family lineage. On a more practical note, ancient China was an agricultural society. Physical labour was in high demand and since men are typically stronger than women, male children were preferred.

To this day, the Chinese word for offspring, *Zi* (子), still means son unless otherwise specified. As an aside, the same character was used as an honorary title for government officials and knowledgeable men like *Confucius* (*Kong Zi* 孔子).

With regards to female rights and equality, things are changing for the better. Women now have the right to inherit a family estate for example. Less importance is placed on passing on the family name and new laws allow women to pass their family name on to their children should they so wish.

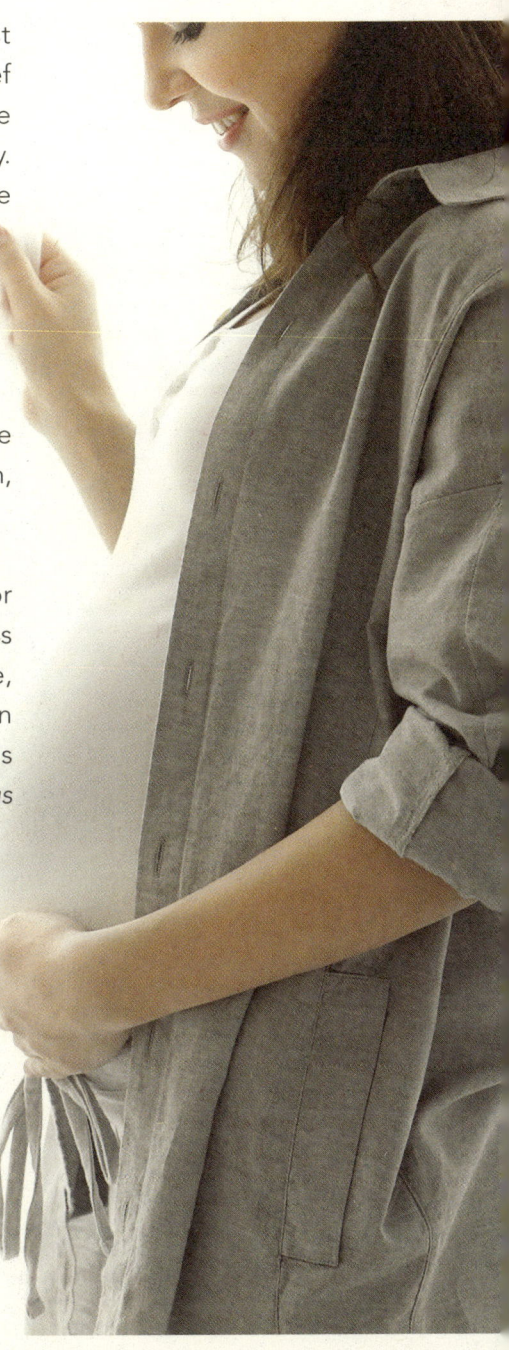

The Three Stages of Childbearing

It should be noted that many of the customs introduced as a result of these beliefs were largely fuelled by the fact that women often died during childbirth or soon after from complications and infant mortality was also very high. Consequently, a number of customs and procedures were developed to improve their odds of surviving. One of the most well-known is post-childbirth confinement which is practiced to this day.

Regardless of which concept a particular household believed in, the people of ancient China generally viewed the entire process of human reproduction as having three stages: the conception stage, the delivery stage and the post-childbirth stage.

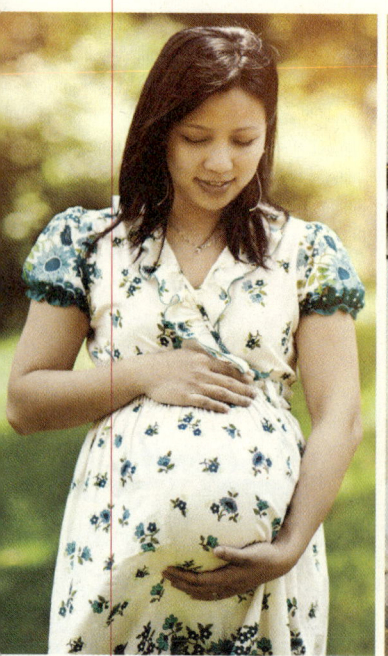
Conception stage

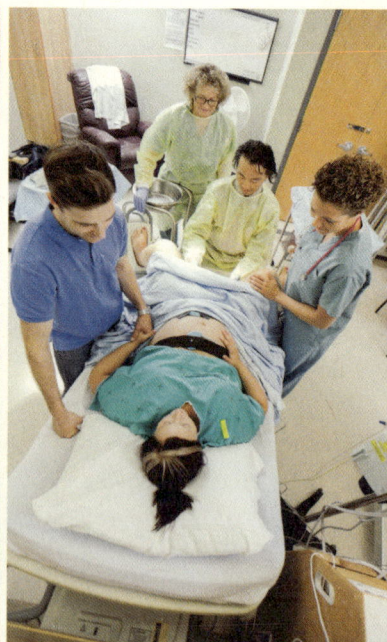
Delivery stage

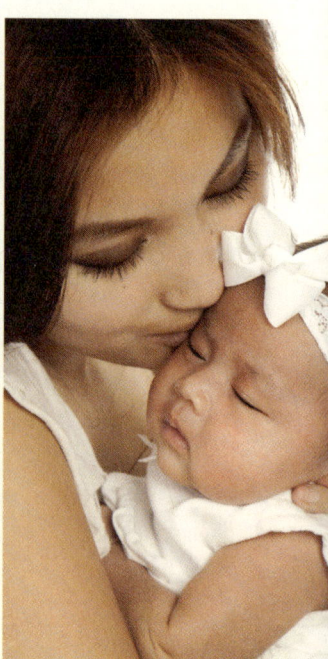
Post-childbirth stage

Conception

Modern science has allowed us to understand conception, pregnancy and childbirth far better than our ancestors. Because of their lack of medical knowledge, the ancient Chinese could only speculate and guess about such matters. Many beliefs and customs reflect this.

As mentioned earlier, it was believed that certain actions increased the chances of producing a son. These were believed to help "summon" or "recruit" a son into a family. Furthermore, it was believed that certain practices could endow the son with special powers and the favour of certain deities.

The most common way people tried to increase their chances of having a son was to appeal to deities associated with childbirth. These included the *Immortal Zhang* (*Zhang Xian* 張仙), the *Lady of the Purple Dawn* (*Bi Xia Yuan Jun* 碧霞元君) and *Guan Yin Pu Sa* 觀音菩薩 in her role as the *Giver of Children* (*Song Zi Guan Yin* 送子觀音). Customs like *Doll-lassoing* (*Shuan Wa Wa* 栓娃娃), paper-cutting (*Jian Zhi* 剪紙), collecting items associated with children and decorating the spousal bedchamber became widespread too.

Worship of the Immortal Zhang (Zhang Xian 張仙)

The *Immortal Zhang* is one of the few male deities associated with childbirth. People worshipped him because they believed he could grant them a male offspring. He could also assist infertile women or expectant mothers dealing with birth complications.

He is usually depicted as an archer with his bow drawn, pointed at the sky. This image has its basis in the belief that eclipses were caused by a gigantic mythical beast called the *Heavenly Dog* (*Tian Gou* 天狗) "eating" the sun or moon. The *Immortal Zhang* would shoot his arrows at the animal to chase it away. It was believed that the Heavenly Dog preyed on young children. By fighting it, the *Immortal Zhang* protected them from harm – a noble deed worthy of praise by those wishing to conceive.

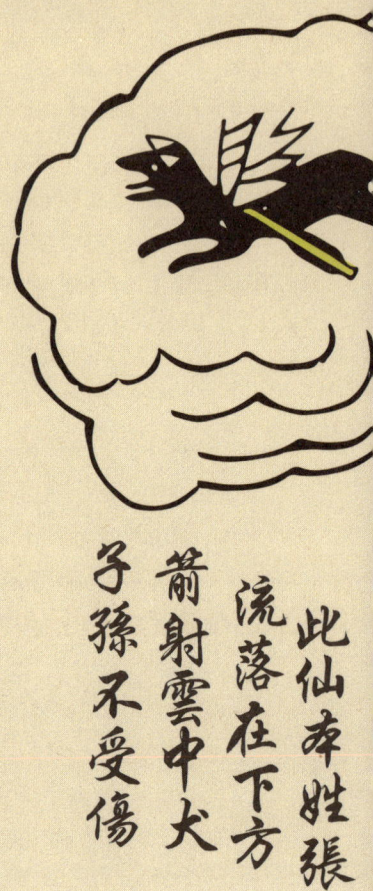

此仙本姓張
流落在下方
箭射雲中犬
子孫不受傷

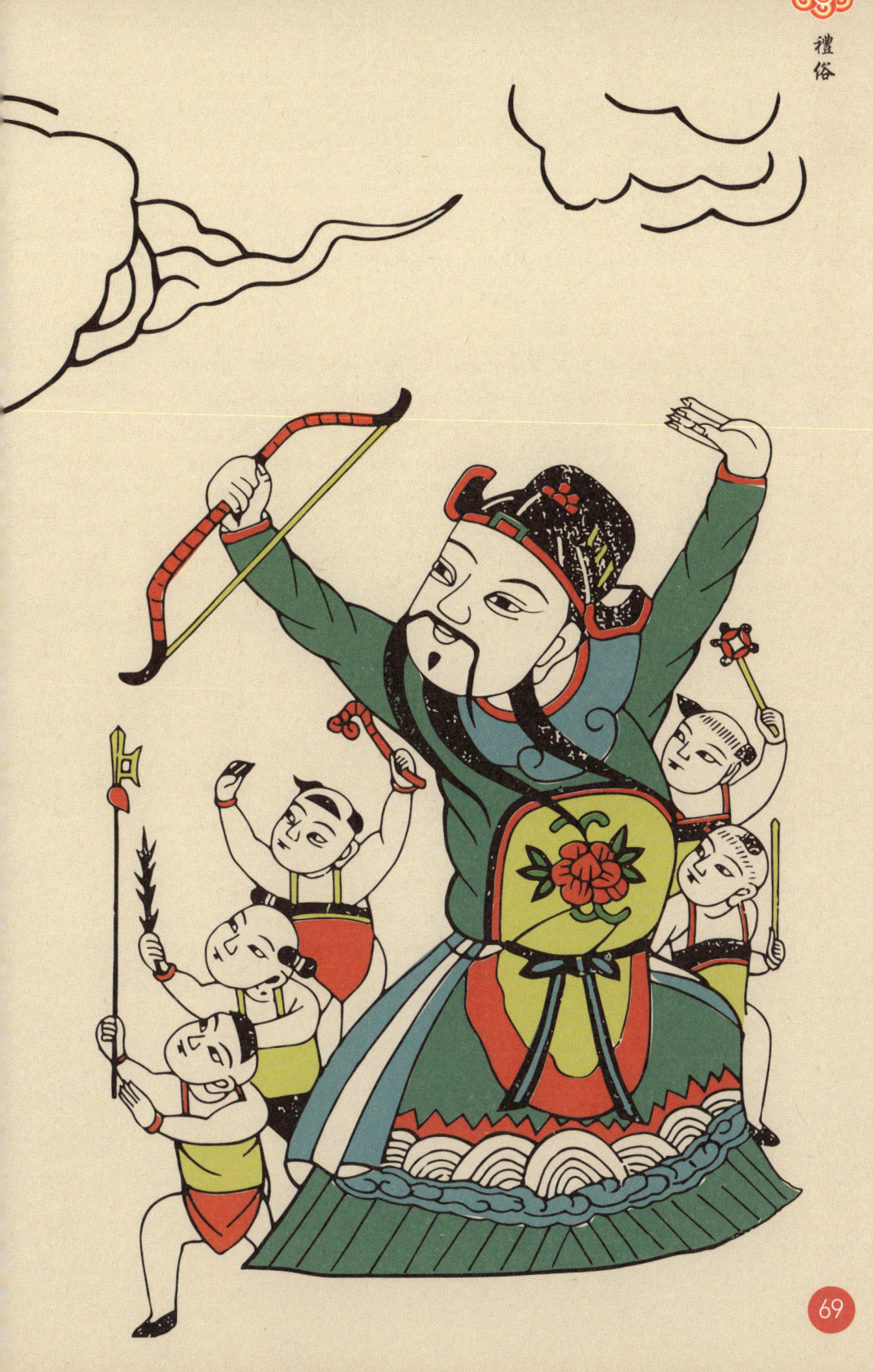

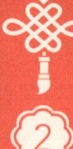

Worship of the Lady of the Purple Dawn (*Bi Xia Yuan Jun* 碧霞元君)

The *Lady of the Purple Dawn* is a Daoist deity associated with childbirth, destiny and the dawn whose name is sometimes translated to *Goddess of Teal Clouds*. Her temple which is called *Temple of the Purple Dawn* (*Bi Xia Ci* 碧霞祠) is located on the historically and culturally significant Mount Tai in the Shandong province. She is the daughter of *Emperor Lord of Mount Tai* (*Dong Yue Da Di* 東嶽大帝) and for that reason is occasionally referred to as the *Goddess of Mount Tai* (*Tai Shan Niang Niang* 泰山娘娘).

Among her many roles, the *Lady of the Purple Dawn* is most famous for being a fertility goddess. Daoists believe that her influence over the process of childbirth is so great that she oversees not only every child's delivery but also their destiny in life. To this day, pregnant women worship her in the hope that she can give their children a bright future.

禮俗

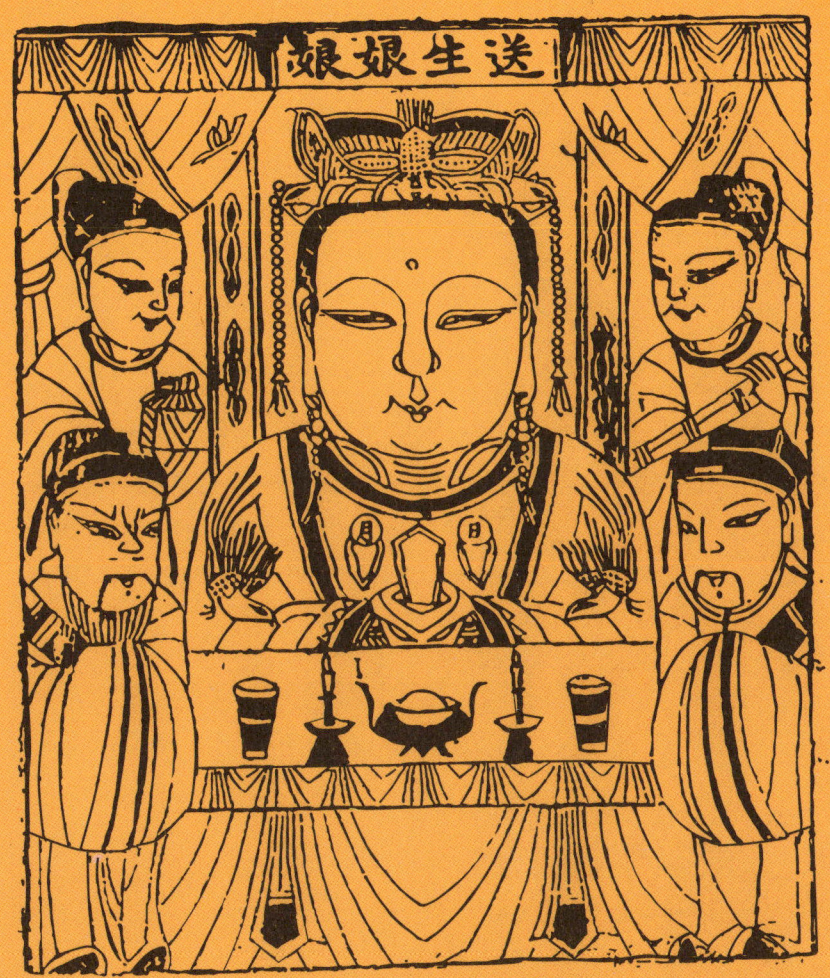

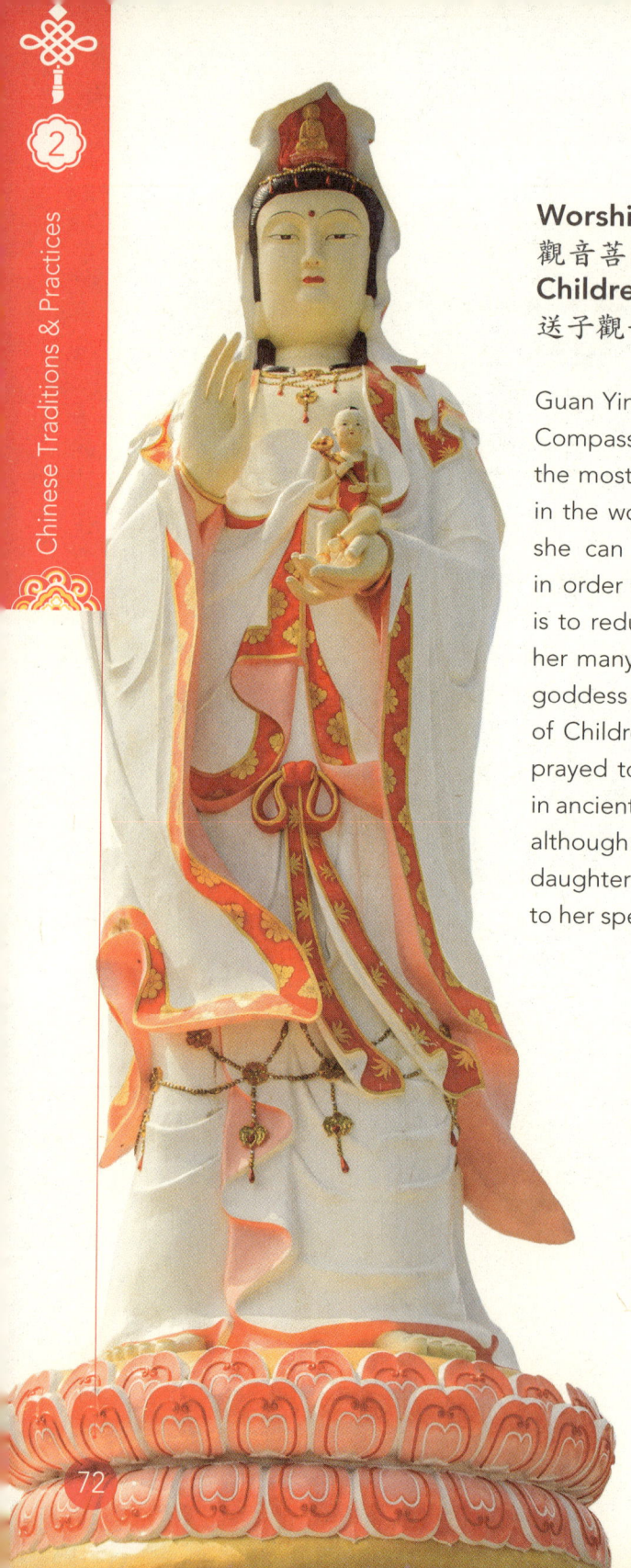

Worship of Guan Yin Pu Sa 觀音菩薩, the Giver of Children (*Song Zi Guan Yin* 送子觀音)

Guan Yin Pu Sa, the Goddess of Compassion and Mercy, is one of the most well-known goddesses in the world. Legend has it that she can take on several forms in order to fulfil her goal which is to reduce suffering. In one of her many forms, she is a fertility goddess with the title "Giver of Children". Expectant parents prayed to the Giver of Children in ancient times for male children although those who wanted a daughter instead could also pray to her specifically asking for one.

On a related note, the Buddhist origins of Guanyin Bodhisattva suggest that she is a somewhat gender-neutral deity. She is traditionally said to be able to take on whatever form she chooses in order to help those in need and thus has the power to determine the sex of children. This is demonstrated in a story in the *Book of Exotic Tales* (*Shu Yi Ji* 述異記) where an old woman with no sons and only one daughter prayed to *Guan Yin* for a son. When she went to sleep that night, she dreamt that the goddess offered her child a red pill. When the old woman woke up, her daughter had become a boy.

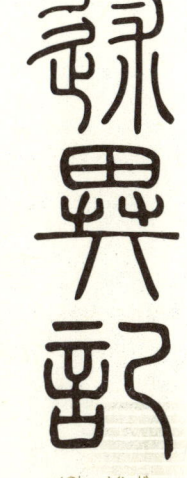

(Shu Yi Ji)
Book of Exotic Tales

Although there are many temples honouring Guan Yin today, people once believed she preferred to dwell in several caves throughout China. Worshippers would therefore travel to these locations to worship her.

Additionally, couples used to secretly take clothing and accessories like shoes or the willow branch she held from statues of her in the belief that these items would increase their chances of having a son. This was possible because such statues of her used to be dressed in real clothing that could be removed.

Doll-lassoing (Shuan Wa Wa 栓娃娃)

In ancient China, some temples had clay dolls or plates called *Dragon Plates* (*Long Pai* 龍牌) which were used by women who wished to have a son. They would loop a red or blue string or tie a coin to said string and then toss the loop at the aforementioned clay dolls or plates. If they managed to catch a doll or plate, they would pray and recite the line, "Son, please come with your mother." (*Er Gen Niang Hui Jia Ba.* 兒跟娘回家吧。) This is because being able to catch the item symbolised the successful "summoning" of a son who was willing to come and be born to the woman in question.

Additionally, there would sometimes be an old woman who either worked or volunteered at the temple whose duties included overseeing this ritual. They would oversee the doll-lassoing ritual. If a woman succeeded in "catching" a son, this old woman would hand her a yellow envelope filled with coins which had "May you have a son" written on it. When she received the envelope, the hopeful mother would rush home and put it under her bed immediately. The belief was that doing this ensured she would have the son she just "caught" in the following year.

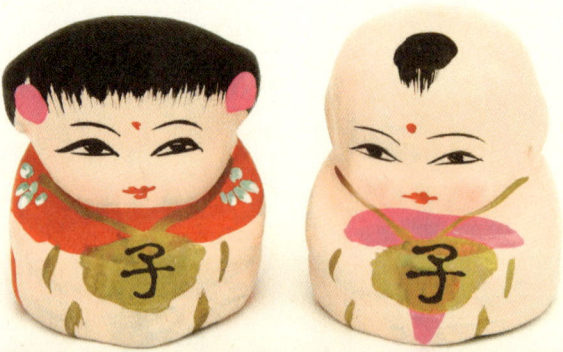

Clay dolls such as these are meant to be representations of the children that hopeful mothers wish to have and "catching" them is believed to lead to a successful conception.

Paper-cutting (*Jian Zhi* 剪紙)

The art of paper-cutting is roughly as old as paper itself which was invented during the Eastern Han dynasty and has its roots in age-old practices related to beliefs and the worship of gods. One such instance is when women who longed for a son would take a piece of red paper and cut it into various patterns and designs associated with reproductive success.

Common designs featured trees with sprawling branches symbolising a large family tree. Lotuses and gourds were also popular as both contain multiple seeds and the Chinese word for seed is the same as the word for son. The flowers of plum trees, peach trees, mulberry bushes, apple trees and Sichuan trees as well as roses were popular too because they symbolised femininity.

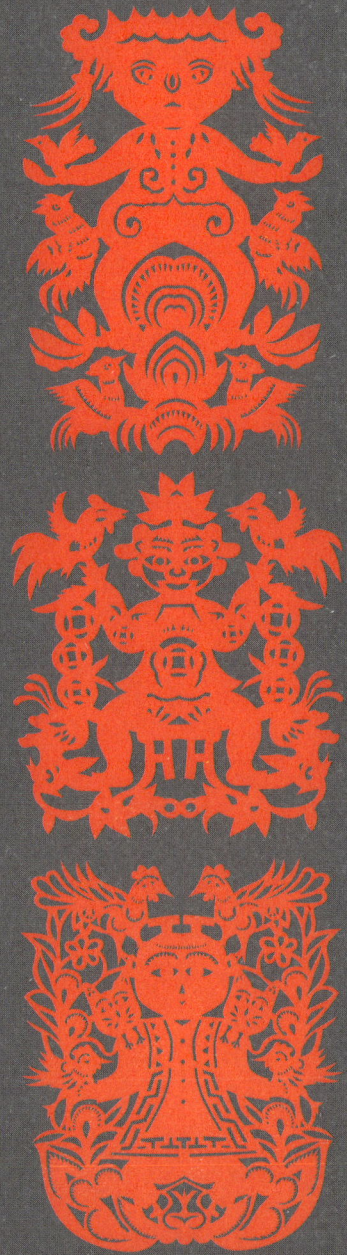

Paper-cutting was thought to have the power to bring about specific outcomes.

Some women liked to use patterns depicting animals like frogs as their rounded bellies made them appear pregnant and they are known to produce a large number of eggs at one time which represents a high fertility rate. Fish were also popular because they produce an immense number of eggs. Another auspicious pick using the same line of logic was rats due to their ability to have multiple pups at one time.

Aside from patterns based on real flora and fauna, designs related to mythical occurrences were equally prevalent. One such design is of the *Child-delivering Qilin (Qi Lin Song Zi* 麒麟送子) which shows a child being brought by a *Qilin*. A mythical chimerical creature with Chinese dragon-like features such as its head and antlers as well as cloven hooves, the Qilin is traditionally associated with a sage or knowledgeable man in some capacity. As such, the delivery of a son to any household by this creature was seen as an incredibly auspicious sign.

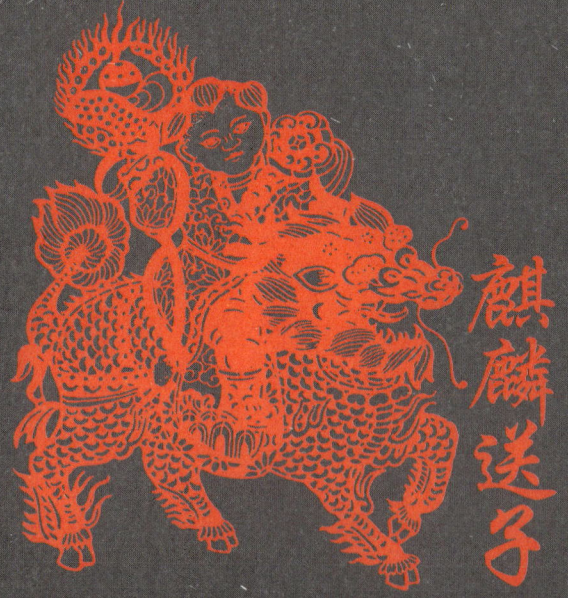

According to ancient beliefs, offspring brought by the *Child-delivering Qilin (Qi Lin Song Zi* 麒麟送子) would grow up to be incredibly intelligent.

Another popular fable used in paper-cutting for the purpose of "summoning" children is the *Marriage of Fu Xi and Nu Wa* (*Fu Xi Nu Wa* 伏羲女媧). In Chinese mythology, the god of creation was a giant named *Pangu* 盤古. After waking up from his slumber inside an egg of chaos, *Pangu* stood up and divided the Earth and sky and then died. His body became all of the features and creatures of the world. Among them was a powerful life form named *Hua Xu* 華胥 which gave birth to a twin brother and sister called Fu Xi and Nu Wa, usually depicted as half human and half snake. As the fable goes, the pair went on to create the human race. It is this aspect of the tale which makes it a popular choice for this occasion.

An animal-inspired story and resulting design which was also favoured is of the *Marriage of the Rats* (*Lao Shu Cheng Qin* 老鼠成親) which ties into the nature of rats as symbols of fertility. This particular picture humanises rats and illustrates them in a marriage ceremony as representative of the couple who desires children. Last but not least is a popular pattern called *Worshipping Heaven and Earth* (*Bai Tian Di* 拜天地) which depicts a typical Chinese wedding. It likens the relationship between a husband and wife to the relationship between Heaven and Earth. In this way, marriage is shown to be a natural and complementary arrangement.

Marriage of the Rats (*Lao Shu Cheng Qin* 老鼠成親) was a popular choice as rats were considered symbols of fertility.

Gathering or Consuming Items Associated with Children

Many cultures have assigned meanings to the flora and fauna of the world based on their appearance and properties. In keeping with this, the people of ancient China associated certain objects and foods with children and would collect or eat them to improve their chances of conceiving. Many of the items in question had a name or key characteristic which was a homophone for the word "son" in Chinese. Other items were chosen for being associated with a high fertility rate.

One well-known food that was associated with children is the watermelon because the Chinese word of seed is the same as the word for son and people associated the fruit's multiple seeds with multiple children. Pomegranates and grapes were also associated with fertility for the same reason. Fish were consumed because of their ability to produce many eggs which is also a sign of a high fertility rate. Last but not least, eggs were chosen due to them being related to the concept of birth.

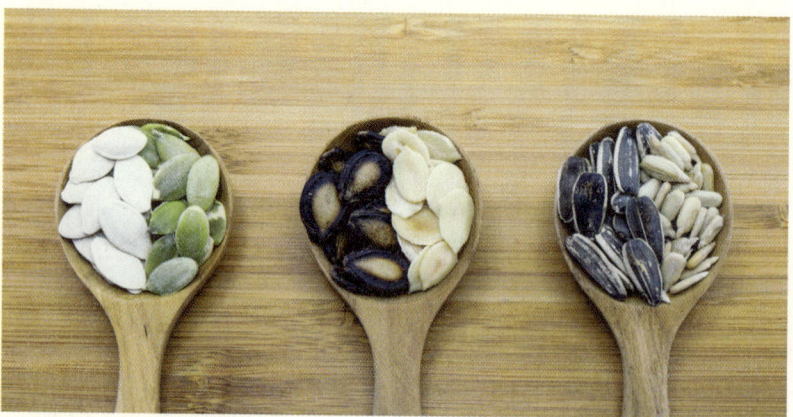

The Chinese word for seed (Zi 子) is the same as the word for son, leading to its association with fertility.

Spousal Bedchamber Decorations

When a woman got married in ancient China she was expected to leave her own family and move into her husband's home permanently. It was customary for her new husband and his family to set up a bedchamber in part to welcome her into a new setting. The bedchamber was then decorated and prepared with great care as it was believed that a well configured bedchamber could bolster a woman's health and fertility.

Decorations related to the God of Joy 'Xi Shen' 喜神 were usually chosen for bedchambers. Xi Shen is an unusual deity because he has no human origins. Instead, he is the personification of happiness itself. As such, the deity is associated with joyful events like marriage and childbirth. For this reason, it was customary to stick pieces of paper with the word "joy" (Xi 喜) on them around the home during weddings, Chinese New Year celebrations and so on.

In order to invoke Xi Shen, a groom and his family would invite him into the spousal bedchamber. As Xi Shen was present in different sectors of a home at different times, they had to use divination techniques like Qi Men Dun Jia 奇門遁甲 to pinpoint his location. They would then paste a piece of paper with the word "joy" written on it onto a surface in the relevant sector. Xi Shen's positive energy could then enter the house and help the bride in question conceive a son. It should be noted that in some parts of China, Xi Shen was considered interchangeable with the God of Fortune, Fu Shen 福神.

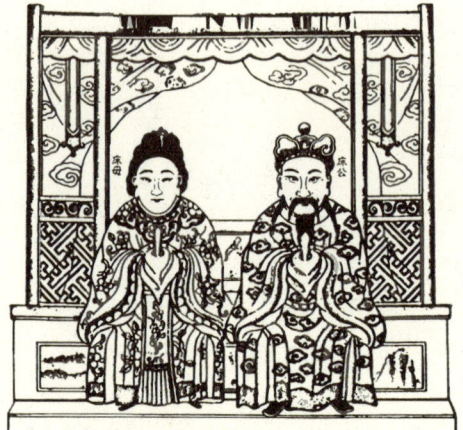
God of Bedchambers (Chuang Shen 床神)

While setting up the spousal bed, families worshipped a pair of male and female deities known as *Chuang Gong* 床公 and *Chuang Mu* 床母 respectively. Together, the duo were known as the *God of Bedchambers* (*Chuang Shen* 床神). Said to be spouses, they are associated with matters related to the bedroom such as sleep, rest, sex, childbirth and recovery from illness.

Due to their roles, they were worshipped when a family was setting up new beds for the new wife. This is practised to ensure the safety of the spouse, the stability of the marriage and the probability of the wife giving birth to a son. Called *Pressing the Bed* (*Ya Chuang* 壓床), this process involved finding an old woman with a husband, son and daughter to make or "press" the bed meant for the future wife. An old woman who was qualified to do this was called a "*Very Fortunate Person*" (*Quan Fu Ren* 全福人).

The actual location of a spousal bed was chosen with great care. It was believed that having the bed in the right place could increase the chances of the new wife getting pregnant. Some families placed the bed in an auspicious corner of the room which was determined using Feng Shui methods. Others based their decision on superstitious beliefs not rooted in Chinese Metaphysics.

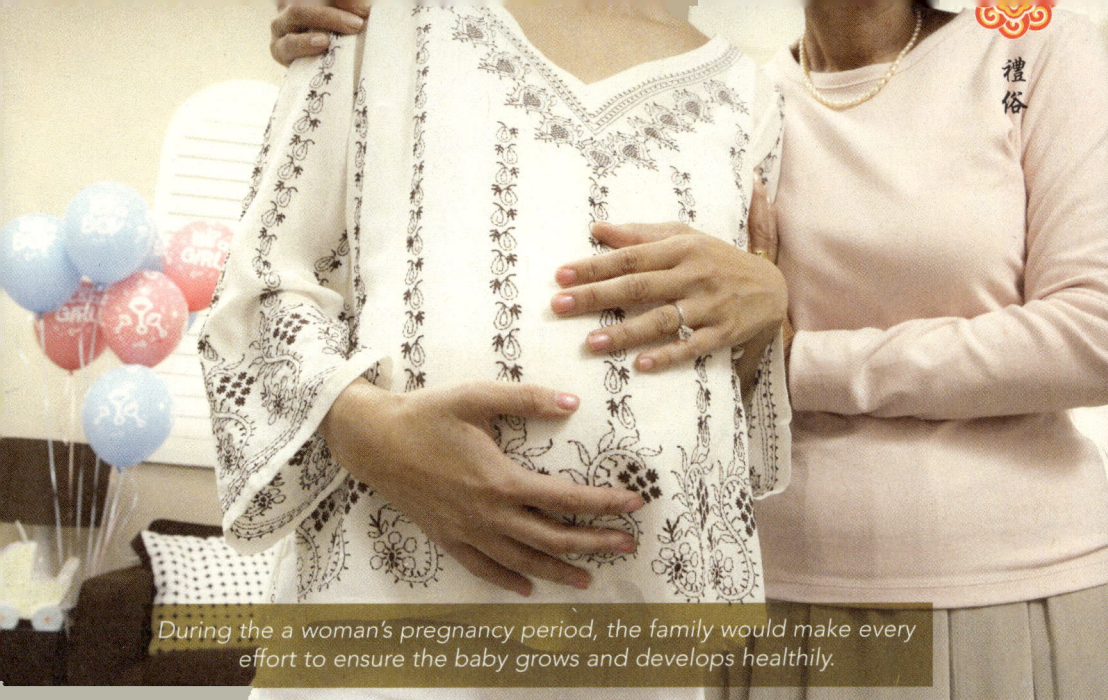

During the a woman's pregnancy period, the family would make every effort to ensure the baby grows and develops healthily.

The Pregnancy Period

Once a child had been "summoned" and a woman was known to be pregnant, she and her family made every effort to ensure that the baby would grow and develop healthily. The expectant mother's diet and daily activities would be carefully monitored and regulated. Other practices such as the quarantine or restriction of the pregnant woman along with the smaller customs that accompanied it as well as prayers to the *Foetal God* (*Tai Shen* 胎神) would also be observed.

As a woman's due date loomed, preparations in the form of decorative choices and items would be made in regard to the delivery room. One such item was the *Birth Pictures* (*An Chan Tu* 安產圖) which were hung up at selected locations in the room depending on the month. Pregnant women in some parts of China also took part in a practice called prenatal education (*Tai Jiao* 胎教).

Today, many of these practices have fallen to the wayside because it is rare for women to give birth at home.

The Quarantine or Restriction of a Pregnant Woman

Pregnant women's movements were restricted to help reduce the chance of complications. They were advised to avoid stress, sex and manual labour during the third trimester of their pregnancies in particular. These wise recommendations are still made today. Aside from that, they were also strongly advised to stay at home throughout this period. However, it should be noted that this can be attributed to the fact that any kind of centralised institution where these women could be quarantined did not exist at that time. As a result, the delivery of the baby would usually take place in the woman's house and the midwife would have to be summoned to the residence. Additionally, pregnant women were considered unclean and forbidden from interacting with their husband's family in any way.

During the quarantine period, it was traditional for a pregnant woman's immediate family to offer an *Urging Gift* (*Cui Sheng Li* 催生禮) which symbolised their wish for the child to be born as quickly as possible. This included clothes for the mother and child like diapers, shoes, hats, underwear or the traditional Chinese bodice (*Du Dou* 肚兜). Alternatively, the family might provide food with special nutritional or symbolic properties like eggs painted with red colouring, noodles representing longevity, longans which embody their wish for many good sons and walnuts which were associated with overall family harmony.

The Foetal God *(Tai Shen 胎神)*

The Foetal God supposedly looked out for the wellbeing of a foetus during pregnancy. It was viewed as more of a supernatural force than an anthropomorphic god. While some sources assert that the Foetal God is a spirit which appears when a woman's egg is fertilised, others claim that the Foetal God is a personification of the foetus itself.

Regardless, the Foetal God and the foetus are deeply connected in Chinese culture. Families tried to avoid doing things which might agitate the Foetal God and, by extension, harm the foetus.

Certain physical activities were believed to be capable of offending the Foetal God. Pregnant women were forbidden from lifting heavy objects, for example, as this was believed to potentially cause a miscarriage. They were also forbidden from tying things up as it was believed their baby would be born with fingers that could not be straightened voluntarily. Cutting or chopping things with sharp implements was forbidden as well as it was believed this could cause the baby to have a deformity like blindness. Aside from that, pregnant women were told not to use a hammer as it would give their baby a cleft palette. Today, pregnant women are not barred from carrying out the majority of these activities because science has proven that they do not lead to deformities or miscarriages. Instead, practical safety precautions rooted in common sense and medical research have thankfully become the norm in the current era.

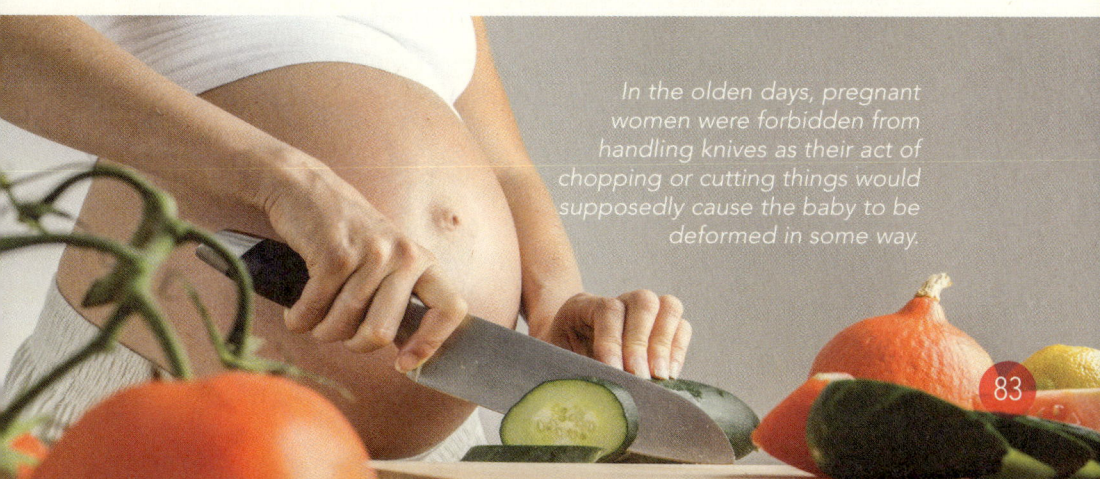

In the olden days, pregnant women were forbidden from handling knives as their act of chopping or cutting things would supposedly cause the baby to be deformed in some way.

The Foetal God was said to move in a different direction and reside in different parts of a house at different times of the year. People avoided making changes to those parts of the home during the times in question so as not to aggravate it.

The table below is a breakdown of the Foetal God's location in a house during each month of the year.

Lunar Month of the Year	Area to Avoid Altering
First	The pregnant woman's bedroom
Second	The windows
Third	The doors and windows
Fourth	The stove
Fifth	The pregnant woman's bedroom
Sixth	The pregnant woman's bedroom, the storeroom and the granary
Seventh	The rice grinder
Eighth	The bathroom
Ninth	The entrance and the porch
Tenth	The pregnant woman's bedroom
Eleventh	The stove
Twelfth	The pregnant woman's bedroom

Preparation of the Delivery Room

During the expectant mother's third trimester, the delivery room would undergo the final stage of preparations. The first order of business was to remove anything red from the delivery room. If a potential delivery room had red walls it was easiest to just use another room. The reasoning behind this was that red might trigger complications as it was the colour of blood. Anything that could make a dripping or rippling sound was also removed because such sounds were associated with severe blood loss.

The Birth Pictures (*An Chan Tu* 安產圖)

It was customary to decorate the delivery room with *Birth Pictures* which were pictures representing stories and scenarios about childbirth. There were a total of 12 Birth Pictures with one for each month of the year. Depending on what month of the year it was at that point in time, the corresponding picture would be hung in the most auspicious sector of the room which was identified using *Ba Gua* 八卦. Some families only hung the corresponding Birth Picture up on the month of delivery.

These pictures generally featured Ba Gua sectors, auspicious and inauspicious stars as well as deities related to childbirth. Accompanying the images were instructions on how to properly take care of a woman who was pregnant or in labour. As such, hanging them up made it easier for people to refer to them. Additionally, they served as a form of prayer to the all-important Foetal God.

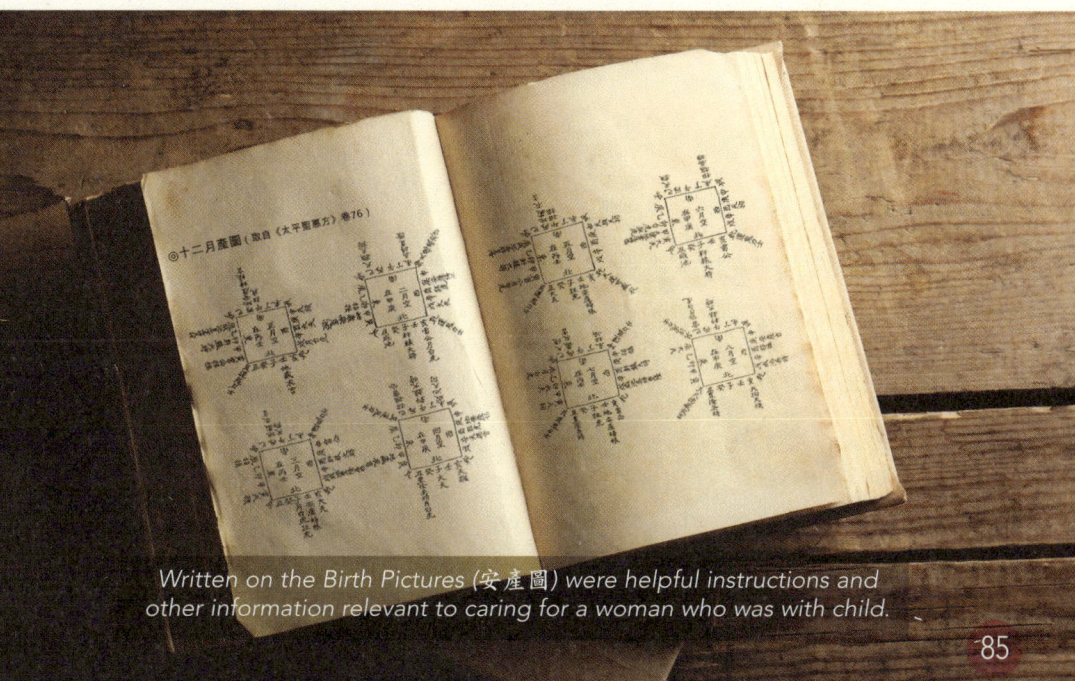

Written on the Birth Pictures (安產圖) were helpful instructions and other information relevant to caring for a woman who was with child.

Prenatal Education (Tai Jiao 胎教)

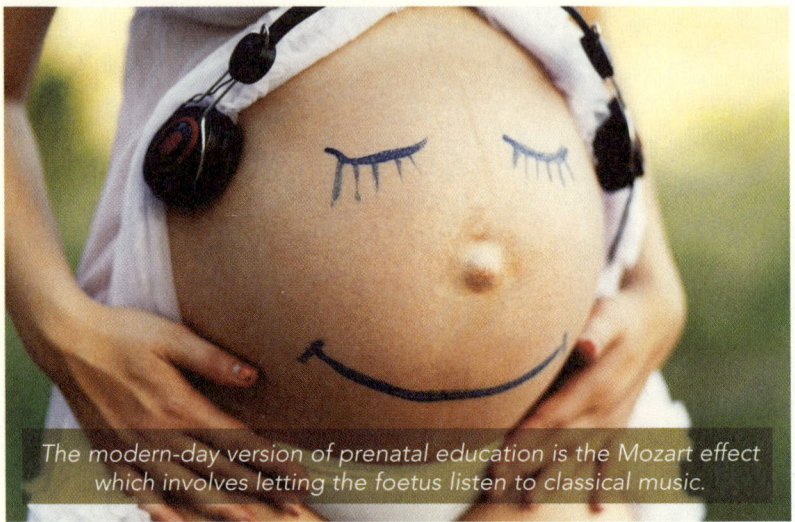

The modern-day version of prenatal education is the Mozart effect which involves letting the foetus listen to classical music.

The concept of prenatal education which literally means "education for the foetus" was based on the belief that a foetus could benefit from its mother's experiences.

According to the classic Confucian text the *Book of Rites* (*Li Ji* 禮記), *King Wen of Zhou* (*Zhou Wen Wang* 周文王) was able to become one of the greatest heroes in Chinese history because his mother Tai Ren 太任 gave him prenatal education. For this, she became a role model for mothers in ancient China especially for her part in establishing the principles of prenatal education called the *Cultivation of External Occurrences* (*Wai Xiang Nei Gan* 外象内感).

According to her writings, everything that a mother experiences with her five senses must be pleasant and beautiful to ensure that her prenatal education is successful. She should go out of her way to avoid contact with unpleasant things, people or events. Furthermore, a pregnant woman's behaviour is considered an "external occurrence" too. Thus, a pregnant woman should behave in an elegant manner and set a good example for her foetus.

Using the source of these principles as an example, Tai Ren supposedly refrained from doing three things in particular which ensured the successful prenatal education of her son. The three actions she avoided were eye contact with unpleasant things, hearing noises and saying arrogant words.

> **On a Personal Note...**
>
> If you think that these ideas are outdated, you probably haven't heard about the Mozart effect. According to its proponents, playing classical music like Mozart to a baby while it's still in the womb can help boost its intelligence.
>
> The link between music and intelligence was first described in a study featured in the scientific journal Nature in 1993. The study found that teenagers who listened to one of Mozart's sonatas temporarily performed better in spatial visualisation tests compared to a control group.
>
> Many people wrongly took this research to mean that listening to Mozart can increase one's IQ. This misconception caught on and people began exposing their children to classical music in the hopes that they would become super intelligent. Some parents took things even further by playing Mozart to their foetus which is very much in keeping with the concept of prenatal education described above.
>
> Unfortunately, there is no definitive proof that this practice works. There is also no definitive evidence that prenatal education itself is beneficial. Any studies which claim to prove its success fall apart under close scrutiny.
>
> Nevertheless, it has been shown that music can improve a person's mood and by extension their performance. This means that your children may well do better when they are allowed to listen to appropriate music. Just don't expect them to turn into the next Albert Einstein!

The Delivery of the Child

When it was finally time for the child to be born, a midwife was summoned to the house to deliver the baby safely. As medicine was less advanced than it is today, many of the practices surrounding childbirth were rooted in superstition. Certain rituals and customs were believed to safeguard the welfare of both mother and child.

One such safeguard was decorating the delivery room in a certain way. Certain restrictions were implemented such as access to the delivery room being severely limited. Additionally, the umbilical cord was cut and the placenta was discarded in a very specific manner.

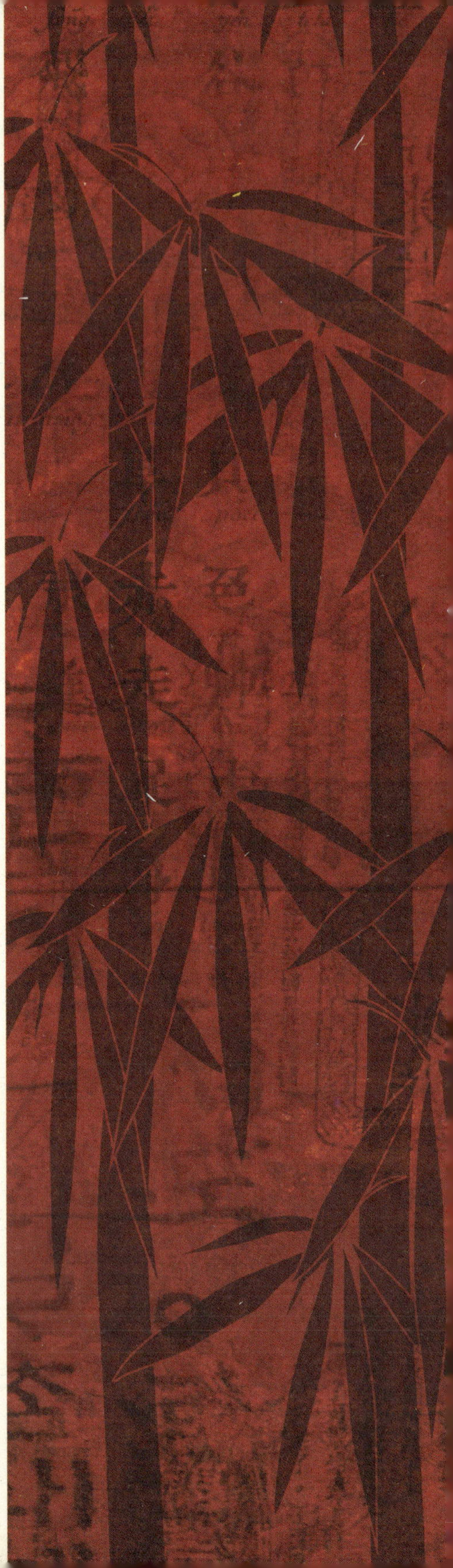

Delivery Room

Work on decorating the delivery room generally began in the third trimester of a woman's pregnancy and was completed in the days leading up to her due date. Several items would be prepared close to the expected date of the child's birth as part of the family's wishes for a strong and healthy son as well as the wellbeing of the mother.

One such item was a pair of chopsticks (*Kuai Zi* 筷子) as the word in Chinese is a homophone for "giving birth quickly" (*Kuai Zi* 快子) which is sometimes read as "quick son". The chopsticks were buried in an auspicious sector of the delivery room in the hopes that they would help the woman make it through labour safely.

Another of these items was the *Braid of Progeny* (*Zi Sun Sheng* 子孫繩) which comprised braids made out of colourful strings and represented the family's wish for good luck. Its strings were coloured red, blue, green or yellow depending on the families' preferences. The braid was usually hung outside the delivery room on a pole or other suitable object.

Once the baby was born, new decorations were added alongside the braid to tell the community whether it was a boy or girl. If the child was a boy, a chilli pepper would be hung as it was seen as a phallic symbol. On the other hand, the sight of shredded clothes on display outside the room indicated that the new-born was a girl.

Restrictions during the Delivery Process

In ancient China, men were forbidden from entering the delivery room at any time. This rule is likely based on the Yin-Yang principle which associates women with Yin and men with Yang. After giving birth, a women's Yin energy levels are supposedly very low. By entering the delivery room, a Yang man could upset the overall balance of Yin and Yang energy, harming mother and child. A possible modern-day explanation for this is that such a precaution was meant to prevent germs or viruses from being brought into the room which could then infect either the mother, child or both.

People who were born in the year of the Tiger were also barred from the delivery room. This was because tigers are fierce animals and allowing a person born in the year of the Tiger was akin to inviting the actual beast into the room. Such a metaphorical animal could scare the child or kill him outright, presumably leading to complications or a stillbirth. It should be noted that this restriction is not supported by Chinese Metaphysics. In BaZi, the Tiger is merely an Earthly Branch depending on a person's date of birth. As such, it lacks the frightful connotation above which was likely made up by people who took the imagery at face value.

The number of people in the delivery room was limited because it was believed that having more people in the room drew out labour. Thus, the less people in the delivery room the better! This could also be explained as a way of minimizing the chances of someone bringing in an infectious illness which could endanger the health of the mother or her child.

Finally, middle-aged women were discouraged from entering the delivery room. This was enforced strictly if the woman in labour was of a similar age. The restriction was based on the belief that such a woman could "steal" a new mother's ability to produce milk for her child.

The Cutting of the Umbilical Cord

Many Chinese stories speak of *a Primal Soul (Ben Ming Yuan Shen* 本命元神*)* which is a divine force that protected a person from coming to harm. Legend has it that an umbilical cord connects one to their Primal Soul even after birth. Cords were therefore handled with great care and cut only with scissors in ancient times. Treating the umbilical cord in this respectful manner supposedly increased a child's chances of growing up to become a healthy adult.

After the umbilical cord was cut, the method with which it was taken care of varies depending on the source. Some took the umbilical cord and sewed it into a hat as this was believed to drive evil forces away. Other families preserved it for the day that their child was ready to make it on their own in the world. By keeping this item close to them at all times, they would presumably be more courageous and face fewer challenges when fighting against unjust lawsuits levelled against them.

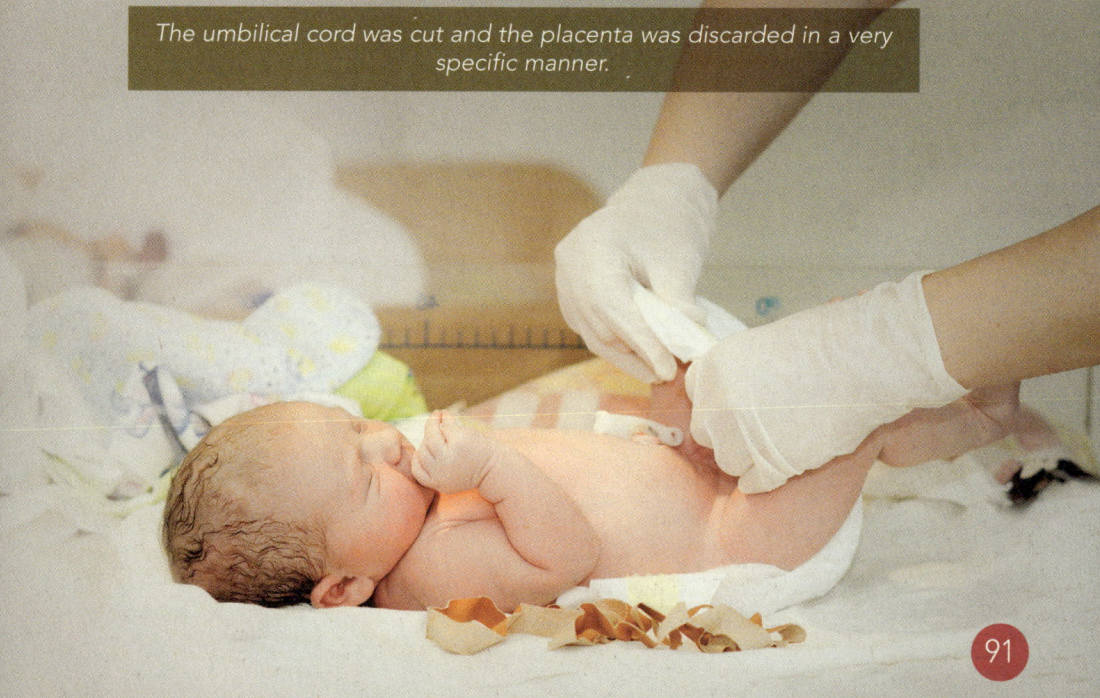

The umbilical cord was cut and the placenta was discarded in a very specific manner.

Disposal of the Placenta

The placenta was also seen as an important link between an infant and the Primal Soul. Dealing with it properly was essential for a child's future wellbeing. It was usually preserved in a jar with lime juice and then buried. The place where it was buried was thought to help shape a baby's destiny, so the burial site was chosen with great care.

Some families buried the placenta under a bed. However, it was apparently not uncommon to make distinctions in order to secure a better future for the child. For example, gender was apparently one of the most frequently used details when it came to determining where the jar would be buried.

In these cases, the placenta for a boy would be buried under the doorsill to symbolise the family's wish for him to be capable of supporting and bringing glory to the family name. Meanwhile, the typical burial place for a girl's placenta was under a tree bearing many fruits to denote their hope for her to have the capacity to produce numerous children.

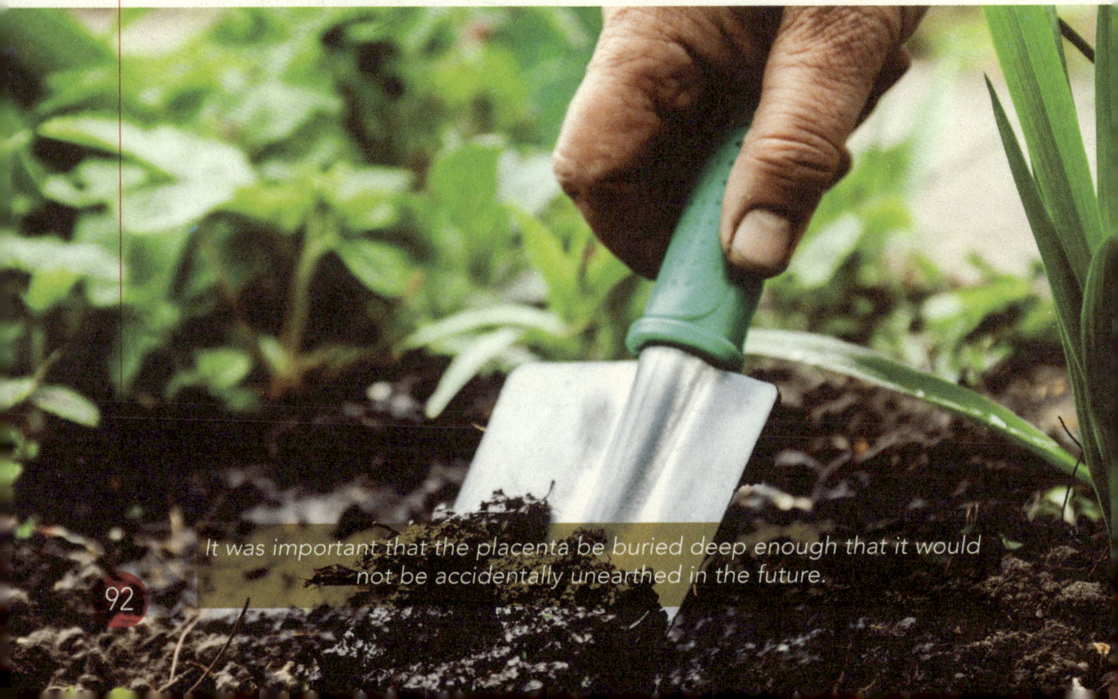

It was important that the placenta be buried deep enough that it would not be accidentally unearthed in the future.

Instead of burying the placenta in a jar, some families opted to wash it with water and then with alcohol before placing it in a jar with a coin. After sealing the jar with cotton, they stored it for three days before burying it. The burial site was located in an auspicious sector for the month. A site that faced the sun was ultimately preferable as the Yang energy of the sun would presumably help ensure that the next child was a boy. Additionally, the jar was buried so deep that its lid was two feet or more below ground level. Doing this supposedly ensured that a child would have a long life.

Meanwhile, certain sources approached the matter from the opposite direction by identifying the kinds of locations which were inappropriate burial sites for the jar of placenta. It was said that placing a child's placenta in these locations would have adverse effects on their wellbeing and fate.

If a placenta was buried in shallow ground, dogs or pigs could dig it up. If this happened, the person it was once connected to would allegedly go insane. If the placenta was eaten by birds, it was believed that the person would die young. Burying it in temples was also a bad idea as it was believed that doing so would leave a child vulnerable to supernatural forces. Choosing to bury the jar in a forest was discouraged as it was thought to increase their chances of being hung.

In a similar manner, ponds were associated with drowning. Burial sites at the side of the road were associated with infertility. Within the home, burial sites near the stove would supposedly leave a person stricken with anxiety. Burying the placenta near a well was associated with blindness or deafness in later life. Last but not least, choosing to burn the placenta was believed to bring about severe skin diseases.

Obviously, this practice is no longer observed today but it is still important to be aware of these ancient traditions. At the very least, they make for good conversation topics.

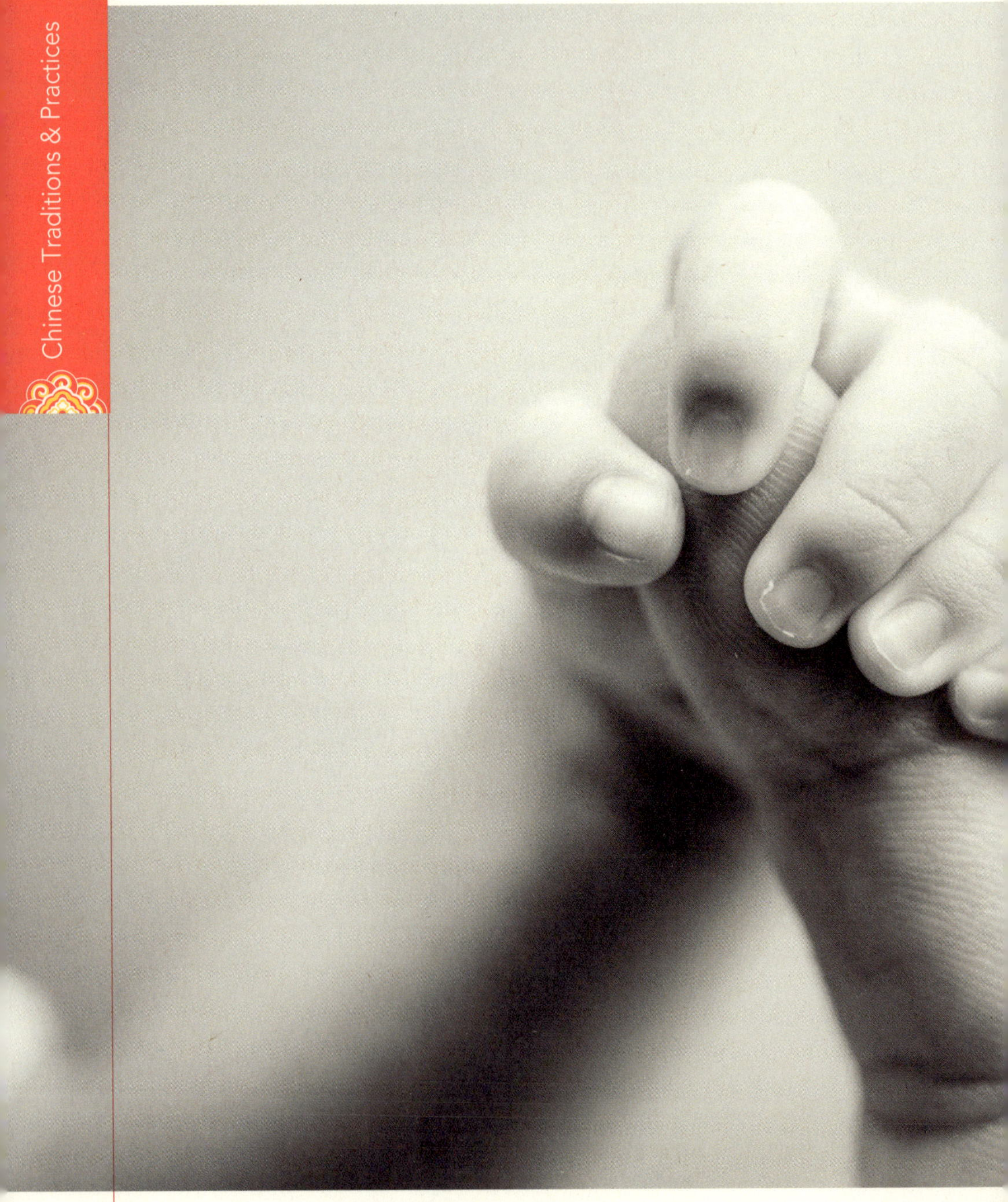

Chinese Traditions & Practices

Post-childbirth

Childbirth was dangerous in ancient China. Because medicine was primitive, certain precautions were taken based on what was known at the time to help reduce mortality rates for mother and child.

One of the most common post-delivery safety measures in this regard is the practice of post-childbirth confinement which is still practised quite frequently to this day. On top of that, there were dietary recommendations aimed at helping the mother make a speedy recovery which she was to follow during her confinement. Aside from this, there were also restrictions placed on the woman in question such as not allowing her to drink water, eat salt, carry babies, have sex or take baths during this period.

Post-childbirth Confinement (*Zuo Yue Zi* 坐月子)

Traditional Chinese medical practitioners recognised that the moments leading up to, during and following delivery were critical to a mother's wellbeing. It was customary to let the new mother rest and recuperate after giving birth. Over time, the idea of a longer recovery period caught on. Eventually, a mother who had given birth was expected to rest for a full month. This confinement period was also referred to as the Sitting of the Month (*Zuo Yue Zi* 坐月子).

Dietary Recommendations

During the post-childbirth confinement period, a new mother was advised to consume certain foods to restore the Yin energy she had lost giving birth. Yin energy loss was linked to the blood loss that was an inevitable part of the birthing process.

The main food recommended by traditional Chinese medicine practitioners for the purpose of restoring the balance of Yin and Yang energy in a woman's body was fruit. Women were advised to consume apples, guavas, grapes, papayas, strawberries, peaches, mulberries and cherries.

Certain vegetables also played a role in speeding up the recovery process, each conferring specific benefits. Spinach was believed to help the body make up for lost blood. Lotus roots could supposedly helped boost the body's depleted Yin energy reserves and provide mental relief. Pumpkin was believed to possess Qi- and energy-supplying properties. Sweet potato leaves were prescribed to help remove toxins from the body. To regain mobility, new mothers could eat okra, also known as "lady fingers". Celery was also part of their diet as it could presumably reduce or prevent constipation.

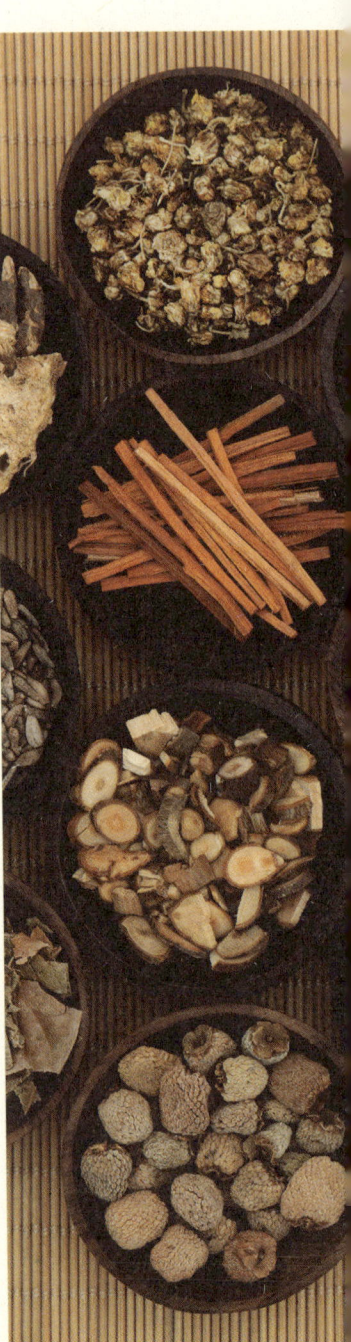

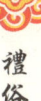
禮俗

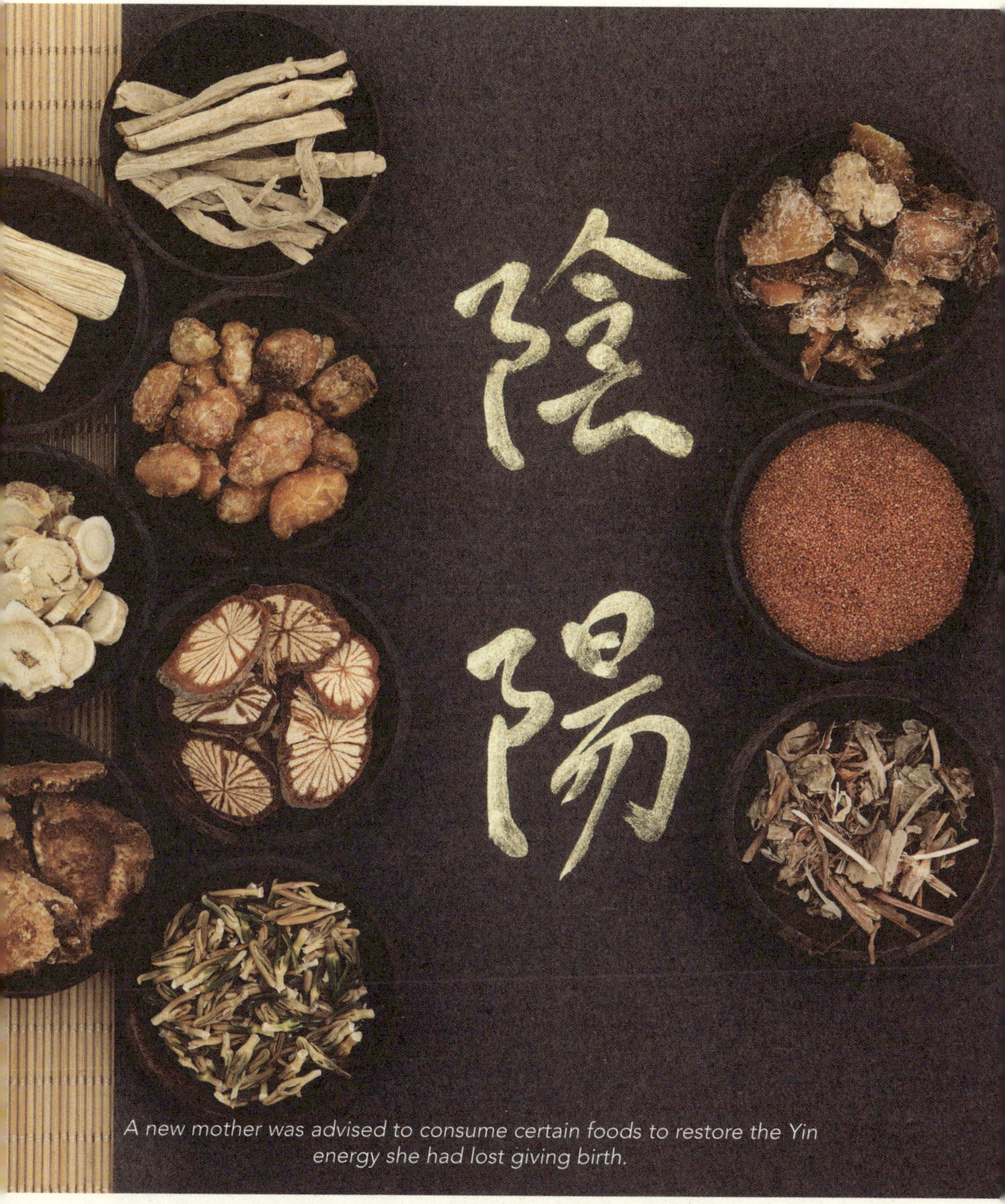

陰陽

A new mother was advised to consume certain foods to restore the Yin energy she had lost giving birth.

Aside from greens, sources of protein were prescribed to improve the quality and volume of a new mother's breast milk. The most readily available sources of protein at the time included pork hocks, peanuts, carp and chicken.

Carbohydrates were also important for a new mother's recovery. Brown rice and noodles were staple foods of the time. Buckwheat and black sticky rice were also consumed to restore the woman's Qi and energy levels. It was believed that adzuki beans could help in regard to the blood loss caused by childbirth. Back pain and water retention problems were remedied with black beans.

A well-known traditional dish given to new mothers was chicken stew with sesame oil and rice wine (*Ma You Ji/ Ji Jiu* 麻油雞/雞酒). Believed to be capable of restoring the new mother's lost blood and energy, this meal is regarded as more of a Yang dish and is linked to "heat" in traditional Chinese medicine. As such, one recommendation when cooking this dish was to use old ginger so that the food not only smelled better but also contained additional Yang energy.

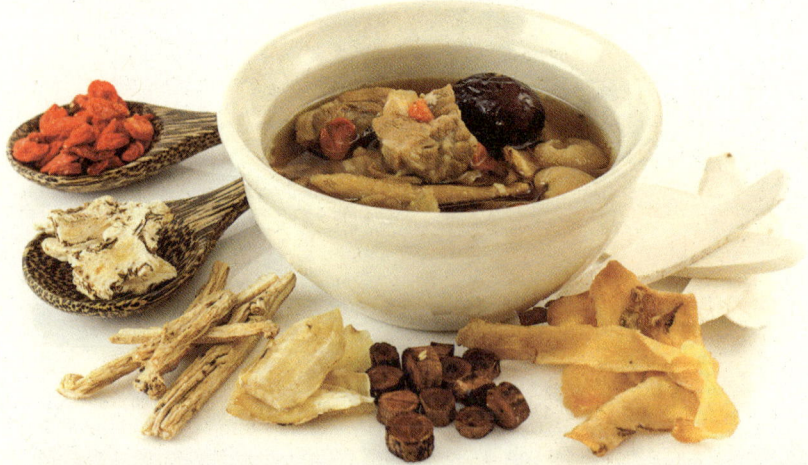

One of the dishes frequently given to new mothers was Chinese herbal soup.

Aside from the aforementioned benefits of eating chicken, the sesame oil used in this stew was also believed to be good for the new mother's health. This has been proven to be true and research has shown that it has hormone-inducing properties which promote contractions as well as help with post-childbirth discharge. Additionally, a third of the unsaturated fat in sesame oil can be converted into a lipid compound called prostaglandin which plays a crucial part in the treatment of pregnancy-induced hypertension.

Nevertheless, it needs to be said that while a new mother in confinement was encouraged to eat all of these foods, there were a number of things to keep in mind regarding this matter as well. Traditional Chinese medicine practitioners advised the woman's family to closely monitor her health and plan her diet according to the state of her wellbeing.

They generally divided the confinement period into three stages with each stage having its own set of dietary recommendations. In the first week after birth, the goal was to reduce toxins in a new mother's body. In the second and third weeks, overall recovery was the goal with particular emphasis being placed on her womb. In the fourth week, high-calorie foods like the chicken stew mentioned earlier were given.

Interestingly, we now know that many of the foods indicated in traditional Chinese medicine possess the properties ascribed to them. Today, doctors recommend many of the same foods to new mothers.

Restrictions during the Post-Childbirth Period

New mothers were subject to a number of restrictions during their confinement period. As some of them have no scientific basis, we can only speculate as to how some came to exist.

For starters, new mothers were forbidden from drinking water in confinement. Food cooked for new mothers had to be prepared with alcohol instead of water. This restriction is still observed to this day. It most likely came about because sterilised drinking water was hard to come by in ancient China and drinking contaminated water could make an already weakened woman seriously ill. As we have much cleaner water today, a new mother can safely ignore this restriction.

New mothers were forbidden from eating salt so everything cooked for them had to be salt-free. This thinking was ahead of its time because today there is evidence that a high salt intake may hamper a woman's ability to recover from post-pregnancy hypertension. Since there was no way to monitor or control a woman's salt intake accurately in the past, complete abstinence from salt was the only option.

During the post-childbirth period, women were discouraged from carrying any babies or taking part in anything strenuous. This was taken to mean lifting anything heavier than the average baby. New mothers were also banned from having sex during their confinement period.

Last but not least, women in post-childbirth confinement were forbidden from taking baths. This rule may be attributed to the poor living conditions and cold weather of ancient China. By avoiding bathing, new mothers with their weakened immune systems were less likely to catch a cold and develop pneumonia. Pneumonia is a serious illness, even with today's medical treatment, so it is understandable that people went to such extreme lengths to avoid it.

> **On a Personal Note...**
>
> I would like to take this opportunity to share my own experience of these customs. When my wife gave birth to our twins, we were subjected to many of these restrictions during the confinement period and some of them were incredibly frustrating for the both of us. For example, my wife wasn't allowed to drink water during the confinement period. She drank red date tea instead which is made by boiling red dates overnight in a slow cooker. This seemed pointless and needlessly complicated.
>
> Now that I know why and how this and other customs came to be, I appreciate the lengths people in ancient China went to in order to safeguard the lives of new mothers. I have also learned that red dates – also called jujubes – are highly nutritious. They provide many health benefits to new mothers.
>
> Obviously, other restrictions are less easy to defend in this day and age. I hope that the information contained herein will help put new parents at ease with regards to how strictly they adhere with tradition. By understanding their origins, we can collectively discard ones that are no longer valid or necessary. The advancements of modern medicine have clearly rendered many of them obsolete. It is, for instance, perfectly safe for new mothers to take a bath or shower to freshen up!

Celebrating a Child's Birth

While a new mother was recuperating during her post-childbirth confinement, her family would herald the safe arrival of a new family member with two customs: the *Bath at Three* (*Xi San* 洗三) and the *Delivery of Good Tidings* (*Bao Xi* 報喜).

Bath at Three (*Xi San* 洗三)

The *Bath at Three* is so named because it was held on the third day after childbirth. The family of a newborn prepared a bath of special water to bathe him or her in. With it, they believed they could symbolically wash away any bad luck that might otherwise befall the child in the future. This ceremony also gave the family the chance to express their gratitude to various deities associated with childbirth for granting them a child. They often prayed to the *God of Bedchambers* (*Chuang Shen* 床神) as well.

The formula for the bathwater varied by region but a typical one included cinnamon flowers, citrus leaves, 12 coins and three clean stones. Each ingredient stood for something. Cinnamon flowers symbolised wealth and privilege – two things that any family would want for their child. Citrus leaves represented happiness and the ability to have many descendants. The three stones were added to represent physical wellbeing and courage. The 12 coins were added to represent wealth and in some cases the 12 Zodiac Animal Cycles of Time (Year, Month, Day and Hour) and abundance as well.

Some versions of the bathwater used for the *Bath at Three* included compounds from Chinese medicine like mugwort which was believed to drive away evil forces.

A more luxurious bathwater formula called the *Fragrant Bath* (*Xiang Tang* 香湯) included peanuts, dates and chestnuts. These ingredients symbolised a family's wish for the child to quickly grow up and form his own family. The objects in question were known as *Zao Li Zi* 棗栗子 in Chinese which is a homophone for the phrase "having descendants early" (*Zao Li Zi* 早立子).

Regardless of what ingredients were used, the bath water was prepared in a standard way. Everything was first put into a container and then brought to a boil. The boiling water was then poured into the bath tub and left to cool. The ceremony began once the water had cooled to an acceptable level.

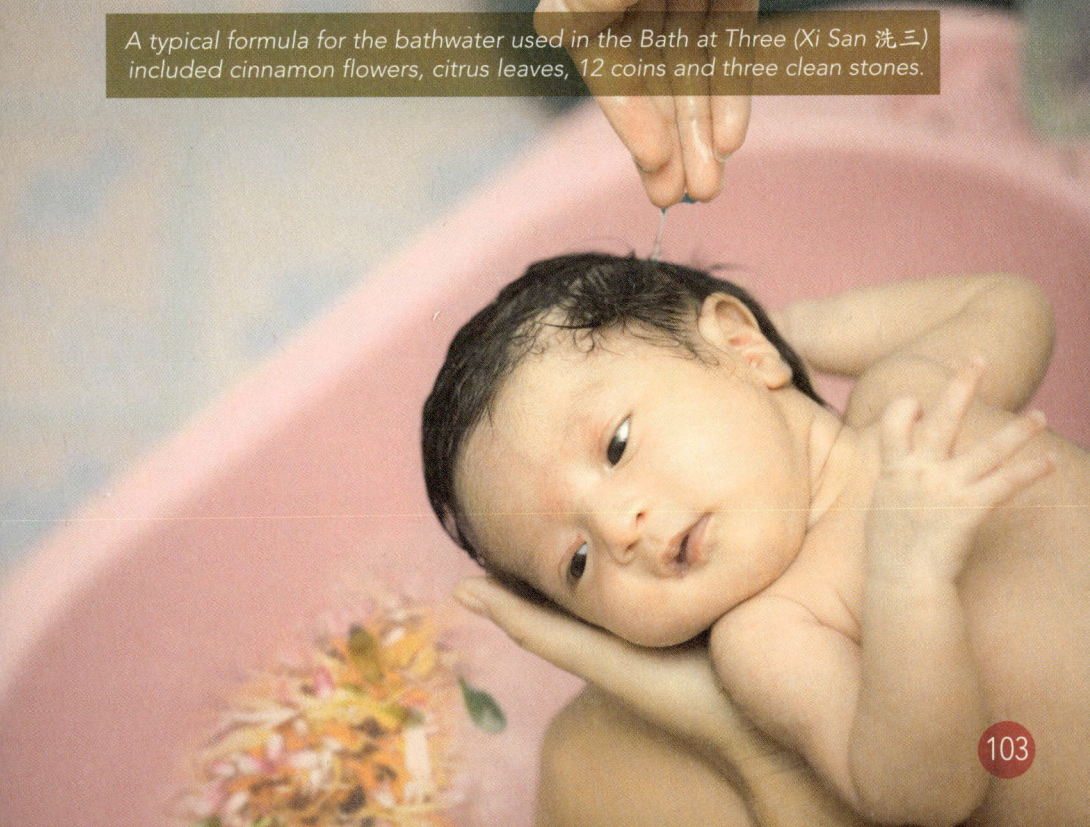

A typical formula for the bathwater used in the Bath at Three (Xi San 洗三) included cinnamon flowers, citrus leaves, 12 coins and three clean stones.

Delivery of Good Tidings (*Bao Xi* 報喜)

When a baby boy was born, his birth father was usually the one to share the good news with the mother's family. Over time, this practice became an official custom known as the *Delivery of Good Tidings* (*Bao Xi* 報喜).

When they heard the good news, the child's maternal family was expected to visit the birth family of its father and bring a congratulatory gift. Usually, this included foods that were suitable for the mother in confinement such as chicken, eggs, rice wine and noodles.

As a gesture of goodwill, the father's family would invite the mother's family over for dinner. The most basic version of this dinner was comprised of chicken stew and Chinese sticky rice – two foods recommended for women in confinement. More wealthy families would serve something known as an *Announcement Feast* (*Bao Jiu* 報酒).

In instances where the marriage was arranged, a separate banquet was held by the birth family of the new mother. The matchmaker who arranged the union was the guest of honour. The banquet gave the family a chance to express their gratitude to the matchmaker for making the union possible.

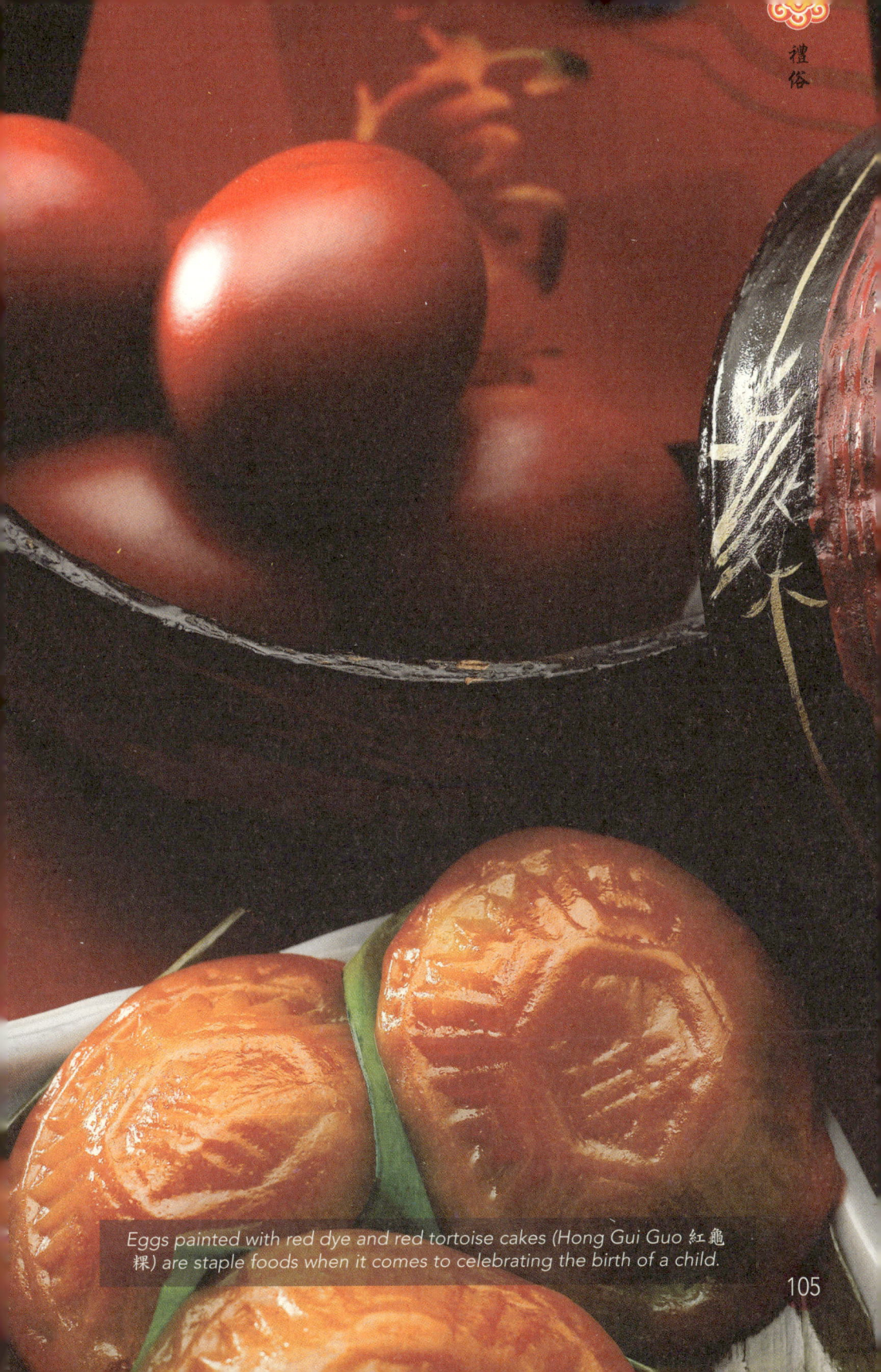

Eggs painted with red dye and red tortoise cakes (Hong Gui Guo 紅龜粿) are staple foods when it comes to celebrating the birth of a child.

The Infant's Full Moon

So named because the end of a month is marked by a full moon in the Chinese lunar calendar, an infant's *Full Moon* (*Man Yue* 滿月) is a significant milestone. It marks the end of a new mother's confinement period and the beginning of regular life for both mother and child.

The *Full Moon* ceremony is complex and lengthy. There are four steps. It begins with a ritual known as the shaving of the baby. This is followed by the worship of the ancestors and the *Suiting-up Ceremony* (*Song Tou Wei* 送頭尾). Finally, everything is brought to a close with the *Full Moon* banquet.

Although the specifics of the *Full Moon* ceremony have changed over time, almost all Chinese parents still practice them to some extent.

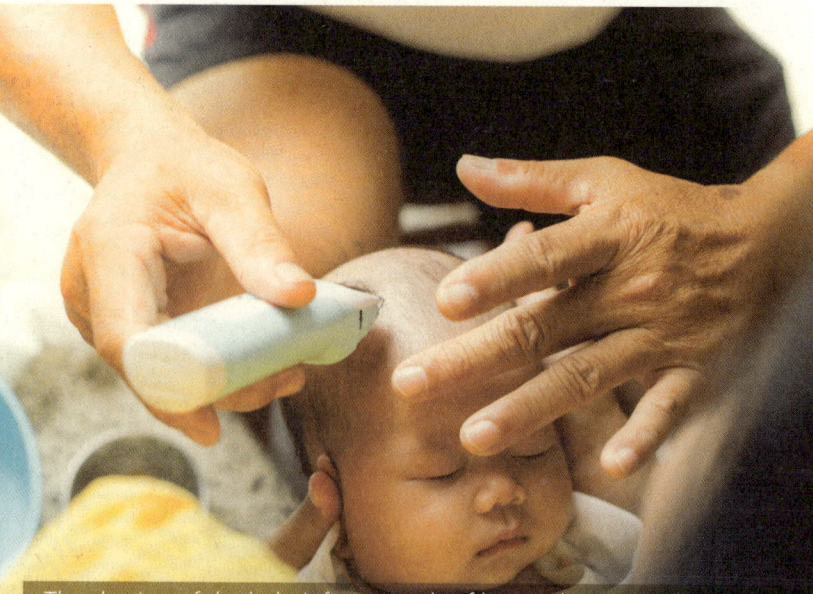
The shaving of the baby's first strands of hair is done on either the day of the Full Moon or the 24th day following his or her birth.

The Shaving of the Baby

It was standard practice in Chinese culture to leave a newborn's hair untouched from the day he was born until the day of the Full Moon. Special attention was paid to the baby's first strands of hair which were called the *Blood Hair* (*Xue Fa* 血髮). It was believed that shaving them off would help the child develop a full head of hair in adulthood.

This was not a compulsory part of the Full Moon ceremony, though. Some families shaved their baby 24 days after birth. The number 24 was favoured because it represents filial piety. This association can be traced back to a collection of folk stories known as the *24 Filial Sons* (*Er Shi Si Xiao* 二十四孝). The 24 sons in the stories are immensely devoted to their parents and they serve as role models for filial piety. By shaving a baby's hair on the 24th day of their life, it was believed they would grow up to become a filial child, too.

Regardless, the hair was collected after it was shaved and used to make a calligraphy brush known as the *Foetal Hair Brush* (*Tai Mao Bi* 胎毛筆). It was believed that the brush would help improve a child's performance in their imperial examinations when they were old enough to take them. This was important

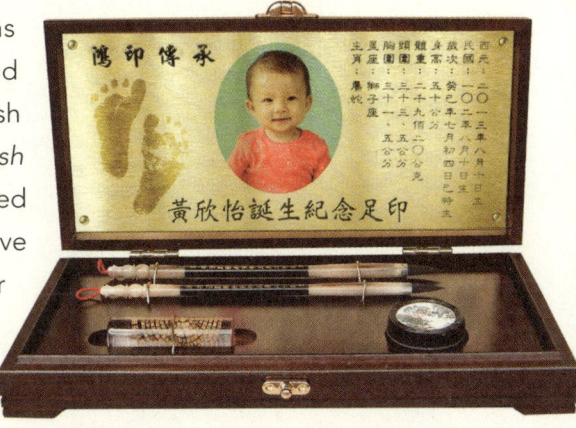

Foetal Hair Brush (Tai Mao Bi 胎毛筆)

as passing the examinations led to a respected government position, wealth and power. The brush was sometimes engraved with a message of goodwill for the child as well.

The final stage of the hair-shaving ritual was a special bath like the *Bath at Three* described earlier. The bathwater formula this time included scallions and eggs. Scallions were chosen because they are associated with intelligence as the Chinese world for scallion is "*Cong*" (葱) which is phonetically similar to the Chinese word for intelligence (*Cong* 聰). Eggs were added to help give the baby clear and soft skin.

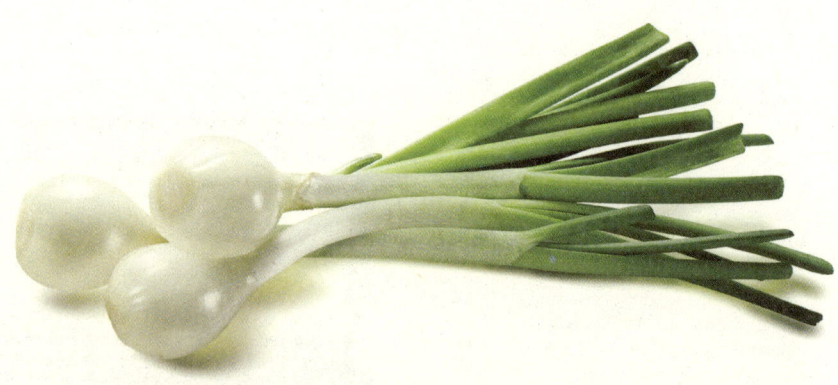

葱（葱代表聰明） Scallions were chosen because they are associated with intelligence as the Chinese world for scallion is "*Cong*" (葱) which is phonetically similar to the Chinese word for intelligence (*Cong* 聰).

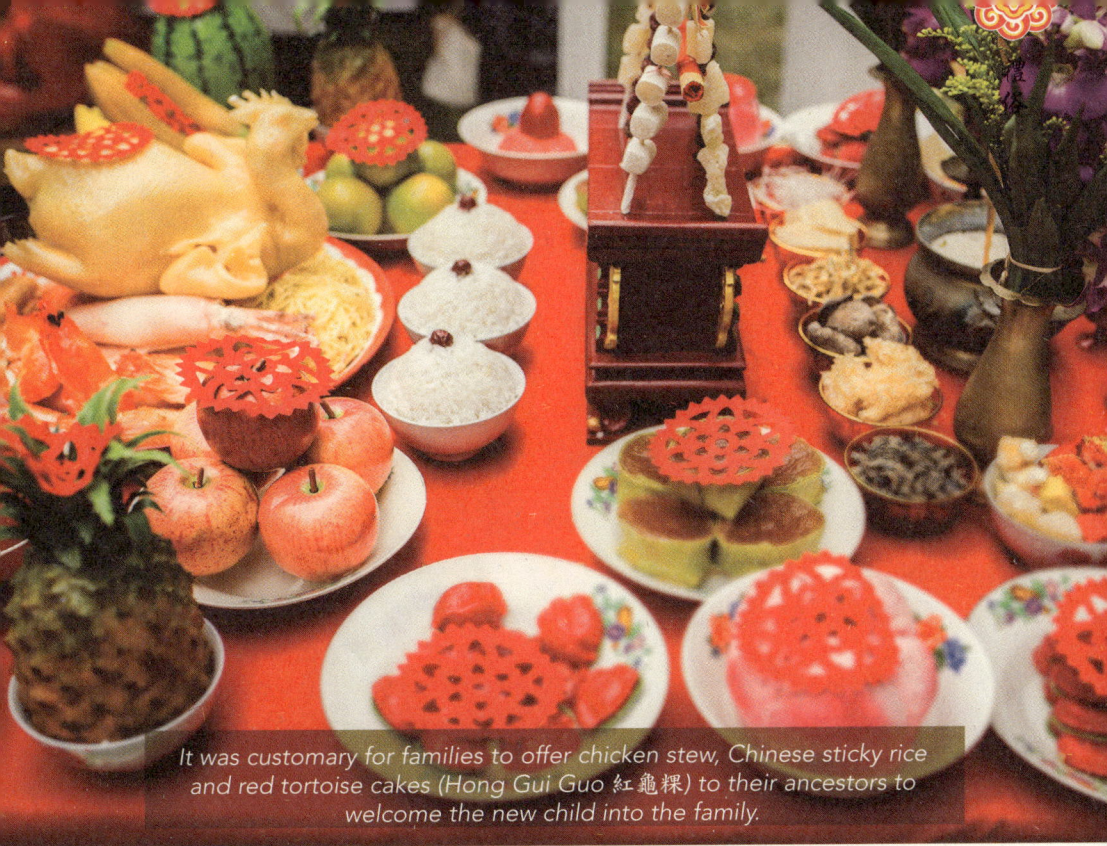

It was customary for families to offer chicken stew, Chinese sticky rice and red tortoise cakes (Hong Gui Guo 红龟粿) to their ancestors to welcome the new child into the family.

The Worship of the Ancestors

After the shaving of the baby, a family would worship their ancestors. They introduced their new family member to the ancestors and then asked for them to bestow blessings upon the child. They also presented the child's BaZi chart to the ancestors for their consideration. It was customary for families to offer chicken stew, Chinese sticky rice and red tortoise cakes (*Hong Gui Guo* 红龟粿) to their ancestors as well.

Honouring the ancestors in this instance was much like other similar ceremonies and included incense burning and prayer. The typical choices of fruits were also laid at the altar as part of the offering.

The Suiting-up Ceremony (*Song Tou Wei* 送頭尾)

Translated literally, the *Suiting-up Ceremony* (*Song Tou Wei* 送頭尾) is called the "offering from the head to the tail". This is an appropriate name as the 12 gifts given by a new mother's family during the ceremony were sufficient to kit a new baby out from head to toe!

The 12 gifts usually offered were:

- A sum of money presented in a red envelope (*Hong Bao* 紅包)
- A hat
- A pair of shoes
- A matching pair of socks
- A pair of trousers
- Diapers
- An item of clothing for the upper body befitting the baby's gender
- A blanket
- A pillow
- A baby sling
- Gold jewellery
- Silver jewellery

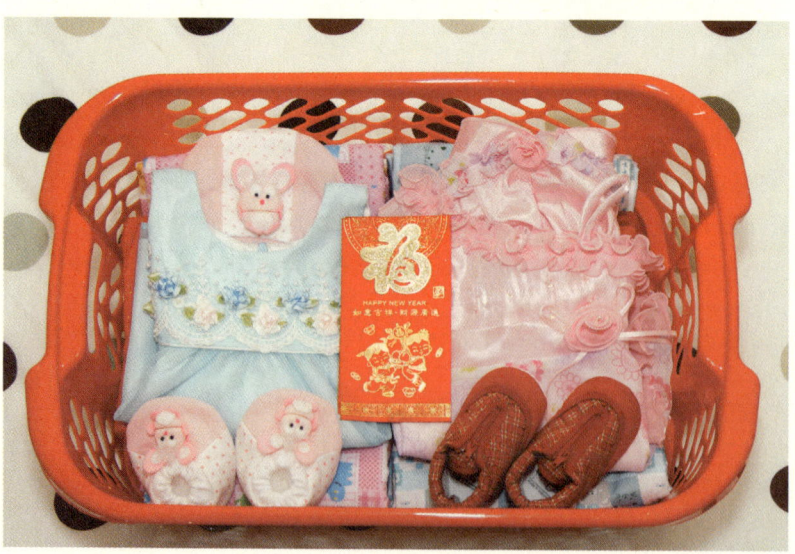

For their part, the new father's birth family offered Chinese sticky rice, cookies and eggs painted red for luck in return.

There were stipulations regarding the 12 gifts listed above, First, it was imperative that the upper body clothing, hat and trousers featured the character "Wan 卍". It is a symbol associated with prosperity, luck, security, glory, and good in many eastern cultures. In China particularly, it was strongly associated with Buddhism and to some extent Daoism as well. The character could be sewn, painted or simply pinned to the clothing but it had to be attached.

Second, two of each gift was given especially if the baby was a boy. This was done in the spirit of wishing the baby to have a lifetime of wealth. If the baby was a girl, the baby sling was omitted. This was because the Chinese word for baby sling (*Bei Jin* 背巾) rhymes with the Chinese word for "daughter" (*Qian Jin* 千金). It was believed that giving a new mother a baby sling might decrease her chances of having a son in the future.

A different group of 12 items were sometimes given. The alternative 12 items were more symbolic than those listed above which were meant to be pragmatic in nature. One of these 12 gifts was rice, representing food and abundance. It was offered in the hopes that the baby would never go hungry in their life. Stones, symbolizing courage and strength, and chives, symbolizing health and longevity, were given too. Chicken and duck eggs painted red were given for good luck, especially in matters of romance. Coins were given to represent wealth along with mugwort which could supposedly ward off negative energies.

The remaining four items were chosen either because they had names that rhymed or sounded like positive words. Longans were given as they were linked to the assistance of Noblemen because they are alternatively called cinnamon beads (*Gui Yuan* 桂圓) which rhymes with Nobleman (*Gui Ren* 貴人). Scallions were provided for reasons mentioned earlier and celery was given because its Chinese name "*Qin*" (芹) is a homophone for the Chinese word for diligence (*Qin* 勤). Finally, garlic cloves (*Suan* 蒜) were given because their name is a homophone for the Chinese word for "calculate" (*Suan* 算), linking them with academic success.

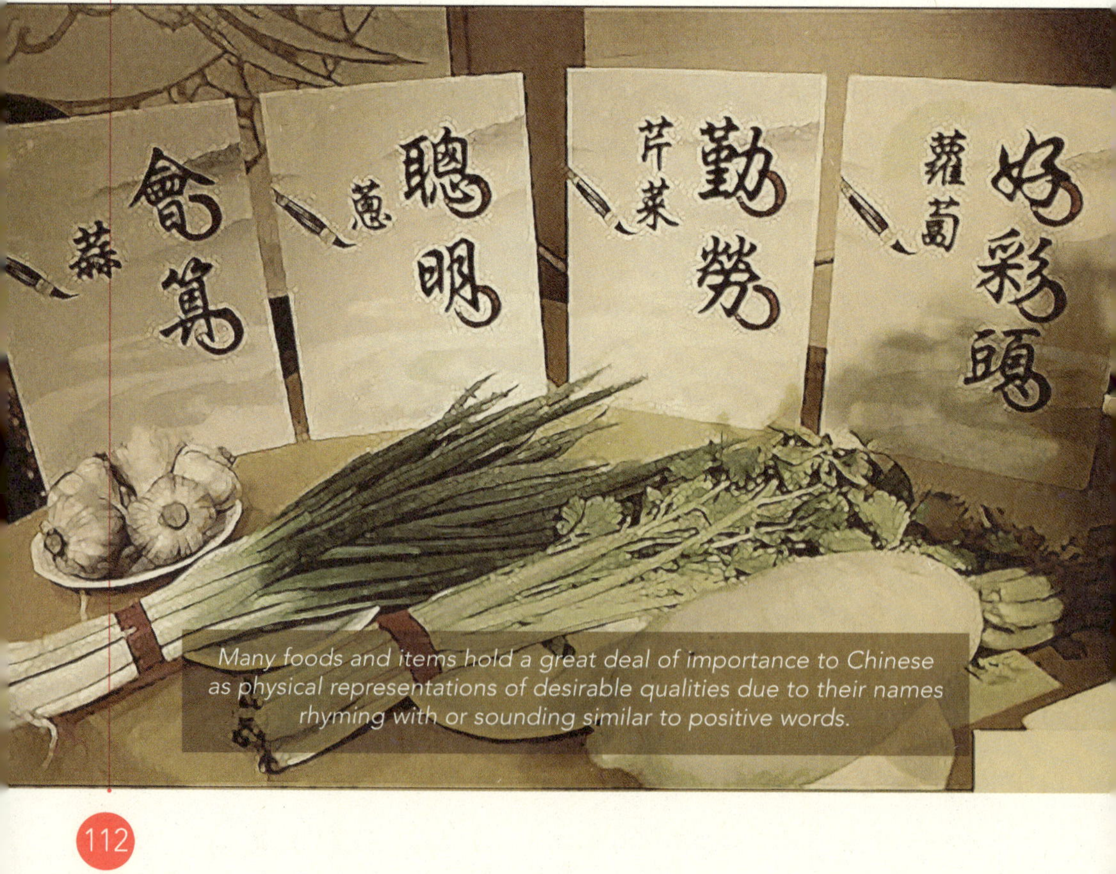

Many foods and items hold a great deal of importance to Chinese as physical representations of desirable qualities due to their names rhyming with or sounding similar to positive words.

The Full Moon Banquet

The Full Moon ceremony culminated in a banquet where a family celebrated with the wider community. It was customary for a new father's family to invite the new mother's family as well as their neighbours, friends and matchmakers to partake in a feast.

Popular dishes in Chinese culture like chicken stew and Chinese sticky rice were served alongside a special soup matched with baked pastries (*Shao Bing* 燒餅). The Chinese sticky rice was accompanied by a braised chicken thigh and two eggs painted with red colouring. This side dish is meant to be interpreted as a phallic symbol.

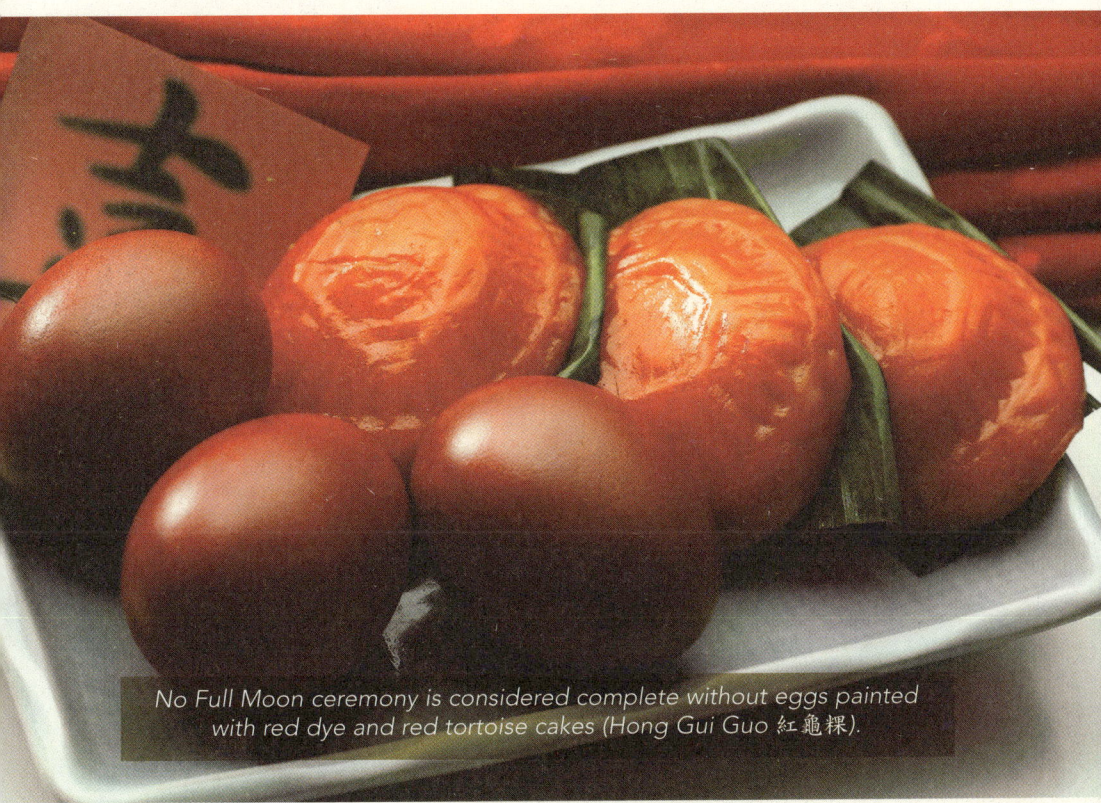

No Full Moon ceremony is considered complete without eggs painted with red dye and red tortoise cakes (Hong Gui Guo 紅龜粿).

The Infant's Hundredth Day

In ancient China, many children didn't make it beyond the first month of their life, much less reach old age. Medical knowledge and expertise were limited in ancient China and so infant mortality rates were very high.

As such, it was customary to celebrate when a child was one hundred days old with a rite known as the *Hundredth Day Ceremony* (*Bai Ri* 百日) or *Prosperity Day* (*Bai Lu* 百祿). It was believed that a child who had survived to their hundredth day stood a good chance of reaching adulthood and old age.

The ceremony consisted of a banquet held by the child's family and several rituals which made use of items like the *Lock of Longevity* (*Chang Ming Suo* 長命鎖) and the *Clothes of a Hundred Families* (*Bai Jia Yi* 百家衣) which are described in detail below. The family also held a small ritual known as the *Drawing of Lots* (*Zhua Zhou* 抓周), also described below. Like the *Full Moon* ceremony, these customs are still observed today.

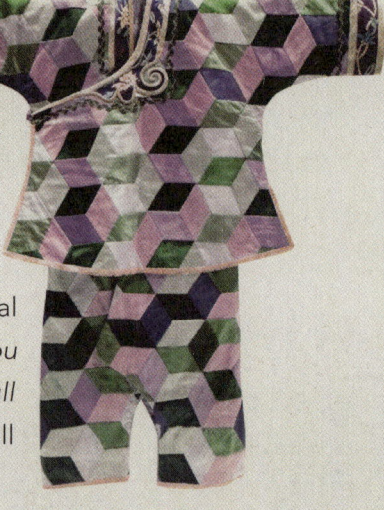

Clothes of a Hundred Families
(Bai Jia Yi 百家衣*)*

The Lock of Longevity (*Chang Ming Suo* 長命鎖)

In this custom, the family of a new mother offered her baby a special gift called the *Lock of Longevity* (*Chang Ming Suo* 長命鎖). This item was a necklace with a charm designed to look like a lock attached to it. While typically made of brass, this charm was sometimes made of gold or silver depending on the family's financial status. It was meant to symbolically secure a child's wellbeing and prevent them from dying young.

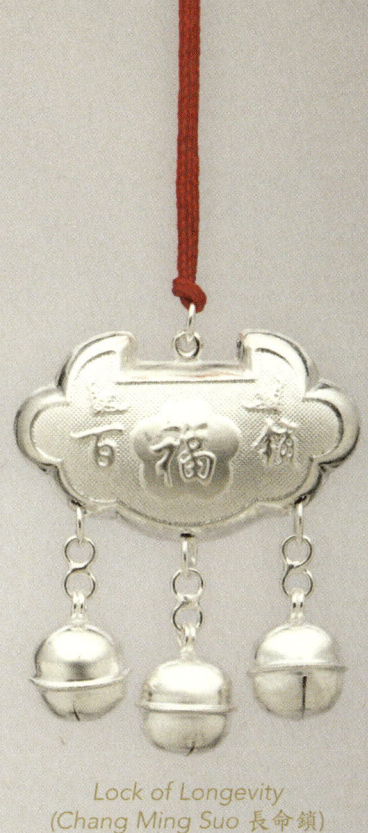

Lock of Longevity (Chang Ming Suo 長命鎖)

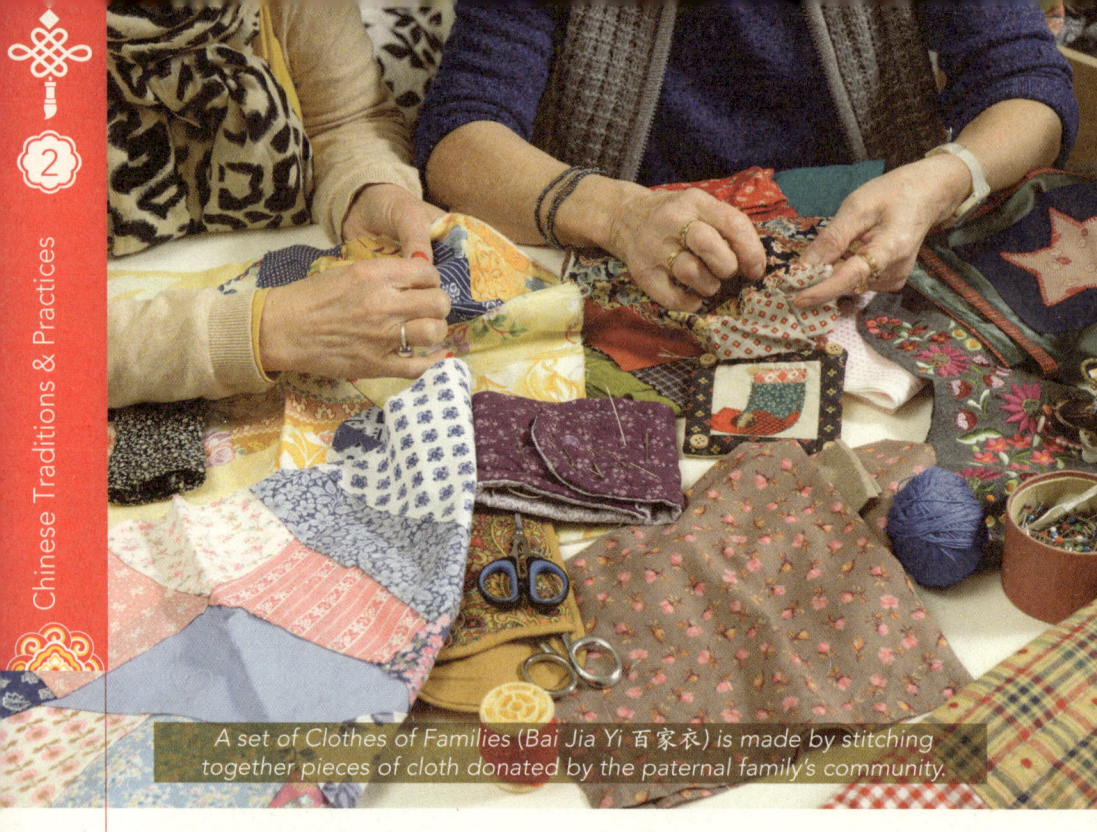

A set of Clothes of Families (Bai Jia Yi 百家衣) is made by stitching together pieces of cloth donated by the paternal family's community.

The Clothes of a Hundred Families (*Bai Jia Yi* 百家衣)

A child's paternal family would prepare something known as the *Clothes of a Hundred Families (Bai Jia Yi* 百家衣*)*. However, this phrase shouldn't be taken literally. In accordance with the custom, a new father's family would make clothing from pieces of cloth donated by the wider community. Like the aforementioned *Lock of Longevity*, the *Clothes of a Hundred Families* were produced with the hope that they would help a child reach adulthood safely. It was customary to use purple fabric and materials as purple is associated with royalty and considered auspicious. Plus, the Chinese word for the colour purple is "Zi" (紫) which is phonetically similar to the Chinese word for "son" (*Zi* 子). Thus, the colour purple is used to represent the desire for a child to grow up and have many children of their own.

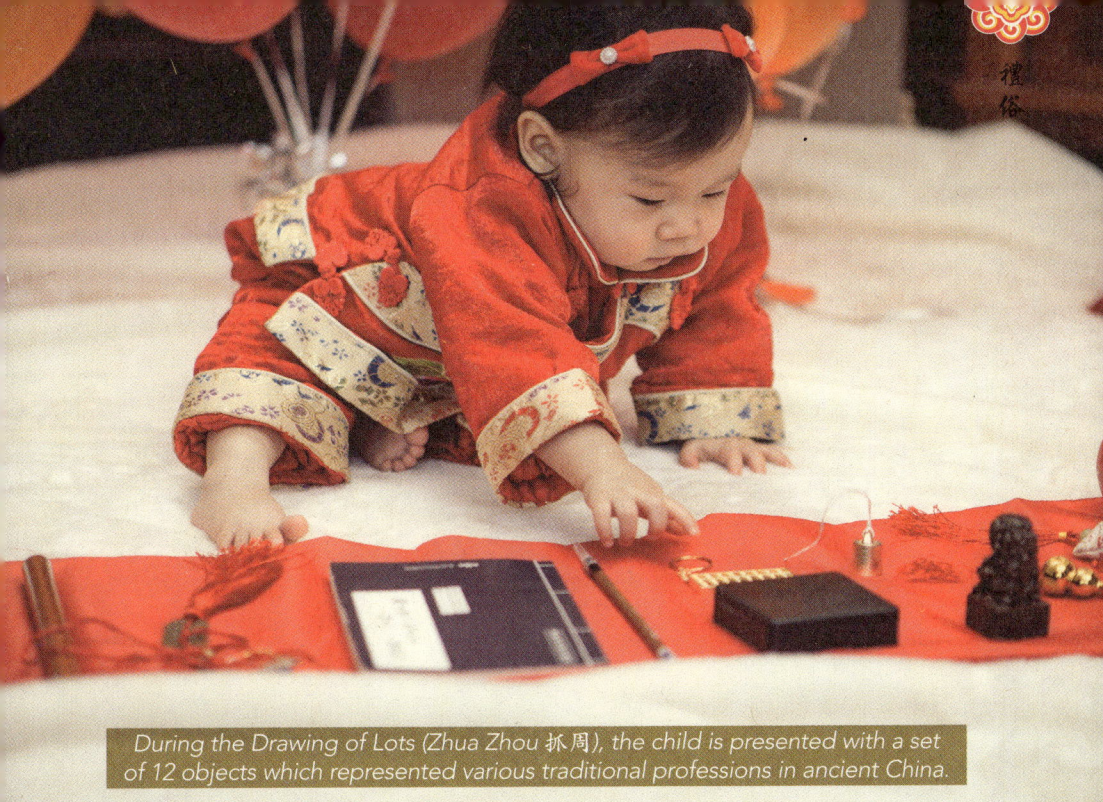

During the Drawing of Lots (Zhua Zhou 抓周), the child is presented with a set of 12 objects which represented various traditional professions in ancient China.

The Drawing of Lots (*Zhua Zhou* 抓周)

Another custom was the *Drawing of Lots* (*Zhua Zhou* 抓周) which literally translates to "Catching Rounds". However, some sources say that this was carried out on the baby's first birthday instead of on the *Hundredth Day Ceremony*. In it, the child's family presented 12 objects on a tray for him or her to play with. The items were chosen to represent various professions in ancient China. Whichever item the child took an interest in indicated their future career.

Many of the items that have been described so far were also used in this ceremony. The scallion represents intelligence, the garlic clove denotes a talent for calculation and the celery signifies diligence. Meanwhile, the braised chicken thigh embodies never-ending prosperity and suggested that the child would never go hungry.

If the child chose a book, it meant they would become an intellectual or excel in the imperial examinations. If they touched an abacus or scale, they might end up as a businessman. Touching a ruler suggested that the child would end up as a carpenter. Touching a calligraphy brush or ink stick suggested they may become a calligraphy artist. If they touched soil, it was thought they would grow up to become a landowner. The final item – a seal – spoke of the possibility that the child might grow up to become a government official.

The items described above have been updated over the years as new jobs have come along. More than 12 objects can be used in this ritual but the number of items must be even. Additionally, the objects must be clearly representative of an occupation or pursuit for the ritual to function. A ball might represent a life in sports or a stethoscope might represent a medical career, for example.

Whether or not the *Drawing of Lots* can accurately predict the future, it remains popular to this day.

Chapter 3

The Joy of Adolescence and the Rites of Adulthood

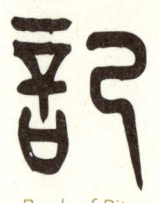

Book of Rites
(*Li Ji* 禮記)

Throughout history, cultures have held rites of passage, often based on their prevailing religious beliefs. Anthropologists assert that rites of passage are a way for societies to recognize and celebrate an individual's change of status. Many rites of passage bestow a person with new rights, like the right to get married. Others also give a person new responsibilities and obligations.

The ancient Chinese had many rites of passage. At first, women were excluded from them. The so called "rituals for becoming a man" or Rite of Manhood (*Cheng Ding Li* 成丁禮) was a collection of largely physical challenges, designed to help usher boys into manhood. The rites tested one's physical strength and included hunting, hair cutting, tattooing and teethbreaking. When Confucianism took hold in China, the "savage" rituals were abolished in favour of more "sophisticated" ones. The shift in thinking around the rituals coincided with a wider transition from a hunter-gatherer society into an agricultural one. The new rites were described in a number of Confucian classics. Today, most of what we know about the rituals of the day comes from the Book of Rites (*Li Ji* 禮記). A significant number of them were based upon Chinese naturalist beliefs, i.e: that everything in the world was created by the natural forces of Yin and Yang. The rituals drew upon other ideas too, however, so a person could participate in them even if they didn't subscribe to naturalist beliefs.

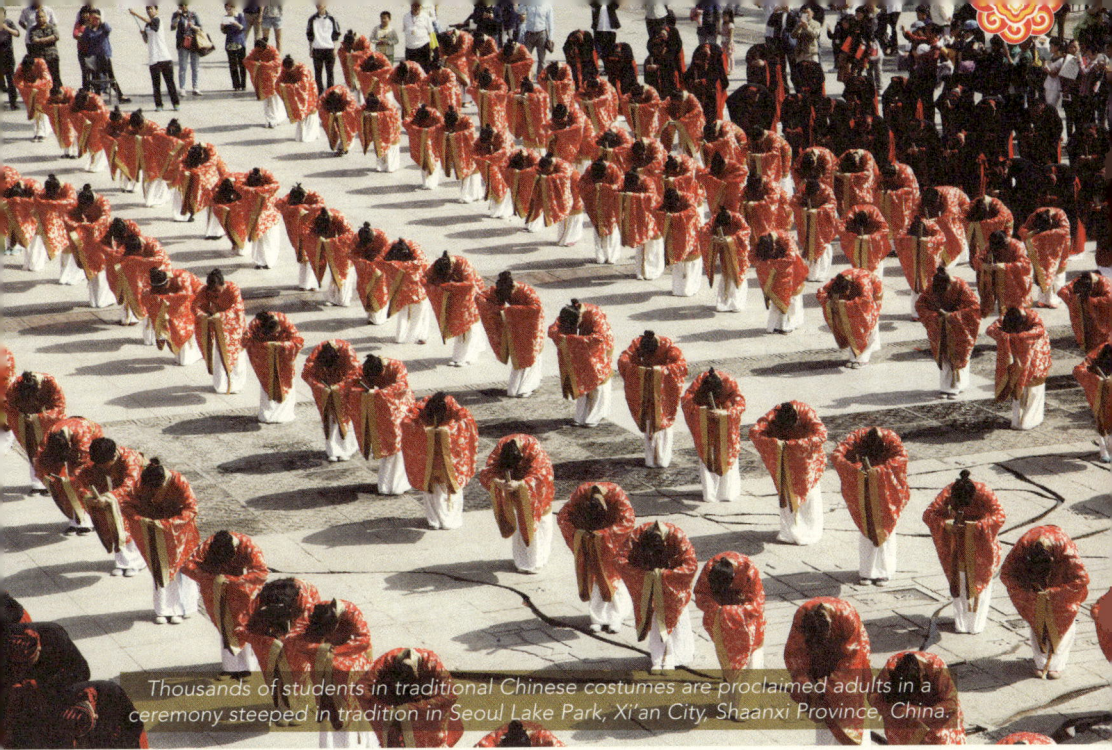
Thousands of students in traditional Chinese costumes are proclaimed adults in a ceremony steeped in tradition in Seoul Lake Park, Xi'an City, Shaanxi Province, China.

Cultures throughout history have celebrated sexual maturity and ancient China was no different. A person's gender, age and class determined which set of rites they underwent when the time came. Boys and girls boys underwent a rite of passage when they turned 16. Boys underwent another ceremony when they turned 20. Reaching adulthood, men were given a Confucian hat and women were given a pair of hair sticks in two rites known as the Capping Rite (*Guan Li* 冠禮) and the Hairpin-wearing Rite (*Ji Li* 筓禮), respectively and the Caps and Hairpins Rites (*Guan Ji* 冠筓) collectively.

Social class divides were even more pronounced in ancient China than they are today and different rites were used by higher class citizens like intellectuals and lower class ones like labourers and farmers. Wealthy families could afford to hold more elaborate rites than commoners. The differences were not just aesthetic, though. People from different classes were given different responsibilities and privileges as they entered new stages of their lives.

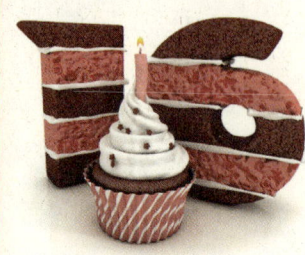

Hitting the Big 16

When the Rite of Manhood mentioned earlier was abolished, it was succeeded by the more measured Rite of Adolescence (*Cheng Nian Li* 成年禮), also known as the "rituals for reaching maturity".

At the time, girls were became women as soon as they began menstruating, typically at the age of 14, 15 or 16. Boys became men when they turned 16, without exception. At the right time, boys and girls underwent the Rite of Adulthood (*Cheng Ren Li* 成人禮).

For middle or upper class girls, the Rite of Adulthood centred around the aforementioned Hairpin-wearing Rite (*Ji Li* 笄禮). Girls who belonged to the poorest social classes practised the less elaborate Rite of Adolescence instead. Notably, the Rite of Adolescence (*Cheng Nian Li* 成年禮) recognized that a young person was ready to work as a paid labourer. It was not unusual for children to work at the time but they only started earning money after completing the Rite of Adolescence. Somewhat ironically, poor families could often only afford to hold the Rite of Adolescence for their eldest son.

Rite of Adolescence
(*Cheng Nian Li* 成年禮)

The Rite of Adolescence ceremony typically began with the boy or girl in question putting on new clothes and shoes to symbolise their "rebirth" into society as an adult. Their parents and family prepared gifts which they then offered to Deities, such as a miniature paper pavilion representing the Seven Star Pavilion (*Qi Xing Ma Ting* 七星媽亭). Other common offerings included joss paper, meat, noodles, doughnut peaches, rouge and lipstick. Next, the child would write a Statement of Gratitude (*Gan Xie Zhuang* 感謝狀) dedicated to the Goddess of the Seven Stars (*Qi Xing Niang Niang/Qi Niang Ma* 七星娘娘/七娘媽). The Goddess of the Seven Stars was believed to protect children and so the statement was a way of expressing thanks for her protection and letting her know that it would no longer be necessary. This document was sometimes produced along with another document addressed to the Goddess confirming that the child had come of age.

After writing their statements, the family of the child in question prayed to the Goddess, bowed and burned incense. After praying, the child presented their statement to her by reading it aloud. He (or she) would then crawl under a table, exit and walk around a miniature paper pavilion three times. Boys walked from left to right while girls were expected to walk from right to left. The rite was concluded by burning joss paper.

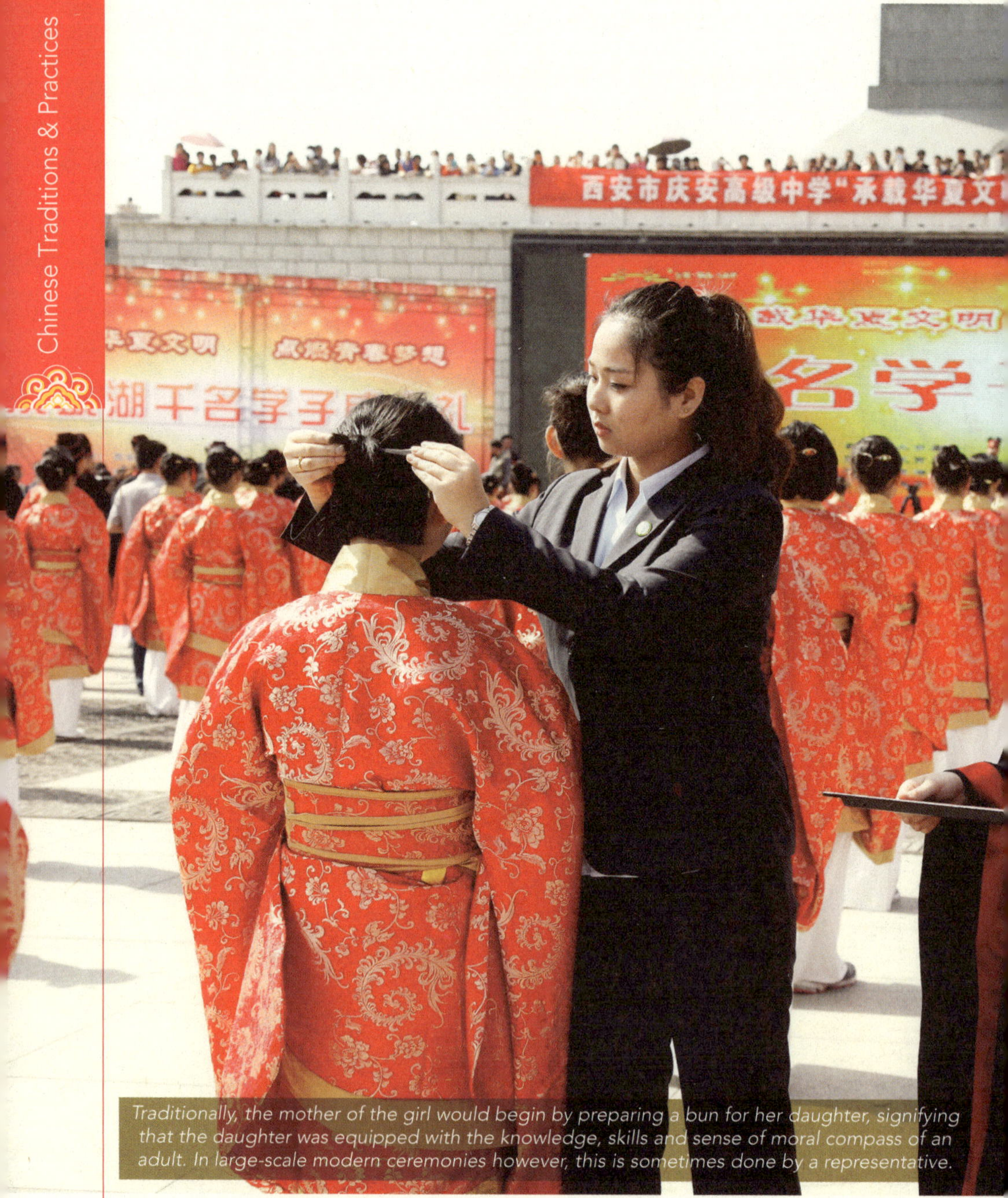

Chinese Traditions & Practices

Traditionally, the mother of the girl would begin by preparing a bun for her daughter, signifying that the daughter was equipped with the knowledge, skills and sense of moral compass of an adult. In large-scale modern ceremonies however, this is sometimes done by a representative.

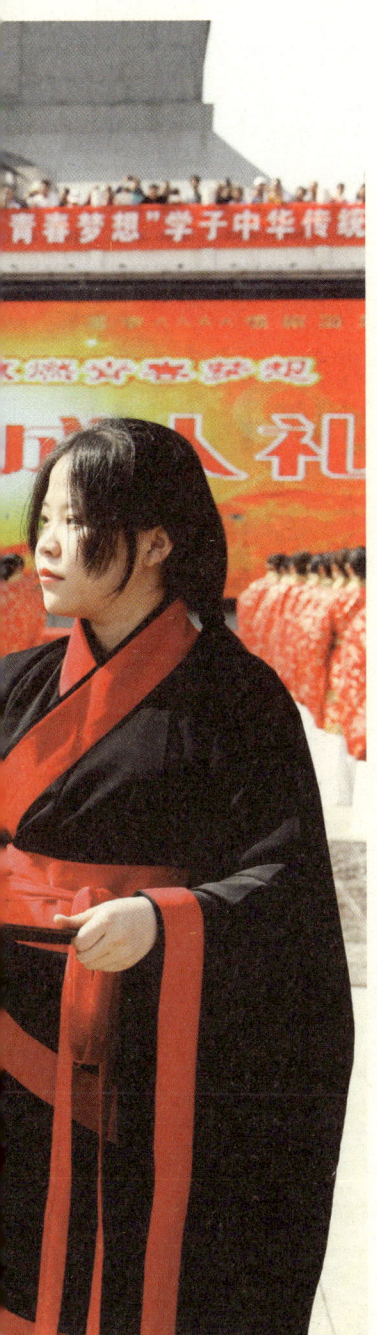

The Hairpin-wearing Rite (*Ji Li* 笄禮)

The Hairpin-wearing rite was held when a girl began menstruating, typically between the ages of 14 and 16. It recognized that she had become an adult in the sense that she could bear children. Women who have completed the rite were eligible for marriage. After the rite, a local matchmaker would take their details and begin searching for a suitable husband in most cases. Of course, some families prearranged marriage for their daughter before she was eligible for the rite. When this happened, the ceremony was sometimes brought forward so that she could get married sooner. The rite was compulsory for any women who was still single by the time she turned 20.

The mother of the girl who was about to pass into adulthood was in charge of conducting the Hairpin-wearing Rite. Although several versions of the rite exist, most proceeded in the following way.

The mother of the girl would begin by preparing a bun for her daughter, signifying that the daughter was equipped with the knowledge, skills and sense of moral compass of an adult.

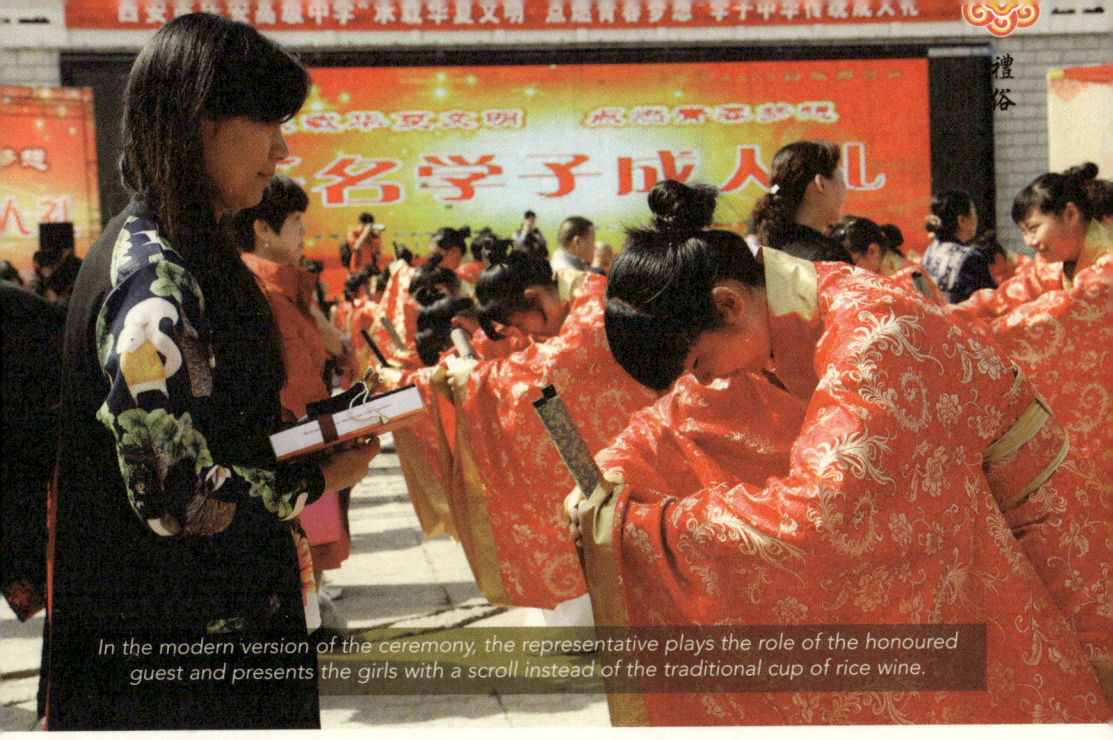

In the modern version of the ceremony, the representative plays the role of the honoured guest and presents the girls with a scroll instead of the traditional cup of rice wine.

When the guest of honour arrived, the mother led her family in a queue-like fashion into the hall. The guest of honour stopped at the gate, facing east, and asked for permission to enter. The nominated family member greeted him, returned to the mother, relayed his request to enter, listened to the mother's response, returned and granted the guest of honour permission to enter.

Entering the premises, the guest of honour could give a goodwill speech at his discretion. He would then bow to the girl before asking her to enter the main hall and stand at his right hand side, dressed in the traditional clothing she had just put on. Next, an exchange of bows between the guest of honour and the girl's mother took place before the mother moved to the centre of the hall. The nominated family member then presented the guest of honour with a hairpin which he in turn placed in the girl's hair, after making final adjustments to her appearance.

With the completion of the hairpin presentation, the final stage of the ceremony began. The nominated family member set up an altar on the west side of the hall, facing south. The guest of honour then led the girl to sit on the right side of the altar, facing south. The guest of honour would then take a cup of rice wine to the altar and give another goodwill speech, facing north. Once he finished his speech, the girl was expected to bow to him and take the cup so that he could return to his original position. Both of them would then bow to the east and the girl would drink the rice wine before leaving the west side of the altar to stand on the east. The guest of honour was then expected to give another goodwill speech and award her a secondary first name referred to as Zi (字) which literally means "word". This custom of adopting an additional first name ties into the ancient Chinese custom of having two first names known the Ming and Zi. In modern Chinese language used today, the word "Ming Zi" can be translated into the word "name" in English.

The hairpin ceremony officially came to an end when the girl gave a goodwill speech of her own. In doing so, she officially became a woman. Afterwards, her family expressed their gratitude to the guest of honour by offering him dinner. Some families opted to pay him for his services and it was customary for him to spend a second night at their home.

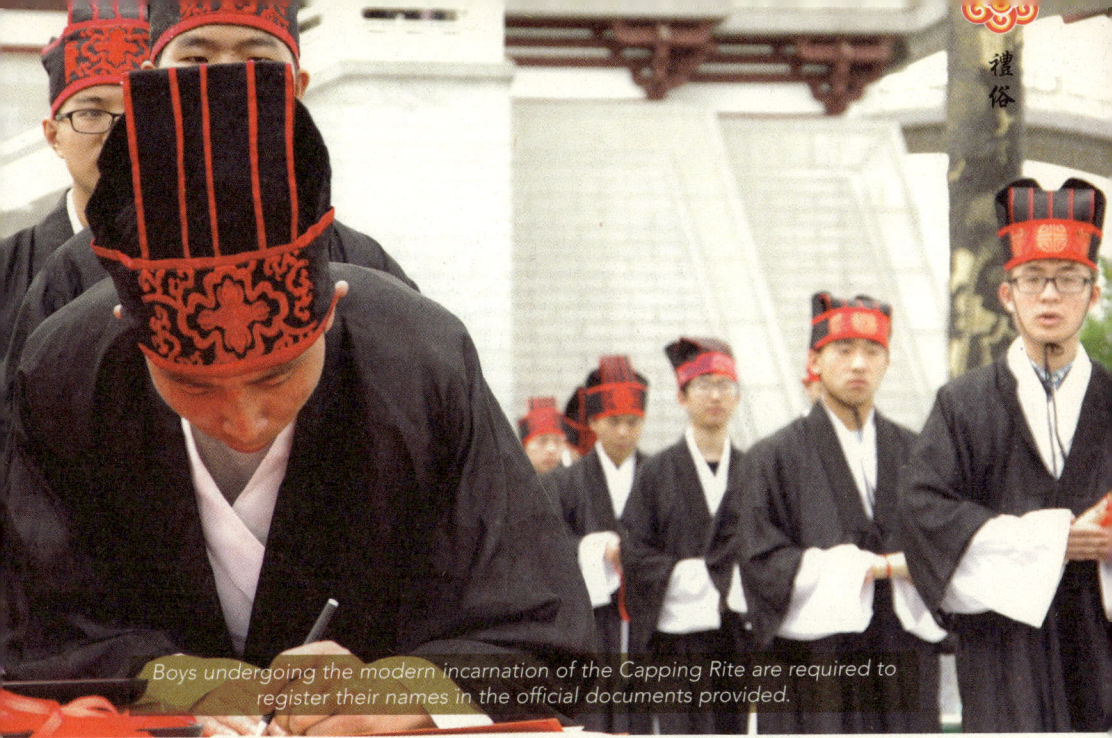

Boys undergoing the modern incarnation of the Capping Rite are required to register their names in the official documents provided.

From Boyhood to Manhood

As mentioned, the Rite of Adulthood for boys in ancient China was the Capping Rite (*Guan Li* 冠禮), held on their 20th birthday. It can be thought of as the direct successor to the abolished Rite of Manhood because it was only applicable to boys.

The Rite of Adulthood was based on the tenants of Confucianism. It differed from the Rite of Manhood in terms of how it defined adulthood. With the Capping Rite, a boy is said to "become a human" (*Cheng Ren* 成人). This unusual turn of phrase can be attributed to the rite's roots in Confucianism, where adulthood has less to do with biology and more to do with adherence to society's moral code. Those who could not live up to the expectations of society were seen as sub-human savages. In accordance with this, the Capping Rite celebrated a young man's knowledge, skill, responsibility and morality instead of their ability to hunt and endure pain.

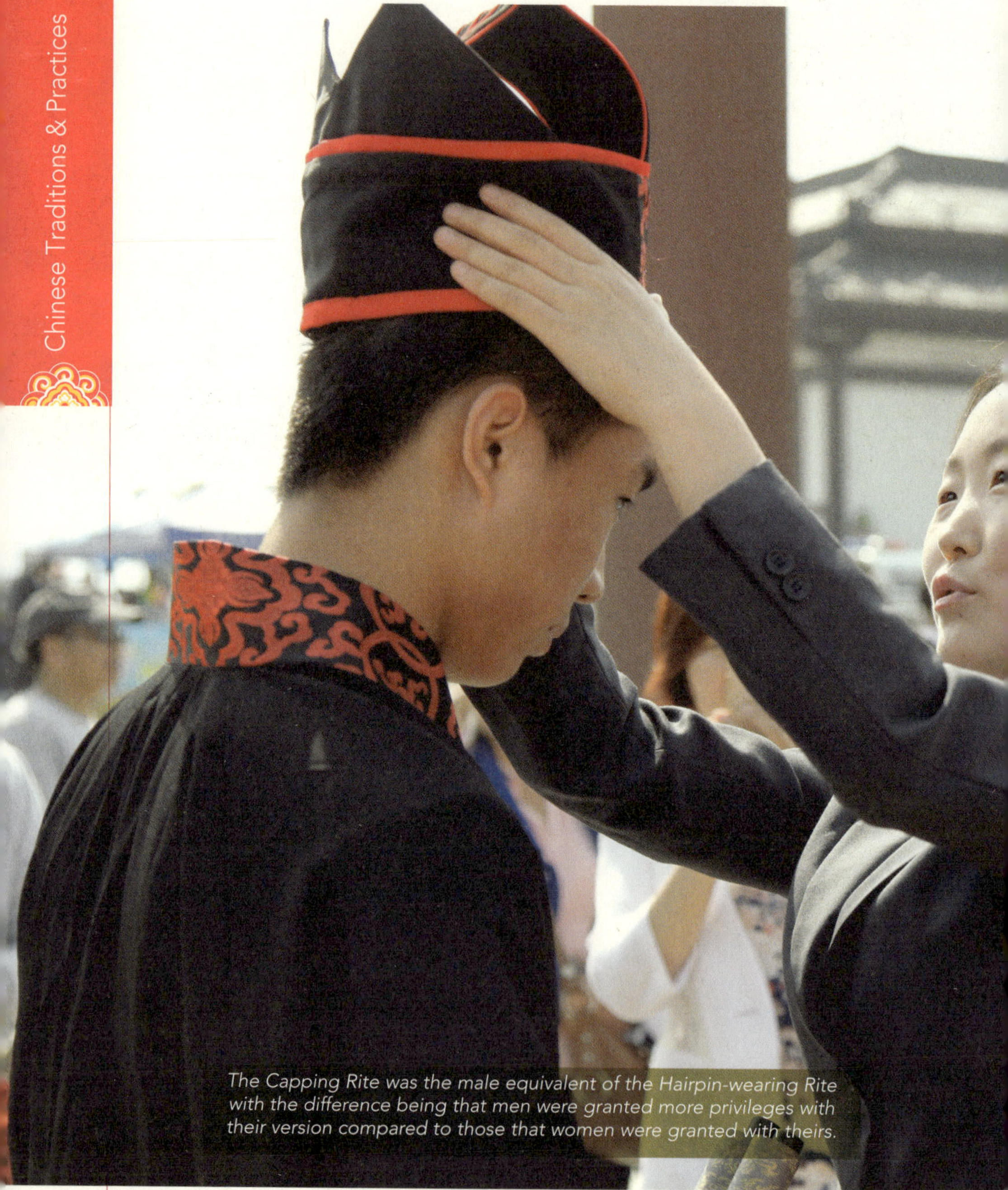

Chinese Traditions & Practices

The Capping Rite was the male equivalent of the Hairpin-wearing Rite with the difference being that men were granted more privileges with their version compared to those that women were granted with theirs.

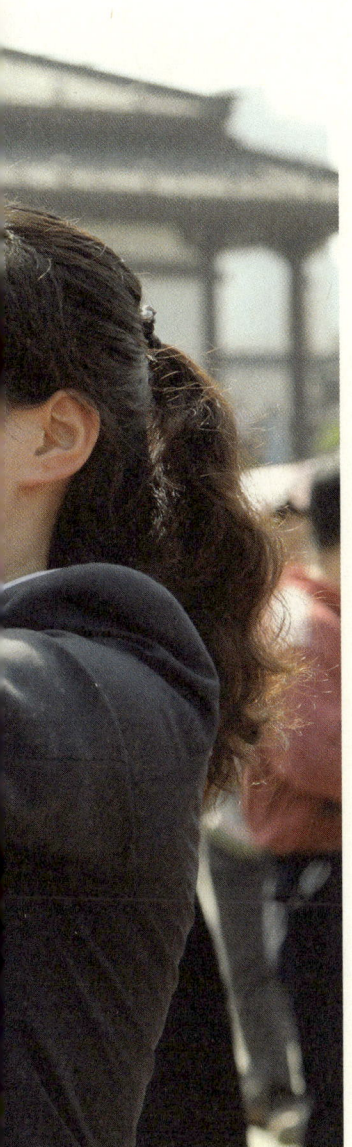

The Capping Rite (*Guan Li* 冠禮)

The Capping Rite was the male equivalent of the Hairpin-wearing Rite, but given the customs of the time, men were granted more privileges with it than women. This is because women of the day were seen as fit for motherhood and little more. Men were seen as more versatile and capable. On a related note, the completion of this rite was a prerequisite for leadership positions of any kind in those days. This is documented in the Book of Rites in a chapter called The Significance of Hats (*Guan Yi* 冠義). In ancient China, hats – the namesake of the Capping Rite - were used to indicate a person's social status. Their usage was therefore regulated, but rules regarding hats varied from one Dyansty to another. For example, poor people were not allowed to wear hats during the time of the Han Dynasty but could wear headbands if they wished.

In the Book of Rites, the Capping Rite is laid out in detail. The first order of duty was to choose a date for the ceremony using Date Selection. (Today, families use a person's birthday or significant date like Chinese New Year for simplicity's sake.) The Book of Rites recommends that the Capping Rite should be held at a family's ancestral shrine but this recommendation is rarely observed today. It can be held in any building with a main hall, like a school.

Mirroring the Hairpin-wearing Rite, the Capping Rite was conducted by the central boy's father with the help of a guest of honour. The guest of honour had to be a high-ranking, well-respected, wise and learned individual with good manners, like a scholar. He was sometimes lined up to mentor the boy once he had become a young man. He was asked to stay overnight with the family before the day of the ceremony.

To kick things off on the day, the father of the boy on the threshold of adulthood would instruct his family to line up at the east side of the venue's main hall, facing west. He would then nominate a family member who was the knowledgeable about the ceremony and Confucianism and assign them the task of welcoming the guest of honour. First, the nominated family member took the boy to a room where he could change into traditional clothing and wait to be called. He then went to stand at the gate of the hall and face west.

When the guest of honour arrived, he stood at the gate facing east and asked for permission to enter. The nominated family member would then enter the hall and inform the father that the guest of honour had arrived. The father was then to lead the family in a queue and enter the hall before going to the gate to invite the guest of honour in. Once the guest of honour had come inside, he could give a goodwill speech at his discretion. He then bowed to the boy who had changed into traditional clothing and asked him to enter the main hall. The boy would then stand at the guest of honour's right side. Next, the guest of honour exchanged bows with the father who then moved to the centre of the hall. The nominated family member presented the guest of honour with a ceremonial hat made of linen, leather and black gauze. The guest of honour made final adjustments to the boy's appearance and then, at his discretion, he could make another speech before placing the all important hat on the boy. As an aside, some versions of the rite see this step repeated as many as three times!

Moving on, the nominated family member prepared an altar facing south at the west side of the hall. The guest of honour led the boy to sit at the right side of the altar, facing south. He then took a cup of rice wine to the altar and gave another goodwill speech, facing north. Once he had finished, the boy would bow to the guest of honour and accept the cup from him, allowing him to return to the centre of the hall. They both bowed to the east before the boy drank the wine presented to him. Once he had finished, he was expected to leave the west side of the altar and stand on the east side of the hall.

To conclude the Capping Rite, the guest of honour gave a final goodwill speech before giving the boy his second first name (Zi 字). It was customary for the boy – now a man – to give a speech of his own to wrap things up. It was also typical for the family to invite the guest of honour to dinner. Some families chose to pay him for his time and most would ask him to stay for a second night.

Chapter 4

Grand Banquets

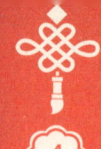

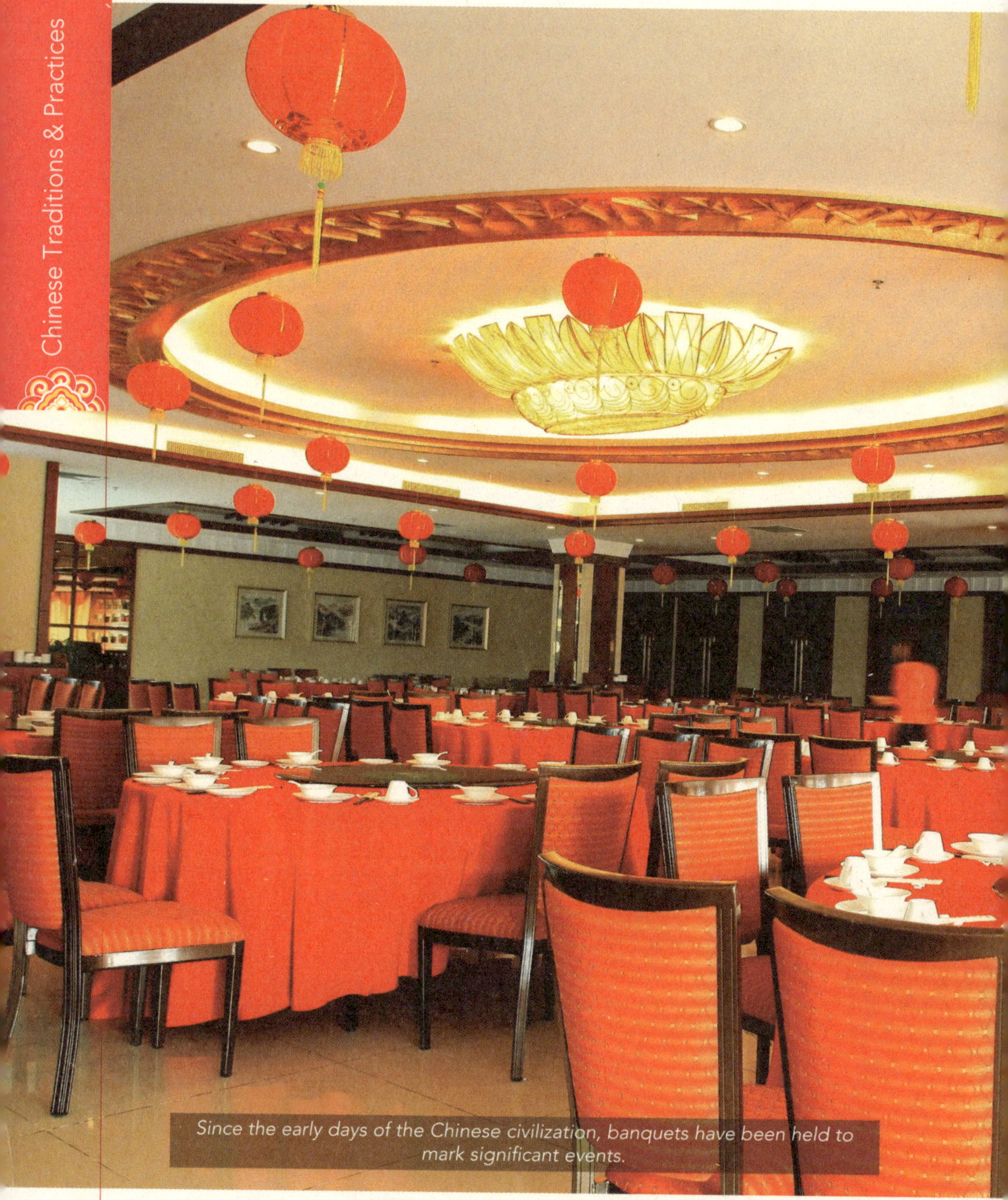

Chinese Traditions & Practices

Since the early days of the Chinese civilization, banquets have been held to mark significant events.

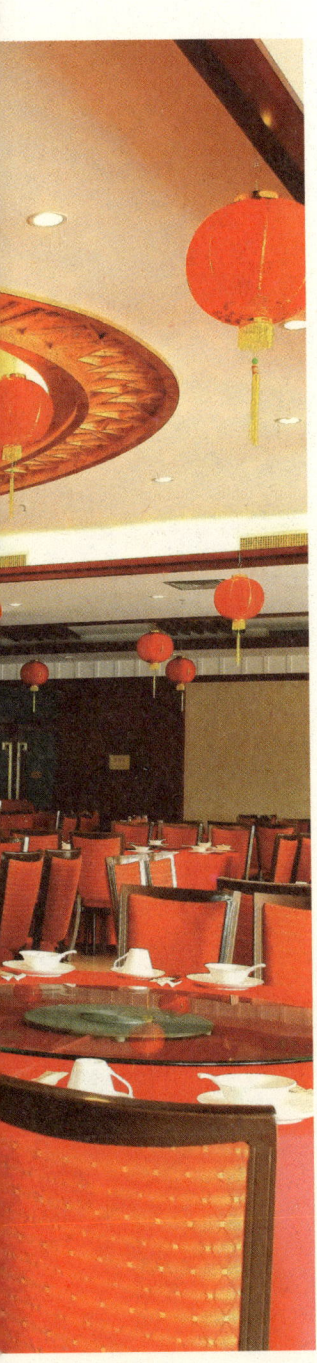

Every culture has its own culinary traditions. The availability of food, religious beliefs and environmental factors all help shape a region's relationship with food. From the simplest meal to the most lavish delicacy; food and the way it is consumed reveals a lot about a country and its people.

As home to one of the world's oldest civilizations, China naturally has rich and complex dining traditions. Grand banquets have been an important part of Chinese culture since before the days of Imperial China. As such, they are associated with many customs and traditions.

Many Chinese dishes reflect the country's agricultural past, like rice which has long been a staple food in China. In the past, rice and other crops were grown in community farms by commoners. Only wealthy people could afford more exotic items like meat, poultry and fish. Fruit was a luxury enjoyed occasionally as a side dish.

Over time, banquets came to symbolise good times and prosperity. At a banquet, guests could choose from a wide variety of dishes and enjoy larger portion sizes. Thus, banquets embodied the Chinese concept of "abundance" (*Feng Sheng* 豐盛).

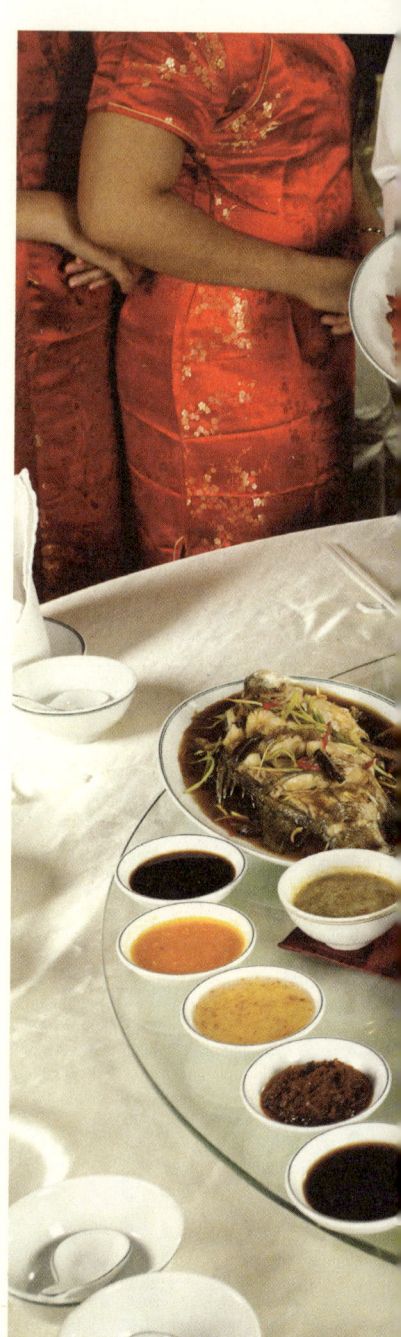

In Chinese cuisine, cooking techniques are just as important as ingredients. As cooking techniques have evolved, so have Chinese recipes. Every region of China has its own distinct cooking style, unique dishes and dietary trends so a banquet's menu varies by region.

At a typical banquet, guests sit around a round table with plates of food in the middle. This arrangement is known colloquially as the Eight Directions Technique (*Ba Fang Cheng Pan* 八方盛盤) and it grants all guests equal access to the food on offer. Some suggest that it is a remnant of pre-Imperial China's matriarchal structure, symbolizing the importance of family and kinship in Chinese culture: communal eating arrangements bring families together.

Over the centuries, the Chinese developed customs that differentiated guests by age and status. These guidelines were eventually refined into a complex set of rites (*Li* 禮), based heavily on Confucian concepts. Some of the rites used in royal banquets are still observed today. Even now, tables and seats at a banquet are arranged to reflect the standing of guests both within their family and in society at large.

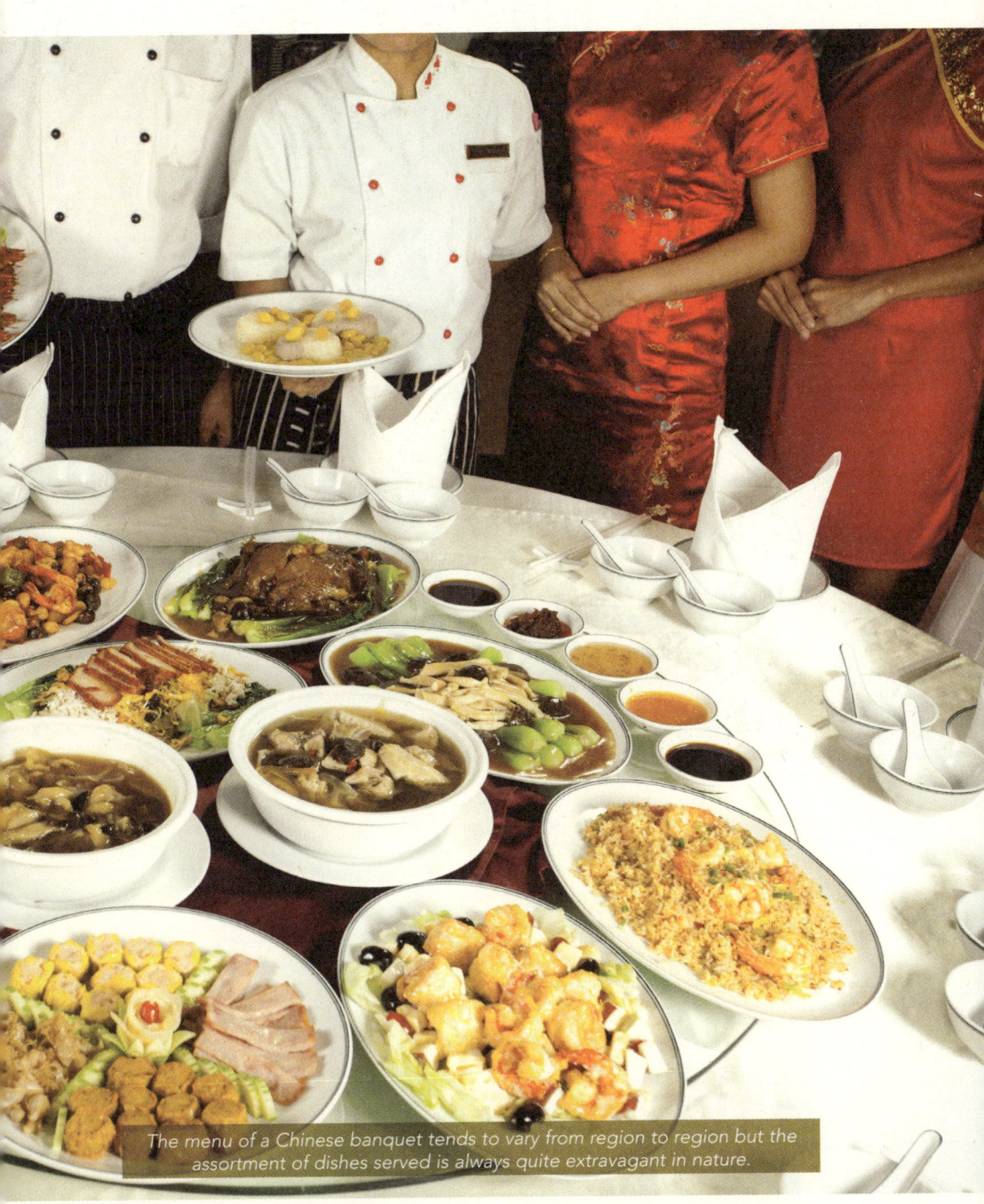

The menu of a Chinese banquet tends to vary from region to region but the assortment of dishes served is always quite extravagant in nature.

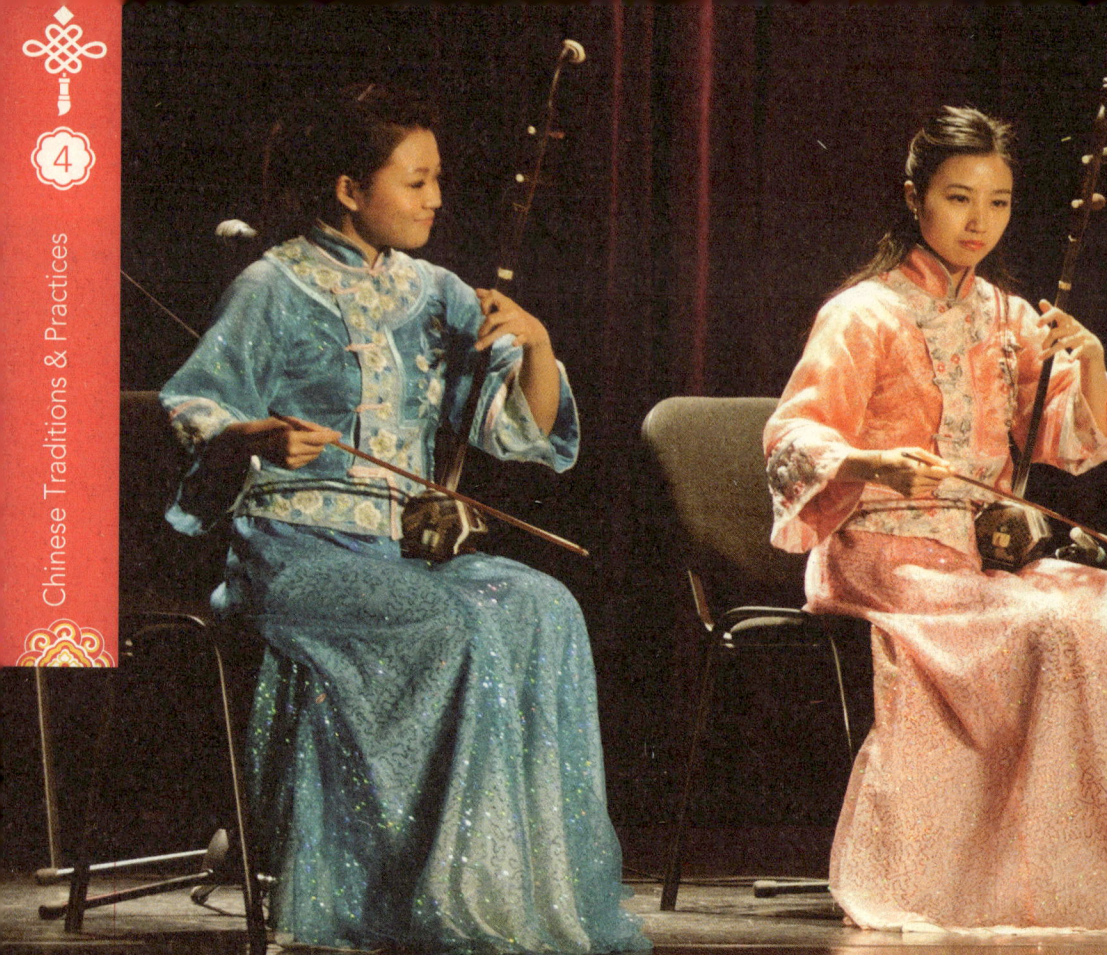

Entertainment often accompanied Chinese banquets in the form of music.

Entertainment often accompanied Chinese banquets. Traditionally, a type of music known as Silk and Bamboo (*Si Zhu* 絲竹) was performed with "silk" string instruments and "bamboo" woodwind instruments.

Seats at a banquet are traditionally assigned to people based on their social status or position in their family as mentioned above. Once guests have arrived and sat down, a nominated person kicks things off by pouring a drink and proposing a toast. This is done as a sign of communal respect.

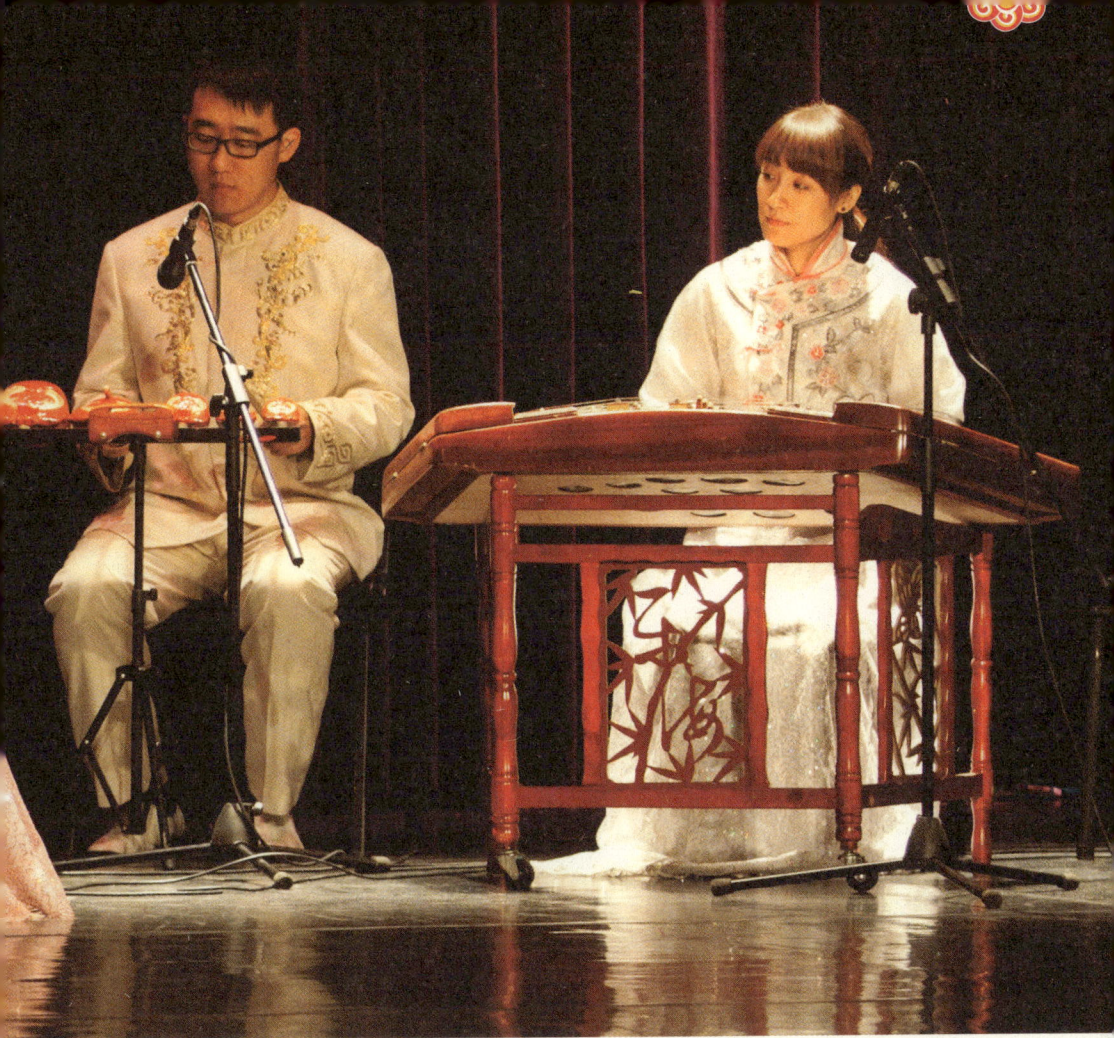

A typical menu starts with a cold appetizer which is followed by hot food and concluded with fruit dishes or dessert. At one time, the oldest and most distinguished guests in attendance ate first, but this is now rare at family banquets. It is still common practice in business or government banquets, however, where rank is clearly assigned.

A second toast may be proposed in the midst of a banquet. Guests who find this coercive may politely refuse or give their drink away. At the end of a banquet, the host may call for a third and final toast to finish things off.

Banquet Invitations

In China, banquets are held to commemorate a special occasion, like a marriage or childbirth. In the past, families used banquets to display their wealth and status, inviting as many people as they could afford to do so. Inviting someone to a banquet demonstrated respect, so it was a good way for a family to maintain ties with neighbors and friends. For all of these reasons, issuing invitations to a banquet was – and still is – a serious matter. Even though banquets are not quite the be all and end all that they once were, proper etiquette is still important.

The protocol of inviting someone to a modern banquet is much the same as it was in ancient China, although modern technology like Facebook and mobile phones make it easy to send out invitations.

禮俗

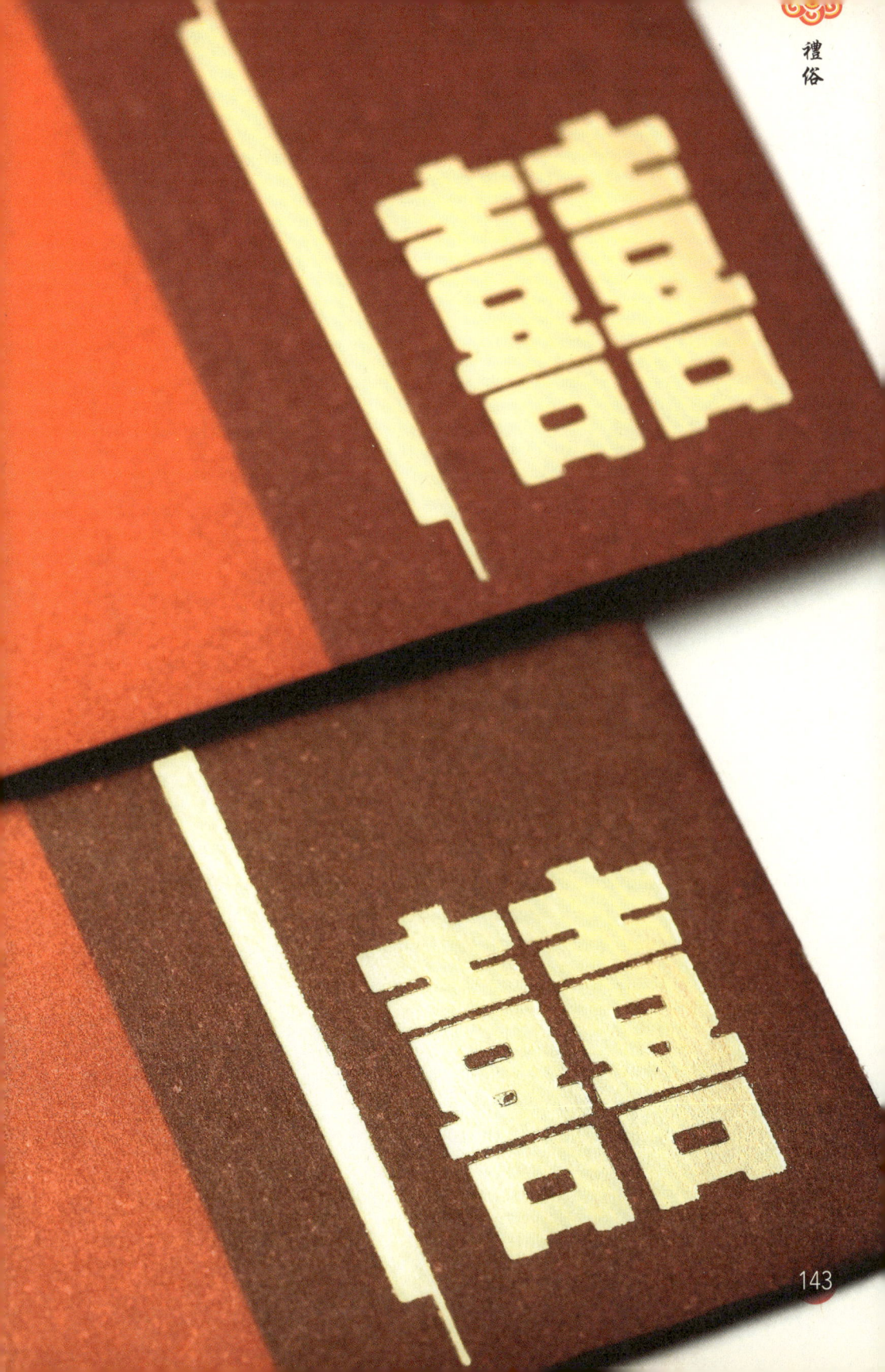

Principles Behind Invitations

In the past, commoners of limited means could only afford to invite their immediate relatives. They would only extend invitations to the wider community for the most joyous of occasions. Today, banquets are much larger and guest lists are far more extensive, often including friends, colleagues and business associates.

There are a few basic principles that one must consider when inviting people to their banquet.

The first principle is "availability" (*Xing* 行). A host should only invite people who they think are willing to attend. Although this seems like common sense, it is an important consideration – inviting a person who is unlikely to attend can damage a relationship (*Guan Xi* 關係) as they will have to decline the invitation and lose "face" (*Mian Zi* 面子).

Next, a host should consider their own social status. Although they may be tempted to invite people of higher social standing, they shouldn't do so unless they have a good personal or professional reason. A person of higher social standing is not obligated to attend a banquet held by someone lower on the ladder. By inviting only appropriate guests, a host can avoid the embarrassment of an honored guest no-show. Again, "saving face" is the goal.

A host must consider a potential guest's occupation, especially in mainland China. A public servant, for example, is likely to turn down an invitation to a banquet unless it comes from a close family member. This is because attending could leave them open to accusations of corruption.

Clarity or "clearness" (*Ming* 明) helps make for a good invitation. When writing an invitation, a host should state the event being celebrated, the time, venue and planned activities in a straightforward manner. The notion of "convenience" (*Bian* 便) is also important. When choosing a time and place for a banquet, a host should think about how far their guests will have to travel. They must also consider their guests' availability before booking the venue. If distance is an issue, a host should consider arranging transportation for guests. The general idea is that a host should make life easy for their guests.

Last but not least is the principle of "sincerity" (*Cheng* 誠). A host must strike a balance between sincerity and politics when issuing invitations to people they dislike. This dilemma isn't unique to China. Around the world, people have to put on a brave face and endure spending time with relatives and acquaintances they would rather not.

If a host feels obliged to invite someone they are not keen on then they should first consider the merits of sincerity. Invitations should not be made lightly.

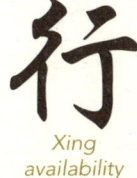
Xing
availability

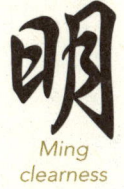
Ming
clearness

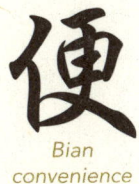
Bian
convenience

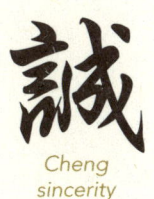
Cheng
sincerity

Issuing Invitations

Invitations to a Chinese banquet are usually written on invitation cards (*Qing Jian* 請柬) and delivered by the host's children who write their own names and titles on them. If the banquet is being held to celebrate a wedding, it is customary for the couple's parents to deliver the invitations themselves.

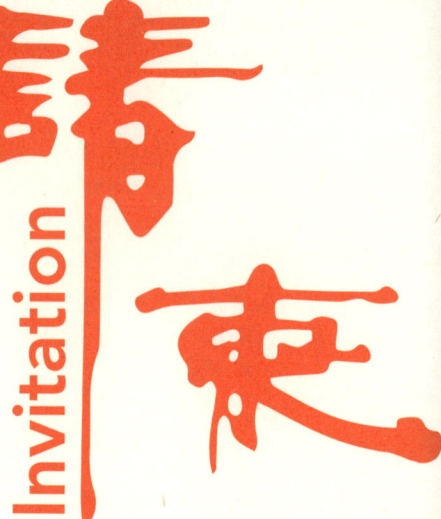

The card which invitations are written on should be made of thick high-quality paper. Yellow or black paper should be avoided. Black is an especially inauspicious colour in Chinese culture.

Everything on the invitation card should be written in black, blue or gold ink with a calligraphy brush or a fountain pen. Red and green ink should be avoided because red ink resembles blood and the colour green is associated with lower-class people in China like prostitutes and corpse burners.

In accordance with tradition, text should be written in the old fashioned vertical way instead of right to left. This is the norm in Taiwan and Hong Kong regardless of what is being celebrated. Of course, many people shun tradition and write their invitations horizontally from left to right instead when using English or simplified Chinese. Some do this because they prefer a more modern or western style.

Invitations are usually written in a set way with a customized message of goodwill.

The text is as follows:

Chinese:

某某先生（女士、小姐）　　，

謹訂於　　（日期和時間）　　
jin ding yu

於　　（飯店）　　
yu

舉行　　（活動或節日）　　, 恭請光臨。
ju xing　　　　　　　　　　　　*gong qing guang lin*

Translation:
We would like to invite _____ [the guest's name and honorary title]
to attend ____ [name of the event]
on ____ [time of the event]
at ____ [location of the event].

Hosts should refrain from asking guests to "please be here on time" (*Qing Zhun Shi Guang Lin* 請准時光臨) which can seem rude. The more pleasant ""when the appointed time is at hand, please come to my place" (*Qing Jie Shi Guang Lin* 請屆時光臨) can be used to make the same point.

Finally, hosts are expected to issue a formal invitation to their guests as a matter of courtesy, even if they have already invited them in person. In such instances, a host may send out an invitation card labeled as a "reminder" (*Bei Wang* 備忘).

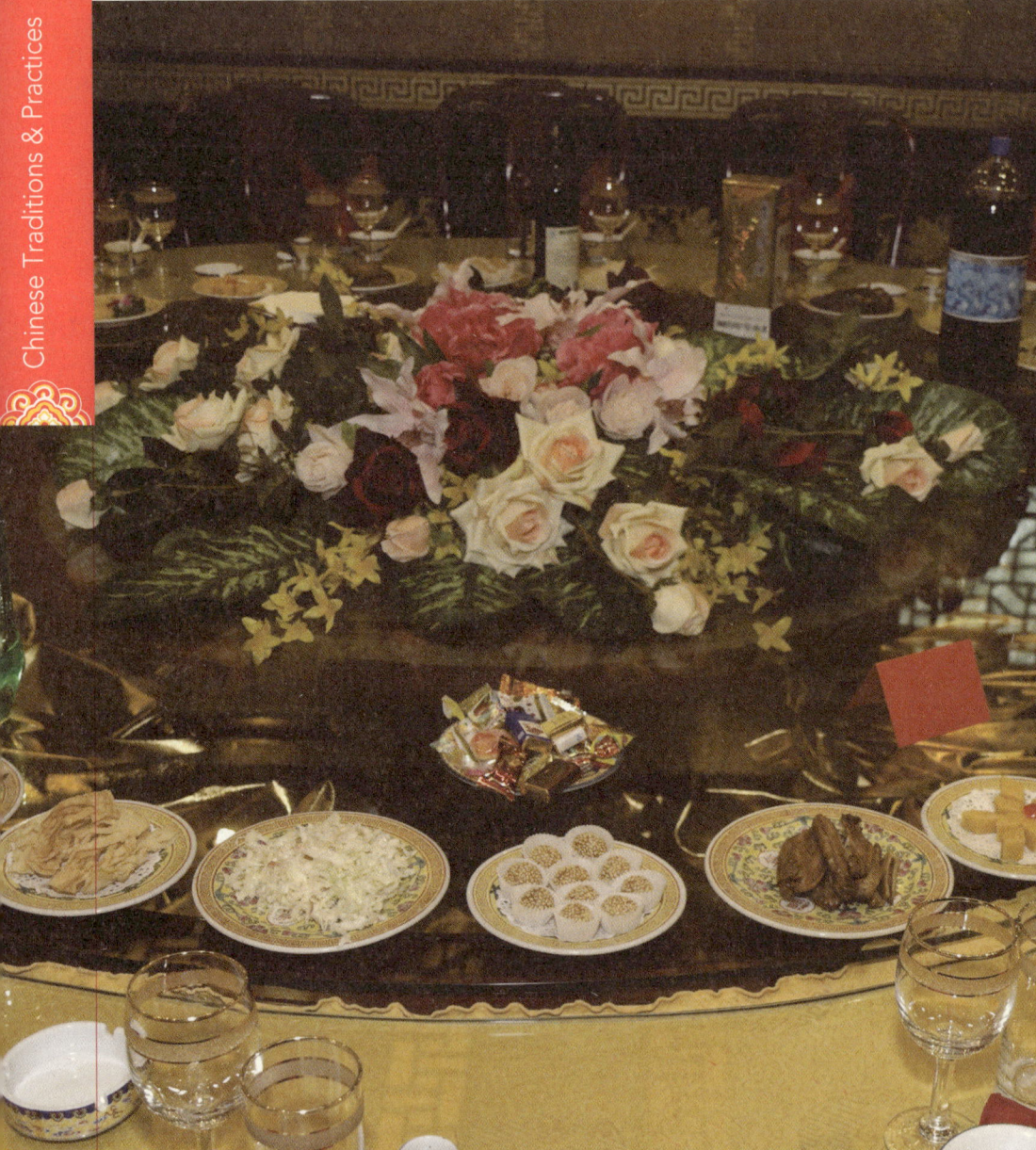

People tend to view the kind of dishes presented at a Chinese banquet as a reflection of the host's fortunes.

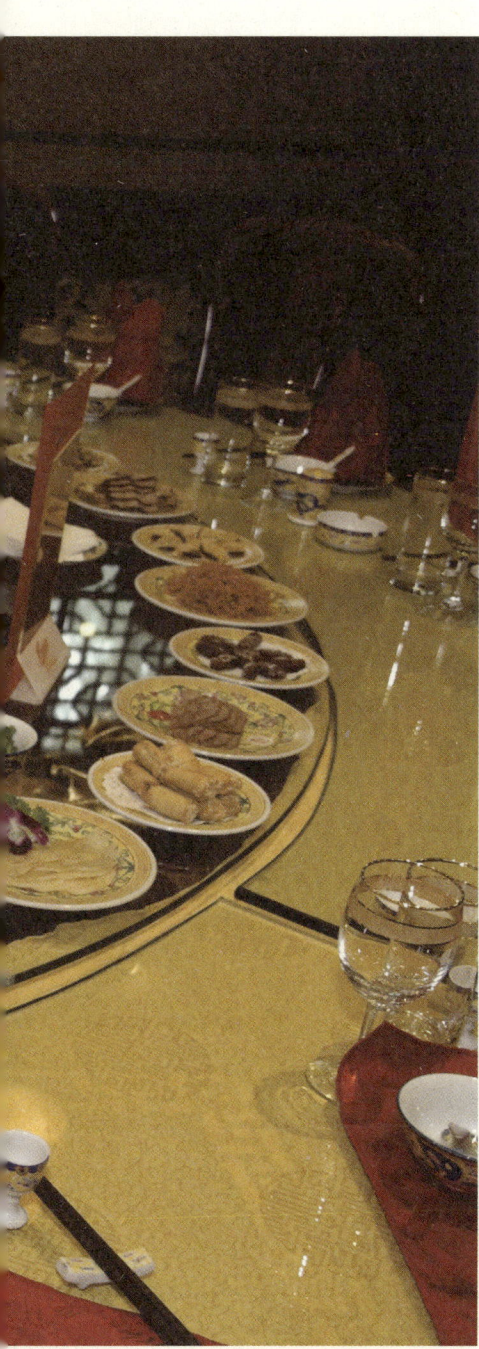

The Ordering Process

The dishes served at a Chinese banquet should be chosen to fit the occasion being celebrated. With that being said, there are a number of staple dishes which are served at almost all banquets.

In some ways, a banquet's menu represents the host's wealth and means. As such, it is often the subject of heavy scrutiny.

The order that dishes are presented in is just as important as the dishes themselves and hosts should adhere to traditional guidelines. The more formal the occasion, the more important the order that dishes are served becomes.

Food Ordering Etiquette

Although it is usually the host's job to choose the menu, they can let a special guest add one or two dishes to the menu if they wish.

Guests are expected to accept the arrangements made by the host and eat what they have chosen.

Whether they consult their guests or not, it is up to the host to take their guest's preferences and dietary requirements into account when creating the menu.

The first thing for a host to consider is their guest's tastes. In China, a host can make educated guesses based on where in the country their guests come. In general, people from northern China prefer salty dishes while people from southern China prefer sweet foods. People from east China prefer spicy food and people from west China prefer sour food. Of course, these are only rules of thumb, but they are as good a starting point as any.

Serving food to guests which goes against their regional preferences might cause offense so a basic understanding of the Chinese palette is important. With that being said, tastes are diverging as a greater variety of food becomes available across the country. People in places like Malaysia and Singapore barely conform to their original regional diets anymore. A wise host should do some research and feel things out for themselves.

Next, a host must think about the age of their guests. If senior citizens will be attending, soft food that is easy to chew and lighter food which is less likely to cause indigestion are appropriate. Clear soup might be a good appetizer for the elderly, as it stimulates the appetite, helping them finish the dishes that follow.

Dishes with a high fat content like meat are suitable for younger guests as they are filling. If there are girls attending then the host should think about increasing the amount of vegetables, sweet and sour dishes or desserts being served. Guests' religious beliefs must be considered, too. Devout Buddhists, for example, cannot eat meat or anything cooked with garlic, chili pepper, chives or onions. If in doubt, a host should ask their guests about their religious beliefs and preferences in advance.

Some guests may have other personal preferences and needs. A host should think about catering for vegetarian and vegan guests. Food allergies must also be considered. Failure to do so could have disastrous effects.

Taking all of the above into account, a host should also make sure that there is enough variety in the menu to please everyone. A good main course should include a balance of vegetables, mushrooms, tofu, seafood, poultry and meat, with appropriate substitutions available for guests with special dietary restrictions or needs.

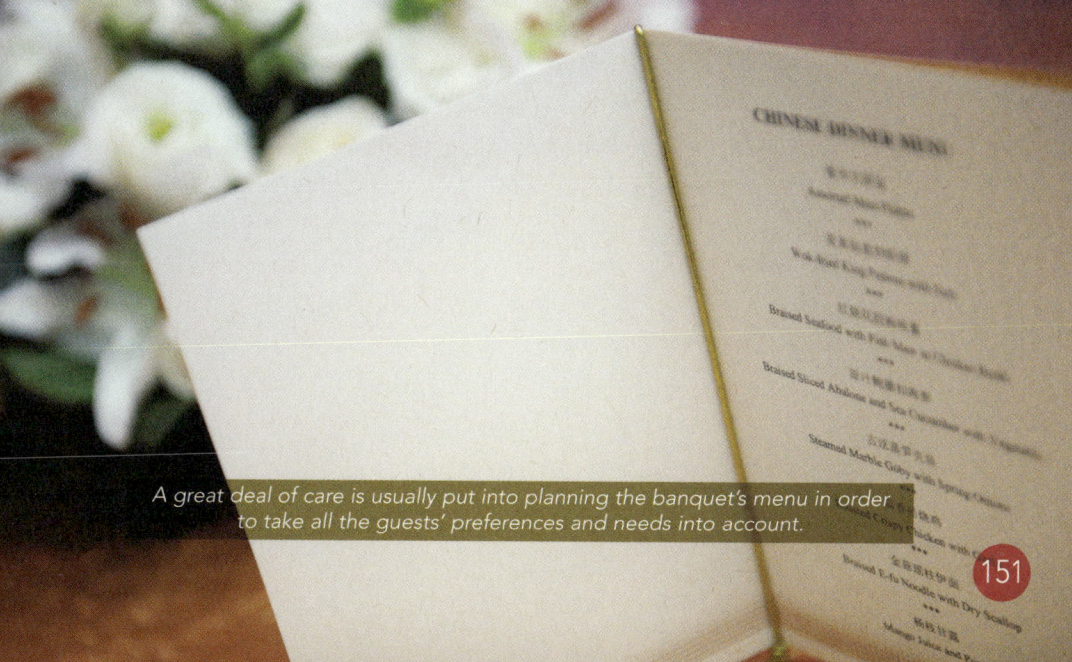

A great deal of care is usually put into planning the banquet's menu in order to take all the guests' preferences and needs into account.

The Banquet's Courses

Chinese banquets consist of several courses served in a particular sequence. Like a three-course Western dinner, a Chinese banquet begins with an appetizer: usually a cold dish. Popular appetizers include raw or cooked vegetables and sliced meat or deep fried dim sum. If there are many guests or it is a formal, important or intimate business banquet then the host may serve two appetizers.

Next comes the main course which usually consists of hot food with a side of rice. In small banquets, the main course tends to have twice as many dishes as guests. More extravagant banquets can feature between 16 and 32 main courses! There should be an even number of courses, because in China it is believed that even numbers are more auspicious than odd ones.

Last but not least comes dessert. In Chinese banquets, dessert is something of an afterthought compared to the appetizer and main course. Typical deserts feature dim sum or Chinese pastries. If the banquet is especially luxurious then dessert may include fruit and bite-sized offerings. Some hosts opt to serve up a plate of fruit alongside a plate of pastries.

The arrangement of the main courses varies. Most banquets held for family events follow the principle of "three dishes and one soup" (*San Cai Yi Tang* 三菜一湯) or a variation thereof. Larger and more formal banquets are more complex. They usually include one or two appetizers, three or four stir-fried dishes, one or two features dishes, one or two kinds of soup and one or two dessert options. It is common to offer two soups at luxurious banquets; one hot and salty to match the hot dishes and one cold and sweet to match the desserts.

At informal banquets, dishes may simply be served up in the order that they are ready. Dessert lovers beware: dessert may be omitted altogether at a small or informal banquet!

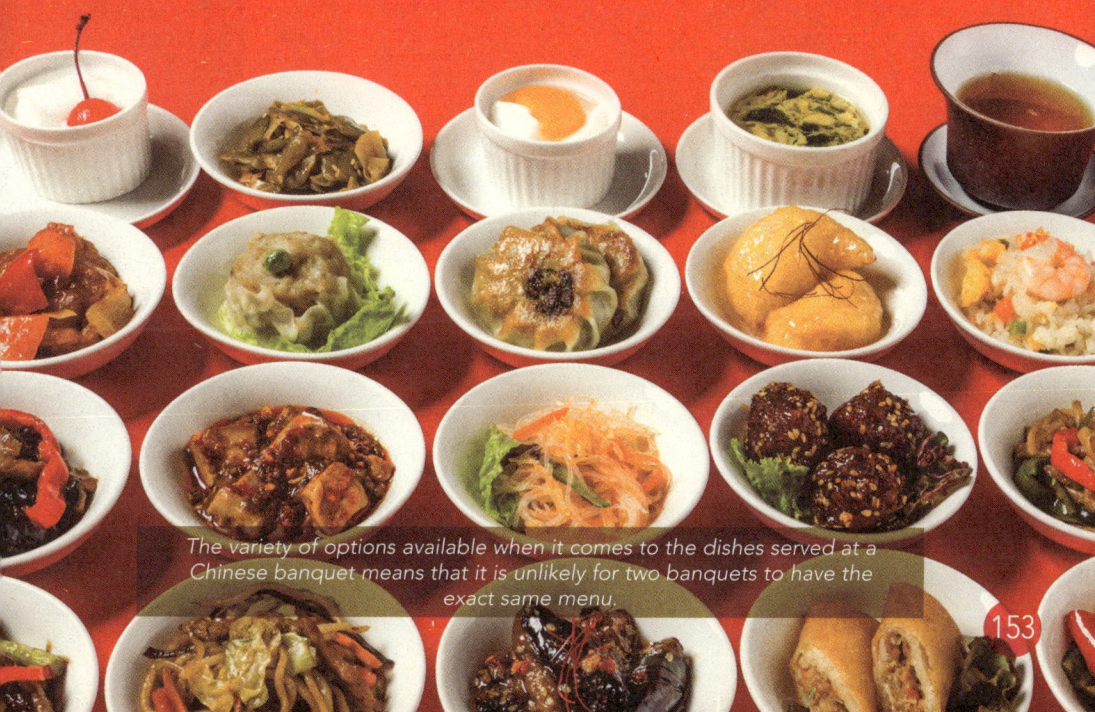

The variety of options available when it comes to the dishes served at a Chinese banquet means that it is unlikely for two banquets to have the exact same menu.

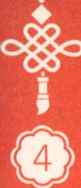

Basic Etiquette

No matter how formal or informal the banquet is, everyone should know the basic etiquette. This ensures that guests do not offend their host and vice versa. The etiquette surrounding banquets reflects the emphasis that is placed on order and respect in Chinese culture.

Basic etiquette involves offering "gratitude money" (*Li Jin* 禮金), sitting in the proper way, using chopsticks in the proper way and eating in the right way, especially if special dishes are served.

The Offering of "Gratitude Money" (*Li Jin* 禮金)

Guests attending a banquet where a birthday, wedding or childbirth is being celebrated are expected to prepare a red envelope filled with money - known as "gratitude money" - and present it to the host when they arrive. If the banquet is being held to celebrate a corporate milestone then this may not be required.

Giving "gratitude money" is important as it allows guests to pay a share of the bill for the banquet. The amount of money that one gives should roughly cover or exceed the cost of their meal. If a guest brings other family members such as spouses and children or a partner then they should give more "gratitude money" to cover their meal too. Paying for one person and bringing others is considered incredibly rude as it gives the impression that that guest is taking advantage of the host. This practice and its related rules are still followed closely today.

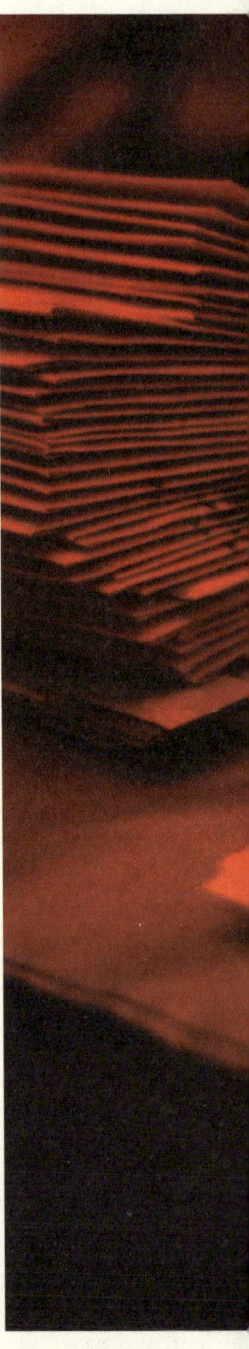

禮俗

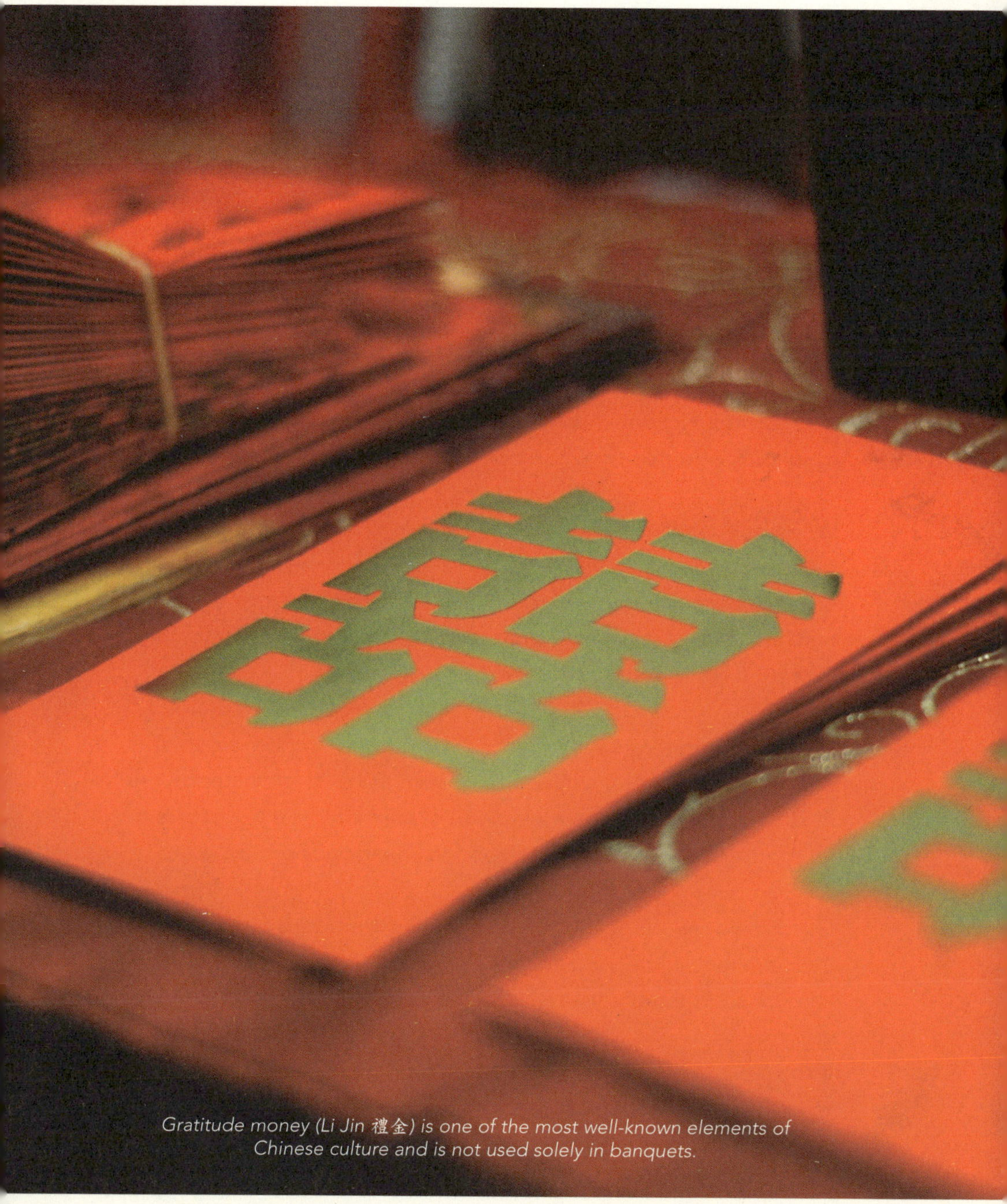

Gratitude money (Li Jin 禮金) is one of the most well-known elements of Chinese culture and is not used solely in banquets.

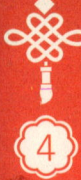

Taking A Seat

Seats at a formal Chinese banquet are arranged to reflect social status by the host: guests are not allowed to choose their seats. Guests should maintain self-awareness and sit with good form: sitting in the wrong way can be seen as rude.

Guests should wait to be guided to their assigned seat by a waiter. Name cards indicate who is supposed to sit where and priority is given to the elderly, honored guests and women. It is polite for guests sitting next to these people to help them take their seats before sitting down themselves. Married men should help their significant other sit down before taking their own seat.

When one reaches their seat they should pull out their chair with their right hand and move in from the left side of the chair. It is uncouth and rude to pull a chair out with one's foot. If there are unfilled seats at a table then a person is expected to move their seat to make it easier for others to sit down.

Informal banquets have much less strict seating arrangements and guests can freely choose their own seats. It is polite for the host to wait until guests have been seated before they sit down. This lets guests find the most comfortable or opportune seats.

Guests are discouraged from dragging an empty seat to a table that is already full. Instead, they should ask a waiter to bring a chair or sit at a table that isn't full.

If the host is the same gender as a guest then they can sit next to or opposite the guest. Otherwise, the host is expected to sit opposite the guest.

According to tradition, all guests should sit with their spine straight, leaning against their chair in such a way that they maintain a distance of 10cm from the table. They should plant their feet on the ground and avoid crossing their legs. Ideally, guests should place their hands on the table or their knees and refrain from moving them around or fidgeting.

As guests sit close together at a banquet, the positioning of elbows is important. Guests should keep their elbows off the table so that their fellow guests have room to eat.

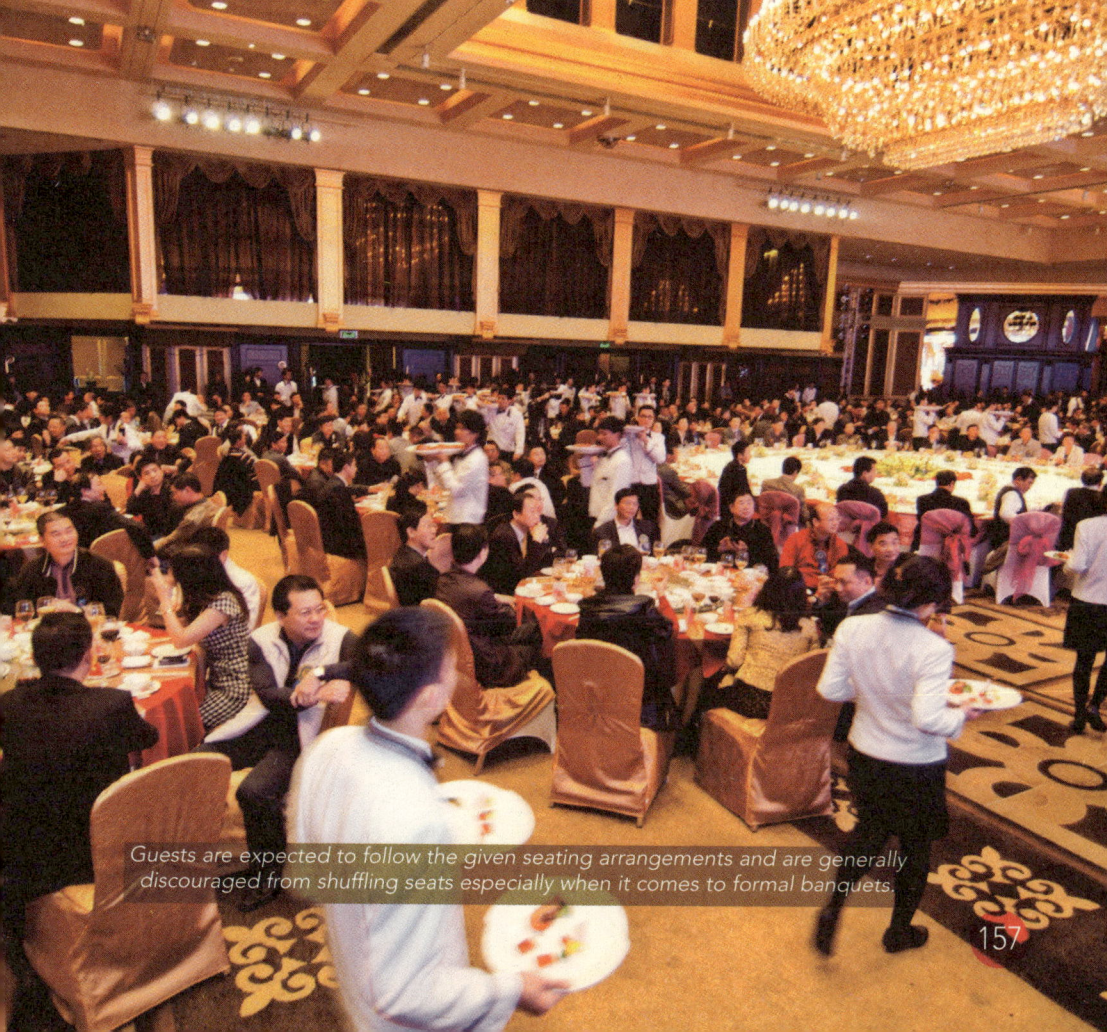

Guests are expected to follow the given seating arrangements and are generally discouraged from shuffling seats especially when it comes to formal banquets.

Using Chopsticks

A host should ensure that the chopsticks they provide for their banquet are all the same length, colour and quality. Every pair of chopsticks should be placed on the table with the tips pointed towards the center of the table.

Traditionally, the correct way to hold chopsticks is with one's right hand, even if one is left handed. The thinking for this is that it ensures nobody interferes with their neighbors attempts to eat. This custom has fallen out of favor in modern times as people can simply make room for left-handed guests.

When putting down chopsticks, one should try not to make any noise as they hit the bowl or plate. This is taboo because it is reminiscent of what Chinese beggars do to attract attention. In addition, one should place their chopsticks on the right side of their glass and never place them on the edge of any communal plates or main dishes.

Guests should never spear food with their chopsticks. If an item is hard to pick up they should use a spoon. Also, it is extremely rude to point chopsticks at someone, especially when talking to them.

In formal banquets, two sets of chopsticks of different colour and length may be provided. The shorter or lighter set is meant for personal use and the other set which is referred to as the "communal serving chopsticks" (*Gong Kuai* 公筷) should be used to take food from communal plates. This special arrangement is used when it is considered rude to use one's personal chopsticks to take food from the communal plates as well as for hygienic purposes.

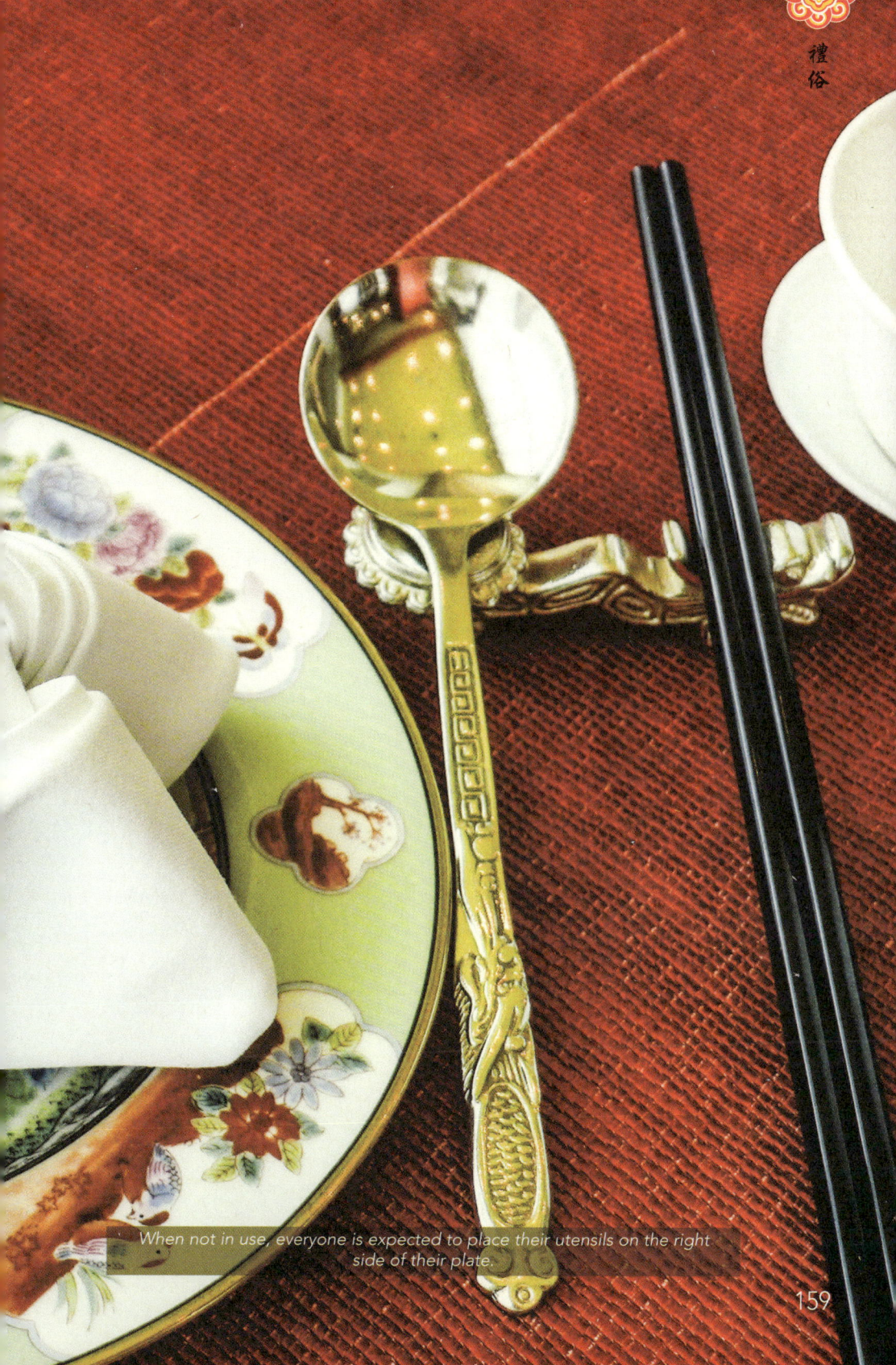

When not in use, everyone is expected to place their utensils on the right side of their plate.

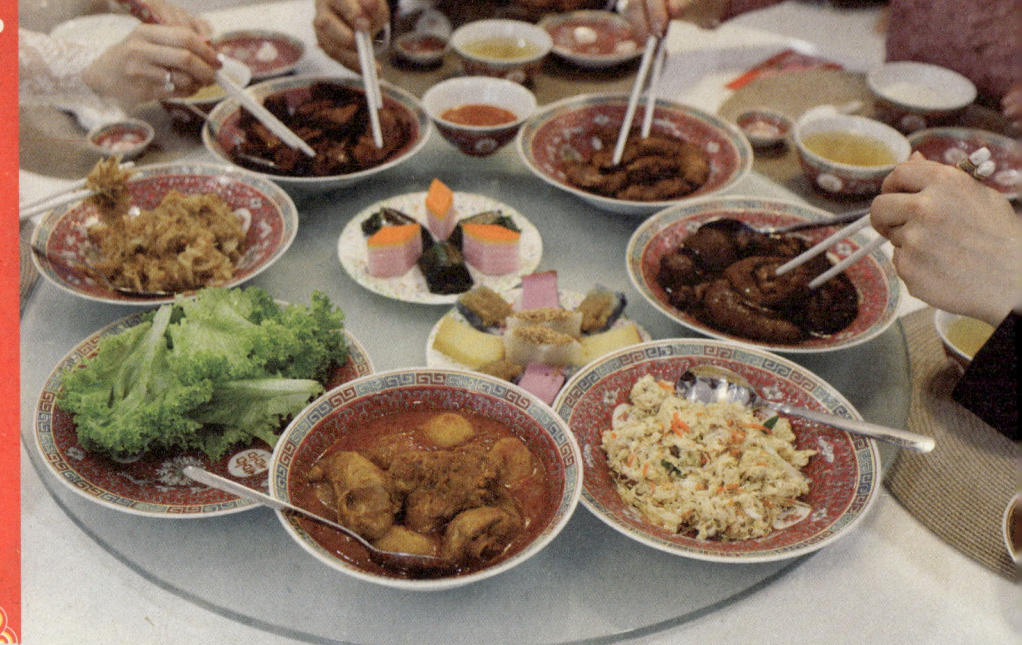

It is only considered acceptable to use one's personal chopsticks to take food from the communal dishes during informal meals such as family dinners.

Table Manners

At formal banquets, each table has a special guest; the host or an honored guest. When food arrives, it is customary for this individual to take their food before anyone else at the table is allowed to do so. Other guests should wait for them to make their move before dishing up.

If a dish is on the other end of the table, it is rude to stretch across the table to get it. The right way to get at it is to make use of the Lazy Susan the food has been placed on. When one spins the Lazy Susan, they should keep an eye out for any other guests who might be trying to get food and stop it when required.

When dishing up, guests should do so promptly and minimize the amount of time that their chopsticks are in contact with the food. The moment a person's chopsticks touch an item they are expected to take it, even if they have a change of heart. Guests should avoid separating food in search of something specific.

Also, if someone else takes an item that a guest had their eyes on they should give it up graciously.

Certain dishes must be eaten in a specific way. Fish is usually served whole and guests should eat it from the head down to the tail. Next they should flip the fish over to access the other side. If a guest finds a fish bone, the appropriate way to remove it is to cover their mouth with one hand and remove the fish bone with the other. Bones should be placed on the side plate assigned to each guest.

When dealing with shrimp or prawns, guests have the option of putting the entire shrimp or prawn into their mouth and using their tongue and teeth to remove the shell. This is only acceptable if the shell has been seasoned along with the shrimp or prawn, however. The most appropriate way to eat shrimp or prawns is to press down on them with one's chopsticks and use one's left hand to remove the shell.

If crabs are on the menu, one may use both hands to deal with their share. A good way to deal with crab is to first remove the top shell and then eat the innards and roe if any can be found. Next, one can split the body in half down the center and eat the meat within. Finally, one can break open the crab's claws and legs using or a wooden mallet or crab cracker to get to the last of the meat.

As an aside, crabs are usually eaten with Chinese wine or ginger. This is because crabs are thought of as "cold" Yin food in traditional Chinese medicine that must be neutralised with Yang ginger or alcohol.

Alcoholic Beverages

Alcohol plays an important role in Chinese banquets and celebrations, much as it does in the west. Globalization has brought a wide variety of alcoholic beverages to China, but wine is still the usual choice for a banquet.

Different wines are indicated for different occasions. As different wines go better with different dishes, it is important to pair the right wine with the right dish. The order in which wines are poured throughout a banquet must be also decided.

Last but not least, host and guests alike must respect drinking and toasting etiquette. Some people have a more fraught relationship with alcohol and this must be taken into account.

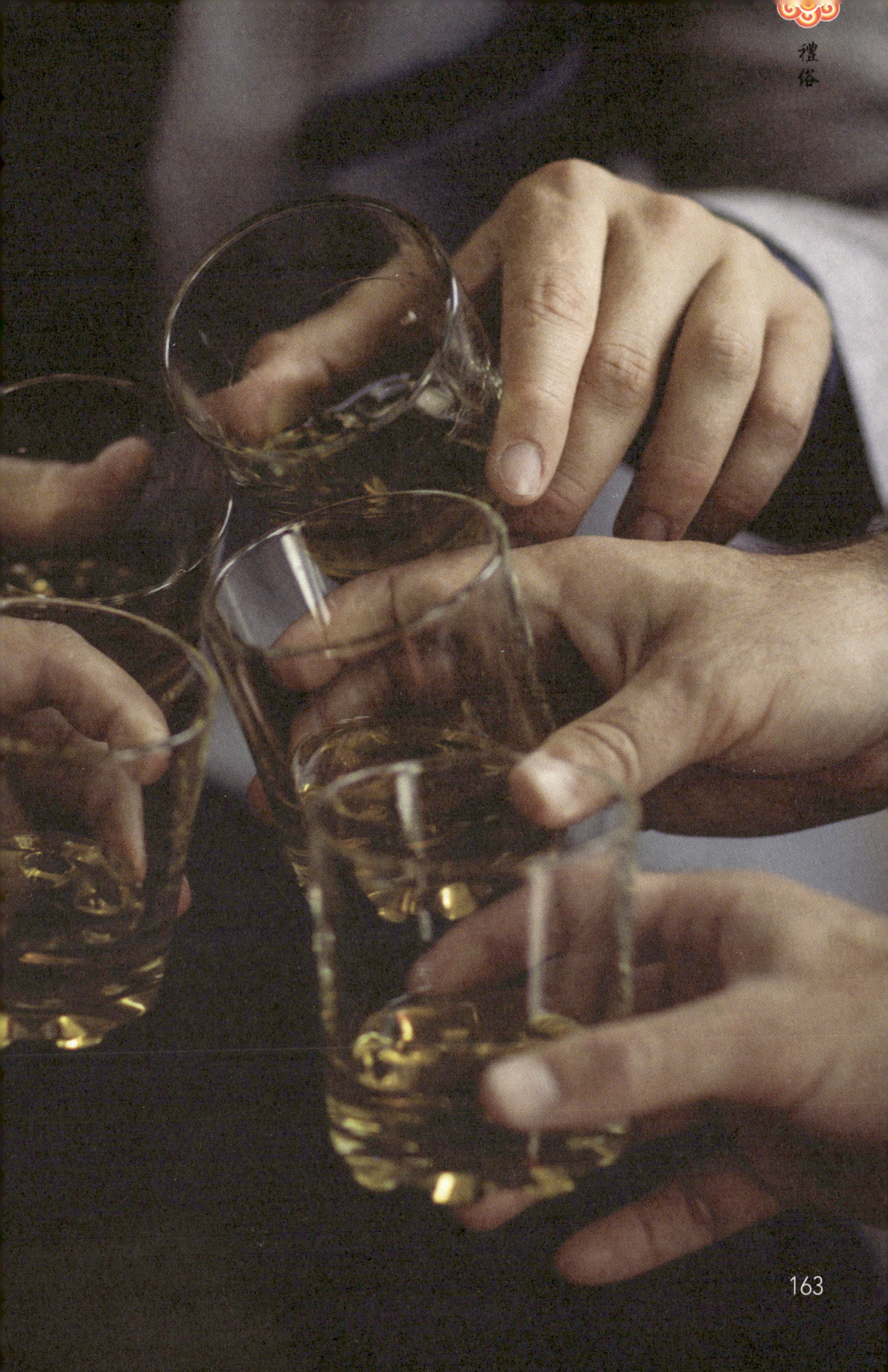

The Wine Selection

When selecting a wine, one should consider how lavish the banquet will be. A host should try to choose a wine befitting the scale and importance of the proceedings. By way of example, a famous white liquor (*Bai Jiu* 白酒) called *Mao Tai* 茅台 is typically reserved for state dinners as it is considered the best and most popular. It is inappropriate to serve Mao Tai at a banquet held for personal reasons unless it is exceptionally extravagant.

Next, timing. A host should choose a wine that suits the season. Many people prefer hot alcoholic beverages such as white liquor in the winter and cool beer during summer. Chinese alcoholic drinks are distilled with different methods so they produce very different effects. For example, white liquor is very strong as it is distilled in such a way as to produce a burning sensation when swallowed, like vodka or whiskey. Many Chinese people believe that drinking white liquor in the winter helps nurture the stomach (*Yang Wei* 養胃).

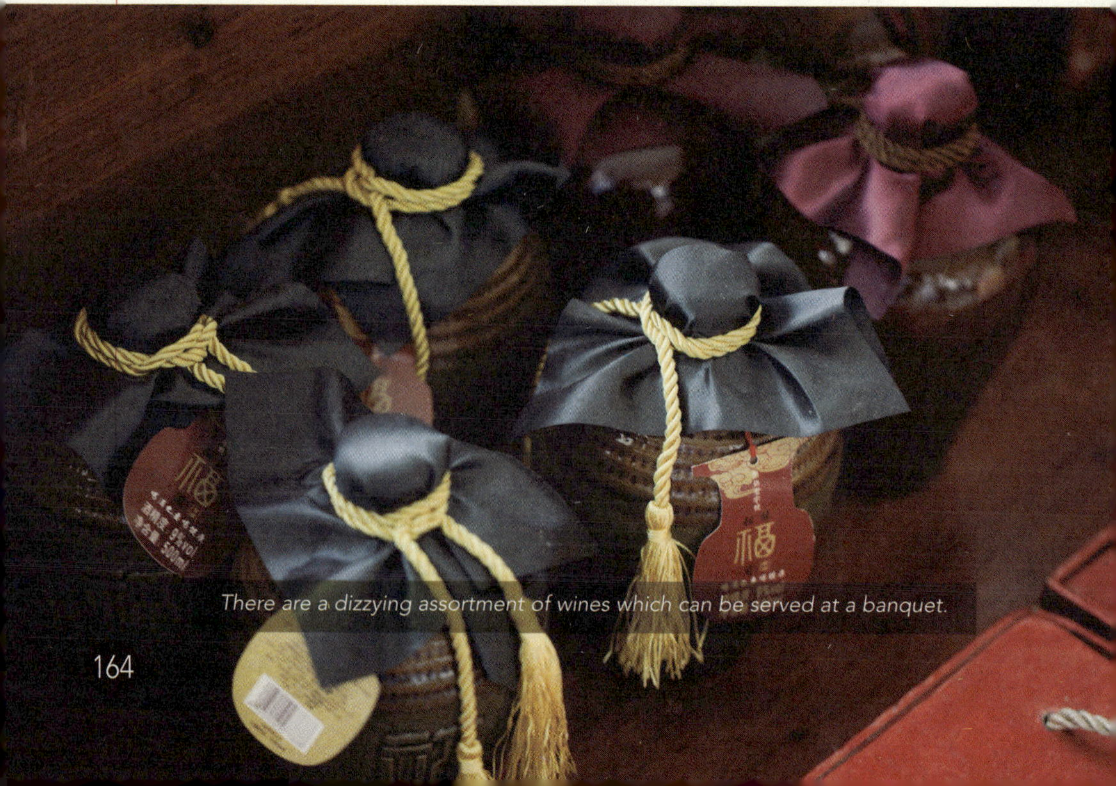

There are a dizzying assortment of wines which can be served at a banquet.

It is best if a chosen wine complements the food as mentioned earlier. Since wine is consumed at the same time as food the taste of one affects the taste of the other.

In most cases, one can exercise their own judgment when selecting a wine. If one wishes to adhere strictly to tradition then grape wines should be served with meat and poultry dishes. Vegetable and seafood dishes should be served with a type of Fen wine (*Fen Jiu* 汾酒) called Green Bamboo Leaf Wine (*Zhu Ye Qing Jiu* 竹葉青酒). An exception is made for crab, which is better complimented by yellow wine (*Huang Jiu* 黃酒). Last but not least, cold dishes go best with feeding rice wine (*Jia Fan Jiu* 加飯酒) which is a type of Shaoxing wine (*Shao Xing Jiu* 紹興酒), itself a variation of yellow wine.

When multiple types of liquors are served, they must be served in a certain order. Lighter wines should be served first, followed by their stronger counterparts. Therefore: sparkling wines are to be served before liquors, young wines before older ones, common types before exotic varieties and dry wines before the sweet ones. In the West, white wine should be served before red wine.

Non-Asian alcoholic drinks are inappropriate for traditional Chinese banquets. Iranian wines are the sole exception as Iran has ties to ancient Persia, so it can be thought of as an Asian country.

Drinking Etiquette

When it comes to drinking, the concept of "face" (*Mian Zi* 面子) is especially important. The concept of "face" is associated with respect and prestige, both of which are at stake at significant events! Guests must keep in mind that banquets are merry occasions and that the host is to be seen as a generous individual at all times.

When someone makes a toast, it is important that they do not "lose face", even if their toast makes a guest feel uncomfortable. Refusing to participate in a toast runs counter to the assumption that banquets are joyous in nature. Doing so would ruin the impression that this event is a festive one and as a result, host and guest alike would "lose face".

To avoid this unpleasant scenario, toasts should be proposed in a non-coercive way. Guests should feel able to drink only what they are comfortable with and no more. After the first toast, guests should feel free to decline further toasts with an indirect refusal.

When pouring alcohol, a host should always err on the side of caution. Once again, this helps everyone "save face". Generally speaking, the host should fill a glass to about 80% of its capacity when pouring Chinese liquor, Western red wine and beer. A host should never fill a glass past 70% full when pouring champagne and no more than 60% of the glass should be filled when pouring Western white wine. When serving brandy, a host should pour until about a glass is about 30-40% full.

Many Chinese make the mistake of thinking that a glass should be filled to the brim because of the saying "the fuller the glass, the deeper the affection" (*Jiu Man Qing Shen* 酒满情深). It was once believed that the amount a host poured reflected their respect for a given guest. In reality, a host should never fill a guest's glass because it makes it hard for them to take a drink without spilling it.

The host should pour drinks for their guests before pouring for themselves. If a guest is doing the pouring then they should fill the host's glass before pouring for anyone else. Regardless, the person who is doing the pouring must pour for everyone at the table because pouring for one person and ignoring others is rude.

To pour, whoever is pouring should first make sure that everyone has a glass of roughly the same size. Next, they should open the bottle in full view of everyone at their table. Pouring should begin with the oldest or most prestigious guests. The guest who has traveled the longest distance to attend should receive preference, too. After attending to the most important guests, whoever is pouring should tend to their table in a clockwise direction. If the guests are Asian, whoever is pouring should pour drinks for men then women. If the guests are not Asian then drinks should be poured for women then men.

Drinks should be poured with a certain technique. Whoever is pouring should ensure that the bottle does not touch the rim of the glass they are filling. They should tilt the bottle slightly when they are almost finished pouring as this will prevent spillage. Separate glasses should be used for each type of wine so that they can be appreciated properly.

Naturally, pouring is usually handled by waiters and waitresses during formal banquets. If this is the case, guests should remain seated and let them do their jobs. It is up to the waiter or waitress attending the table to pour drinks properly and in the right order, starting with the most prestigious or oldest guest, then the host and then other guests.

A Gesture of Gratitude

Guests can show their gratitude to whoever pours their drinks with a special gesture. To do so, one pinches the thumb, index finger and middle finger on their right hand together and knocks on the table with their knuckles. Funnily enough, this is known as "knocking one's knuckles" (*Kou Zhi Li* 叩指禮). Its modern counterpart is much simpler. One simply taps the table with the tip of their right index and middle fingers.

The gesture is part of a legend involving Emperor Qianlong (*Qian Long Di* 乾隆帝) at the height of his powers. During one of his southern inspection tours - which he conducted anonymously with one of his servants - he decided to sit down and have a drink at a little tea house located in the city of Xiguan in Guangzhou.

The waiter serving the unassuming Emperor brought him two cups with tea leaves rather than two full cups of tea. Another waiter then came to the table with a bronze kettle in his right hand. He lifted the cover of the tea cup with his left hand and proceeded to pour the hot water within the cup from eye level. To the Emperor's amazement, not a single drop of water missed the cup.

Surprised by both the waiter's skill and pouring technique, Emperor Qianlong asked him why he served tea in this manner. The waiter smiled and replied that the local tea was made with shrimp bubble water (*Xia Pao Shui* 蝦泡水), so named for the bubbles that appeared when it boiled. He went on to explain that it was necessary to pour the water from height to ensure that it was fragrant.

Fascinated, the Emperor promptly got up to try and do it himself. He took the bronze kettle, mimicked the waiter's earlier stance and poured the water into his servant's cup. This shocked the servant, as according to the rules of the imperial court, it was an honor if the Emperor poured someone tea. The only proper response would be to kneel on the floor and bow until he hit his head on the ground repeatedly in gratitude, but to do so would expose the Emperor's identity.

In desperation, the servant used an unusual gesture as a substitute. He bent his right index and middle fingers, shifted his body so that he appeared to be kneeling while still seated and then rapped the table with his knuckles several times. A waiter who saw this was puzzled by the servant's strange behavior and asked him to explain what he was doing. Finding himself in a difficult position, the servant responded with a half-truth and said that it was a gesture of thanks one could make to someone who had poured them tea.

Over time, the gesture became popular. Eventually, it became a standard part of tea-drinking etiquette.

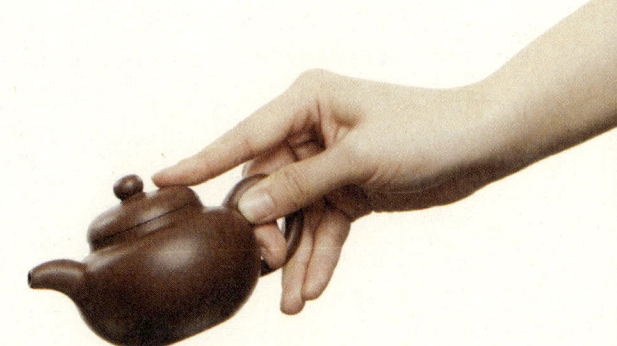

Making A Toast

Once the banquet has started, the host or a merry guest may feel like proposing a toast. This can be done in a formal or informal manner. Different expectations accompany each.

It is customary for the host to propose a toast between the main courses and before dessert. They customarily read a speech prepared in advanced, arranged so as not to disrupt guests' eating.

More informal toasts can be made any point during a banquet. Anyone can make such a toast whenever they have the urge to do so. With that said, guests should only do so if they have a good reason and if it will not inconvenience or embarrass other guests. It might be best to wait until the person a toast is intended for is not in the process of eating or accepting someone else's toast, for example. Women are discouraged from toasting to the health of guests, especially if no other toasts have been made.

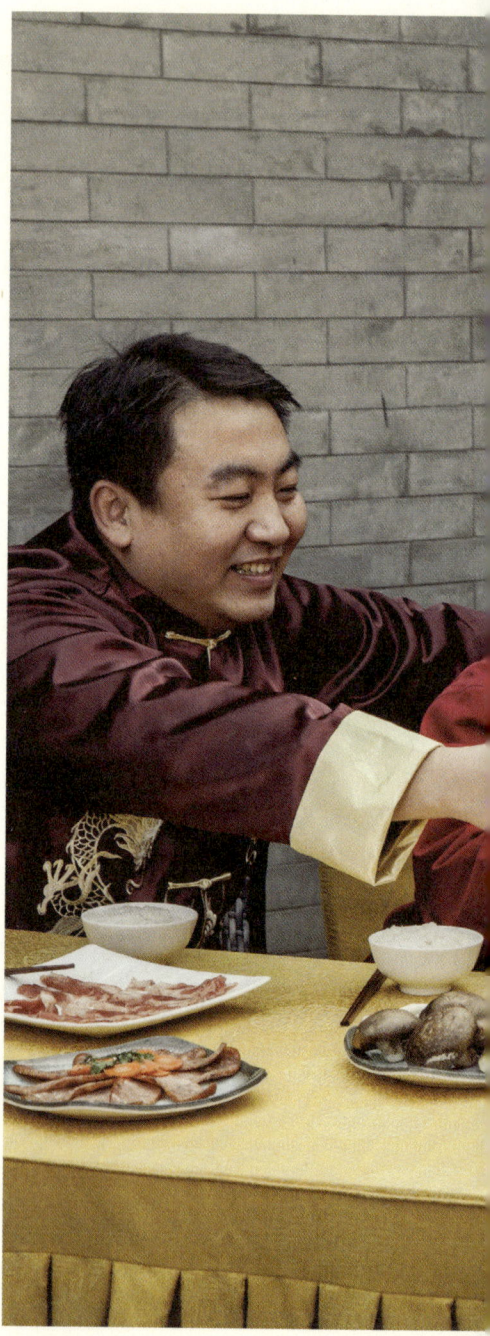

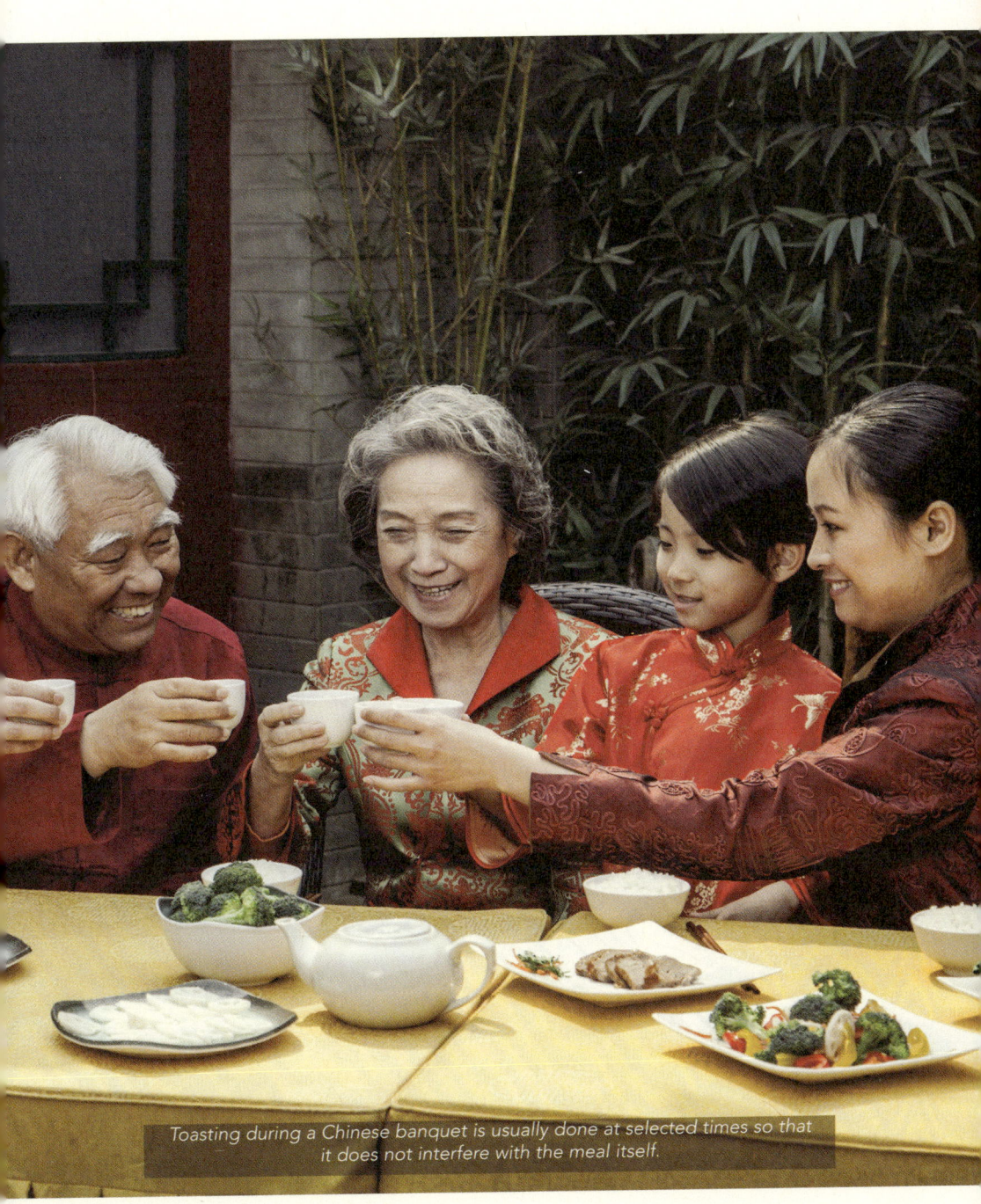

Toasting during a Chinese banquet is usually done at selected times so that it does not interfere with the meal itself.

If a host likes, they may use a polite proposal (*Wen Jing* 文敬) to convey their message at the start of a banquet. To do so, they stand up and give a short speech before they propose a toast. Guests are expected to stand up as well and remain standing until the speech is over.

Once they have made a toast, the host should finish their drink in one go and turn their glass upside down. This demonstrates that they have consumed all of their drink and demonstrates the respect that they have for their guests. Their guests should then finish their own drinks. If the host has a strong constitution, they may repeat this process at every table.

A type of toast that guests may propose is known as the "returning of respect" (*Hui Jing* 回敬). To do so, a guest waits until the host has proposed a toast and then reciprocates with another round of drinks in thanks.

If a guest has close ties to the host then they can propose a fun-filled mutual toast (*Hu Jing* 互敬). This involves two guests proposing a toast to one another and trying to drink each other under the table. They can justify their proposal with the flimsiest and most absurd reasons as it is merely an excuse to get a person to drink. If the recipient of the toast cannot find a witty way to refuse it, he or she must drink. This custom is based on the belief that good humor, food and drink are what bind people together and it is done in good fun.

Finally, there is the punishment proposal (*Fa Jing* 罚敬). Whoever makes a punishment proposal must find a way to paint their target's behavior in a negative light using the most ridiculous logic possible. Naturally, their victim must be punished with alcohol for their wrongdoing. As an example: a host might propose a toast for guests who arrived late to the banquet in order to "punish" them, making them consume a number of drinks for everyone's amusement.

Regardless of what method is used, there is an accepted order in which toasts should be proposed and etiquette surrounding them. In general, toasts should be made to older guests before younger ones, guests with more social status before those with less and toasts should be proposed in a clockwise direction.

At the end of a toast, some like to throw in the Chinese equivalent of "bottoms up" or "cheers" with the phrase "empty your glass" (*Gan Bei* 乾杯). It is similar to the Japanese phrase "kanpai". To do this, one must rise from their seat, hold their glass up with their right hand, support the bottom of their glass with their left then say the phrase clearly. While speaking, they must look the recipient of the toast in the eyes and smile. They can also give a short goodwill speech at their discretion. The recipient of a toast that ends in this way must immediately stand up with their glass in hand, raise their glass to face level, repeat the phrase and finish their drink. If the person in question has a low tolerance for alcohol then they can drink whatever amount they are comfortable consuming. If they cannot drink alcohol at all then a glass of water or a carbonated drink will suffice. Once they have consumed their drink they must make eye contact with the person who proposed the toast and smile. This concludes the toast.

Contrary to popular belief, it is not necessary for people participating in a toast to clink their glasses against others'. If this is done, it is usually in imitation of the host who may chink his or her glass against older or more powerful guests' glass.

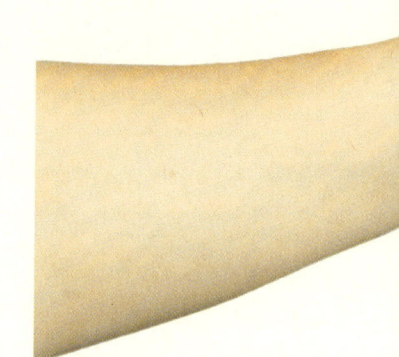

Guidelines For Making A Toast

As mentioned before, a toast proposal can seem coercive: the recipients of a toast are expected to accept it and finish their drinks lest they offend the person toasting them. It is therefore the responsibility of whoever proposes a toast to do so responsibly and tactfully.

If the recipient of a toast is a woman then getting them to drink lots of alcohol is in poor taste. Trying to get a person with a low tolerance for alcohol to drink should also be avoided. Passive people will likely consume whatever amount of alcohol they are asked to without complaint, so toast proposals directed at them should not be overdone. If the recipient of a toast is known to be going through a rough patch, proposing a toast to them is probably not a good idea as alcohol can amplify negative feelings. Finally, alcoholics should never be the target of a toast proposal.

In any case, timing is also important. An appropriate time to propose a toast is when the main course is being served. Proposing a toast at the end of the banquet is unwise, as most guests will be approaching their limit with alcohol and some may have to drive home in short order.

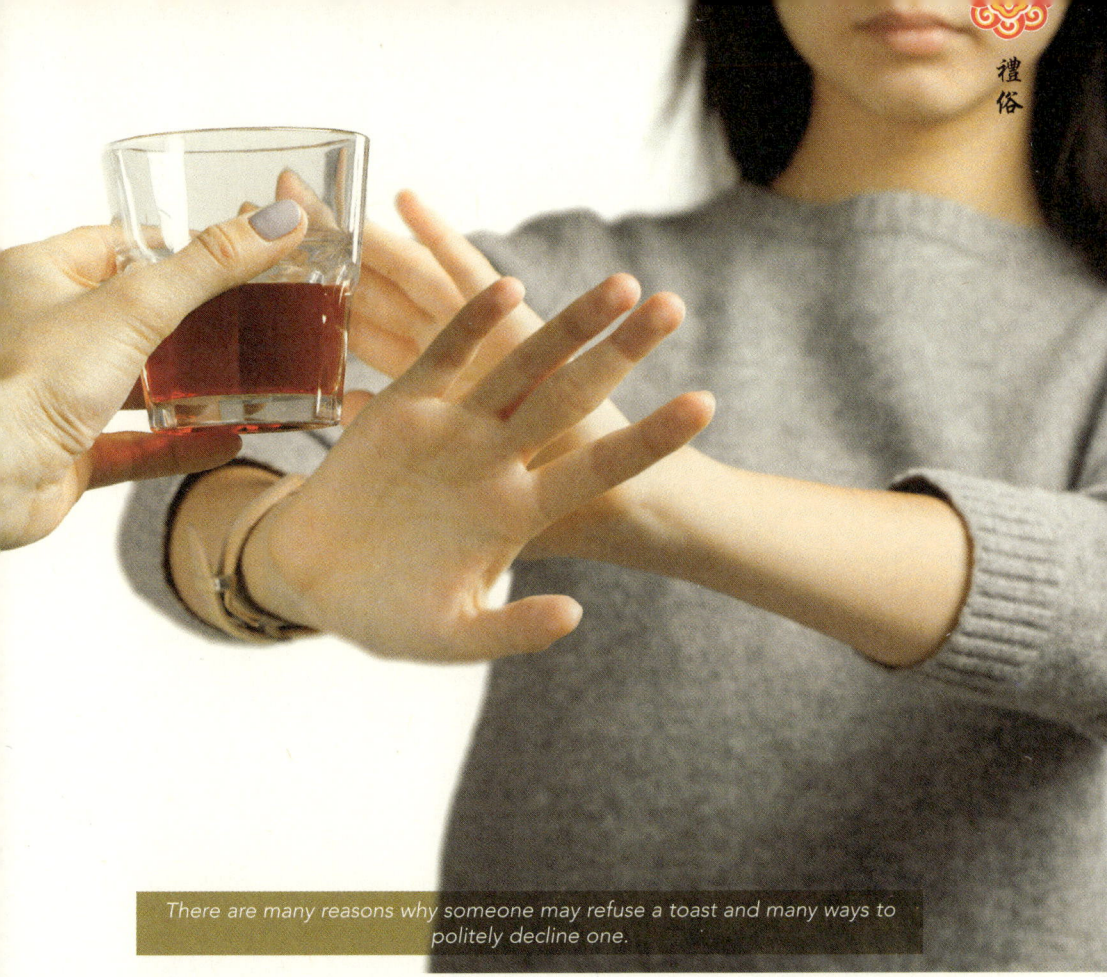

There are many reasons why someone may refuse a toast and many ways to politely decline one.

Declining A Toast

The subject of a toast can politely or indirectly refuse without causing anyone to "lose face". A simple way to do this is to create a distraction by changing the topic of conversation or redirecting the attention of whoever proposed the toast to someone or something else. If this is not possible, one can feign illness or pain to avoid drinking more than they can handle. The key to success with this tactic is to fake symptoms in a plausible way. One can also claim that they are taking medication which does not mix well with alcohol. This is a good tactic as people are unlikely to press the issue further. Finally, anyone driving home after the banquet has a solid out.

Alternatives

There are several ways that a person can take part in a toast without consuming too much alcohol.

Instead of drinking wine with their food, a person can reserve it for toasts. This will minimize their overall consumption of alcohol. Alternatively, one can simply drink tea instead of wine.

Another option is to switch drinks when Chinese liquor or vodka is served. A skillful guest may be able to swap their alcohol for a glass of water or carbonated drink to accept a toast. The only risk is that anyone caught doing so might be forced to drink twice the original amount of alcohol as "punishment".

One can dilute the alcohol in their system by drinking more water or eating soup. As an added benefit, this will mean more trips to the bathroom where alcohol can leave the system. Drinking water also helps prevent dehydration and reduce the severity of hangovers.

Those who plan on drinking a lot should eat a decent amount of food. Drinking on an empty stomach makes it easier to get drunk. Having food in one's stomach slows down the rate at which the body absorbs alcohol. Foods that are high in protein or fat are particularly effective.

Finally, there is the neutralisation method, based on the Chinese belief that certain foods neutralise alcohol in one's body. These include fish stock, honey water, tomato juice and bananas.

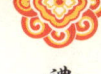

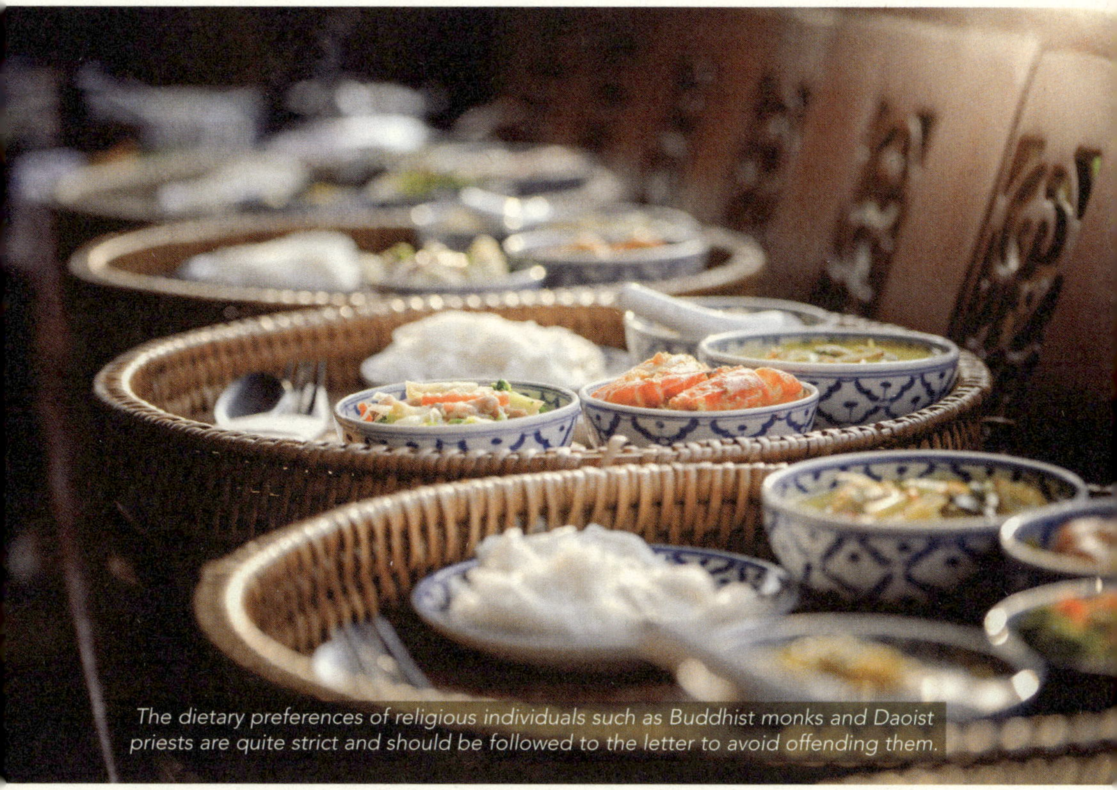

The dietary preferences of religious individuals such as Buddhist monks and Daoist priests are quite strict and should be followed to the letter to avoid offending them.

Buddhist Monks and Daoist Priests

Most religions have restrictions and stipulations concerning food. Some religions have very specific rules about the way in which food can be prepared and served. These stipulations are usually rooted in superstitious beliefs or pre-existing folklore.

Buddhism and Daoism both have stipulations with regards to food that must be respected when preparing the menu for a banquet. This is especially the case if a Buddhist monk or Daoist priest is attending!

Buddhist Monks

Contrary to popular belief, Buddhist monks are not all vegetarian. Even so, many people associate Buddhism with vegetarianism. The version of Buddhism prevalent in China is more closely tied to vegetarianism than others.

The original principles of Buddhism do not prescribe a vegetarian diet. Monks who subsist on offerings may graciously accept any food offered to them, including meat. Buddhist monks learn not to make demands, like asking for a specific dish or asking that certain ingredients are not used.

Monks may eat meat, provided that it is "clean", having been prepared in accordance with three rules known as the Three Aspects (*San Jing* 三淨). First, Buddhist monks themselves are prohibited from slaughtering animals. Second, livestock must not be slaughtered specifically to fulfill a monk's desire for meat. Last but not least, monks must not witness the slaughter of livestock that they will eat.

The vegetarian aspect of Chinese Buddhism is the result of several different factors. In the Mahayana branch of Buddhism, a vegetarian diet is strongly advised. Vegetarian philosophy also overlaps with Confucianism values like compassion. In the past, Emperor Wu of Liang (*Liang Wu Di* 梁武帝) used his power to promote Buddhism in ancient China. At one point it became the official state religion and as a result, vegetarianism became religious law for a time.

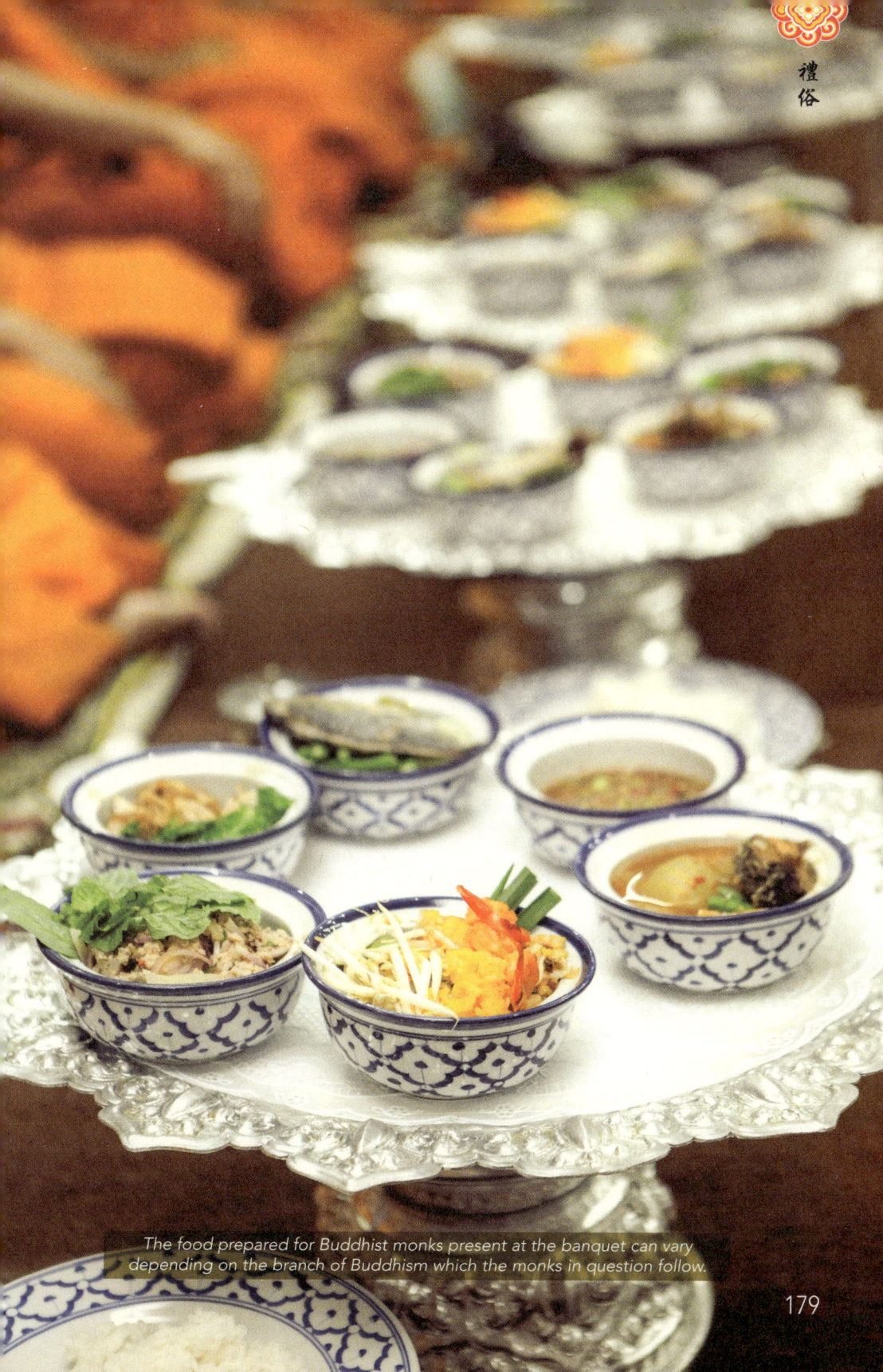

The food prepared for Buddhist monks present at the banquet can vary depending on the branch of Buddhism which the monks in question follow.

With the introduction of vegetarian laws, vegetarian dishes were developed by the people of ancient China. This eventually led to the development of a set of principles for the serving of food to Buddhist monks at banquets. The strictest of these stipulations concerns timing: Buddhist monks cannot consume food after noon unless they are ill. If so, they are allowed to have a "medical meal" (*Yao Shi* 藥食) at supper time to provide their body with extra nutrition for recovery.

Dishes for Buddhist monks should be prepared separately from dishes made for other guests. They can eat vegetarian cold dishes made of fruit and stir-fried vegetables. Cooks must take care not to use animal fat or any kitchen utensils which have come into contact with animal fat when preparing dishes for Buddhists.

For their main course, monks can be served a combination of three types of mushrooms and six types of edible fungi (*San Gu Liu Er* 三菇六耳). This includes the common mushroom, straw mushroom, button mushroom, jelly ear, snow fungus, yellow ear, elm fungus, rock tripe and golden fungus. Those who are new to the Buddhist way of life may be served a dish containing pieces of bean curd made to resemble meat as they adjust to their new diet.

Buddhist monks should be served tea instead of alcohol. Tea helps Buddhists cultivate the Three Virtues (*San De* 三德): stimulation, digestion and abstinence. Tea is a stimulant because it contains caffeine, which can help a monk stay awake and meditate at night. Tea is also believed to cleanse one's palate and repress sexual desire.

Daoist Priests

Daoist priests view eating as something to be celebrated: they see eating as a way to cherish life itself. This is underpinned by two Daoist goals: the goal of living as long as possible (ideally forever) and the need to cultivate compassion. Daoists differ from Buddhists in that they believe all life forms are equally sentient and sacred. Thus, they harbor a deep respect for nature and seek to minimize their impact on the environment.

Daoists believe that different kinds of food contain different amounts and types of Qi. Because of this, Daoist priests and adherents strive to maintain a diet with balanced Qi content. In the first instance the Five Spices (*Wu Hun* 五葷) - garlic, leek, mustard, coriander and onion - are off limits because they contain too much Yang Qi which makes it too difficult to balance the Qi in one's diet.

It is believed that Daoist immortals subsist on pure Qi. In emulation of this, Daoists observe a practice called "avoiding grains" (*Bi Gu* 辟谷) which are seen as secular food. Some edible fungi, honey and Ganoderma mushrooms are ideal foods like their Buddhist counterparts. This is due to their perceived ability to preserve Qi and grant longevity.

Bi Gu
avoiding grains

Because these foods are not usually available at Chinese banquets, Daoist priests and adherents can be given a vegetarian main course instead. These dishes should have little to no seasoning and must be completely devoid of the Five Spices.

Chapter 5

Houses and Homes

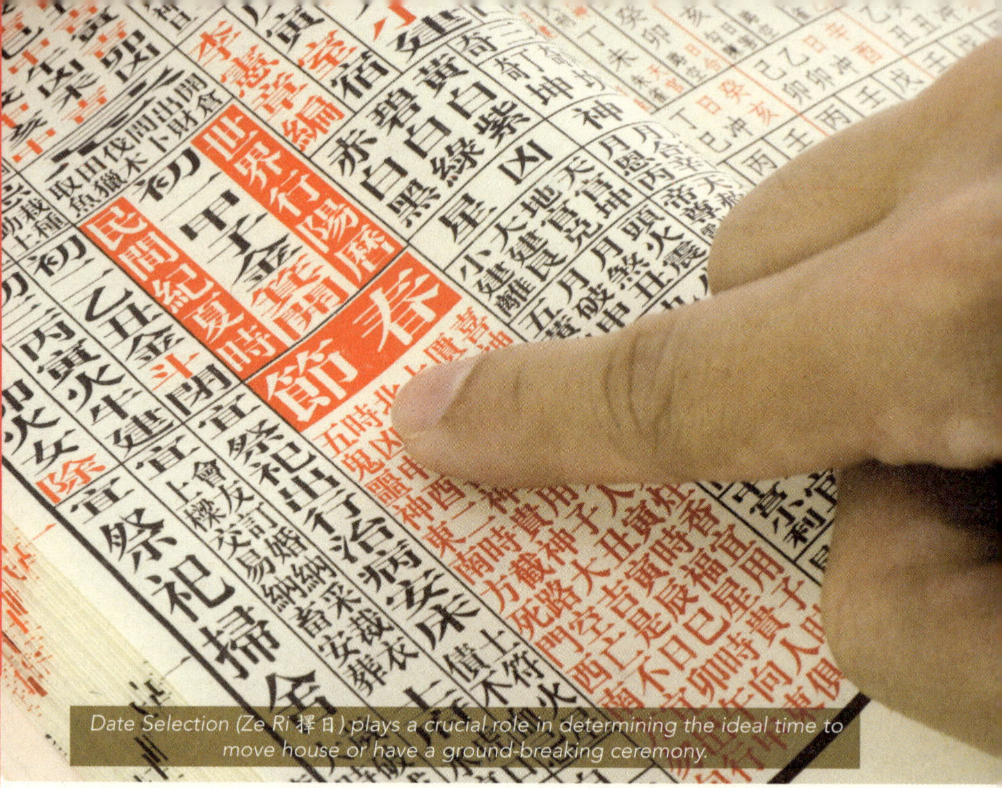

Date Selection (Ze Ri 择日) plays a crucial role in determining the ideal time to move house or have a ground-breaking ceremony.

Throughout history, the concepts of home and family have been intertwined. The ancient Chinese placed a great deal of importance on the concept of the ancestral home; the shared birthplace of a lineage of male descendants.

The strong attachment that the ancient Chinese felt to their ancestors stems from China's history as an agricultural society. The ancient Chinese sustained themselves with agriculture and it was customary for land to be passed down from generation to generation. Understandably, a link between a person's ancestral home and their family developed over time.

Because of this, moving to a new home was a big decision for a family. Renovating or changing an existing home was a significant event, too. Customs and rituals developed around both. Some were based on religious beliefs and others drew upon concepts from Chinese Metaphysics.

Feng Shui has a major role to play in decisions about the home as it is all about the impact that a living environment or Yang house has on its occupants. By ensuring that a new home is Feng Shui compliant and in keeping with Feng Shui's best practices, people can usher in positive energy. Good Feng Shui fosters family harmony, longevity and peace of mind and can also help improve a person's fortunes – helping them advance in their personal life and career.

Date Selection (*Ze Ri* 擇日) complements Feng Shui by helping one choose the most opportune time to move house or have the ground-breaking ceremony based on the premise that Qi fluctuates over time. By choosing the right time to move or renovate, one can benefit from good Qi or mitigate the effects of poor Feng Shui such as the presence of negative energies.

Last but not least is BaZi. BaZi is an intricate system that lets people understand more about themselves and map out their destiny using their date of birth. It is associated with Date Selection and the notion of "clashing". By examining a person's date of birth from a Bazi point of view, one can determine which dates or hours they should avoid certain activities.

Although people are no longer tied to an ancestral home in the way they once were, many of the customs and beliefs held by the ancient Chinese have survived. People continue to utilize Feng Shui when renovating their home or looking for a new one. Date Selection and BaZi charts can still help one make the most of their residential choices. Many religious customs concerning the home have survived to the present day, too.

Moving House

In ancient China, families moved far less often than they do today. Moving house was a complex process with many associated rituals and traditions. All the same, many customs from ancient China persist to this day and moving house has arguably become a more complex process today thanks to centuries of developments in Chinese Metaphysics.

The first step in moving house is of course finding a new home. Although moving house may seem like a daunting process as there are so many things to consider such as furnishings, the local amenities and more, it needn't be if one prepares adequately.

Many buyers wish to live in a house with good Feng Shui. To facilitate this, they can either learn about Feng Shui or consult a Feng Shui practitioner. Many contemporary property developers employ Feng Shui consultants to assess their Feng Shui compliance before they start construction. This means that most modern properties have reasonably good Feng Shui. (More information on this can be found in the Feng Shui for Homebuyers series).

Once a new house is ready, a homeowner can hold a moving in ceremony to mark the occasion. A Date Selection specialist can help them choose the most auspicious day to officially move in and celebrate.

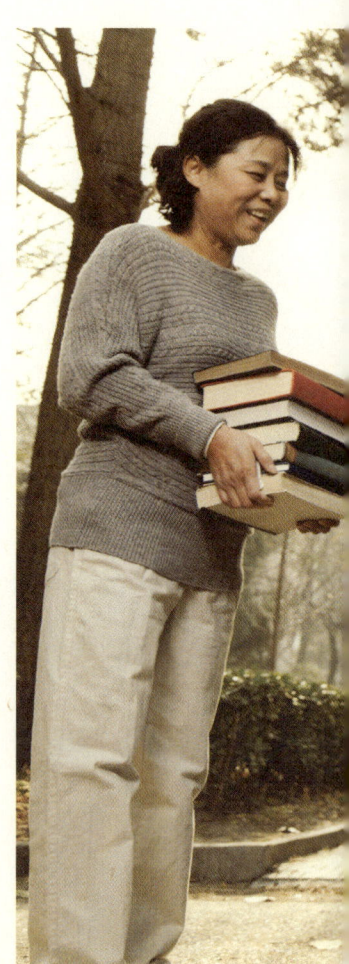

Moving in ceremonies help get rid of negative energy or Killing Qi (*Sha Qi* 煞氣) and bring in positive energies or Fortunate Qi (*Fu Qi* 福氣). They also serve a religious purpose, placating deities and a person's ancestors. By carrying out rituals and adhering to tradition, a homeowner can avoid incurring the wrath of the deities associated with the home.

For most people, everything begins with an essential choice: where to call home?

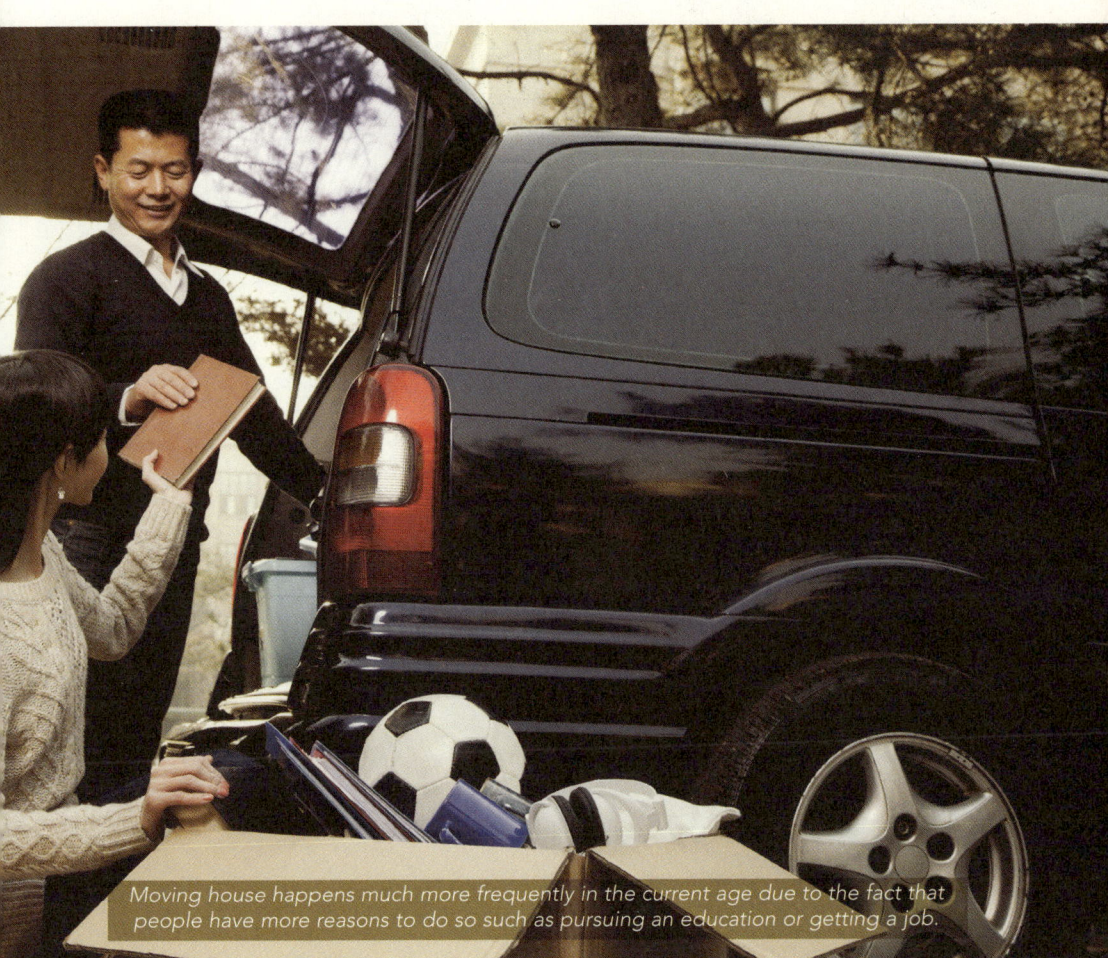

Moving house happens much more frequently in the current age due to the fact that people have more reasons to do so such as pursuing an education or getting a job.

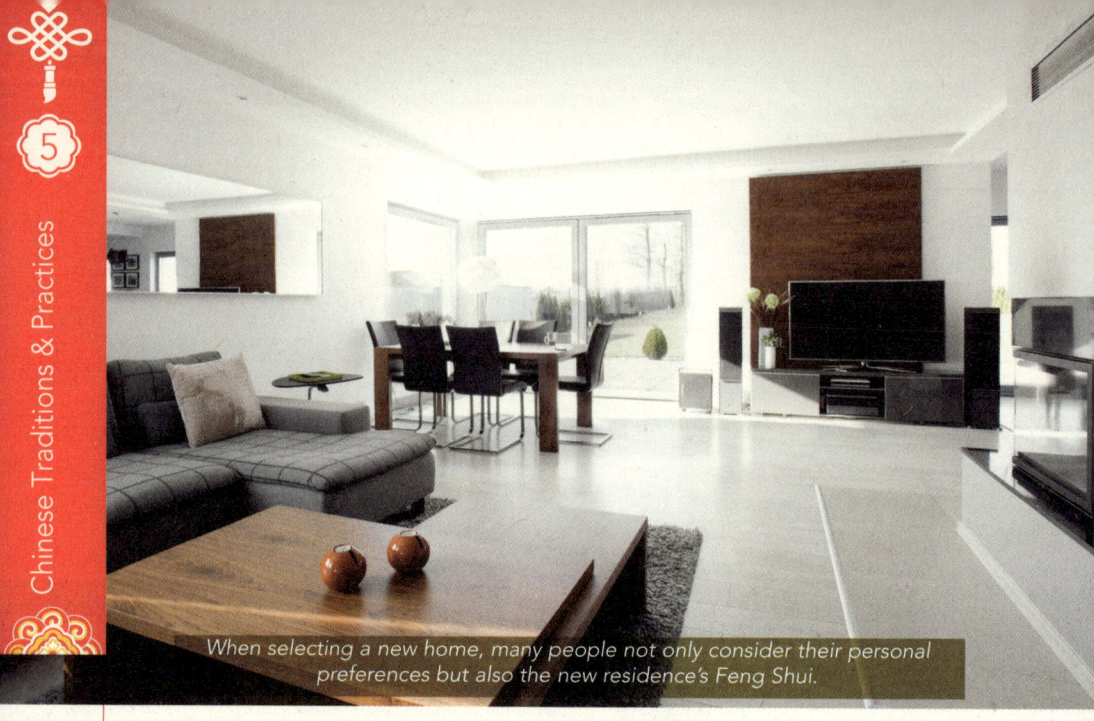

When selecting a new home, many people not only consider their personal preferences but also the new residence's Feng Shui.

The Home Selection Process

Regardless of why a person wants to move, choosing the right home is important. When selecting a new home, everyone has different criteria and preferences. Some people have superstitious beliefs that influence their choices. For example, some people are averse to homes with blue roof tiles and white paint because they are associated with funeral parlours and memorial halls. This is an example of a personal preference with non-basis in Feng Shui principles. There are many other principles which do have their basis in genuine Chinese Metaphysical concepts, however.

The focal point of Feng Shui is a vital force known as Qi that influences all living beings. The practice of Feng Shui is all about managing a living space so that Qi is present, balanced and flowing. The retention of dissipation of Qi wherever people are can affect their health, wealth, energy levels and luck among other things. Since most people spend a lot of time at home, a home's Feng Shui has a large effect.

The most significant Feng Shui factors are Environment, Building, Time and People. One must consider the impact of all four to gain a complete understanding of a home's potential Feng Shui compliance.

The Environment factor is determined by the natural landforms surrounding a property which affects its Qi quality. The Building factor is determined by a home's architecture which determines its internal Qi flow and accumulation. The Time factor refers to the element of timing with regards to harnessing Qi. The People factor concerns individual differences: as everyone is different, the effects of a property on people varies.

It is easiest to begin a Feng Shui investigation by first considering a home's Environment.

First, if a home is exposed to strong winds then buyer beware! Feng Shui principles state that strong winds blow auspicious Qi away, preventing it from accumulating in a home. On the other hand, the complete absence of wind is also undesirable, as wind is needed for auspicious Qi energy to flow.

Another Feng Shui rule of thumb asserts that homes with entrances facing a narrow alley should be avoided, a narrow alley being one between three and five meters wide. The Feng Shui principle behind this is Sky Crack Sha (*Tian Zhan Sha* 天斬煞) which is said to signify repression. Extrapolating from it, a narrow alley may stifle a person's progression in their chosen career. Apartments with long hallways were once seen as undesirable, too. This was because long hallways were dark, which negatively affects the flow of Qi energy around a residence. The advent of bright indoor lighting and air conditioning has negated this. Modern hallways adequately circulate both air and Qi and are no cause for concern.

Feng Shui principles discourage living on a slope, as Qi will simply flow down the slope and away from one's home. Conversely, a wall in front of the house would obstruct the Qi and not allow it to enter the home.

In ancient China, homes facing a temple or administrative office were seen as undesirable. Police stations are the modern equivalent of administrative offices. According to Feng Shui, the problem with temples is that they accumulate Yin Qi 陰氣 and may be haunted by wandering spirits seeking to enter the afterlife. Yin Qi is also associated with police stations in the sense that they are "haunted" by a near-constant criminal presence.

For more examples and further guidance on selecting the right home, consider looking into the Feng Shui for Homebuyers series!

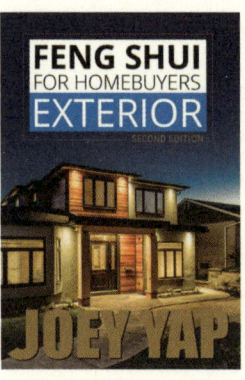
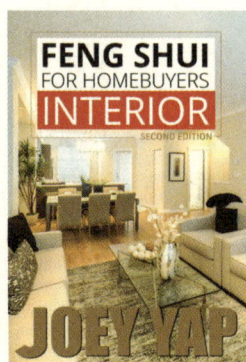
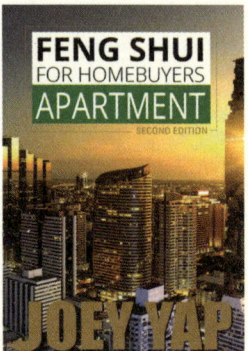

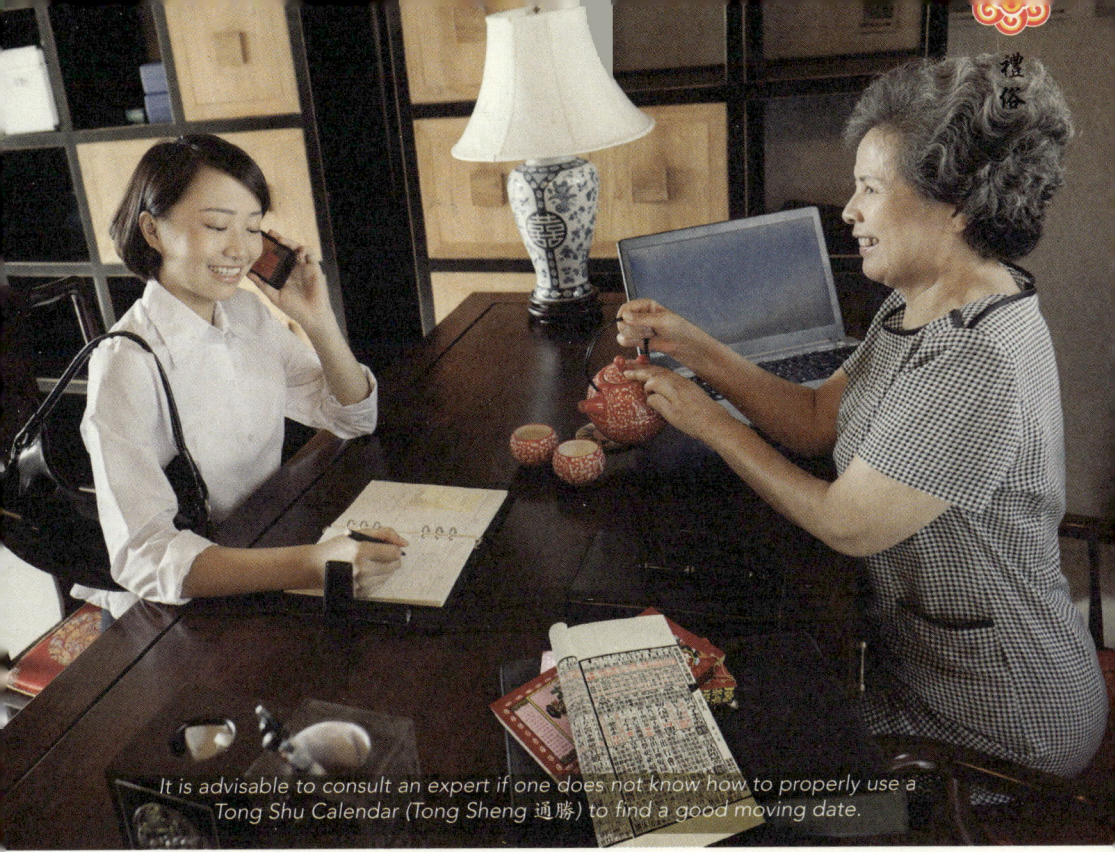

It is advisable to consult an expert if one does not know how to properly use a Tong Shu Calendar (Tong Sheng 通勝) to find a good moving date.

Preparations Before the Move

After choosing a new home and dealing with all the necessary paperwork, the next step is to prepare for the big move. The most pertinent question is: when should one actually move? Date Selection provides the answer. First, a homeowner should consult their Tong Shu Calendar (*Tong Sheng* 通勝), find a good moving date and write it down. Next, they should check that the date doesn't clash with the Chinese zodiac sign of any family members. They can do this themselves if they are experienced with Chinese Metaphysics or else consult a Chinese Metaphysics practitioner. To produce accurate guidance, they will require the location of the house and the tentative location of the main bed. BaZi charts for family members and anyone who will participate in the moving in ceremony are also useful. This can help them choose the perfect day and hour for the big move.

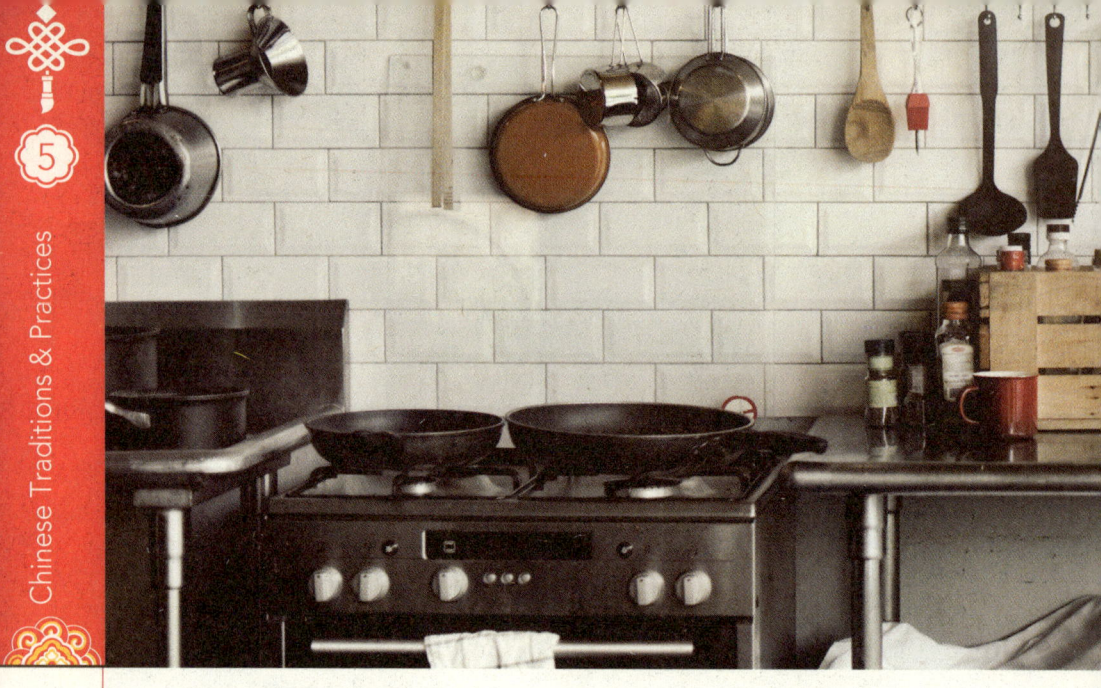

As mentioned, certain times can clash with people's Chinese zodiac sign. The main clashes are as follows:

Chinese zodiac sign	Not Suitable
Rat (*Zi* 子)	Horse (*Wu* 午)
Ox (*Chou* 丑)	Goat (*Wei* 未)
Tiger (*Yin* 寅)	Monkey (*Shen* 申)
Rabbit (*Mao* 卯)	Rooster (*You* 酉)
Dragon (*Chen* 辰)	Dog (*Xu* 戌)
Snake (*Si* 巳)	Pig (*Hai* 亥)
Horse (*Wu* 午)	Rat (*Zi* 子)
Goat (*Wei* 未)	Ox (*Chou* 丑)
Monkey (*Shen* 申)	Tiger (*Yin* 寅)
Rooster (*You* 酉)	Rabbit (*Mao* 卯)
Dog (*Xu* 戌)	Dragon (*Chen* 辰)
Pig (*Hai* 亥)	Snake (*Si* 巳)

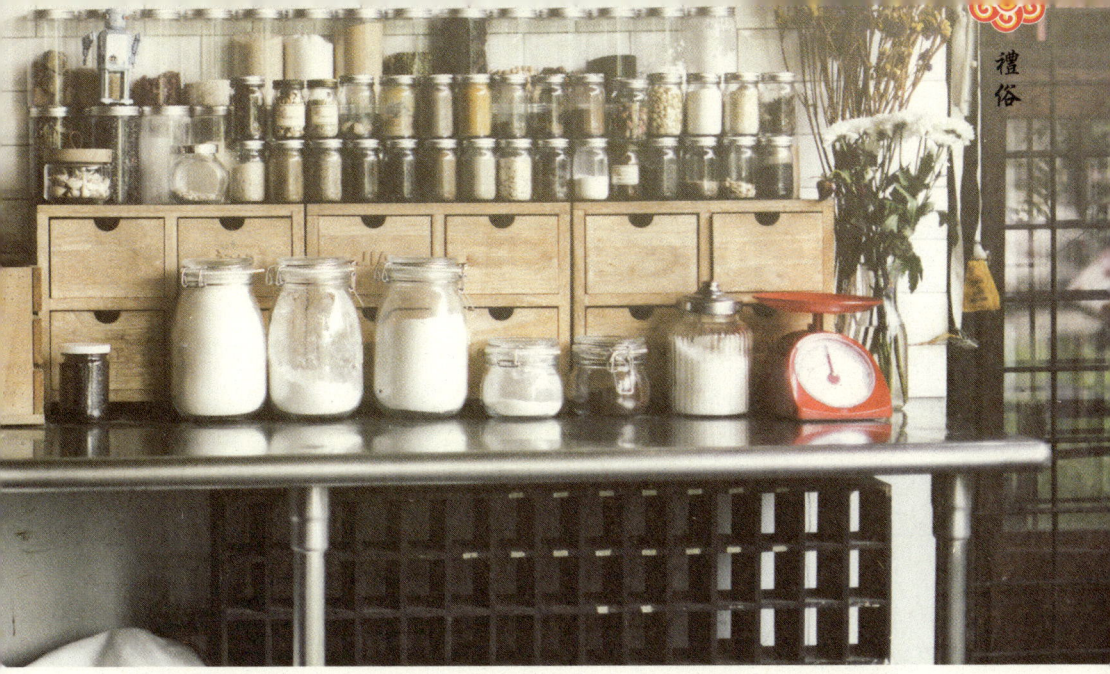

Traditionally, pregnant women were not allowed to move house because doing so might provoke the Foetal God (*Tai Shen* 胎神). In order to appease the Foetal God, pregnant women were expected to rest in their existing home until after they had given birth. If her family moved while she was still carrying, she could only join them after delivering her child.

In any event, a new homeowner would start preparing for the moving in ceremony as soon as the time was right by moving the newest pieces of furniture into their new home. This custom was based on cultural beliefs that have no basis in Feng Shui: it was a purely symbolic act meant to represent breaking away from one's past. Older pieces of furniture were only moved after the completion of the moving in ceremony.

After moving their newest furniture, a homeowner moved seven items representing the life of an ordinary person into their new kitchen. Traditionally, these included firewood or gas as well as foodstuffs like rice, cooking oil, salt, sauces and pastas like soy sauce, tea leaves and vinegar. In modern times, some of these can be swapped out for electric kitchen appliances that produce heat, representing prosperity.

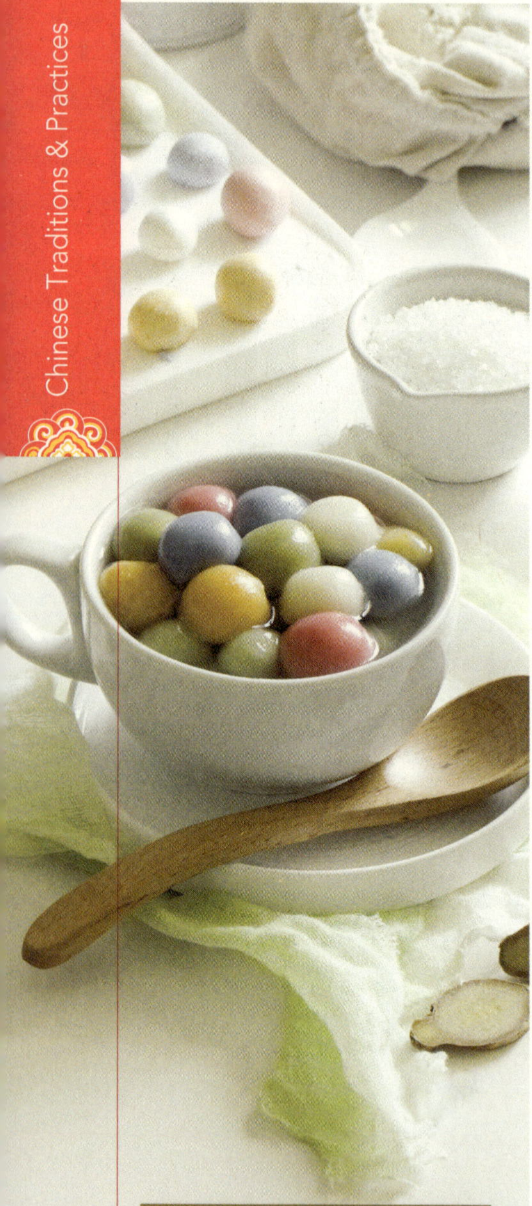

To prepare for their upcoming house cleansing and moving in ceremonies, homeowners had to procure a dozen bowls and chopsticks. They would also need crockery to make *Tang Yuan* 湯圓, sweet glutinous rice balls served in hot water. They would also prepare a rice container with a piece of red paper bearing the Chinese word for "full" (*Man* 滿) on it which is meant to signify that the household will never go hungry. The container was left outside until it was time for the moving in ceremony.

Of course, no Chinese celebration would be complete without red envelopes (*Hong Bao* 紅包). Before moving, it was customary for a homeowner to put a specific amount of money into an envelope, typically 168 units of the local currency as the pronunciation of the number in Chinese is Yi Liu Ba 一六八 which is a homophone of the Chinese phrase "lifelong prosperity" (*Yi Lu Fa* 一路發). They would also need two dozen coins for the moving in ceremony which will be used to symbolically welcome wealth into the house.

Tang Yuan 湯圓 are a key part of the moving in ceremony.

Before moving, a homeowner had to pack sharp objects with care so that knives, scissors and the like were not exposed to the air. Kitchenware to be unpacked after other items. It was believed that breaking these "rules" could bring injury or harm upon a homeowner.

Last but not least, a homeowner would need a new broom and dustbin to place would place at the entrance of their new home before the house cleansing ceremony.

The common version of this rite today involves the homeowner shutting off the power in their new home for more than three days before moving in. On the day of the move in ceremony itself, a coal fire would be lit outside the house and tended until the coals turned red-hot. Called the *Housewarming* (*Ru Huo* 入伙) ceremony, these coals would then be taken inside and to the kitchen.

In the kitchen, the coals were to be used to boil water and make hot drinks which would be consumed by the family members. The homeowner was then allowed to switch on the power in the house as well as open all the windows. If the house had an altar, the family would offer prayers to the local deities before having a light meal. If not, the family would skip the prayers and go straight to eating. Additionally, this meal was to be cooked using the water boiled with the coals brought into the kitchen.

The House Cleansing Ceremony

In most cases, a simple house cleansing ceremony was started the day before the moving in ceremony. Ideally, it was held at the Snake Hour (Si 巳) which corresponds to the period between 9:00AM and 11:00AM. A more exact time can be derived with advanced application of Qi Men Dun Jia.

To carry out the house cleansing ceremony, a homeowner created a mixture of equal parts rice and salt. An alternative mixture could be made with five types of beans, namely mung beans, adzuki beans, black beans, soy beans and runner beans.

Regardless, the homeowner would scatter the mixture in every corner of every room in their house to drive away any evil spirits and Yin energy that might reside there. If the homeowner was married, he was to lead his wife through the house as he went. He would also open the windows in each room as he went. Once the homeowner had spread the mixture in all the rooms, they closed the windows, which brought the first half of the cleansing ceremony to an end.

It must be noted that some variations of this ritual took up to three days. In this case, the homeowner was expected to keep the lights on for three days after scattering their mixture.

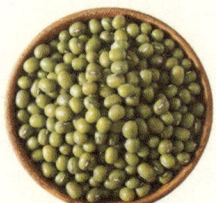
Mung beans

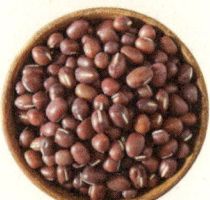
Adzuki beans

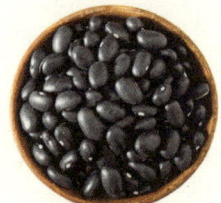
Black beans

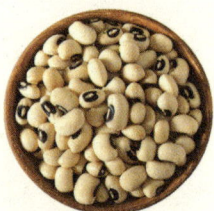
Soy beans

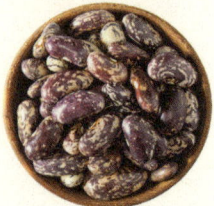
Runner beans

The Moving In Ceremony

The moving in ceremony began with prayers to the guardian of the local residence, which could be either Tu Di Gong (土地公) or Da Bo Gong (大伯公). Da Bo Gong was seen as the divine equivalent of an area's administrative figure. Offering prayers to him is akin to informing a local official that one is moving into the area. While this ritual of praying to the local deity is being conducted, the main door of the house is left closed.

After praying to their chosen deity, the home owner will fill a grill or pot with coal and light the coal to create an intense fire. This was known as the Housewarming (*Ru Huo* 入伙) ceremony and the fire symbolised purification and prosperity. After the fire has settled down, the coals are taken inside to the kitchen.

Next, the homeowner will open the main entrance to their home and chant, "May the Door of Wealth open for me. May money and jewellery tumble into the house." (*Yuan Cai Fu Zhi Men Wei Wo Er Kai, Jin Yin Zhu Bao Zhuang Man Wu.* 願財富之門爲我而開，金銀珠寶裝滿屋。) He will then throw the two dozen coins he had prepared in advance through the doorway and roll eight oranges into his house. The coins and oranges symbolise the money and jewellery in the aforementioned mantra.

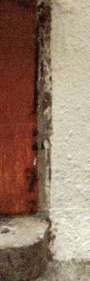

Street shrines dedicated to the local Tu Di Gong (土地公) are a common sight in Chinese neighbourhoods.

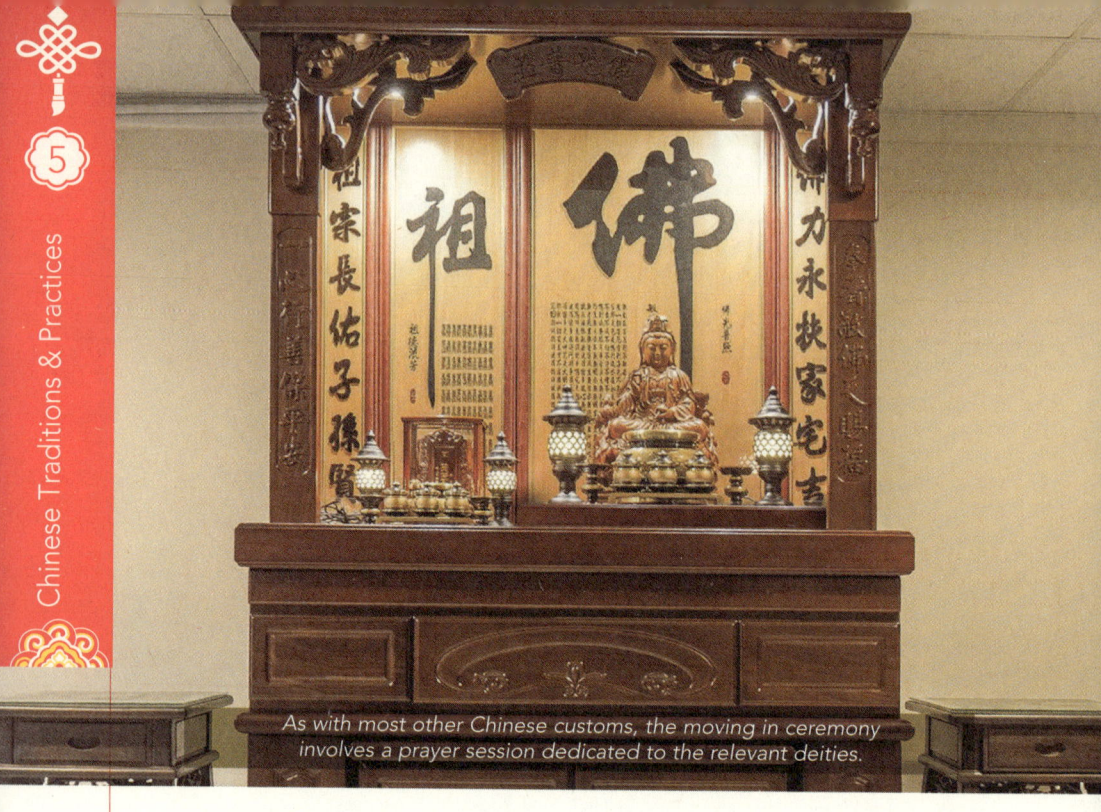
As with most other Chinese customs, the moving in ceremony involves a prayer session dedicated to the relevant deities.

Having thrown his coins and oranges around, the homeowner will bring any statues of deities or ancestral tablets from their old home into their new one. It is important that he did this before he allowed any other family members to enter his new home. The homeowner has to carry them without assistance as a show of respect.

Once he had taken his statues inside, he will finalize the location of his altar before placing the statues and/or tablet in their place. The homeowner then made time to pray to the deities and offer them roast pork, poultry or fruit. It was custom to place a bundle of red flowers in a vase on the altar, too. This was done to symbolise prosperity as well as Peach Blossom Luck and was believed to help bring the homeowner good relationships with others. Flowers with thorns or sharp petals were off limits as it was believed that pointy objects could adversely affect a home's atmosphere. It must be noted that this belief is often mistaken for a Feng Shui principle as such flowers have no real effect on the flow or state of Qi in a home.

After setting up their altar, a homeowner will paste pieces of red paper onto various objects in their house as this was believed in the olden days to be effective in helping to accumulate "auspicious energy" known as Happiness Qi (*Xi Qi* 喜氣). The pieces of red paper were stuck to cooking oil containers, rice containers, bowls and chopsticks, symbolizing a stable and ordinary life where food is readily available. They were also placed on clothing associated with each family member as well as cleaning equipment like brooms or vacuum cleaners, symbolizing the fulfilment of the family's basic needs.

Having completed all of the steps above, a homeowner could finally lead his family into the house. A red envelope containing an auspicious amount of money is given to each family member when it was their turn to enter. Family members carried auspicious items like dumplings, oranges or fish as they entered, exchanging kind words with the homeowner as they did so.

At this point, the second half of the house cleansing ceremony begins. Using the broom they had procured in advance, the homeowner will sweep the entire house. They begin by cleaning the innermost room and gradually move through the residence, finishing at the door. Before cleaning each room, the homeowner will open its windows and knock on a corner a few times. Next, they will gather all the dust, trash and mixture used in the first half of the house cleansing ceremony and put it in the centre of the room. They will then take everything out of the house and dispose of it, symbolically ridding the house of any lingering negative energy.

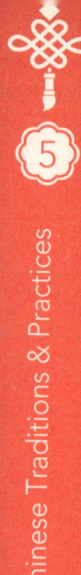

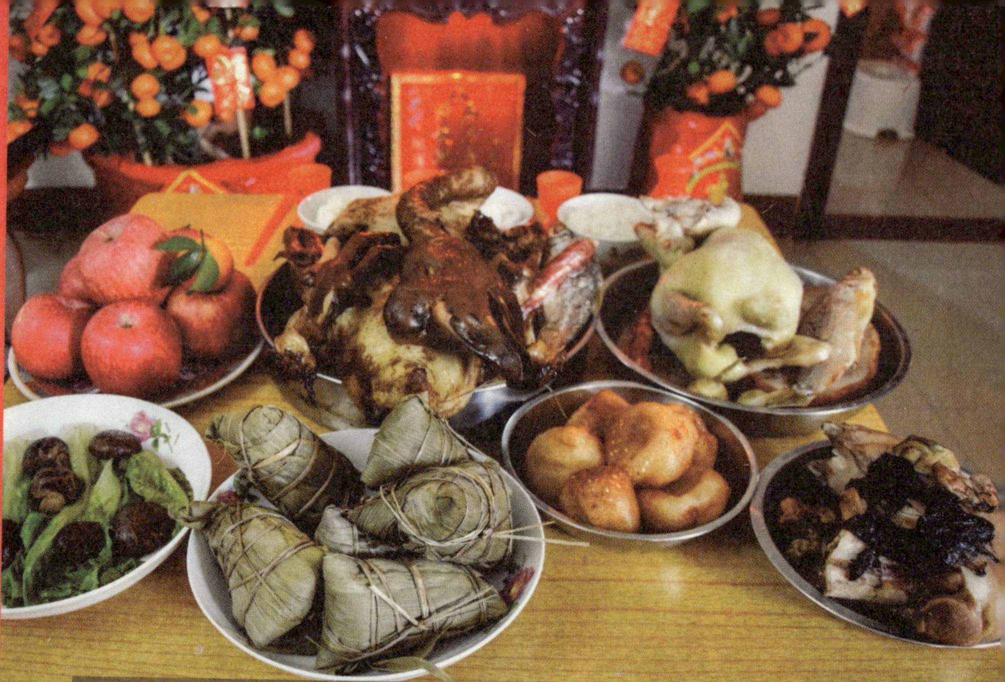

Food offerings which usually include pork, poultry or fruit are usually placed at the altar of the deities as part of the ceremony.

With the house cleansing ceremony complete, it was time to make Tang Yuan. The homeowner will place his kitchenware and appliances in their proper places. The rice container prepared earlier is filled with rice and the kitchen basin with water. These actions once again symbolise abundance. With both filled, the homeowner can make enough Tang Yuan for his entire family, cooking it using water boiled with the hot coals from earlier. Tang Yuan was chosen for its shape which is associated with family unity. Its sweetness evokes happiness.

Aside from this, family members present were discouraged from taking a nap in the afternoon on the day of the moving ceremony. This was because it was believed that carrying out such a "low-energy" activity would invite negative energies that would make them ill in the future. Instead, they had to be joyful and celebrate the occasion so as to bring in vibrant Yang energy that would "energise" the house.

To bring the moving in ceremony to an end, everyone offers prayers to the *Lord of the Foundation* (*Di Zhu Shen* 地主神), the personification of a building's foundation. As a subordinate of Da Bo Gong, the Lord of the Foundation is believed to watch over a house and all who reside in it. It was believed that every house had its own Lord of the Foundation who served as the police or an authority figure protecting its occupants.

Due to the perceived closeness between the Lord of the Foundation and a family compared to Da Bo Gong, the act of offering prayers to him was complex with many stipulations.

Prayers to the Lord of the Foundation was saved for the evening because Yang energy is too strong in the morning. The ideal time to pray to him is between the Horse (Wu 午) and Goat (Wei 未) Hours which are 12:00PM and 3:00PM, but no later than the Monkey (Shen 申) Hour which is 5:00PM. If it was night time, prayers could be postponed until the next day.

The location and design of the altar dedicated to the Lord of the Foundation is important. As the deity usually resides at the back of the house or the kitchen alongside the God of the Stove (*Zao Shen* 灶神), it was customary to pray to him there. The altar dedicated to him is never taller than 40cm as the deity himself was only 100cm to 200cm. It was believed that a tall altar might intimidate him. The altar was never placed facing the back door as doing so might draw inauspicious energy into the house. Prayers to the Lord of the Foundation were accompanied by the placing of braised chicken thighs or a lunch box containing chicken thighs at the altar.

During the entire moving process, there should be no ongoing family conflict: one mustn't pray to the Lord of the Foundation if they are in a bad place emotionally. If an argument erupts, amends must be made before things can proceed. As a moving in ceremony is meant to mark the beginning of a new chapter in one's life, praying to the Lord of the Foundation in the wrong frame of mind can jeopardise a family's wellbeing. Furthermore, the homeowner was forbidden from being angry at children in particular during the ceremony.

When praying to the Lord of the Foundation, a homeowner could have a personal mental conversation with the deity as part of his prayer. This was believed to help establish a bond between the deity and the homeowner. Afterwards, the homeowner took a pot of coal to his backyard and burnt joss paper for the deity, asking for his protection. In certain parts of China, there are stores that sell joss paper specifically designed for the worship of this deity.

It should be noted that many of these ancient Chinese customs are not linked to Feng Shui and those who still follow them use simplified versions of these complicated practices. Many do not even pray to any deities and simply focus on making sure the move-in process resonates with vibrant energy and positive emotions.

Extended Customs Potentially Practised After Moving In

- The moving in ceremony usually ends after prayers to the *Lord of the Foundation*. Some families opt to carry out additional rituals, however. These lasted for a week or two after the regular moving in ceremony. One ritual was the house cleansing ritual known as *Fire under the Roof* (*Huo An* 火庵). To carry it out, a homeowner would keep the lights on in his new home for at least 24 continuous hours over a three-day period.

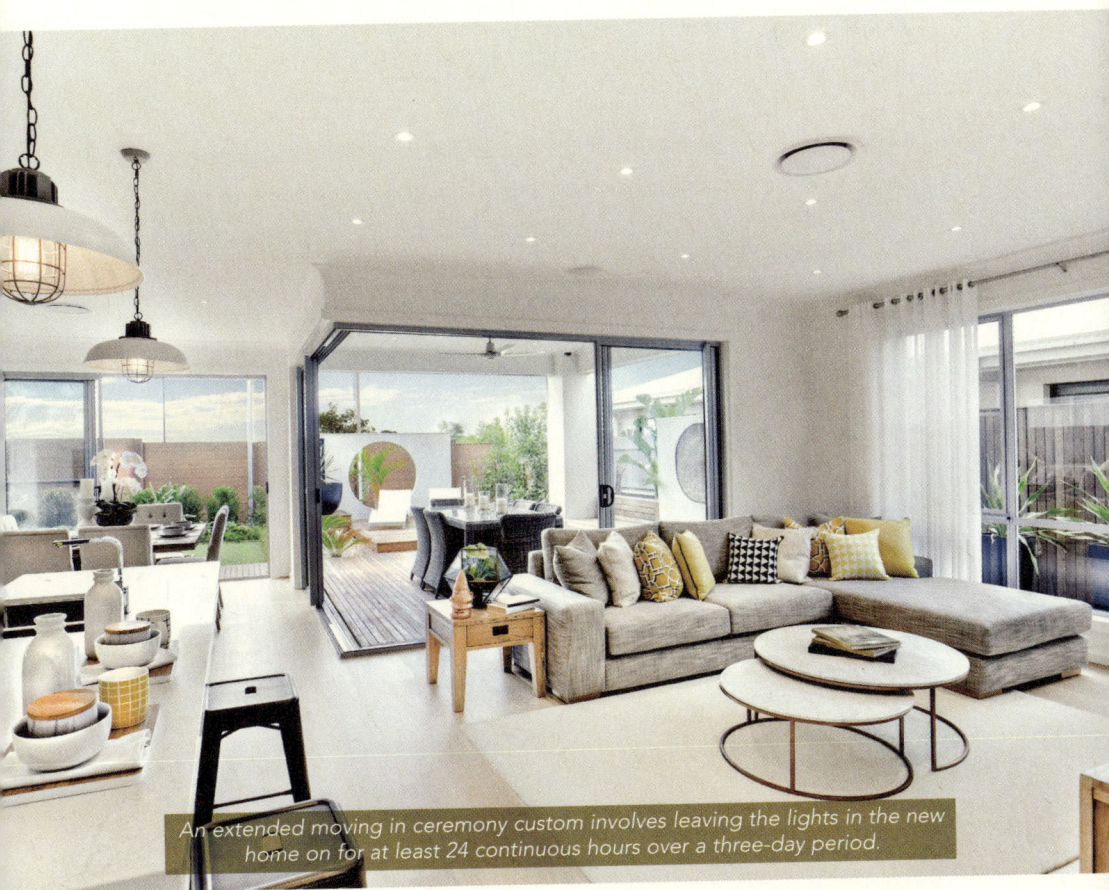

An extended moving in ceremony custom involves leaving the lights in the new home on for at least 24 continuous hours over a three-day period.

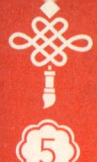

風生水起

"The Wind Emerges and the Wave Rises"
(Feng Sheng Shui Qi)

During the regular moving in ceremony, some families chose to keep their kitchen basin full for one to three days, either retaining water in the basin or leaving a tap running. The running tap symbolised sustainability, invoking an old Chinese phrase which asserts that "a tiny stream often lasts the longest distance" (*Xi Shui Chang Liu* 細水長流).

In modern times, some families add an electric fan to the mix and leave it on for the same duration. They do this in recognition of the two core components of Feng Shui: Wind and Water. The underlying imagery is that the wind from the electric fan is auspicious Qi and the water in the tub is akin to the Dragon Vein. Together, the fan and water symbolise a scenario called "The Wind Emerges and the Wave Rises" (*Feng Sheng Shui Qi* 風生水起) which symbolised a booming business. Once again, it must be said that this recent custom is based on a rather superficial understanding of Feng Shui and it cannot actually affect the Qi energy in a home. It is often mistaken for a genuine Feng Shui custom but it is based on more general cultural beliefs.

Last but not least is a custom known as *Settling the Incense* (*An Xiang* 安香). This involved keeping the censer which was lit during the moving ceremony continuously burning for 24 hours over 12 days. Doing so allowed the incense to settle throughout the house.

On A Personal Note…

When moving in and house-warming ceremonies were first introduced, they were meant to be fun and enjoyable. A new home is something worth celebrating. Over time people have become extremely uptight about doing everything by the book and moving in ceremonies have become stuffy affairs. Far from bringing a new homeowner joy, they can cause considerable stress and frustration. As such, they no longer fulfil their original purpose of ensuring that the new homeowner is able to move into his new house in a good state of mind.

If you are happy when you move into your new home, you bring positive energy into it. If you can feel the warmth and joy of everyone celebrating the occasion then you have accomplished what you set out to do. Don't feel hemmed in by rules and restrictions, because they can detract from the original purpose of the ceremony and negate its effects.

In short, have a good time and enjoy yourself!

House Construction

Some aspiring homeowners choose to purchase a plot of land to develop on rather than a completed house. Although it is becoming less common for homeowners to do this as empty land is snapped up quickly for large-scale developments, there are still occasions when plots of land are sold to individual buyers. In such cases, a buyer should bring an experienced Feng Shui consultant into the fold as early as possible.

When a Yang House – a home – is being built, a *Ground-moving Ceremony* (*Dong Tu* 動土) should be held. This refers to the first time the housebuilder drives his draw hoe into the ground where the house will be built. Its equivalent when building a Yin House – a grave site – is called the *Ground-breaking Ceremony* (*Po Tu* 破土).

In Chinese, the two customs are literally called "moving the ground" and "breaking the ground". While the act itself is similar, this naming distinction was made solely to differentiate the two since one is linked to life while the other is related to death. Additionally, "breaking the ground" carries no implications of innovation or the creation of something new.

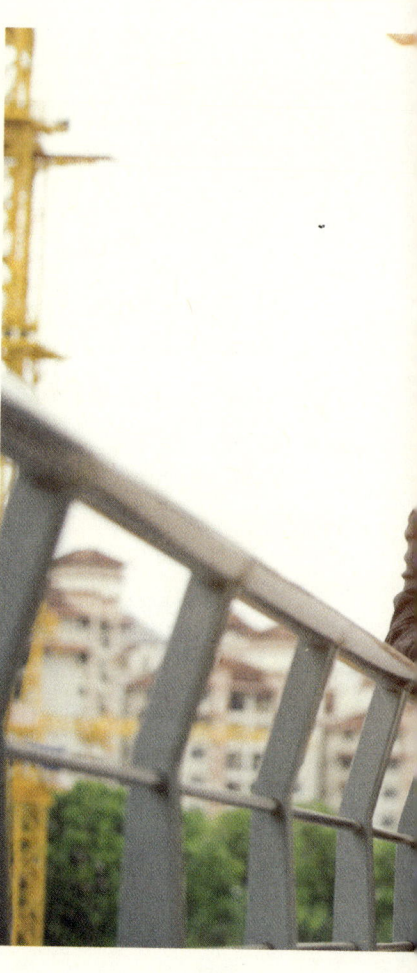

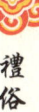

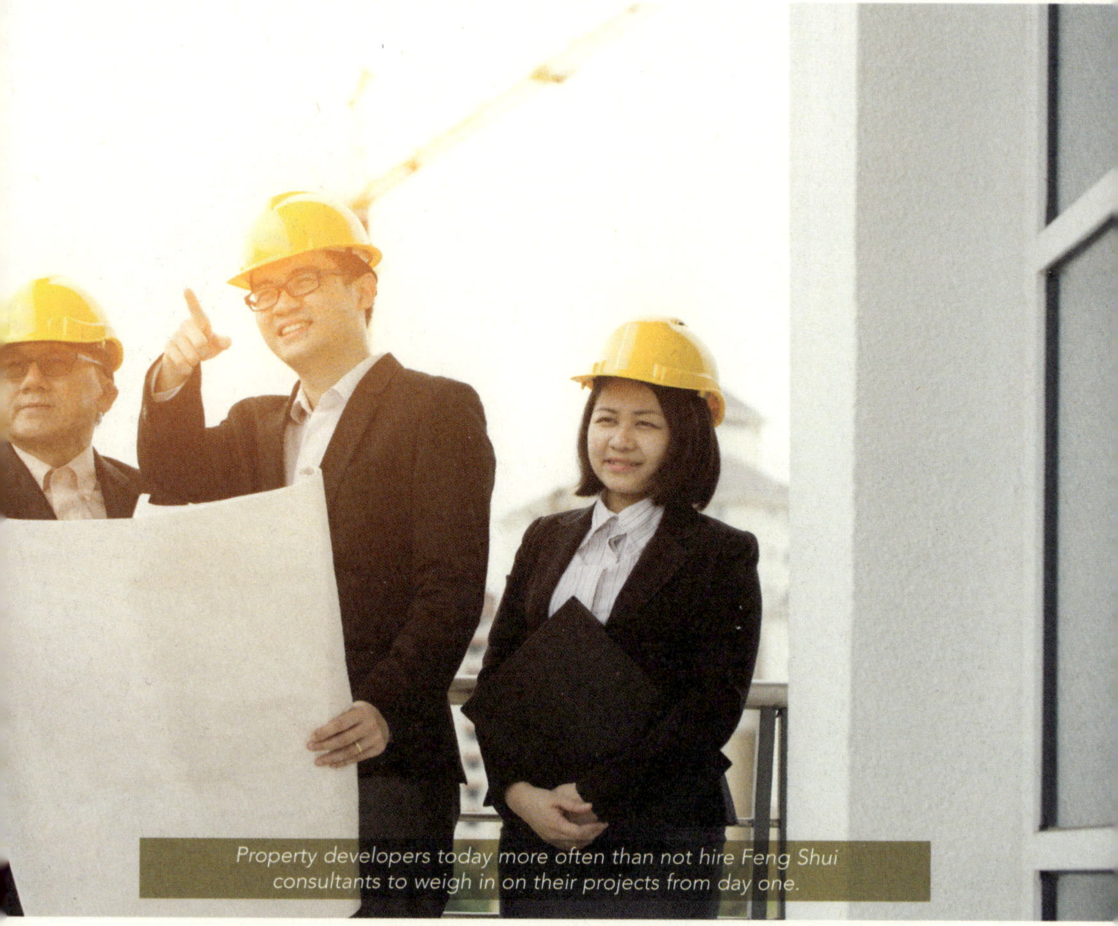

Property developers today more often than not hire Feng Shui consultants to weigh in on their projects from day one.

On the other hand, the term "ground-breaking" used today is an English term and this of course means that its definition is rooted in a different line of thought. For explanation's sake, ground-breaking in English refers to the introduction of new ideas or endeavours. Its definition with respect to the ceremony is an act which marks the beginning of a new construction project.

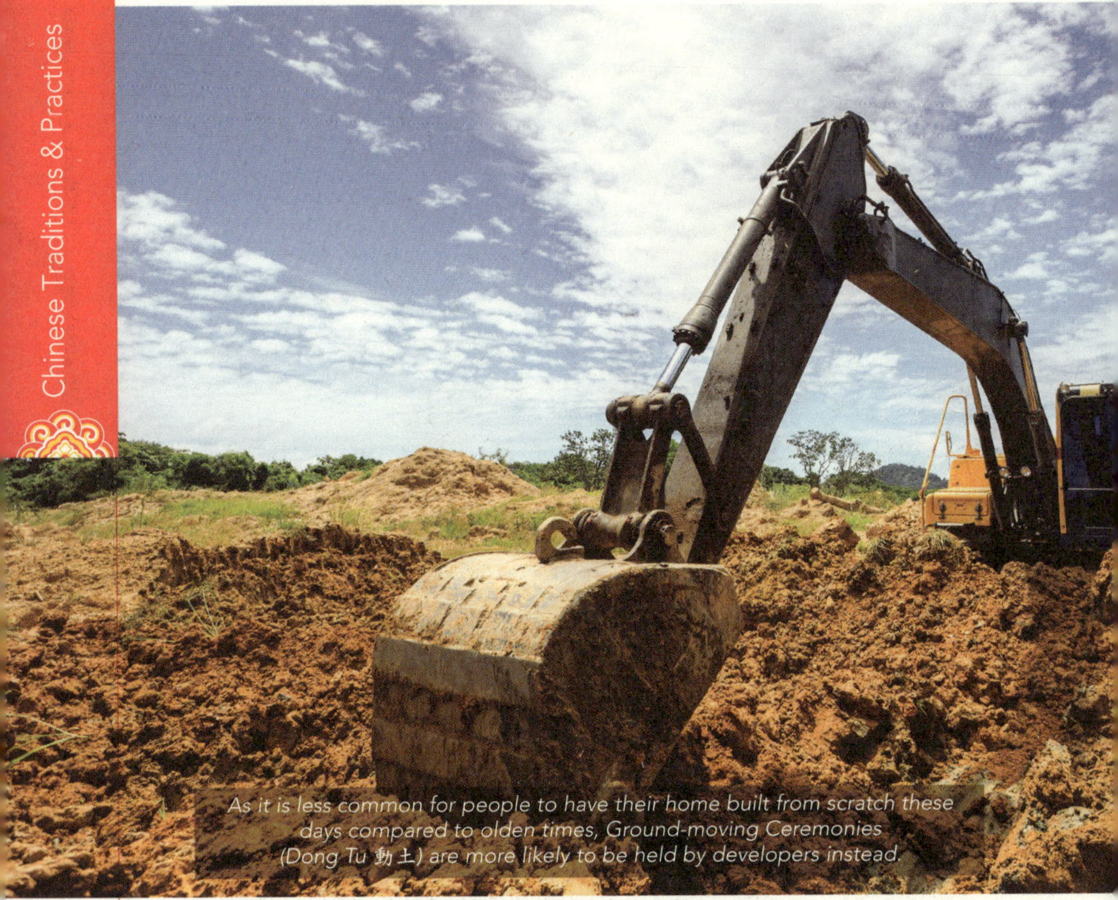

As it is less common for people to have their home built from scratch these days compared to olden times, Ground-moving Ceremonies (Dong Tu 動土) are more likely to be held by developers instead.

The Ground-moving Ceremony (*Dong Tu* 動土)

The Ground-moving Ceremony lets a homeowner formally notify local deities that the location has become a construction site. Prayers are offered during this ceremony to divine beings so that they may drive away inauspicious forces and negative spirits. The ceremony is also believed to help prevent construction workers from offending local divinities and subsequently reduce the chances of on-site accidents occurring during the construction period.

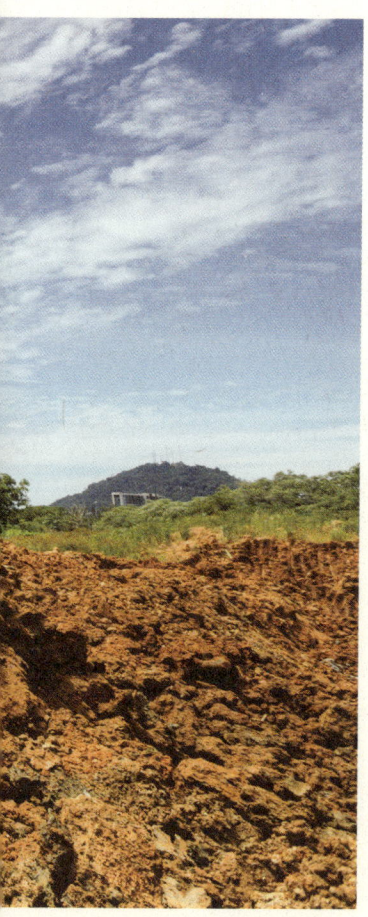

Long ago, the custom was conducted by a Daoist priest accompanied by the landowner. In modern times, however, it is usually conducted by a Chinese Metaphysics practitioner and the real estate developer.

It is important that the ceremony isn't held in the sector where the Grand Duke resides. The sector where the Three Killings, *Robbery Sha* (*Jie Sha* 劫煞), *Calamity Sha* (*Zai Sha* 災煞) and *Annual Sha* (*Sui Sha* 歲煞), are located should also be avoided.

The timing of the ceremony is also important. An auspicious Date and Hour must be chosen. Offerings must be also be prepared for presentation to the local deities usually consisting of meat, poultry, fish, incense, ceremonial candles, flowers, fruits and joss paper.

At the auspicious Hour that has been chosen, the individual conducting the ceremony should lead a prayer session accompanied by the homeowner or real estate developer followed by the recitation of a chant. If several representatives of a development company are present, they are to form a row with the eldest person in the middle. They must also be positioned according to the Feng Shui orientation of the project.

After a round of prayers, the people who have been tasked with "moving the ground" should pick up their tools and ready themselves. They should hold their tools in their left hand and ensure that their left hand and left foot are positioned in front of their right foot. This is because the left represents Yang and the right represents Yin.

Digging should begin in the middle of the construction site. Ground should be moved a total of three times while the allocated workers hold their breath. They must then repeat the process at all four corners of the site. After moving ground at all four corners, the joss paper and/or incense prepared earlier would be burned and the firecrackers lit, thus ending the ceremony and officially "registering" the construction site with local deities. Meanwhile, the simplified and modern version of this merely involves a quick prayer.

In contrast to the steps outlined above, another approach based on the principles of Chinese Metaphysics involves the use of a Qi Men chart to locate the sector where positive Qi in the area gathers. This sector is then "activated" by digging into the ground there at the right hour. To identify the correct time and place, it is best to hire a professional Chinese Metaphysics practitioner.

As an aside, disruptive renovation works should be kept to a minimum after a house is completed. This is especially true in the time just after residents have moved in. If renovations are unavoidable, an auspicious date should be chosen to start them.

Home Renovations

Home renovations were once regarded as something that should be avoided at all costs as they were believed to disrupt a home's Qi. Renovations were only commissioned when absolutely necessary and there were many stipulations surrounding them.

Today, renovations have become commonplace and people worry much less about any disruptive effects. Nevertheless, many people observe certain customs when they go about renovating their property.

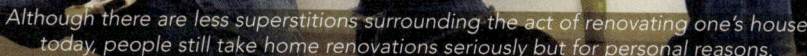
Although there are less superstitions surrounding the act of renovating one's house today, people still take home renovations seriously but for personal reasons.

A Cultural Approach to the Renovation Process

The first step in the renovation process is choosing the right date to begin! As usual, this can be done with Date Selection. To choose a date, a homeowner can either consult their Tong Shu Calendar (Tong Sheng 通勝) or consult a Chinese Metaphysics practitioner who is proficient in Date Selection to do so.

Choosing the best date possible will ensure that the renovation will go well and only positive energies will flow throughout the house. Even in a worst-case scenario, it is highly recommended that a good date be chosen so as to neutralise the negative energies.

Once a date has been chosen, a homeowner should pray to the Lord of the Foundation (*Di Zhu Shen* 地主神) mentioned earlier and inform him of their plans to renovate their home. Those who are unfamiliar with this ritual should just make some sincere prayers and offerings where appropriate to the "Divine Energies of the Earth". Renovation work is like the Ground-moving Ceremony (*Dong Tu* 動土) as both are disruptive in some way. Renovation work should not be done in the Grand Duke or Three Killings sectors. If this cannot be avoided then a homeowner can ask a Buddhist monk or Daoist priest to provide them with a special talisman designed to neutralise inauspicious energy released during renovation.

Renovation should never begin outside the home. This is because work on the exterior of a house can imprison or disrupt the flow of Qi into the home. If possible, renovation work should begin inside the home and progress outwards to maintain adequate Qi flow. Renovation work should start in an auspicious corner of the house, identified by a Qi Men practitioner using a Qi map. Doing this will stir up the auspicious Qi gathered there and allow it to circulate around the home. Construction workers can then continue their work following the path of the displaced Qi.

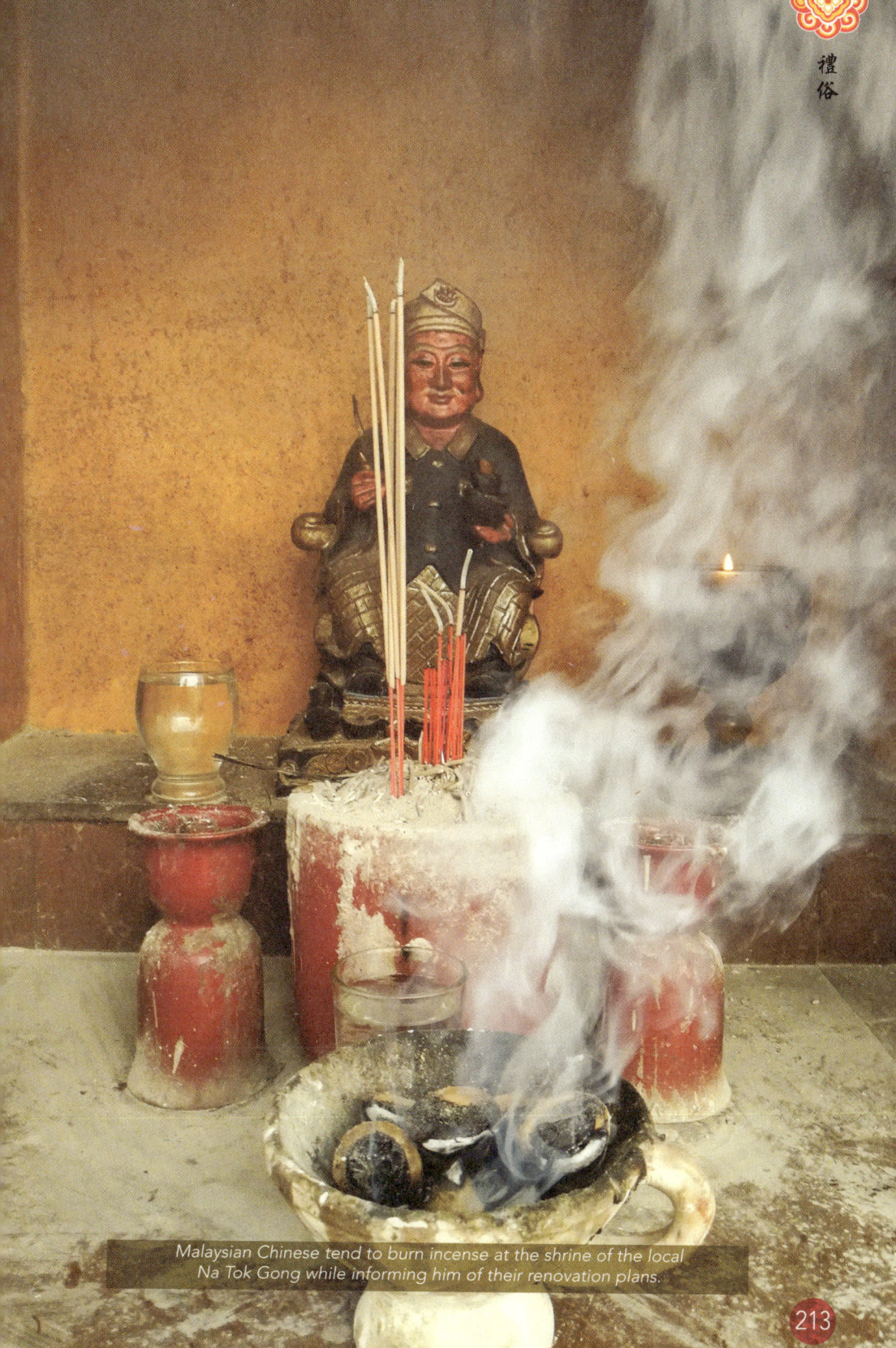

Malaysian Chinese tend to burn incense at the shrine of the local Na Tok Gong while informing him of their renovation plans.

Restrictions Related to the Renovation Process

Homeowners should move out during an extensive renovation, especially if the renovations include the installation of new windows and window frames. This advice is based on the notion that a home represents a homeowner's body. By making holes in walls or taking out windows, one may increase a homeowner's chance of getting into an accident or coming to harm because this severely disrupts the Qi flow.

To prevent this, a homeowner and their family should find somewhere else to live for the duration of renovation work. According to Feng Shui principles, certain sectors within a home might contain adverse Qi. By changing the structure of a home in any serious way, one might inadvertently activate the negative Qi.

Special care must be taken when a home has a pregnant resident. In these cases, precautions must be taken so as not to offend the *Foetal God* (*Tai Shen* 胎神). To appease the Foetal God, family members should place a mark where the Foetal God is located and ask construction workers to stay away from it. In addition, they can paste a *Foetus Protection Talisman* (*An Tai Fu* 安胎符) on the pregnant woman's bed. This has the effect of protecting both the unborn foetus and the Foetal God. This spiritual custom is traditionally performed under the supervision of an experienced Daoist priest.

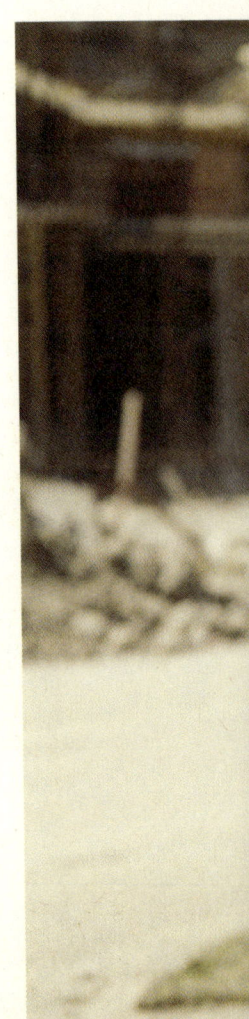

Women – pregnant or not – were once advised to stay away from the construction site on the first day of renovation. Women on their periods were advised to avoid it as well with the exception of the homeowner's wife.

These stipulations were all built on antiquated ideas and most are no longer observed. A modern Feng Shui approach to renovation involves simply identifying the appropriate date for renovation and starting in the right sector.

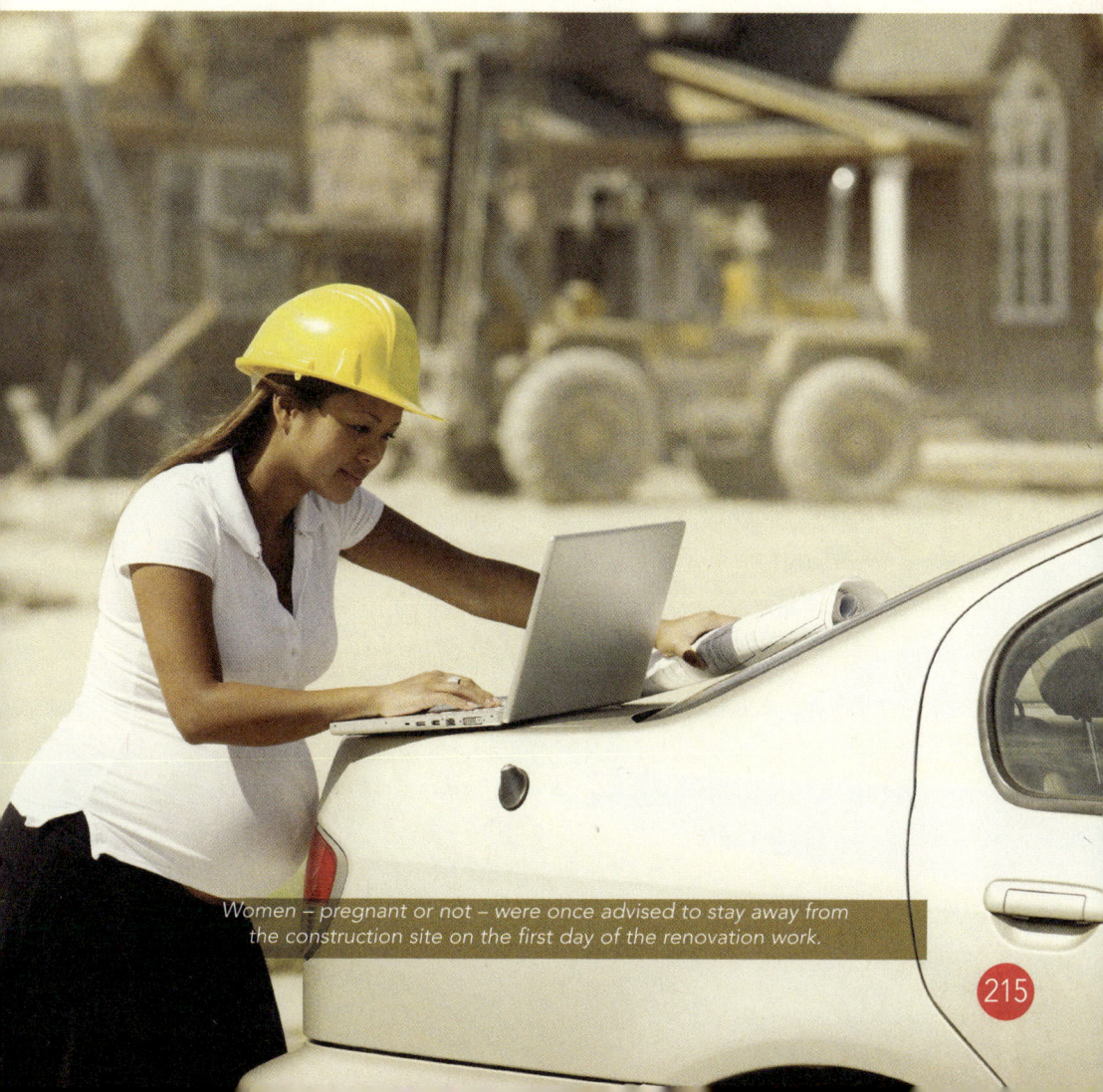

Women – pregnant or not – were once advised to stay away from the construction site on the first day of the renovation work.

Other Beliefs Related to the Renovation Process

Some believe that a homeowner can complement their BaZi chart by using certain materials during renovation work. According to this theory, a person with very little Wood element in their BaZi chart might use wooden materials to compensate. And those with BaZi charts deficient in the Earth or Metal elements could use metal or rock in their home, perhaps installing stainless steel kitchen furniture or granite features for example.

Some people also believe that the intelligent use of colour can also make up for deficits in a home owner's BaZi chart. People who subscribe to this notion believe that green decorations can benefit a person who has insufficient Wood element in their BaZi chart, blue, teal or black decorations can benefit a person with insufficient Water element in their BaZi chart and that red, purple or pink decorations can benefit those with little Fire element in their BaZi chart. The same people also believe that gold, white and grey decorations can make up for a BaZi chart that has little Metal element and that a person with too little Earth element in their BaZi chart can make up for it with yellow, brown or dark brown decorations.

It should be stressed however that none of these recommendations are based on hard and fast Chinese Metaphysics principles, even though they incorporate elements of Chinese Metaphysics. They are mainly based on superstitious beliefs and wider cultural beliefs. In genuine Chinese Metaphysics practice, none of these things actually serve any purpose in improving one's fortunes.

Chapter 6

Funeral Customs

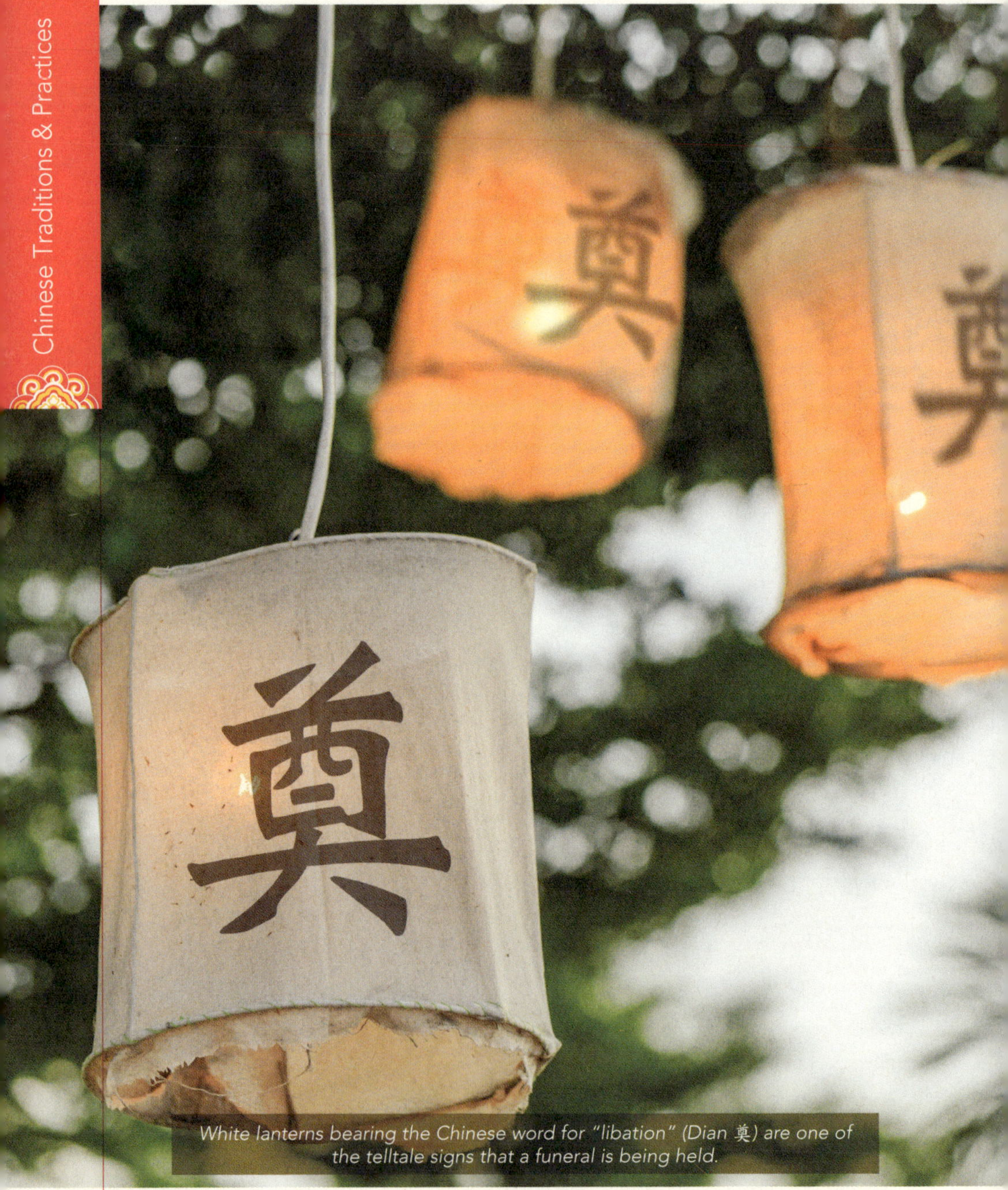

Chinese Traditions & Practices

White lanterns bearing the Chinese word for "libation" (Dian 奠) are one of the telltale signs that a funeral is being held.

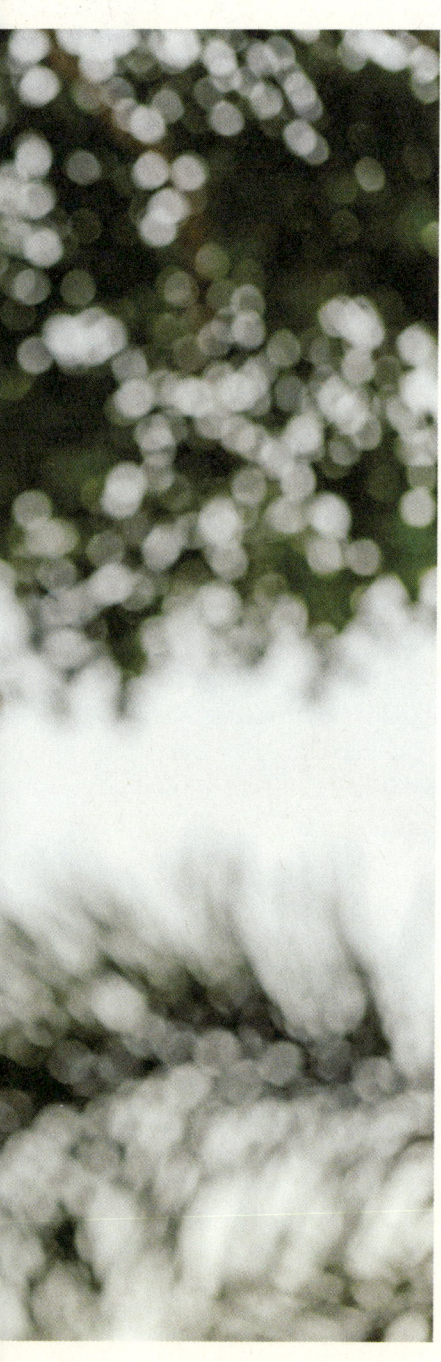

Like many modern Chinese cultural practices, Chinese funeral customs draw upon Confucian principles. With that said, many predate Confucianism. As a matter of fact, early funeral rites are the basis for some Confucius philosophies in the first place!

Confucius himself was inspired by the ancient Chinese funeral rites to develop a way of living in social harmony and practising good moral conduct. When thinking about funeral practices Confucius thought primarily about the way that a son might bury his father: demonstrating filial piety in doing so.

Confucius believed that filial piety was a fundamentally natural, good and moral emotion. He also found compassion and mutual love (*Ren* 仁) important. These concepts are integral to all Chinese funeral customs based on Confucian principles.

Confucian influence is evident in the emphasis on rituals and closure in Chinese funeral customs. Confucius believed that well defined rituals (*Yi Li Zhi Sang* 以禮治喪) could help a grieving person experience the right amount of poignant mourning or calm sadness (*Ai* 哀).

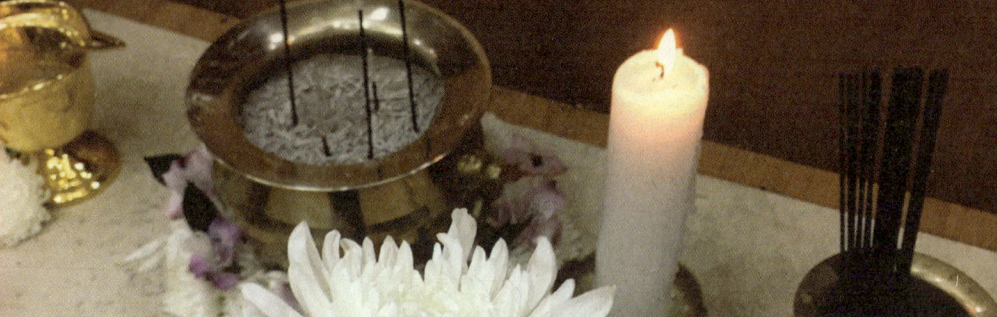

Confucius believed that any decent man would take a long time to recover from losing his parents and obtain full closure. As such, he believed that while a man was grieving they would not be in the mood to dress up, eat or enjoy anything. He therefore advocated for three years of simple living after a death – three years being the amount of time an infant takes to learn how to stand on its own two feet. By taking three years to mourn, a son could symbolically honour and repay his parents for ushering him through the first three years of his life. Confucius later standardised his thinking and laid out an "official" grieving procedure. He asserted that grieving was a sign of compassion and that any son who did not sufficiently mourn the loss of their parents must lack basic decency.

Initially his views led to the development of overly complex Confucian funeral rites. The ancient Chinese likely felt that they had a lot to live up to and that only the most elaborate displays of grief and filial piety would suffice. Over the years, Chinese funeral rituals have been simplified but they still adhere to the same basic structure.

Overall Chinese funeral proceedings consist of several steps: the planning of the funeral (*Zu* 卒), the preparation of the obituary and body of the deceased (*Lian* 殮), the Visitation (*Bin* 殯), the funeral, the burial (*Zang* 葬) and the post-funeral practices which include either the Closure (*Ji* 祭) or something else like it.

Planning the Funeral

The Chinese word for finality (*Zu* 卒) is closely associated with death: specifically, the period of time where a person is aware of their impending demise. If a dying person was still of sound mind they would use the time to prepare their will and make decisions about their funeral rites in a process known as Approaching the End (*Lin Zhong* 臨終). During this time, a dying person's family was morally obligated to accompany them until they passed. This was known as a Farewell (*Song Zhong* 送終).

Once a person had died their family was expected to unite and collectively take care of their funeral arrangements. Shortly after a loved one's death, a family could carry out a rite called Soul Conjuring (*Zhao Hun* 招魂) in an attempt to call them back to the world of the living.

When some people are about to die they refuse to let their children bid them farewell. In the past, some did this as a way of punishing their offspring. In the most extreme cases they also prohibited their children from returning to their household after their death, even when they lived in the same town or city.

The family of a dead person was expected to wear appropriate mourning clothes throughout the grieving process, wearing specific outfits depending on their relationship with the deceased. At other times they could wear plain white clothes instead. Traditionally, family members were expected to adhere to the dress code for 3 years. Today, 3 years is considered excessive and many family members observe a 3 month or 100 day mourning period instead.

The Farewell (*Song Zhong* 送終)

In accordance with tradition a person coming to the end of their life would write their will in front of their entire family during the Farewell. Their will would dictate their last wishes, preferred medical treatment methods, how their wealth and property should be divided among their family and their desired funeral arrangements. Wills had to be written in an official manner and contain realistic requests so that they could be substantiated and then carried out.

Today, people have more affairs to put in order and writing a will is a complex undertaking. Legal professionals suggest that people should write their wills when they are lucid and mentally capable of understanding their options. One should never write a will without legal oversight either.

In any case, once a person had written their will their family would carry out several rituals for them as they approached the end of their life.

In the first of these they would remove the incense burner from it's place at the family altar and cover the ancestral tablet (*Zu Xian Pai Wei* 祖先牌位) or divine tablet (*Shen Pai* 神牌) with red paper. This was done so as to prevent the deities from witnessing a death out of respect for them.

When the dying person was very close to the end they would give cash known as "last money" (*Shou Wei Qian* 手尾錢) to their descendants. Traditionally, this consisted of silver nuggets or whatever else they had left after paying for their funeral services. This tradition has survived to the present day but it is now a largely symbolic gesture: it represents the act of passing on one's wealth. Many family members keep whatever they are given as "last money" as a memento.

Families sometimes placed a bowl of rice near a dying person's feet which was meant to represent their last meal (*Jiao Wei Fan* 腳尾飯) as a mortal and first meal as a spirit. This presumably spared them from making the journey to the underworld on an empty stomach. To mark the rice as an offering, they stuck a pair of chopsticks into it. To this day, people are discouraged from sticking their chopsticks into their food because it evokes this tradition.

After a person had died, select members of their family were put in charge of their funeral, forming something known as a Funeral Service Committee (*Zhi Sang Wei Yuan Hui* 治喪委員會). Sometimes they were joined by professional funeral organisers, but not always. Regardless, the committee was usually led by the deceased person's eldest son unless he was dead, too. If this was the case, then a standard line of succession was used to appoint the next most suitable relative, like the dead person's second son. If they had no living sons then their grandson would be chosen instead. If they had no male offspring at all then their daughter would be put in charge and so on.

Among other responsibilities, the person in charge of the Funeral Service Committee was expected to produce 10 death certificates for funeral service providers, to notify banks and so on.

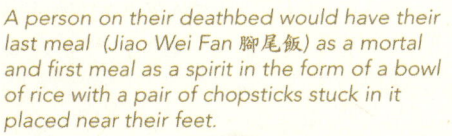

A person on their deathbed would have their last meal (Jiao Wei Fan 腳尾飯) as a mortal and first meal as a spirit in the form of a bowl of rice with a pair of chopsticks stuck in it placed near their feet.

The Soul Conjuring
(*Zhao Hun* 招魂)

In the past, some families observed a tradition known as Soul Conjuring. The tradition is rarely practised today.

The people of ancient China believed that after a person died their soul remained aware of what was happening in the mortal realm. This gave rise to the practice of Soul Conjuring where families made a last ditch effort to reach their loved one and coax them back to life. Anyone who refused to take part in the ritual was considered unfilial.

The Soul Conjuring ritual began after a family had finished crying which they were forbidden from doing before their loved one had actually passed. To conduct the ritual, a selected family member took the deceased person's clothes to the roof of their house and stood on the apex of the roof facing North. Holding a shirt collar in their left hand and its lapel in their right they waved the shirt in the air and wailed the name of the dead followed with a request: "please return" (*Hui Gui Ba* 回歸吧).

North is a Yin direction, so by speaking the North direction, it was believed a person was more likely to attract the attention of the dead. According to records of the ritual in classical texts, a person could further increase their chances of success by using mortuary clothes instead of regular clothes. However, these traditional practices are largely symbolic in essence. We all know, it is not possible to bring the deceased back to life. It's an act to demonstrate filial piety.

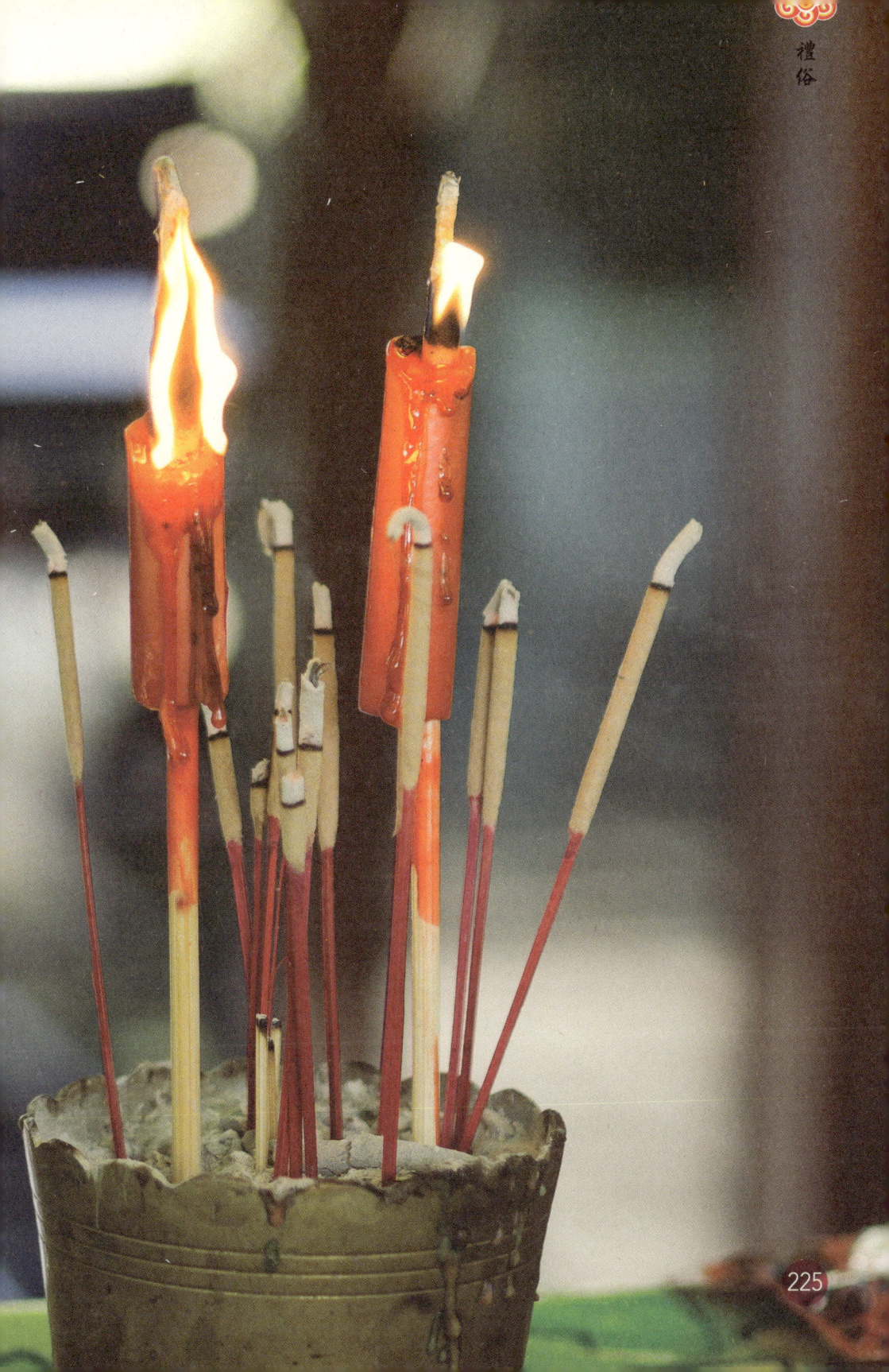

The Mourning Clothes

Mourning clothing were meant to indicate a person's relationship with the deceased and as such they were not made in a homogeneous way.

Mourning clothes were traditionally made out of hemp. The coarseness of the hemp used for each item of clothing and their design were meant to reflect the degree of sadness it's wearer had. A bereaved father would wear full coarse-cut clothes (*Zhan Shuai* 斬衰) made from the roughest hemp fiber without seams on it's edges. This reflected the immense sadness of a father who lost their child. If the deceased was a mother, uncle or brother then the appropriate mourning clothes were sewn coarse-cut ones (*Qi Shuai* 齊衰) instead; identical to full coarse-cut clothes in terms of material but with seams instead. If the deceased person was an uncle, married female relative or cousin then fine hemp clothes (*Da Gong* 大功) made of cooked fine hemp fiber were worn. Last but not least, light hemp clothes (*Si Ma* 緦麻) made from the finest possible hemp fiber were appropriate for great grandparent or in-law deaths.

Over the centuries mourning clothing customs have been simplified and tweaked. Today they are rarely worn in accordance with tradition. Modern families opt instead to wear white shirts and black pants. Some pin small squares of hemp and different coloured pieces of cloth called mourning pins (*Xiao* 孝) to their shirtsleeves. The combination they use indicates their relationship with the deceased. If the dead person was a man then one should wear mourning pins on their left sleeve and if they were a women then one wears them on the right.

In ancient China people wore mourning clothes after a king passed away. This custom was developed by Confucius who lived in the time before China was united. At that point in history China had several kingdoms ruled by respective kings instead of a single Emperor. People of the day were expected to mourn their king's "collapse" (*Beng* 崩) as intensely as they would mourn their own father's passing. This was especially true for people who served as counsellors in the royal court. This level of mourning actually became mandatory during the reign of the Han Dynasty (206 BC-220 AD).

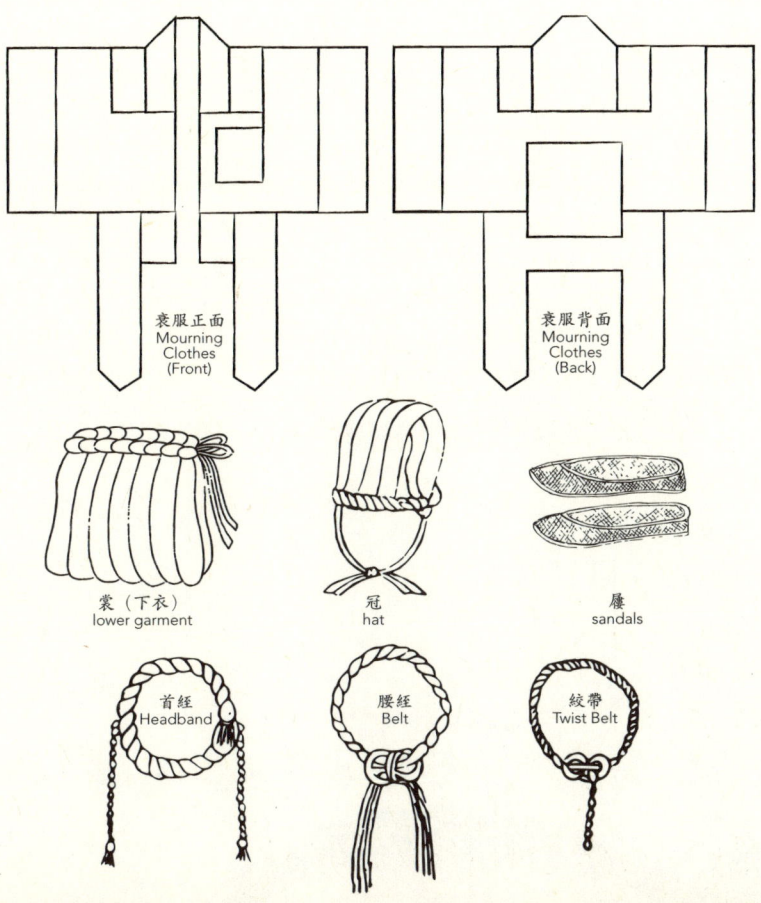

Illustrations of the traditional mourning attire of ancient China

The Obituary

After the Soul Conjuring ritual had come to an end a bereaved family issued an obituary as part of the preparations (*Lian* 殮). Traditionally, families would issue an obituary 10 days before the funeral of their loved one - this ensured that any relatives who lived far away had enough time to make travel arrangements in order to attend.

Obituaries had to be written in accordance with very specific rules. In the past, they were often written by a professional funeral service provider. Nowadays, it is common for families to simply inform a newspaper of their loss and have them write and publish an obituary instead.

Normally whoever was tasked with writing an obituary used B4 paper and then folded the paper four times. White paper was preferred but it was acceptable to use light yellow paper if white was unavailable. Pink and red were not allowed as the two colours symbolise happiness in Chinese culture.

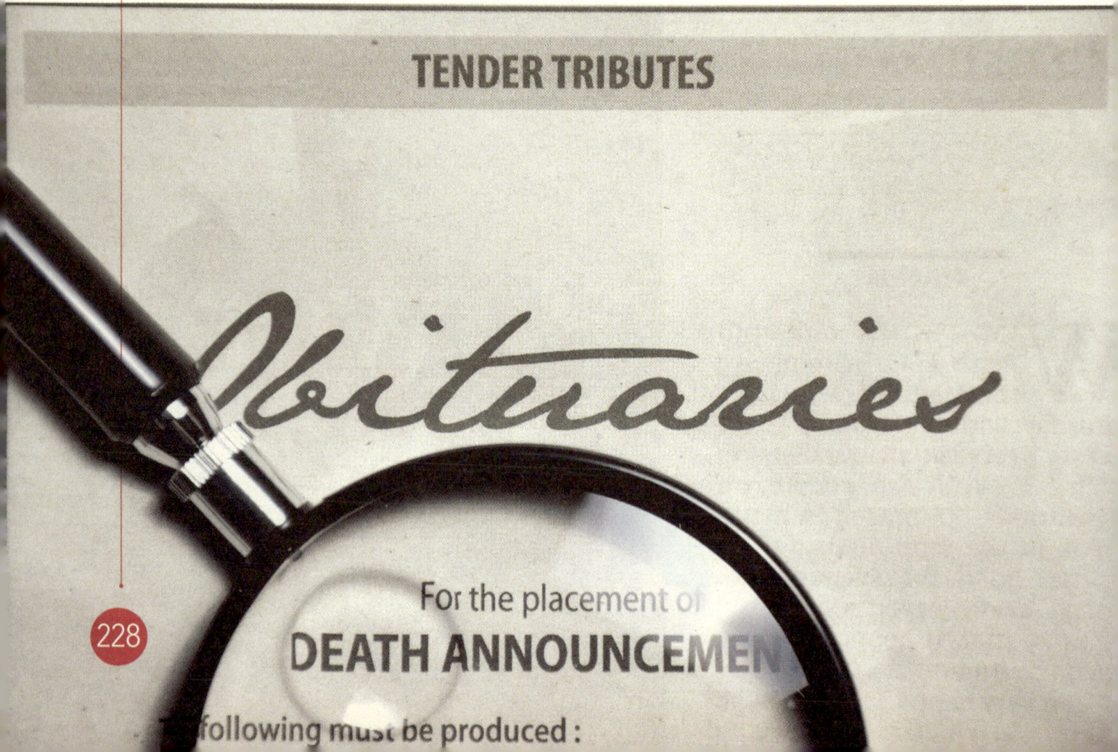

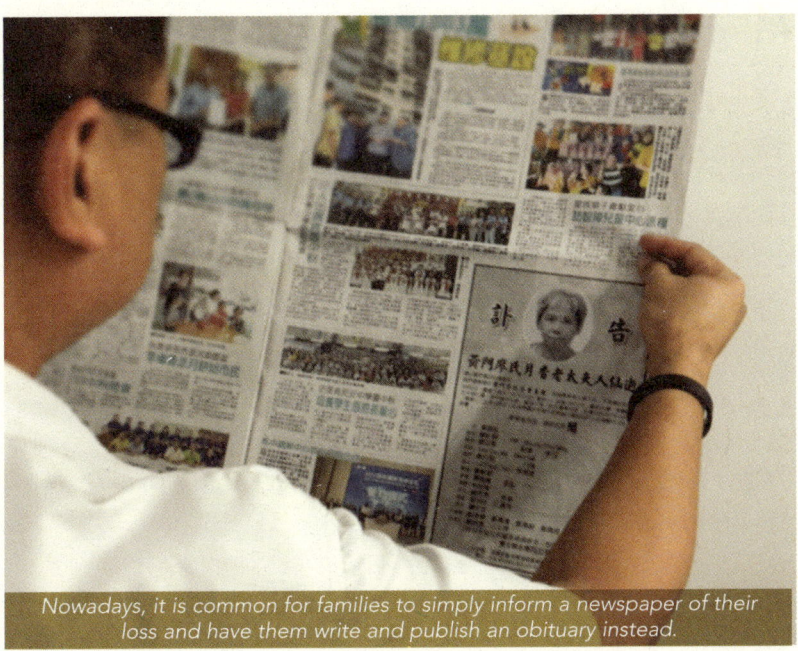
Nowadays, it is common for families to simply inform a newspaper of their loss and have them write and publish an obituary instead.

Naturally, the font used for a traditional Chinese obituary was neat and easily readable. In accordance with tradition the Chinese phrase for an obituary (*Fu Wen* 訃聞) must be written in a specific way. The first half of the phrase means "unfortunate" (*Fu* 訃), especially in the context of death. As such, it must be written in black. The second half of the Chinese phrase for an obituary means "notification" (*Wen* 聞) and should be written in red. This auspicious colour has long been used to help offset the dark nature of the subject matter.

A traditional obituary contained the deceased person's personal information and the names of family members, listed according to their relationship with the person.

Minor Preparations (*Xiao Lian* 小殮)

Once an obituary had been issued, a funeral committee saw to it that the body of the deceased was cleaned, dressed and placed in a casket ready for viewing: a process known as the Minor Preparations (*Xiao Lian* 小殮). Today the Minor Preparations are often combined with the Major Preparations (*Da Lian* 大殮) which are described in more detail later.

Traditionally the Minor Preparations proceeded in the following way. First, the body of the dead was carried to a bed reserved for the ritual. Buddhist families followed this step with a round of prayer, gathering around the body and chanting Buddhist mantras for eight hours. They did this because Chinese Buddhists believe that a person's soul remains aware of events in the mortal world, even after death. With their mantras, Buddhist adherents hoped to help souls find peace. Some families prayed during the Soul Conjuring stage rather than during the Minor Preparations.

After this optional round of prayer, members of the same sex as the dead person washed their limbs and hair. In the past, the water used so called "lively water" (*Huo Shui* 活水) in contrast to well water, called "dead water" (*Si Shui* 死水).

Once the dead person had been cleaned and dried, their family would prepare mortuary clothes known as the Longevity Clothes (*Shou Yi* 壽衣) for them. Before putting them on, they would wrap the body in new cotton cloth. Wealthier families could use silk instead of cotton cloth if they wished. If the deceased was male then their family could gave them a green or teal Confucius hat. Mortuary clothes were used because the ancient Chinese believed it was inauspicious for a person to be buried naked.

After dressing the deceased their family would present a Farewell Offering (*Ci Sheng* 辭生) to their soul with the oversight of a Daoist priest. Usually the offering took the form of a regular meal. Next, the family relocated the body of the deceased to a special bed for viewing. Only later, after the Minor Preparations were complete, would they be placed into a casket proper.

In accordance with tradition, the area are around the body had to be decorated. Normally families chose to decorate deathbeds with the deceased's clothing, shoes and personal effects. Cats were forbidden from jumping on deathbeds or over a dead person's body as it was believe this would precipitate bad luck. These decorations were of course different if the body was to be placed in the casket.

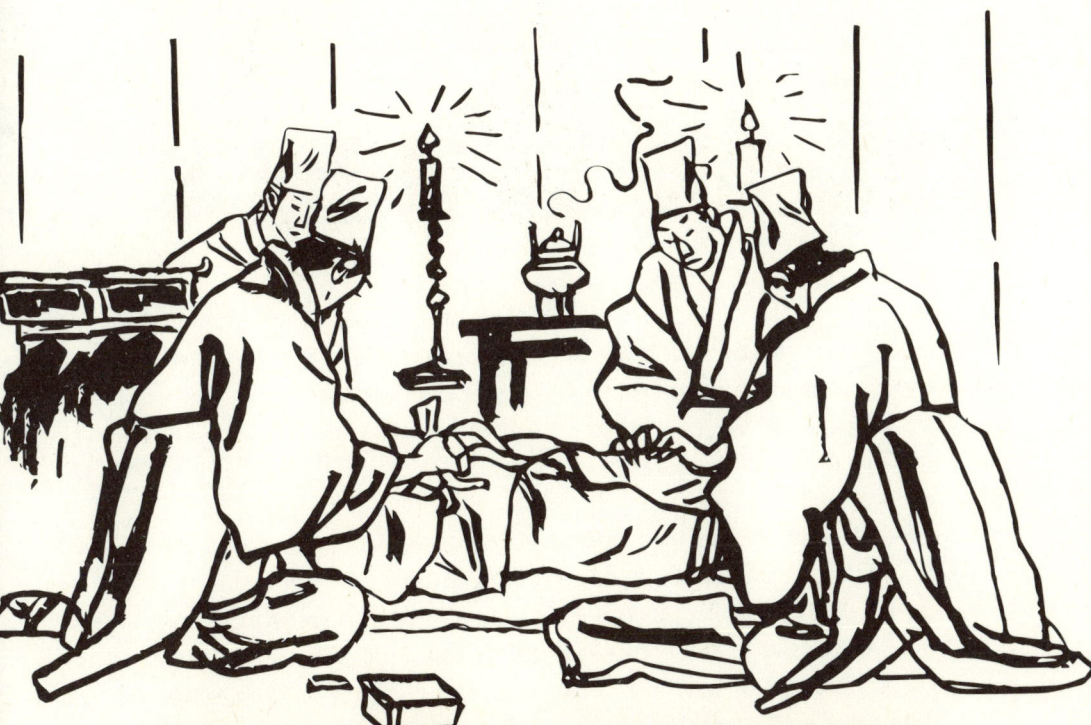

The Minor Preparations (*Xiao Lian* 小殮) revolved around preparing the body for viewing.

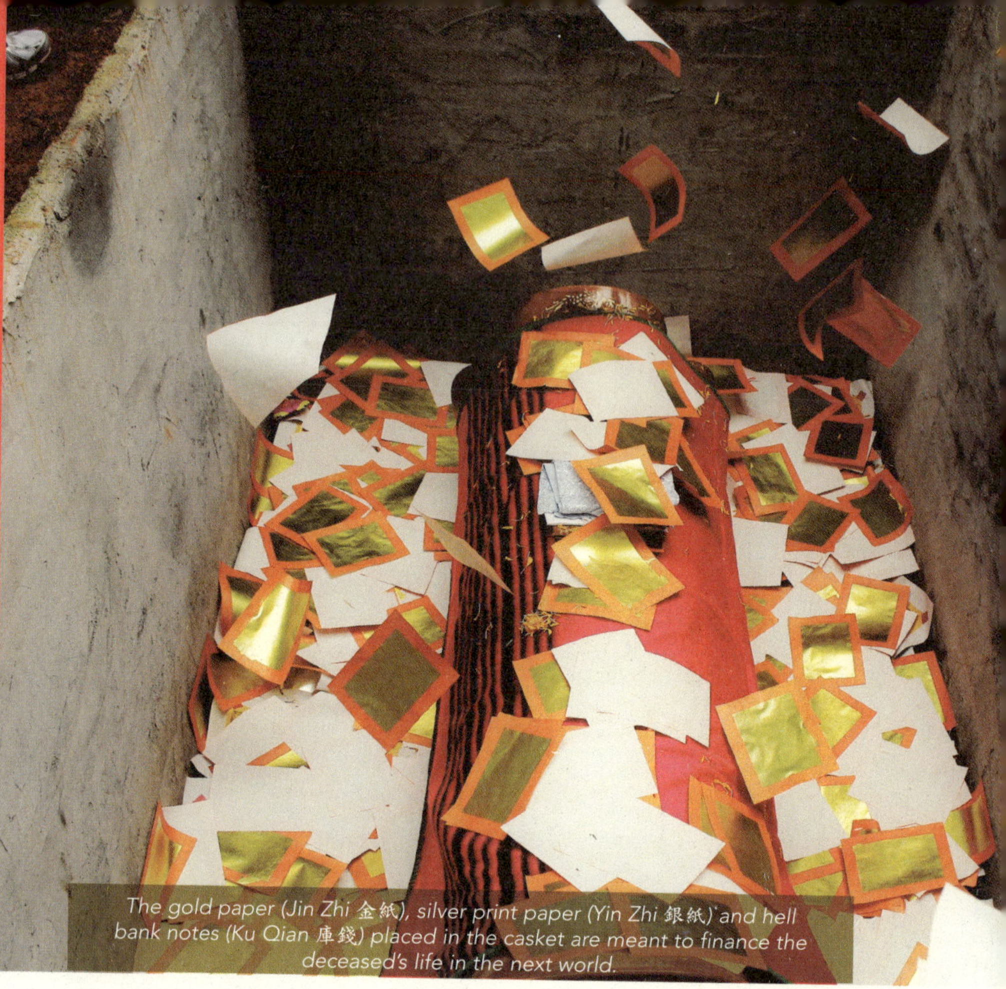

The gold paper (Jin Zhi 金紙), silver print paper (Yin Zhi 銀紙) and hell bank notes (Ku Qian 庫錢) placed in the casket are meant to finance the deceased's life in the next world.

Before putting a body into a casket, the outside of the casket was coated with Tung oil and lime to prevent leakage. Three layers of joss paper including a layer of gold paper (*Jin Zhi* 金紙) followed by silver print paper (*Yin Zhi* 銀紙) and finally hell bank notes (*Ku Qian* 庫錢) were used to help the deceased pay their way in the afterlife.

After preparing the joss paper, a family would place a wooden board decorated with a seven-star pattern referred to as the Board of the Big Dipper (*Qi Xing Ban* 七星板) on top of it. Next, they prepared the deceased's pillow, filling it with silver print paper instead of feathers. With this, the casket was considered complete and a body could be placed inside it along with various personal effects as described.

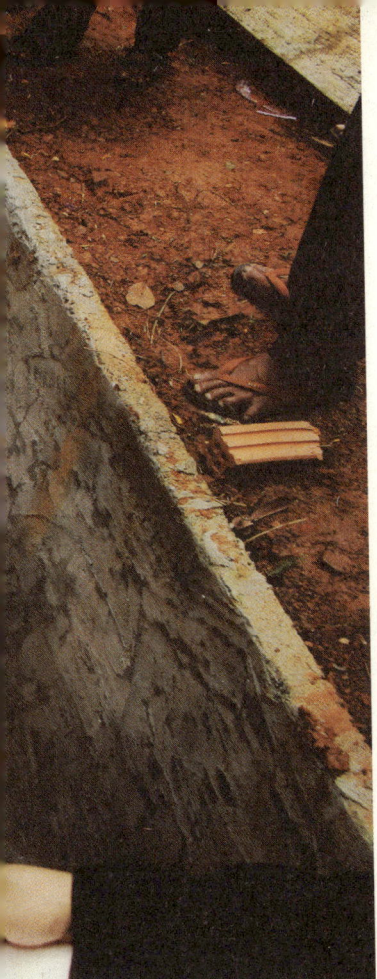

In the final stage of the Minor Preparations, a family would place items into the deceased's mouth in a custom called Feeding (*Han Lian* 含殮). Usually this was done with a handful of rice grains but wealthier families could use money, silver coins, pearls or even jade objects. The purpose of this act was to care for the soul and ensure that it wouldn't be reincarnated as a hungry ghost (*Er Gui* 餓鬼). It was also seen as an expression of filial piety and compassion. Any family which denied the dead this custom would be seen as cruel and unfilial.

Once the Feeding practice was completed, the family would cover the deceased's face with a piece of yellow or white paper or cloth in a custom known as the Veiling. This was done because the Chinese believed that the dead person's ghost might find their dead body's appearance unflattering. As such, the veiling was a simple courtesy for the dead. It also spared living people from the frightening sight of a corpse.

After a veil was in place a body was deemed ready for viewing. Anyone who wished to see the deceased's face could temporarily remove the cloth or paper being used to cover it, as long as they obtained the family's permission to do so.

The Visitation

The stage after the Minor Preparations (*Xiao Lian* 小殮) where relatives or close friends of the deceased were allowed to view the body was traditionally called the Visitation (*Bin* 殯).

During the Visitation period a family was allowed to grieve in public while wearing mourning clothes. The duration of the Visitation could be extended while a family searched for a place with the correct Yin Feng Shui to bury their loved one.

After finding the right location, families prepared a table in the area where the body was laid out and placed an incense on it: an offering to the dead person's soul. The family would also hire a Buddhist monk or Daoist priest to perform the necessary rites. All in all, this part of the funeral process could last several days until it was an auspicious time to move on.

In the past, two viewings were held after the Minor Preparations had been completed, namely the Private Session (*Jia Dian* 家奠) and the Public Session (*Gong Dian* 公奠). The two viewing sessions could last between one and three days or more. During one of these days, families would hold a wake (*Shou Ling* 守靈) at night. Once both viewing sessions were over they could proceed to carry out the Major Preparations (*Da Lian* 大殮) and ultimately seal their dead loved one's casket.

In modern times, the Visitation step is limited to a day or two.

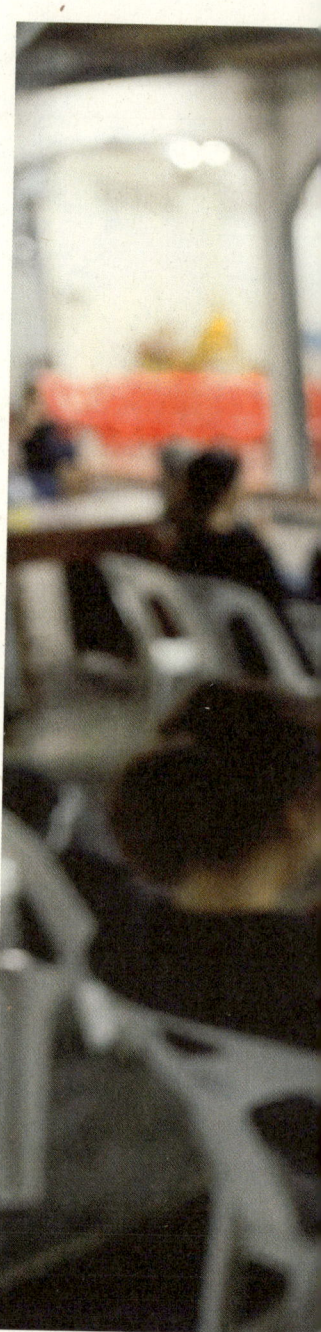

禮俗

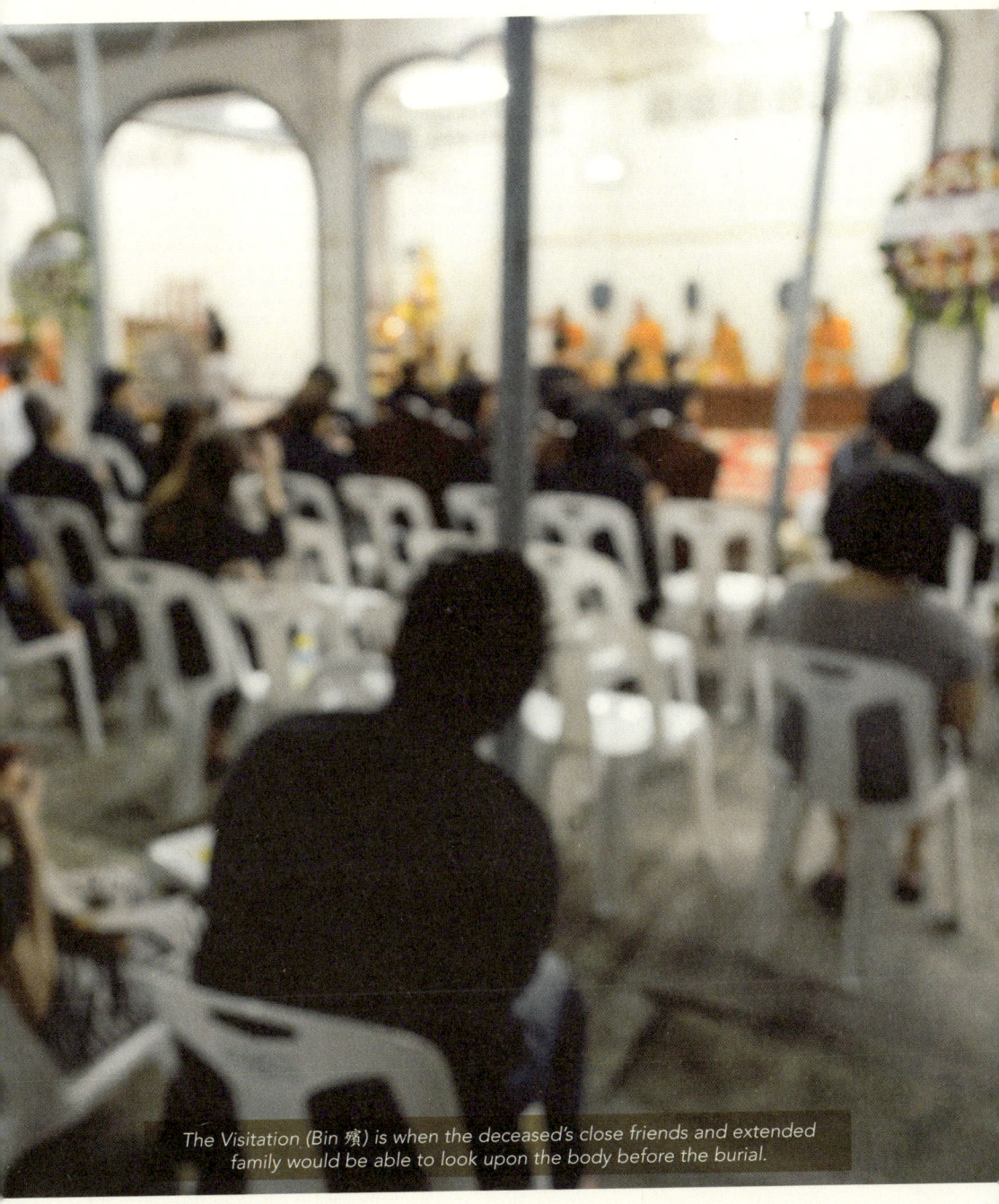

The Visitation (Bin 殯) is when the deceased's close friends and extended family would be able to look upon the body before the burial.

The Private Session (*Jia Dian* 家奠)

Traditionally, the Private Session was a viewing held in a funeral hall, reserved for the family of the deceased.

The Private Session only began once everyone had arrived. Attendance was compulsory for all family members and by this point it had usually been several days since a person died: plenty of time for anyone travelling overseas to arrive.

In a traditional Chinese funeral, the deceased person's body was already on their deathbed when it was time for a Private Session to begin. Once it did, the body was moved into their casket for the viewing. This part could at times overlap with the Major Preparations where the casket would be sealed immediately afterwards. As the Minor Preparations and the Major Preparations are often combined in modern funerals this step is largely irrelevant today as a body would already be in its casket by this point.

Some families expected everyone in attendance at a Private Session to openly display sadness – anyone who didn't was seen as unfilial. In the past, Private Sessions took a long time but today they only last around half an hour at the longest.

During the Private Session many families prepared an offering known as the Five Sacrifices (*Wu Sheng* 五牲) for the prayer session to follow. The offering contained pork, chicken, duck or goose, seafood and animal guts and was placed on a table in the funeral hall.

Next, families changed into their mortuary clothes and took turns praying to the deceased. These prayers were led by the deceased's oldest son or highest-ranking relatives.

Once everyone had finished their prayers, families would kneel in front of the body of the deceased. Buddhist monks or Daoist priests hired for the ceremony would then chant mantras or read Daoist scripts associated with the Private Session. This step took some 40 minutes and all family members were expected to remain kneeling throughout. It was not uncommon for family members to wail in grief at this point.

To conclude the Private Session, a family simply left the immediate vicinity of the body. In modern funerals the Private Session is followed immediately by the Public Session and burial.

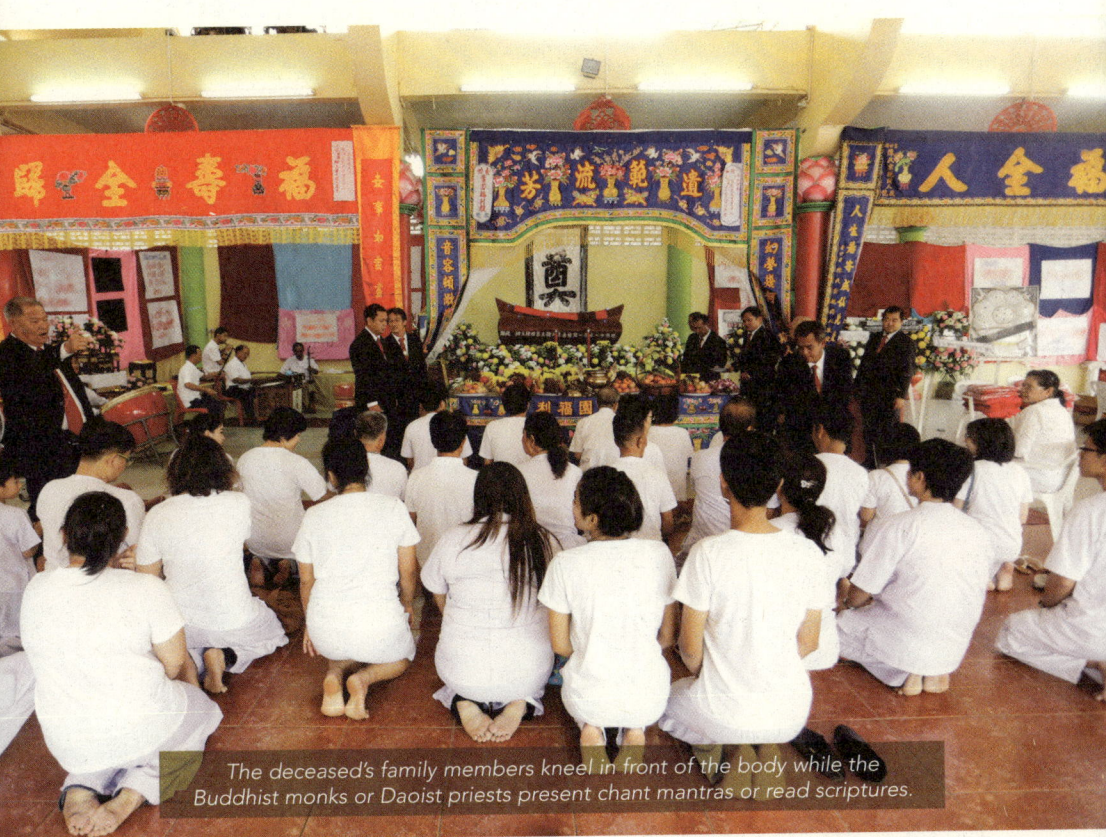

The deceased's family members kneel in front of the body while the Buddhist monks or Daoist priests present chant mantras or read scriptures.

The Wake (*Shou Ling* 守靈)

Traditionally, a wake was held on the day that a person passed away, lasting until they were buried. After moving a dead person's body to their deathbed, members of their family would take turns sleeping and watching over the body on mattresses placed on either side of it. Male relatives of the deceased stayed on the left side and female relatives stayed on the right.

The purpose of a wake was twofold. Firstly, wakes were believed to help prevent the deceased from "clashing" with any other souls that might be present - it was believed that by keeping watch over a body, filial children would scare other souls away. On a practical level, relatives could protect a body from animals like cats who would otherwise be tempted to bite or maul at it. This could otherwise supposedly create static and cause the body to rise: an extremely inauspicious occurrence.

Today, these beliefs have been largely cast aside.

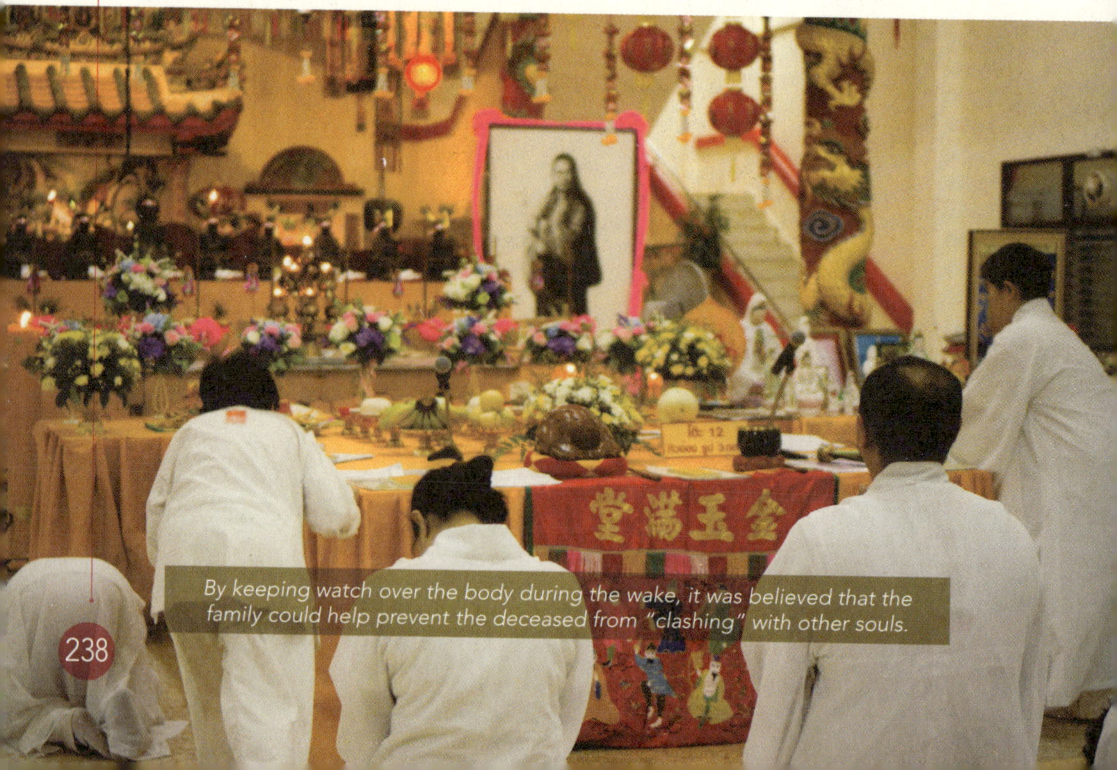

By keeping watch over the body during the wake, it was believed that the family could help prevent the deceased from "clashing" with other souls.

The Public Session (*Gong Dian* 公奠)

As its name implies, the Public Session gave the general public an opportunity to enter the funeral hall, mourn the passing of the deceased and pay their respects.

Public Sessions were meant for people who knew the deceased but were not related like friends, neighbours, colleagues, business associates and fellow club or organisation members. Such people were notified about the specifics of the Public Session in the dead person's obituary. If the dead person was a famous figure like a politician then complete strangers could attend the Public Session.

Attendance aside, there were few differences between the Public Session and Private Session.

Buddhist or Daoist ceremonies were not performed at a Public Session. Loud or overt displays of grief were also frowned upon. This aside, a Public Session was like a shorter repeat of the private one, proceeding as follows.

At the appointed time, guests arrived at the funeral hall and present a white envelope (*Bo Jin* 帛金) filled with money to the family. In this way, guest's offered financial assistance during the hard time. The sum of money within the envelope had to be an odd number as even numbers were seen as inauspicious.

What constitutes an "odd" amount of money varies by country today. In a Malaysian Chinese funeral, RM110 in the form of 11 RM10 notes is appropriate as the odd number of notes fulfils the criteria of an "odd" amount of money. In Hong Kong the total amount given should be odd, i.e: HKD101.

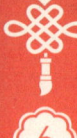

Traditionally, once all the guests had arrived and entered the funeral hall, the host – usually one of the deceased's family members – announced the beginning of the Public Session. This was followed by a eulogy and a minute of silence for guests to quietly mourn. Afterwards, a family member from the Funeral Service Committee would express their gratitude to everyone in attendance.

Next an honourable guest – like the deceased person's workplace supervisor – offered the deceased person some incense and gave a memorial speech ending with a bow to a picture of the deceased as a display of respect. The family of the deceased traditionally reciprocated the gesture. Any other guests who wished to pay their respects then formed a line. When their time came, they offered incense and bowed to a picture of the deceased.

Once all guests had said their goodbyes then the Public Session was over.

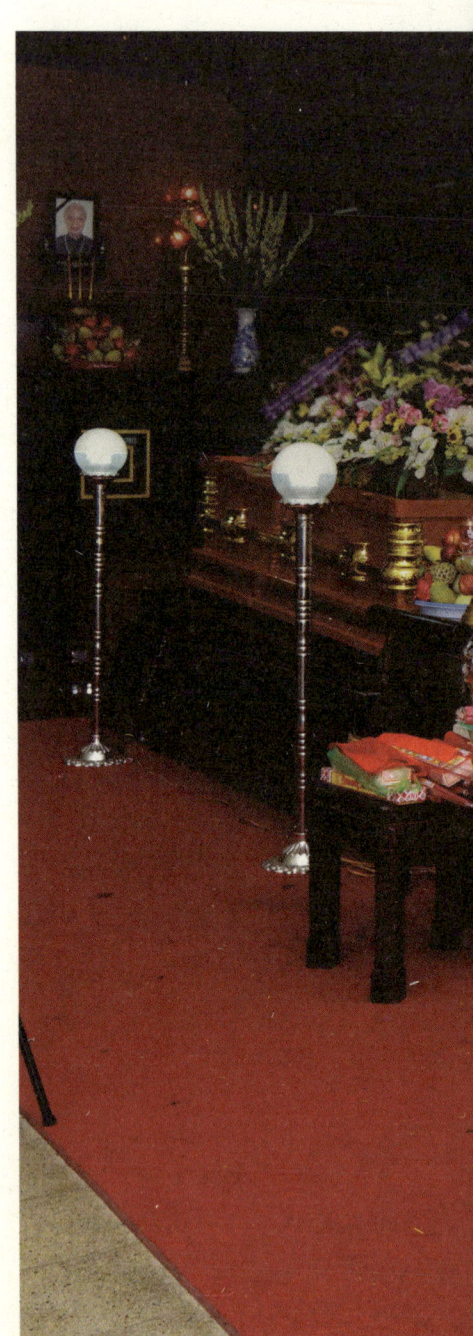

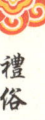

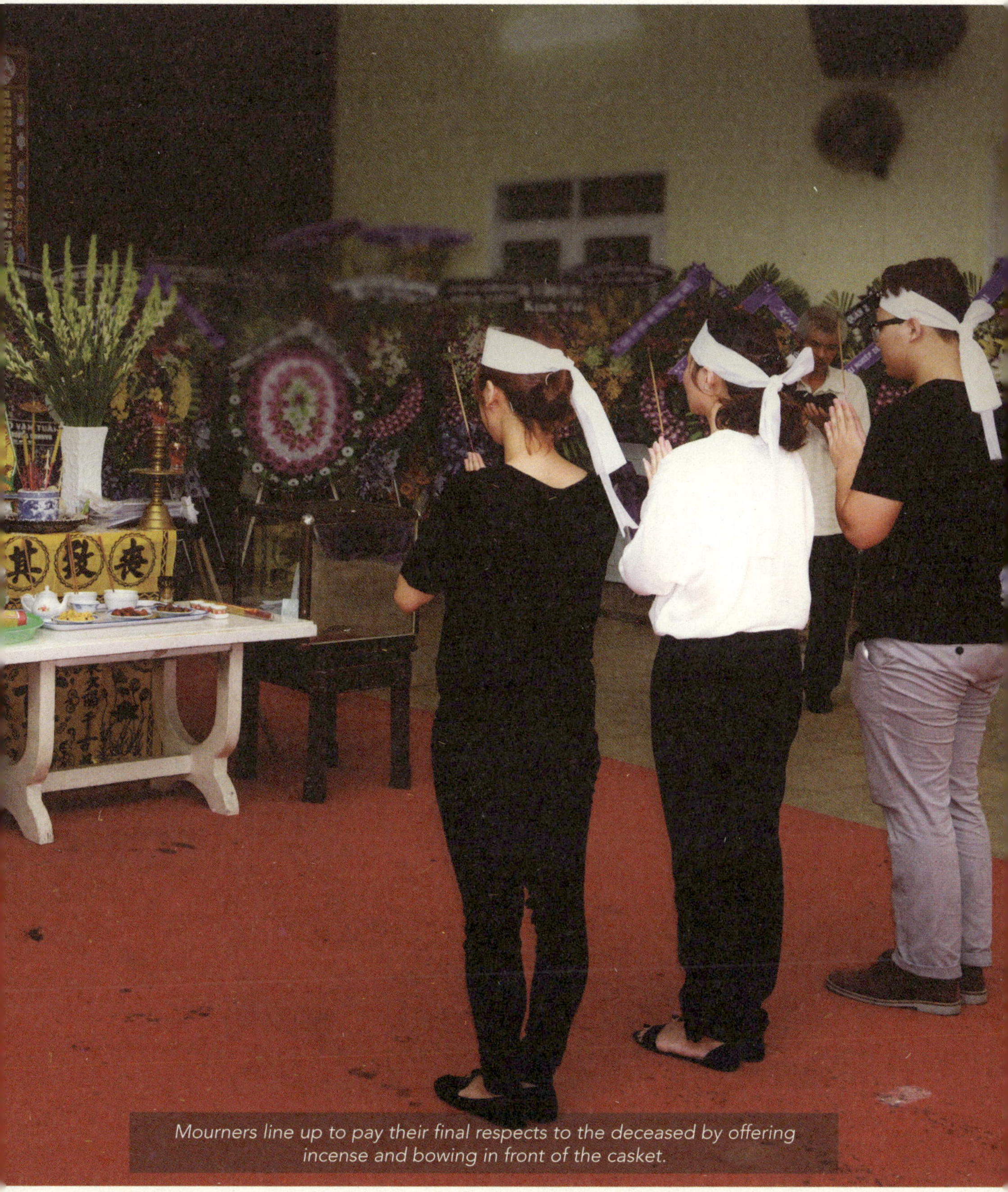

禮俗

Mourners line up to pay their final respects to the deceased by offering incense and bowing in front of the casket.

The Funeral

After the Public Session had ended a family could proceed with the funeral itself.

In accordance with tradition funerals began with the Major Preparations (*Da Lian* 大殮). After they were complete, family members prepared to join the funeral procession (*Chu Bin* 出殯) by changing their mourning clothes.

In recent times, funerals differ significantly from their traditional counterparts.

In the past, the funeral itself was usually held the day after the Public Session. In modern times, both are usually held on the same day for convenience. Modern funerals also combine the Minor Preparations and the Major Preparations. Most notably, bodies are placed immediately into a casket rather than onto a deathbed and then into a casket. Because of this, funeral service providers can skip parts of the Major Preparation process.

Although burials are the traditional option, cremation is acceptable if a person requests it in their will. In countries like Singapore where spare land is in short supply, it is actually encouraged.

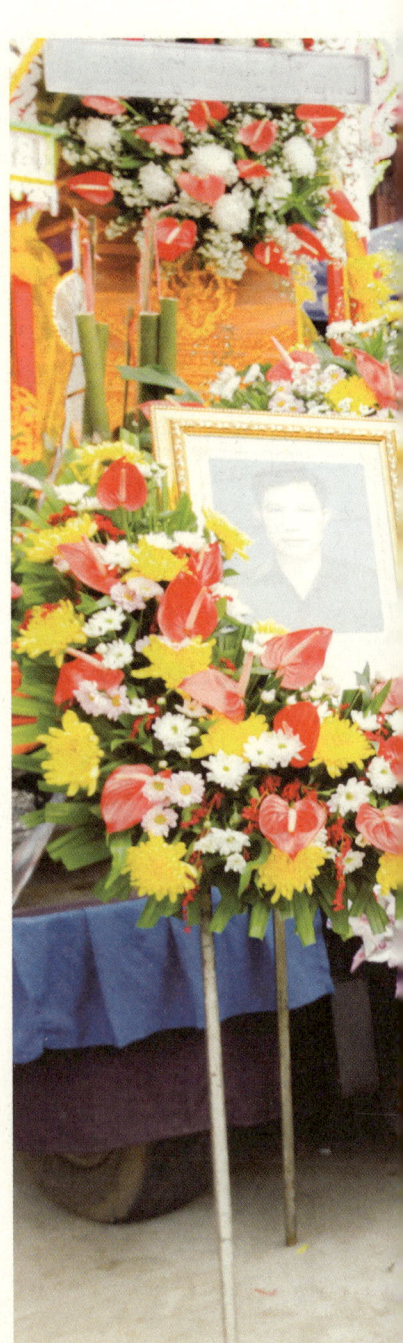

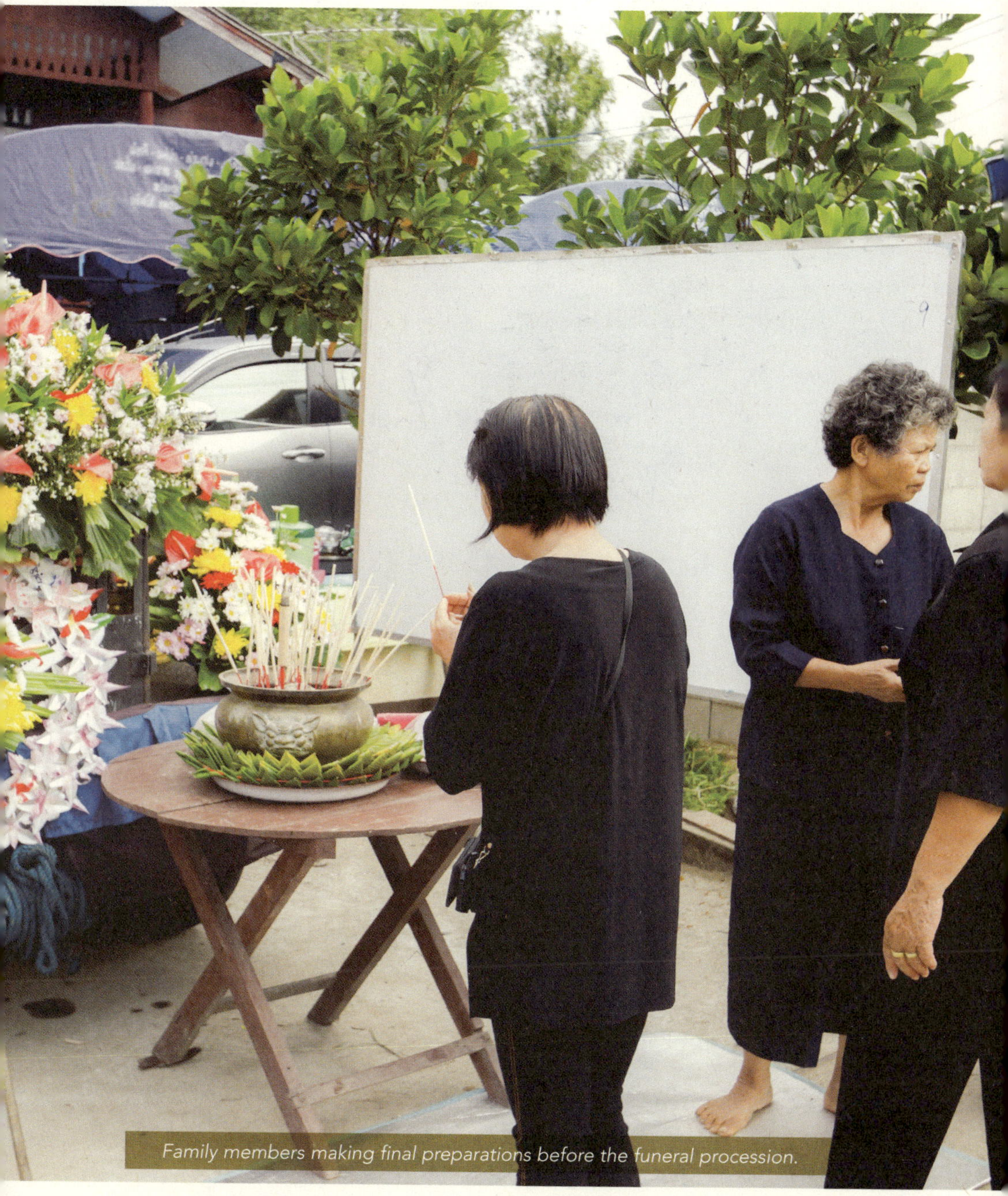

禮俗

Family members making final preparations before the funeral procession.

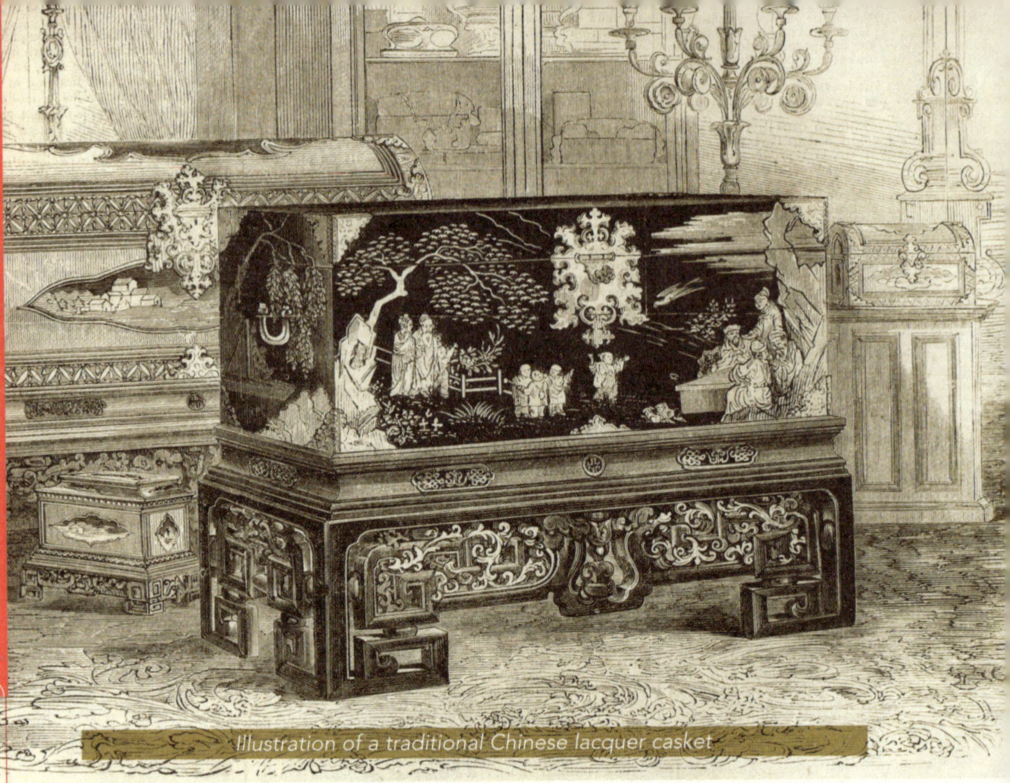

Illustration of a traditional Chinese lacquer casket

The Major Preparations (*Da Lian* 大殮)

In the past, the Major Preparations included removing a dead person's body from their deathbed at the end of the final viewing session and placing it in the casket. In accordance with tradition, this was followed by an offering of Five Sacrifices identical to those presented during the Public Session.

Next, the attending Daoist priest recited relevant chants in a custom known as Starting the Hood of the Car (*Qi Che Tou* 起車頭) or simply Starting. The chants were led by the leading family member and professionals hired for the ceremony, including the aforementioned priest, casket service supervisor and their subordinates. The leading family member was chosen based on their proximity to the deceased. If the deceased's father was still alive then they would be made the leading member. If not, their uncle, son or brother would be chosen with age being given priority. Traditionally, the same system was used for married women: in death, they were thought of as part of their birth family again.

Once the right family member had been chosen a family would prepare a tray, axe, red envelope and five nails with colourful pieces of cloth attached to the end of each one. The envelope was filled with money for the casket workers. As for the five nails; the one held by the leading family member was considered the Master Nail (*Zhu Ding* 主釘) while the rest were held by the casket workers and called the Auxiliary Nails (*Fu Ding* 副釘).

To kick off the Starting ceremony, a casket worker would guide the leading family member through the process of sealing the casket. While the worker sang Daoist chants, they would guide the leading family member to hammer the Master Nail into the end of the casket where the deceased's head was positioned. The workers would then hammer the remaining Auxiliary Nails into the four corners of the casket. Once this was done, the Starting ceremony was over and a family could change into mourning clothes and began preparing for the funeral procession as mentioned earlier.

As modern Chinese funerals combine the Minor and Major Preparations, the distinction between them has become blurred. In modern times, bodies are placed inside their casket before the first viewing takes place. Thus, Major Preparations today consist of little more than nailing a casket shut and preparing it for a funeral procession. From there on, the Major Preparations have remained unchanged.

While the majority of the family members present were changing, the loading (*Shang Kang Chuang* 上扛床) of the body in preparation for the funeral procession took place. This was done using something known as a bier (*Kang Chuang* 扛床), - basically a frame that a casket is placed on to facilitate easily lifting.

Traditionally, family members who were chosen as pallbearers were tasked with doing this and carrying the lifeless body throughout the entire funeral procession. In modern times, families are entrusted with carrying a casket to a funeral coach hired for the ceremony which then leads the procession. In this case a bier is needed to initially lift the casket, load it into the funeral coach and eventually lower it into the grave.

Once a family was ready, a marching band hired for the ceremony would lead the funeral procession. The eldest son of the deceased would lead the rest of their family behind the band. Additionally, the eldest son would carry a bamboo walking stick referred to as the Wand of Sorrow (*Shuai Zhang* 衰杖) to stop them from collapsing during the journey. This walking stone is known colloquially as the Wailing Stick (*Ku Sang Bang* 哭喪棒) – a pejorative term which can be used in an insulting way.

When everyone was ready to begin marching (*Song Zang* 送葬), the eldest son was expected to pick up a clay pot and smash it while crying in a custom called the Pot Smashing Ritual (*Shuai Pen* 摔盆). If the pot did not shatter, he was expected to step on it immediately. With this auspicious ritual complete the marching could begin.

Throughout the journey to the burial site, the marching band would play funeral music in order to inform passers-by of their purpose. Additionally, a Funeral Lantern (*Sang Deng* 喪燈) was placed at the front of the procession while a Happiness Lantern (*Xi Deng* 喜燈) was placed at the rear.

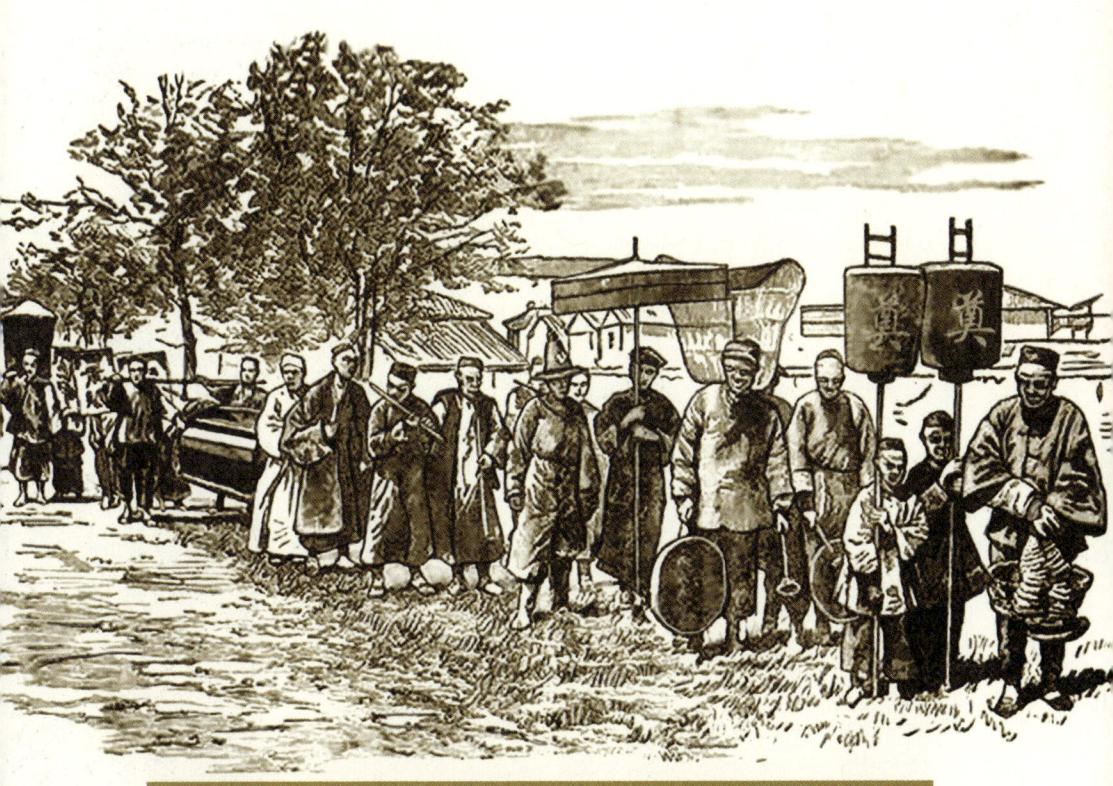

Nowadays, the transportation of the casket is handled by people hired for the task instead of the family members like in ancient times.

When the procession arrived at the burial site, the bereaved family lit a torch and tosses it into the grave. This practice, known as the House Heating Ceremony (*Nuan Wo* 暖窩), was done to make the tomb more comfortable for the deceased. The practice is based on the Feng Shui principle that tombs are Yin Houses. Throwing a torch into a tomb is very much like lighting the fireplace in a new home from a Feng Shui perspective.

The Burial

The idea that ancestral burial sites exert an influence on living descendants has existed since ancient times in China, along with the Feng Shui concept of Yin Houses. In the past, however, only the rich and powerful could afford to select their ancestral burial sites. Commoners could not afford to hire Feng Shui masters and thus they were unable to choose suitable burial plots let alone obtain them. Convenience was far more likely to influence the average person's declension making than Feng Shui considerations.

Those who had a little more money than average but couldn't afford to preselect their burial site could choose to have their family rebury them in a place with better Feng Shui in the future. In this instance their first, temporary burial was known as their Inauspicious Burial (*Xiong Zang* 凶葬) and their ultimate burial was known as their Auspicious Burial (*Ji Zang* 吉葬).

Nowadays funeral services are far more affordable and accessible. "Moving house" for the sake of procuring a burial plot with better Feng Shui is too much to ask for most people now and it is understandably no longer the norm.

A basic Chinese grave is prepared several days ahead of the funeral. A square hole is dug roughly 2.7m into the ground, wide enough for a casket. In the past, families would pray at their ancestral tomb and offer joss paper to the gods before digging a grave. Today grave digging is usually handled by a third party as part of a funeral service.

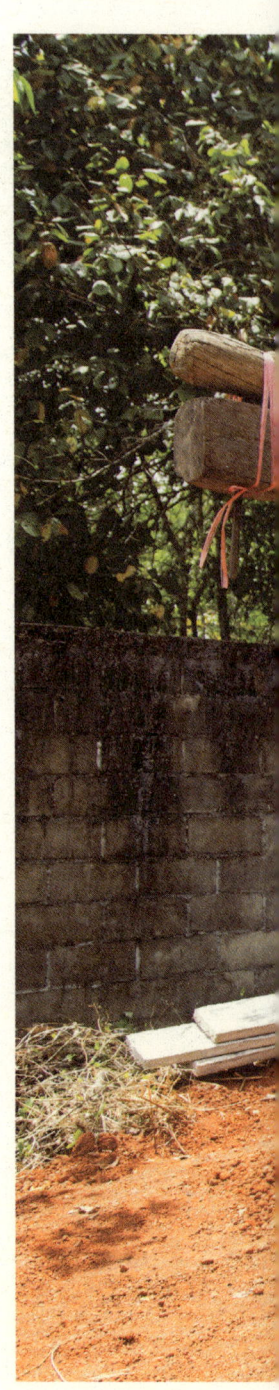

禮俗

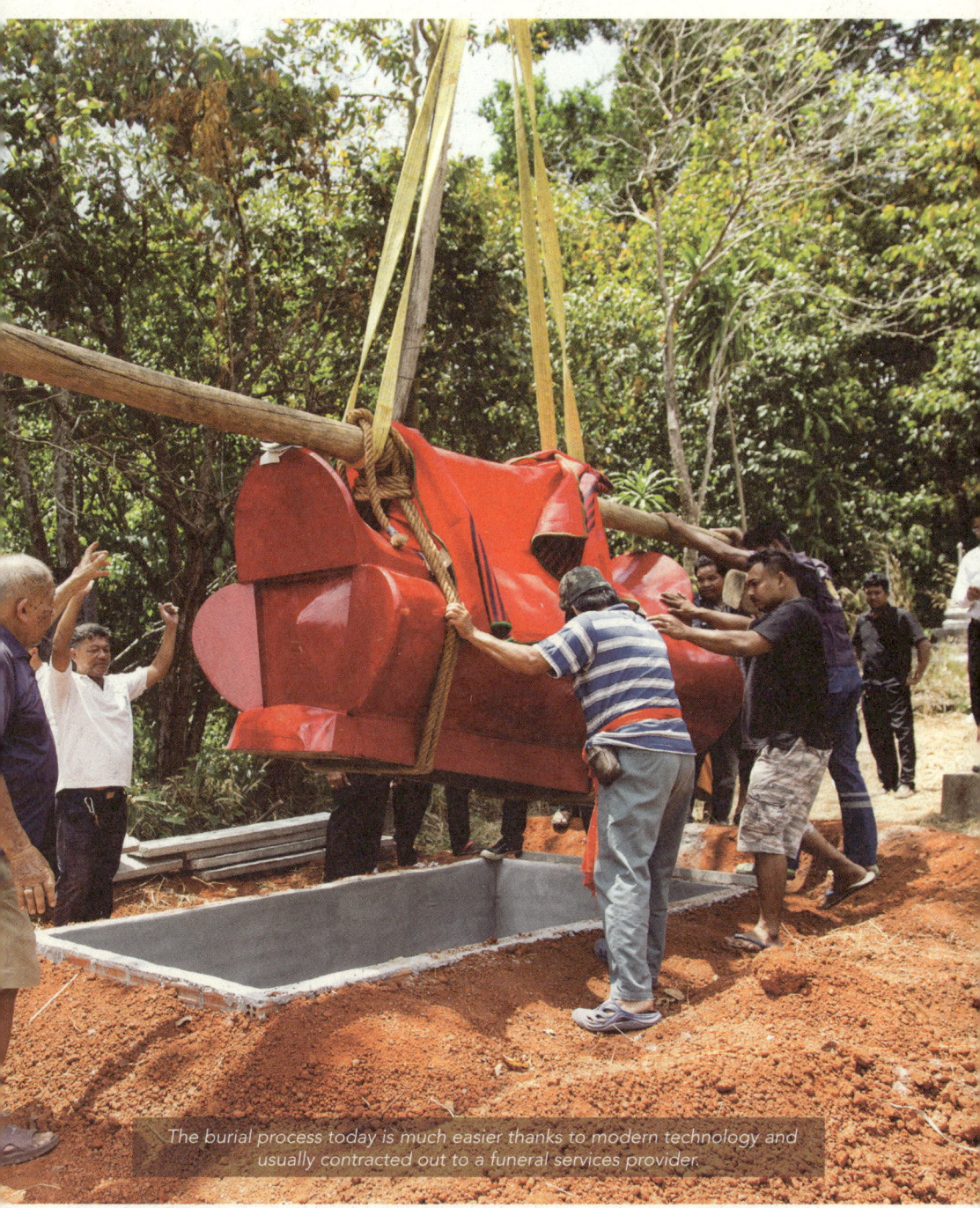

The burial process today is much easier thanks to modern technology and usually contracted out to a funeral services provider.

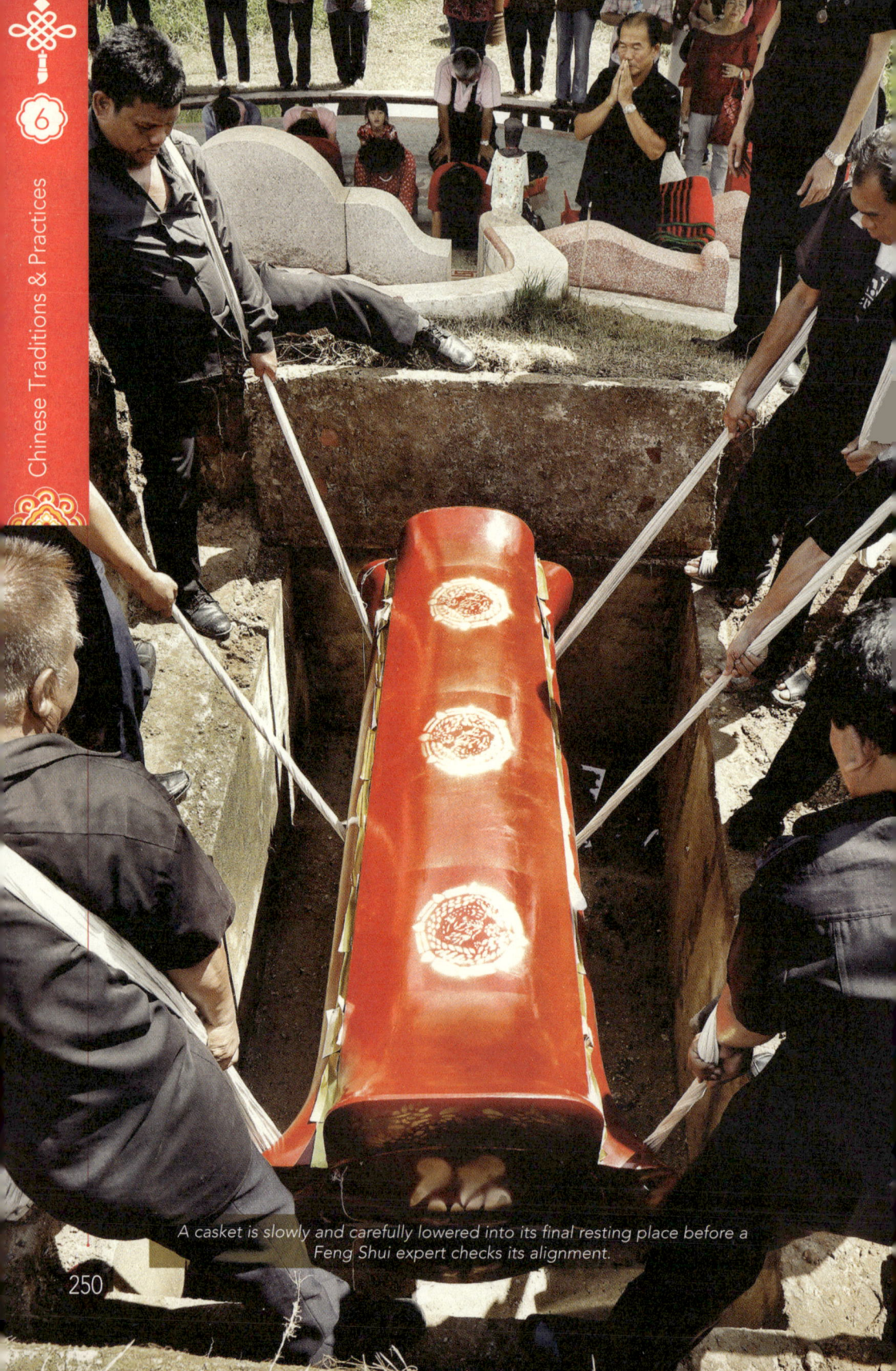

A casket is slowly and carefully lowered into its final resting place before a Feng Shui expert checks its alignment.

The Inauspicious Burial (*Xiong Zang* 凶葬)

Traditionally, families carried out the temporary inauspicious burial for hygienic reasons. Once a body was safely underground, they had free reign to find a proper burial site for them.

Although the Inauspicious Burial is a temporary one it has always carried a great deal of importance. As such, an auspicious date had to be chosen for an inauspicious burial. To do this, families viewed the deceased person's BaZi chart – a destiny chart plotted using their time of birth. The deceased's next of kin's BaZi charts were also taken into account unless they had an impractically large family. In such cases only their immediate family members and eldest grandchild were take into consideration.

On the day of the funeral the casket was placed next to the burial pit when the procession arrived at the burial site. Once family members had paid their respects, casket workers would break off a small portion off the foot of the casket for the purposes of ventilation and allowing putrefaction fluids to flow out. This procedure was known as Releasing the Stopper (*Fang Shuan* 放栓) and it also helped hasten the decomposition of the body.

Next, the casket was lowered into its grave and its alignment was checked by someone with Feng Shui experience. The ropes used to lower the casket were then removed and the casket was covered with a red cloth and a dash of rice wine. Next the deceased's eldest son was expected to grab a handful of soil and scatter it over the casket. Each of the dead person's relatives then lined up to do the same. Once everyone had finished the funeral service provider would bury the casket with the family's assistance.

Once a grave was covered, a tombstone was to be put in place and the Worshipping of the Deity of Earth (*Si Hou Tu* 祀後土) would begin. This was done with the intention of protecting the grave and the deceased. The ceremony was usually overseen by a Feng Shui master, Daoist priest or Buddhist monk hired for the funeral.

In the following ceremony, the deceased's soul was invited to temporarily reside in an item called a spirit tablet (*Shen Zhu Pai* 神主牌). This tablet was placed in front of the tombstone and was protected from the elements with a black umbrella held by a family member. Attendees then presented five offerings which included prosperity cakes (*Fa Gao* 發糕), rice, wine and silver joss paper before praying and burning joss sticks.

Next, a custom named Calling the Dragon (*Hu Long Yi Shi* 呼龍儀式) was conducted by the priest or monk present for the purpose of activating the Qi of the burial site. This ensured that the deceased's descendants were blessed and protected from misfortune.

At the conclusion of the funeral, the eldest son or the family member chosen to fill that position would change into fresh clothes and place the spirit tablet inside a container filled with rice for the journey home. During this return journey, the order of the lanterns were to be reversed with the Happiness Lantern leading the procession and the Funeral Lantern borne by those at the rear. When the procession arrived at the relevant house those who did not follow the procession for whatever reason had to come out to invite the spirit tablet inside.

Once the spirit tablet had been removed from the container of rice it was placed on an altar along with a photograph of the deceased. The deceased person's family then offered prayers again along with flowers and fruits. They then bowed three times. They repeated the whole process in the morning and evening for seven or one hundred days, a ritual which ties into the post-funeral ceremonies described in the next section.

The Auspicious Burial (Ji Zang 吉葬)

Several years after the Inauspicious Burial, the body of the deceased was excavated for their Auspicious Burial.

The waiting period between a person's Inauspicious Burial and excavation varied. In general, older people were left in the ground for longer. If it was discovered that a person's body had not decomposed properly yet then they would be buried for another 11 months.

People who died before their 16th birthday were not exhumed. People who died before the age of 30 could be exhumed after five to seven years and people who were approximately 40 could be exhumed in six to seven years. People who died aged around 50 could be exhumed after six to nine years had passed.

Regardless, when enough time had passed an auspicious date and time was chosen to exhume the deceased person's bones. In preparation, family members were contacted, offerings were made and a burial urn was purchased. The urn had to be large enough for human remains and they often had a decorative exterior.

On the day of exhumation, the burial plot was cleansed. Sandalwood powder was then placed on the ground and two paper ingots were placed on top of it. Holding seven pieces of joss paper in both hands, the specialist hired for the ceremony would light the papers and read a special incantation.

Next, everyone attending the event was expected to pray to the deceased and the Deity of Earth before digging could begin. Once the grave had been dug, the unenviable task of collecting the dead person's skeleton could begin: first the arm bones, then the shoulder bones, the torso and finally the skull.

It was important to ensure that the bones were never exposed to direct sunlight so a canopy or large umbrella was usually erected above the grave. The individual collecting the bones was required to address the deceased in a formal manner and family members were expected to withhold their tears – crying was seen as inauspicious.

When all 206 bones had been retrieved they were first arranged in the form of a person and then cleaned. Sandalwood powder was then burned for the purpose of smoking and dying the bones. The skull was wrapped in silk then gauze with excess material tied up to form a pigtail. The deceased's bones were painted with cinnabar to represent circulating blood. The same cinnabar was also used to paint facial features on the silk covering the skull. The whole skeleton was then linked with willow branches and red string so it could retain its structure.

Having been properly cleansed in advance, the burial urn was ready to serve its purpose. Joss paper arranged in the shape of a lotus flower was placed at the bottom before the bones were arranged in a foetal position inside the urn. Great care was taken when handling the bones, as it was believed that improper treatment of them could have unpleasant consequences for a family. For example, if a person's knee bones were positioned in a way that suggested they were kneeling then it was believed that all of their descendants would be followers not leaders.

Before the skull was placed inside, another stack of joss paper styled to resemble a lotus flower was placed inside. If the dead person was male then the skull was positioned tilted upwards slightly. This was believed to help their descendants "lift their heads" and prosper. If the dead person was female then the skull was tilted slightly downwards. This was believed to help their descendants care well for their families.

Before closing the urn, families asked for divine intervention to help with any illnesses they might have had. The ossuary where the urn was then placed was then "officiated" by placing two joss paper ingots inside and reciting an incantation while holding seven pieces of lit joss paper in each hand and drawing a talisman.

The urn had to be put in place 20 minutes after this step so as to prevent it from cracking due to the heat of the fire. During this process, a specialist would recite auspicious words while holding his right hand in a position referred to as a Daoist Hand Form or Mudra. Once inside the ossuary, the urn was sprinkled with water. This was done to wash the urn as well as help settle the earth under it so that it was less likely to fall over in the event of something such as an earthquake.

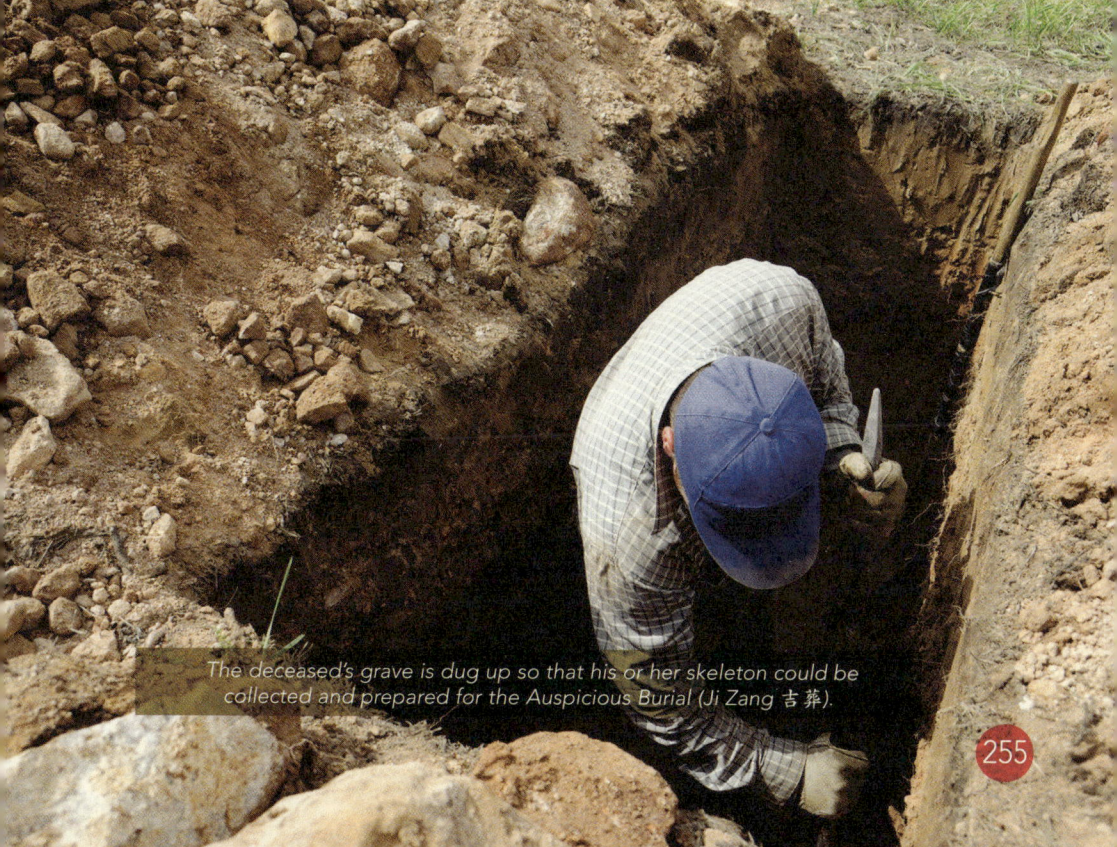

The deceased's grave is dug up so that his or her skeleton could be collected and prepared for the Auspicious Burial (Ji Zang 吉葬).

The Installation of the Tombstone

After the urn was placed in the ossuary, it was time to install the tombstone. The tombstone could be installed immediately or on another auspicious date.

To begin the installation of the tombstone, a ritual specialist would draw a talisman over it with their fingers while reciting a special incantation. Next, they tilted the tombstone backwards slightly. This represented the wish for the dead person's descendants to "lift their heads" and prosper. It was important that the tombstone conformed to the Gold Division – a formula used to determine it's alignment based on Feng Shui principles. At the same time, a measurement for the drain outlet of the half moon terrace in front of the tombstone was taken. The future locations of the Deity of the Earth's shrine and incense burner were chosen, too.

After doing all of the above, the gods were invited by prayer to give their blessings and protection. The family of the deceased then offered prayers and wine to the Deity of the Earth before praying directly to their dead relative. This officially brought the Auspicious Burial to an end.

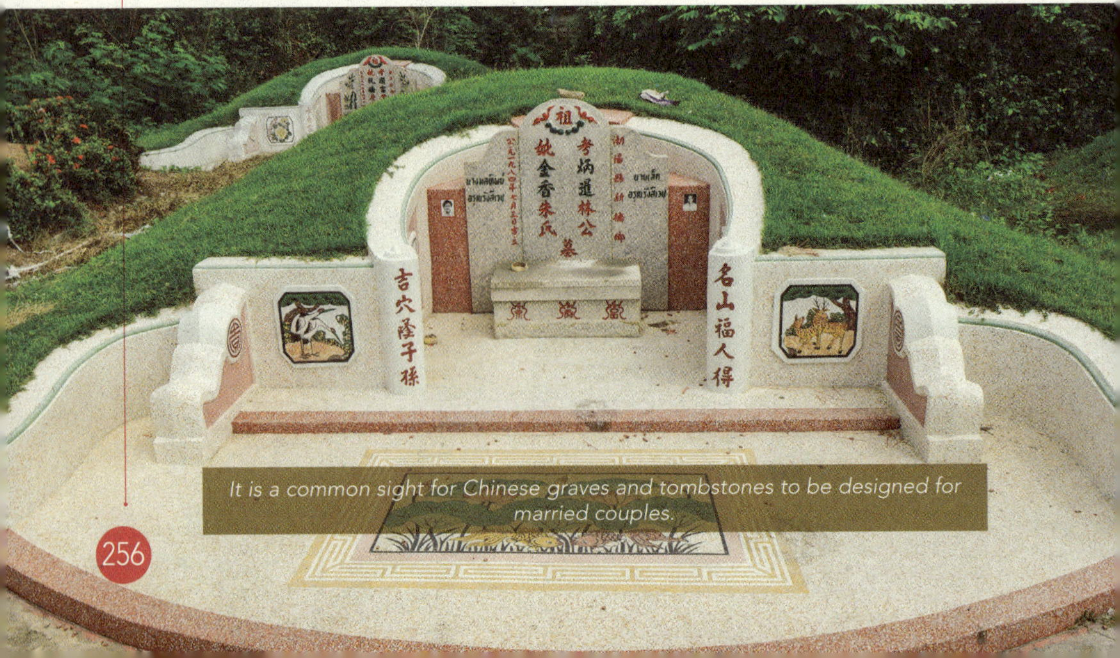

It is a common sight for Chinese graves and tombstones to be designed for married couples.

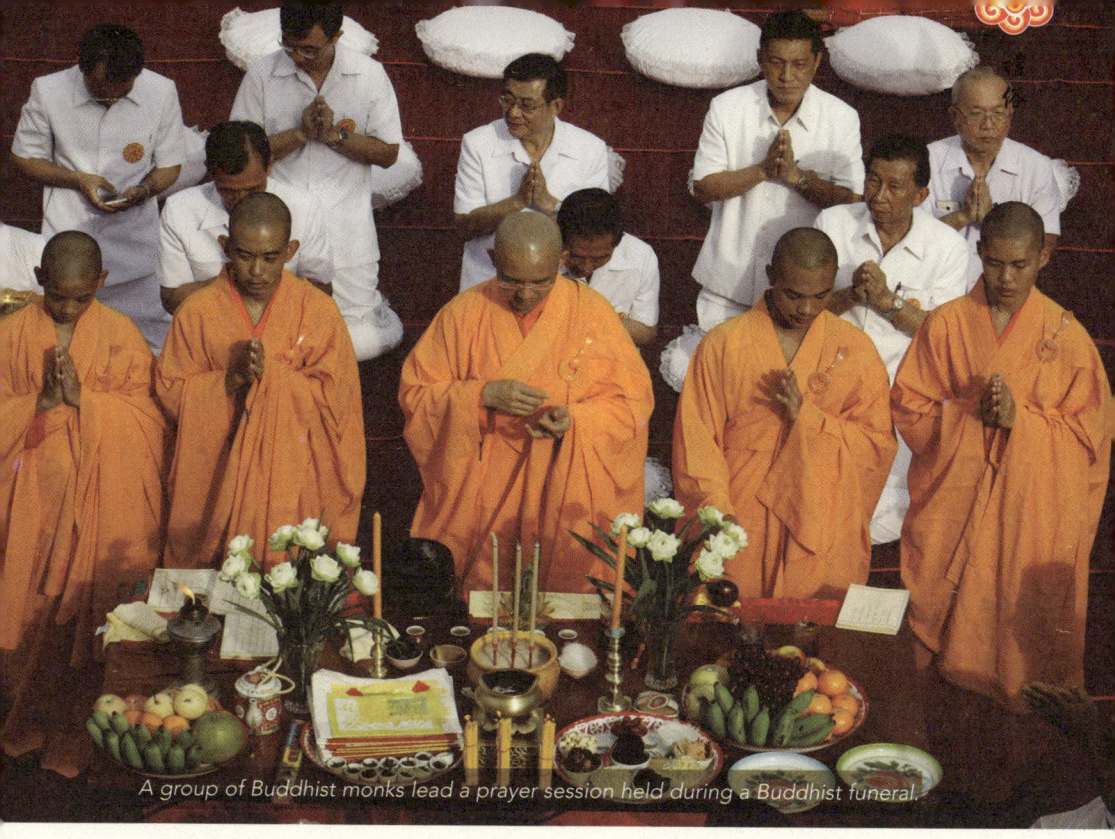
A group of Buddhist monks lead a prayer session held during a Buddhist funeral.

Post Funeral Practices

A Chinese funeral officially ended once a person had been buried. There are a number of post-funeral practices and ceremonies which families could observe including religious post-funeral ceremonies and a purely Confucian approach known as the Closure (*Ji* 祭). Many families carried out post-funeral traditions in the belief that they would help the soul of their loved one. On a more practical note, post-funeral traditions have helped many families come to terms with their loss.

The most well-known of post-funeral ceremonies are the Rite of the Seventh Day (*Zuo Qi* 做七), the Night of the Soul's Return (*Hui Hun Ye* 回魂夜) and the Hundredth Day Ceremony (*Bai Ri* 百日).

The Rite of the Seventh Day (*Zuo Qi* 做七)

The Rite of the Seventh Day is so old that its exact origins are unclear. Several different religions have laid claim to it including Daoism and Buddhism.

In Daoism, the number seven is special because it is related to the human soul: Daoists believe that a person's soul is comprised of 10 parts, divided into three Spirits (*Hun* 魂) and seven Primal Spirits (*Po* 魄) (Both words can be also be translated as "soul").

According to Daoist teachings, the three Spirits governed a person's mind and judgement and the seven Primal Spirits controlled their biological functions and impulses. Daoists would say that an intellectually disabled person has a missing or damaged Spirit but that their Primal Spirits are intact. If their intact Primal Spirits were damaged by a metaphysical accident, however, then they would surely perish as their soul would be fully compromised.

Daoists believe that a person takes 49 days to move from one stage of life to the next. For example, they believe that a newborn baby takes 49 days to develop a sense of reasoning. By the same token, a dead person's seven Primal Spirits must take 49 days to leave the mortal world. Because seven squared makes 49, the number seven is highly significant to Daoists.

Daoists conduct the Rite of the Seventh Day with the hope of resurrecting the deceased. In their eyes, there is a small chance that the soul of the deceased can be recalled before they depart for the underworld. Daoist families traditionally hold a ceremony seven times - once every seventh day - after a funeral until 49 days have passed.

Interestingly, the number seven is also special in Buddhism because it is associated with the concept of reincarnation.

Chinese Buddhists have incorporated many local myths and ideas over the centuries into their doctrine. Among these is the notion of 10 Courts of Hell (*Shi Cheng Di Yu* 十層地獄). According to Chinese Buddhist beliefs, a person's soul goes to Hell first regardless of their conduct in life. They can only be reincarnated after they have passed through all 10 courts. In this context, the number seven refers to the first seven Courts of Hell. Furthermore, it is said that the soul moves from one Court to the next every seven days. The Yama Kings (*Yan Luo Wang* 閻羅王) oversee each of the 10 Courts of Hell and sentence the dead based on their actions in life.

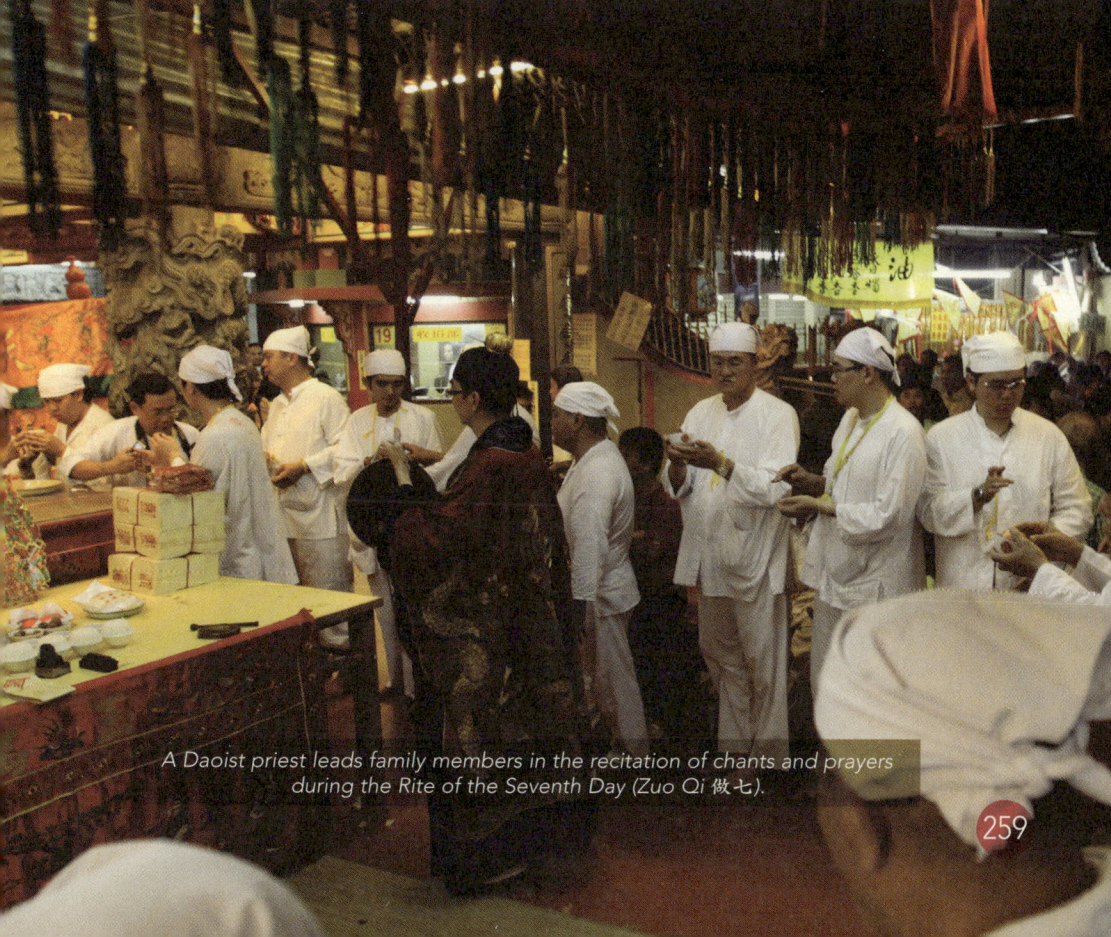

A Daoist priest leads family members in the recitation of chants and prayers during the Rite of the Seventh Day (Zuo Qi 做七).

In the context of Chinese Buddhism, the Rite of the Seventh Day serves as an attempt to appease the Yama Kings and help a soul make it safely through the 10 Courts of Hell. For this purpose, Chinese Buddhists conduct a ceremony seven times – once every seventh day – after a funeral just like Daoists. All being well, the deceased person's soul will be reincarnated in human form. A child who did not follow these practices properly was seen as unfilial and disrespectful. Additionally, this behaviour would presumably cause their ancestor to be reincarnated as an animal such as a pig.

Regardless of their aims, Daoists and Buddhists carry out the Rite of the Seventh Day in the same way. It usually begins in the Zi (子) hour of the day which spans 11pm to 1am. To begin the ceremony, a family puts on their mourning clothes, lights three incense candles and offers them to the Yama Kings. Next, they light another incense candle and pray directly to the soul of the deceased. They then give the soul approximately 20 minutes of peace to enjoy the incense.

After 20 minutes or so, families throw moon blocks (*Jiao Bei* 筊杯) and ask the dead person if they are done. If the moon blocks indicates "yes" then the rituals ends. If they indicate "no" then the family must wait a little longer and ask again. This process is repeated until the moon blocks give a positive answer. At this point, Buddhist monks or Daoist priests hired for the ceremony may chant mantras and scripts.

In a luxurious variation of the Rite of the Seventh Day, some families offer the Three Sacrifices (*San Sheng* 三牲); pork, poultry and seafood.

The Night of the Soul's Return
(*Hui Hun Ye* 回魂夜)

In accordance with tradition, The Night of the Soul's Return or First Seventh Night takes place seven days after a person is buried. It is centered on the notion that a dead person will return to their home in spirit seven days after their body was buried.

Records of this tradition date as far back as the Northern Qi Dynasty (550–577 AD): The Book of Northern Qi (*Bei Qi Shu* 北齊書) states that prayers and rituals were performed every seventh day after the death of Emperor Le'An (*Le An Wang* 樂安王).

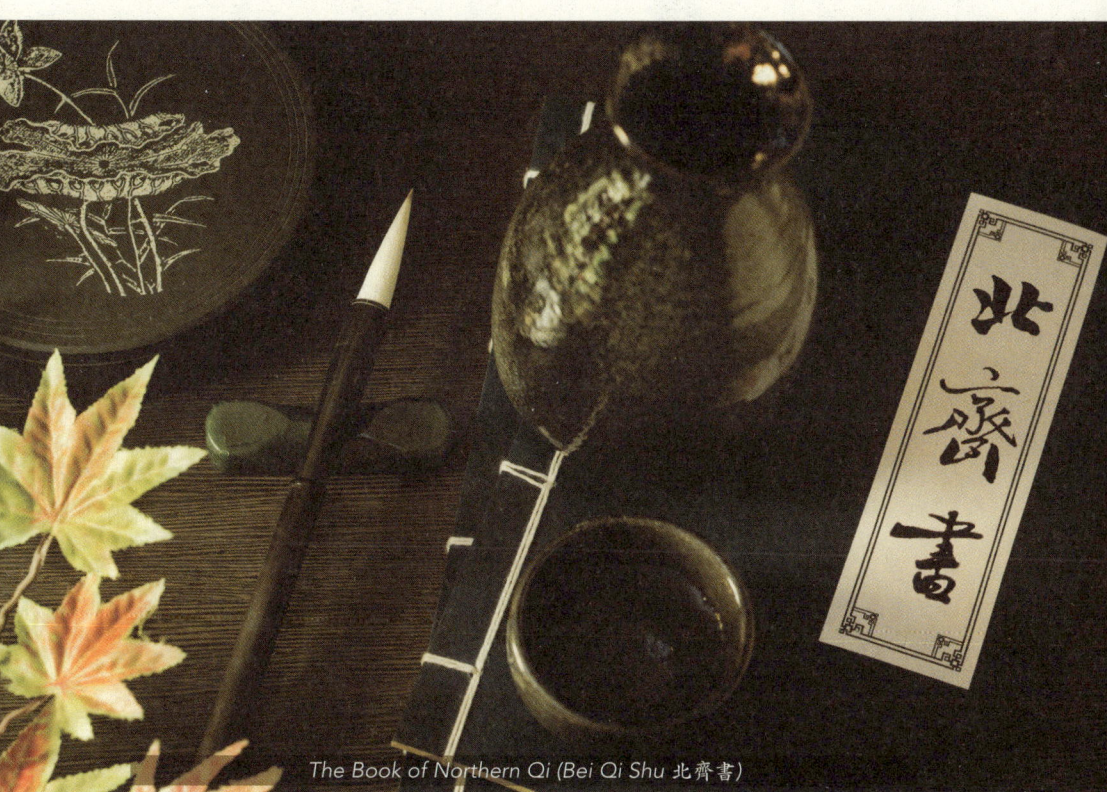

The Book of Northern Qi (*Bei Qi Shu* 北齊書)

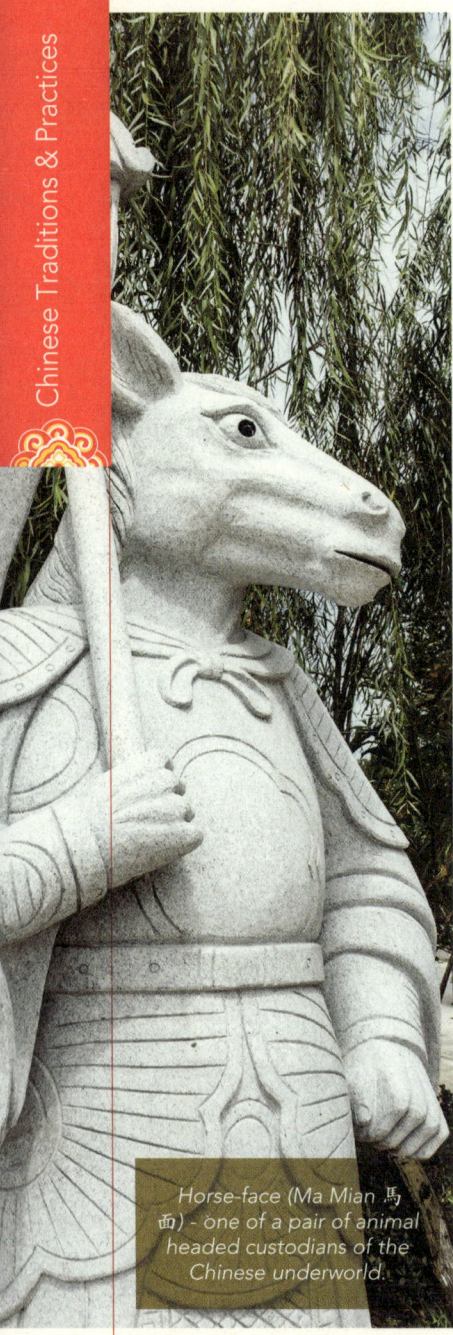

Horse-face (Ma Mian 馬面) - one of a pair of animal headed custodians of the Chinese underworld.

Some believe that this custom is based on the Buddhist idea that humans have seven types of consciousness. The first six of these are the "common" types of consciousness of the eyes, ears, nose, tongue, body and mind. The seventh type of consciousness is the soul. As death comes for someone, their senses fail them one by one. Some Buddhists believe that the soul leaves the physical body once all of a person's organs have shut down, taking on a gaseous form known as an intermediate body (*Zhong Yin Shen* 中陰身) before it moves on to its next living incarnation.

Buddhists believe that souls in this state who could not bear to part with their loved ones or were worried about their family's wellbeing could return to their homes. Such attachments to the mortal world can cause them to transmigrate to the realm of ghosts, although their karma ultimately determines their fate.

Buddhists believe that if a deceased person led a virtuous life then their good karma will help them move quickly to their next incarnation. In contrast, a thoroughly immoral person will be sent to hell immediately. Because most people have both good and bad karma, Buddhists believe that most souls remain in an intermediary state for some 49 days. During this time, they wander the physical world in search for a way to be reborn.

In order to help their loved ones achieve rebirth, Buddhist family members are encouraged to chant the Buddha's name, recite sutras, perform good deeds and give blessings on their loved one's behalf. As mentioned earlier they also conduct rituals every seven days during the 49 day period after a person dies while their soul searches for the path to the next life. During this time Buddhists are advised to stick to a vegetarian diet as meat is considered a luxury in Buddhism. Abstaining from it can supposedly help ensure their loved one is reincarnated into a good life.

On the "first" seventh day after a funeral, a Buddhist family prepares for the Night of the Soul's Return by making a wonderful feast for the deceased which they do not eat themselves. This feast should include the departed person's favourite fruits and snacks. Beef and horse meat is avoided because of the Buddhist belief that the underworld custodians who escort the dead back to their homes on the night in question are Ox-head and Horse-face (*Niu Tou Ma Mian* 牛頭馬面) and Black and White Impermanence (*Hei Bai Wu Chang* 黑白無常). Many families burn a ladder made of joss paper to symbolise the dead's ascension to a higher plane of existence.

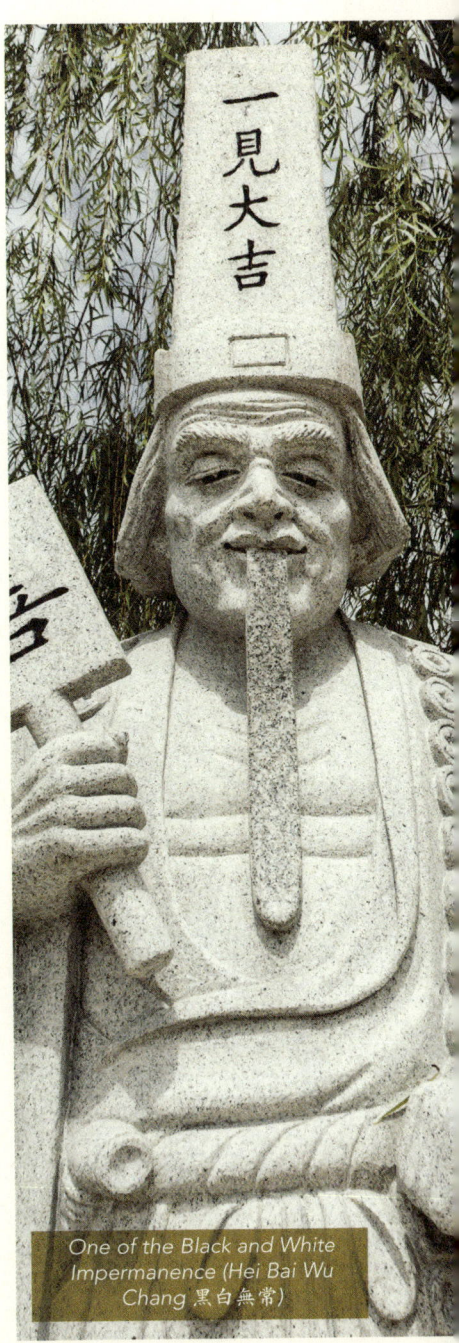

One of the Black and White Impermanence (Hei Bai Wu Chang 黑白無常*)*

Traditionally, families don't pray at their loved one's grave on the seventh day. This is because of the belief that a person's "death certificate" is only issued by the underworld seven days after a person dies. To pray to the underworld might cause confusion among the underworlds' officers and prevent them from issuing a "certificate". If this happened, the departed might end up being "registered" as a wandering ghost, free to haunt their family and home unintentionally.

Pregnant women, children and bespectacled family members are traditionally kept away from the rituals because of the belief that the recently deceased or their underworld custodians might bring bad luck upon them. Families try not to argue during the Nine of the Soul's Return so as not to distress the soul of the deceased.

When night falls, a family stays in their rooms so that the deceased won't see them when they arrive and find it even harder to move on to their next life. Some families sprinkle salt, flour or another powder on the floor to see if the deceased leaves signs of having visited. They may also place a bowl of clean water symbolizing the absolution of past sins and five grains to protect against bad luck by the main door. To avoid bad luck they should dispose of these items the next day.

Families are taught not to be afraid if the recently deceased appears to them as an apparition or in a dream. As a loved one in life, they are unlikely to cause harm. Many believe that if a deceased person makes an appearance it is because they have a message, warning or request which ought to be heeded. The recommended course of action is to listen attentively and fulfil any requests that are made so that the deceased can find peace and move on.

The Hundredth Day Ceremony (*Bai Ri* 百日)

A hundred days after a person's death their family was no longer expected to openly express grief. They could stop wearing mourning clothes and put on dark, conservative clothing of their choosing instead. At this point, families held the Hundredth Day Ceremony.

According to Buddhist beliefs, a soul takes a lot longer to pass through the eighth through tenth levels of Hell compared to the first seven. As such, a person's soul is still passing through the eighth level of hell a hundred days after their death. The Hundredth Day Ceremony serves to guarantee their safety as they pass through hell and ensure that they are reincarnated as a human. In this way the Hundredth Day Ceremony is a continuation of the Rite of the Seventh Day.

Daoists believe that once 49 days have passed, a person's soul has no chance of being resurrected. As such they attach no special meaning to the Hundredth Day Ceremony and simply hold it out of respect for the dead.

When holding the Hundredth Day Ceremony, a family would offer the Three Sacrifices and flowers, bow to the local *Tu Di Gong* (土地公) and bow to the deceased. This simple ritual usually marked the end of the post-funeral proceedings, especially in modern times. There are other ceremonies but most families omit them for the sake of convenience.

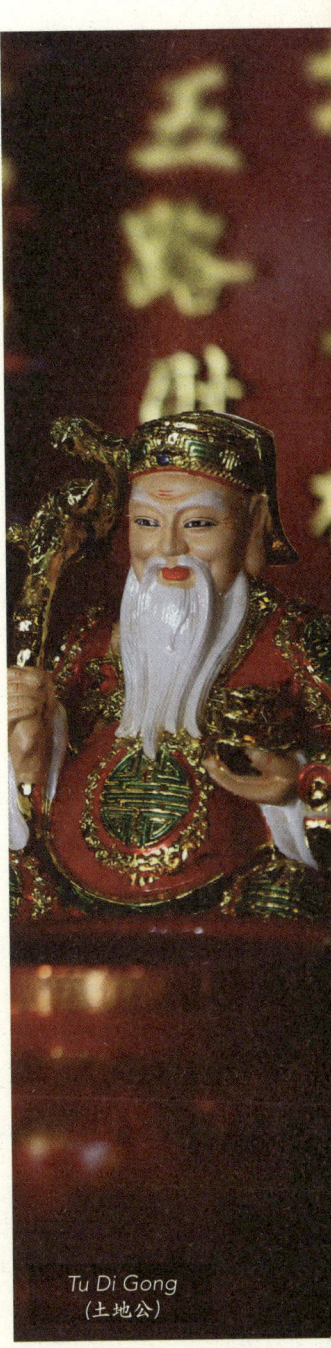

Tu Di Gong (土地公)

The Closure (Ji 祭)

The Closure ceremony was created in accordance with the Confucian emphasis on filial piety.

In short, the Closure is an official mourning period of three years where family members – eldest sons in particular – wear mourning clothes.

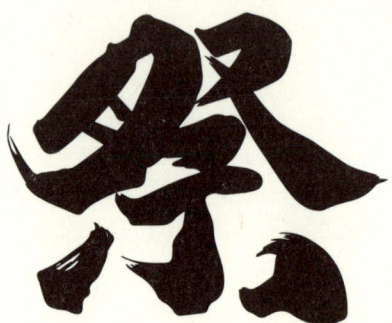

Closure (Ji 祭)

The practice is rooted in a story told by Confucius about a discussion with one of his disciples, *Zai Wo* (宰我).

As the story goes, *Zai Wo* asked Confucius, "Is it not too long a time for one to spend three years mourning his deceased father? If a righteous man (*Jun Zi* 君子) does not practices his rites (*Li* 禮) for three years, then no one would. If a righteous man does not play music for three years, then there would be no music. Is death not a natural cycle much like how old crops are reaped and new crops are grown?"

Confucius replied with another question: "If your father died, would you find peace in eating his crops and wearing his clothes like usual?" *Zai Wo* replied that he would.

Confucius continued: "If you can still manage to find peace after your father has passed away, then go ahead… A righteous man would find his food tasteless and his music meaningless while his mind would be in a constant state of unrest. Because peace eludes him in the wake of his father's passing, he would not practice his rites or play any music. If you can find peace in such a situation, you may go ahead and do so."

Hearing this, *Zai Wo* fell silent. Confucius addressed the rest of his disciples. "*Zai Wo* has no sense of compassion (*Ren* 仁). It took a man and a woman three years to raise a child so that he can walk and now he cannot even be bothered to hold a proper funeral for his father. Is he unable to at least repay the debt he owes his father for those three years?"

This story is most probably the basis for the three-year mourning period of Confucian funerals. It is interesting to note that neither Confucius or his most famous successor Mencius (*Meng Zi* 孟子) mourned for three years after their own losses. The practice was made official by other Confucian disciples.

In any case, the Confucian view is that a normal person should be overwhelmed with grief for three years after their father or king dies. During this time, a person ought to grieve and behave in accordance with Confucian expectations: mourning people can be judged by their adherence to several restrictions.

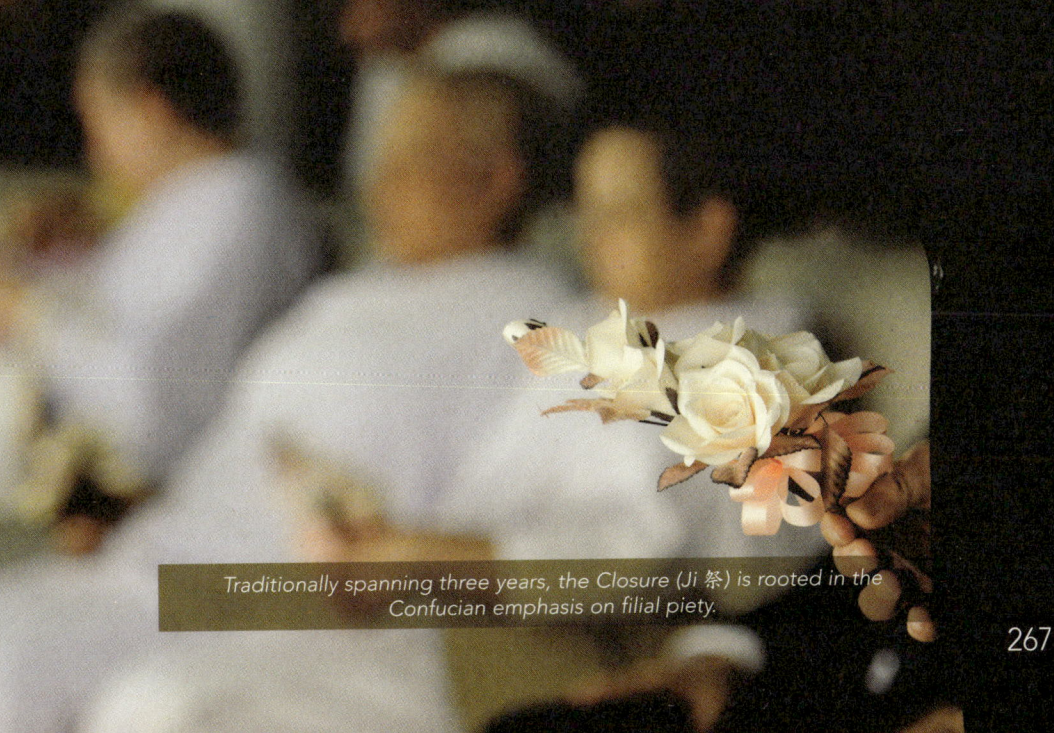

Traditionally spanning three years, the Closure (Ji 祭) is rooted in the Confucian emphasis on filial piety.

The first restriction concerned language: one should remain silent as a sign of their grief, breaking their silence only to talk about subjects related to the deceased or the funeral. Bouts of crying were permissible. Grieving people were only allowed to talk about subjects related to the deceased or the funeral.

Grieving people were also expected not to eat for the first three days of a funeral. After that they were allowed to eat porridge made from a single handful of rice once a day. After three months they could add crops to their diet. They could only add fruit and vegetables to their meals after a full year. Alcohol and meat were forbidden for three years. Today, the three-year mourning period is no longer a compulsory part of Chinese funerals although it lives on somewhat in spirit. The restrictions described above have fallen out of favour – many people opt instead to wear a variation of the mortuary pin used during the funeral to their everyday clothes as a sign that there are grieving.

Today, something known as the Three-year Ceremony (*San Nian* 三年) is often held three years after someone's death. This modern adaptation of Confucius' three-year mourning period is identical to the Rite of the Seventh Day in terms of the steps which are carried out and today it marks the end of the Closure custom.

Chapter 7
The Traditional Chinese Way of Doing Business

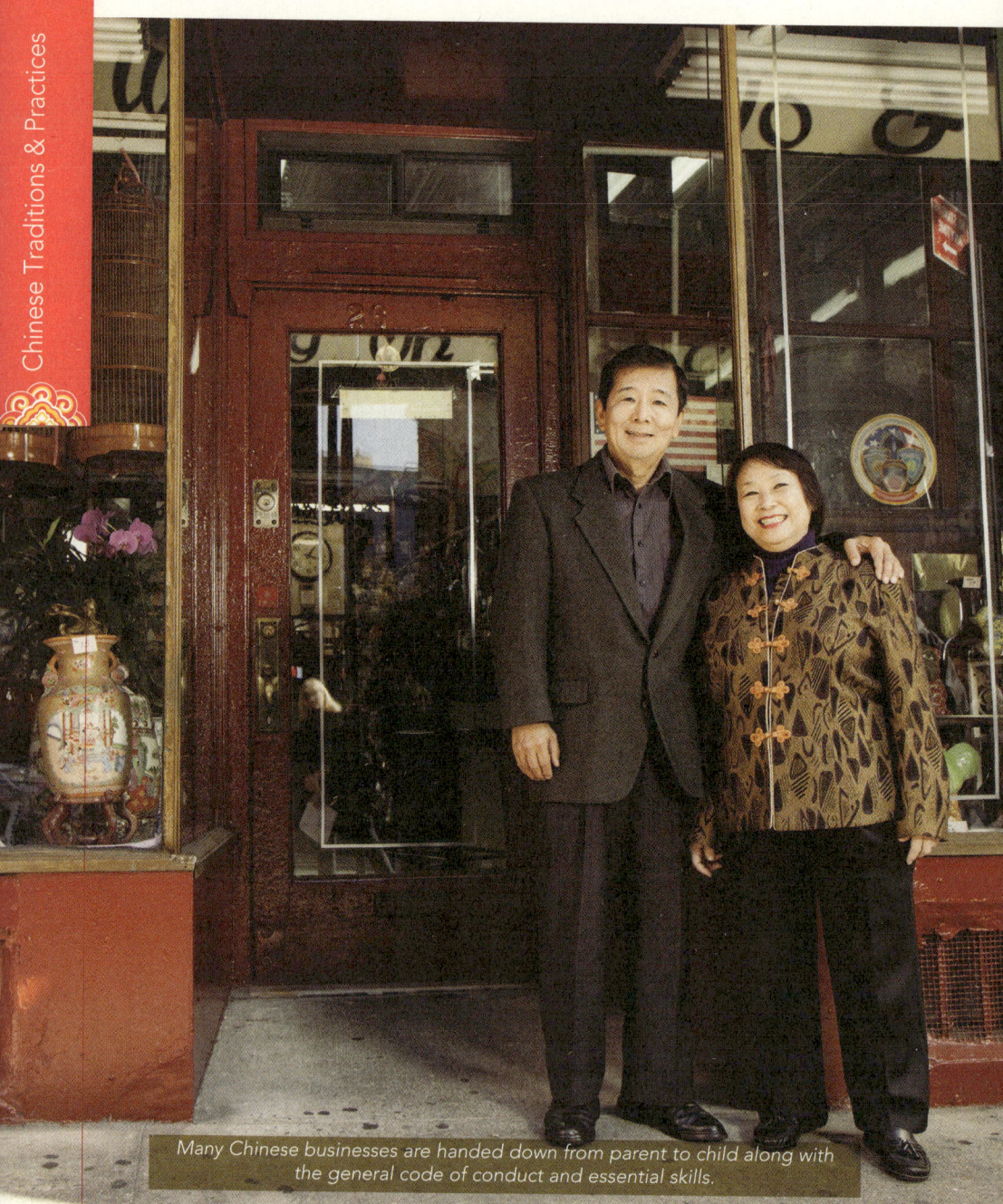

Many Chinese businesses are handed down from parent to child along with the general code of conduct and essential skills.

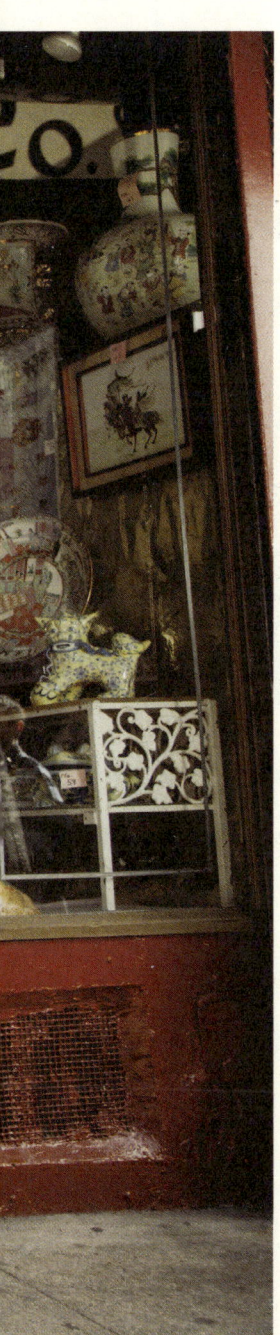

As ancient China transitioned from a hunter-gatherer society into an agricultural one, trade between settlements became crucial. As trading increased, new infrastructure and transportation methods were developed. Eventually trade routes were established to facilitate the movement of goods and people throughout the country.

Over time, merchants and businessmen learned that good etiquette, strong business ethics, luck and a decent knowledge of Feng Shui could boost their chances of business success. As this knowledge caught on, new customs and traditions arose. Merchants and businessmen who learned the code of business conduct passed it on to their children and apprentices who in turn did the same, ensuring they that it would never be forgotten. As globalisation and technology have helped trading grow, these customs and traditions have evolved, too.

In Chinese business, the quintessential qualities of respect and good manners are of great importance. In China, a person has to be confident, respectable and perceptive to build business relationships and succeed in their chosen market.

The code of conduct surrounding business is a complex mix of traditional beliefs and practical wisdom. Some rules and customs have their basis in true Feng Shui principles, others were created in the belief that they bring good fortune and stave off bad luck.

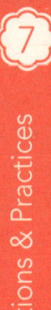

Although it is more of a Western tradition, ribbon-cutting has now become a common part of the opening ceremonies of Chinese companies as well.

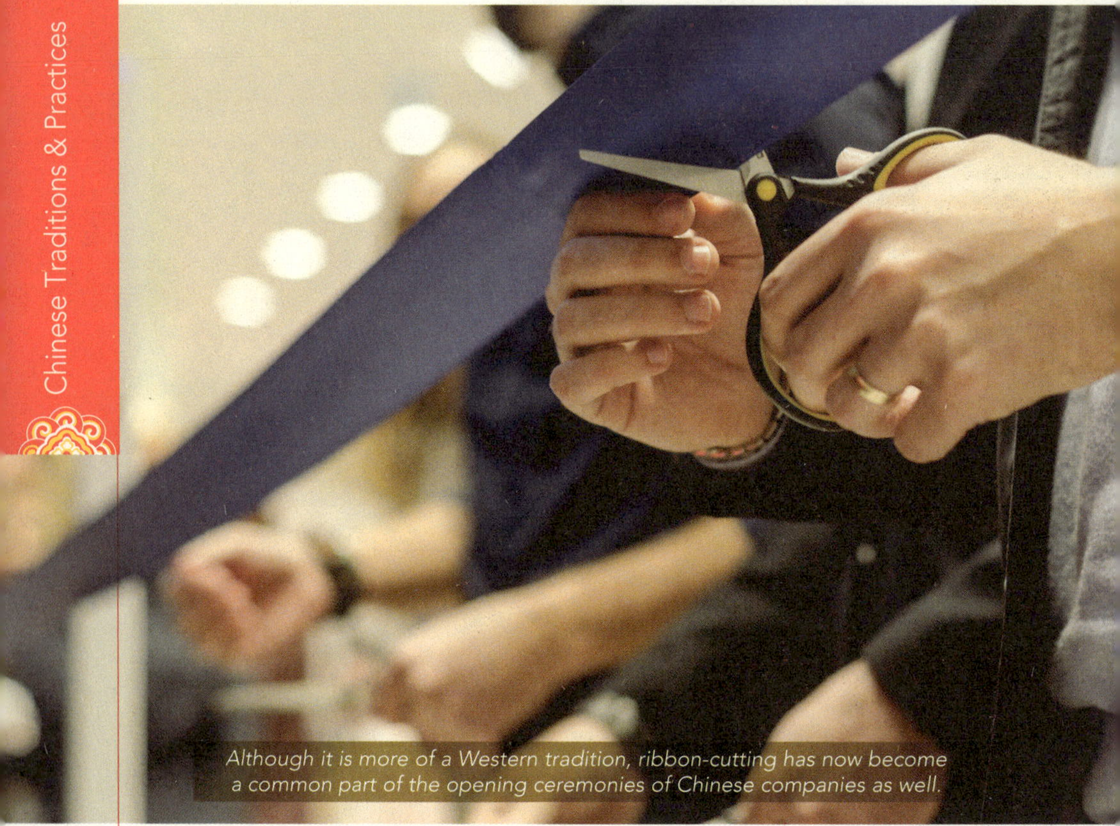

The Opening Ceremony

When a new business is launched, an opening ceremony called a Business' Commencement (*Kai Shi* 開市) can be held. It may draw upon Chinese Metaphysics or a business owner's religious beliefs. Regardless, the opening ceremony can be likened to the moving ceremony that a family holds when they move into a new home. The two ceremonies are almost identical, save for a few specific details and the place where they are held.

The Business' Commencement (Kai Shi 開市)

To hold a Business' Commencement ceremony, one must first choose the right date to "open shop". A Chinese Metaphysics practitioner can use the Art of Date Selection (Ze Ri 擇日) to identify the most favourable time and day for the ceremony.

It must be noted that there is no such thing as a perfect date for this ceremony - every person who works in a business affects its auspicious Qi. A day that is auspicious for a business owner might be inauspicious for a given employee and so on. To overcome this one should consider the business owner's BaZi Chart then take steps to ensure that any employee who "clashes" with a good date cannot have a negative influence. The employee in question can either take the day off or perform a small rite to neutralise the "clash", conducted after the main Business Commencement ceremony. To do this, the employee takes an empty red envelope and writes "May the Opening Ceremony be Auspicious" (Kai Gong Da Ji 開工大吉) on it. They then place the envelope on the table to mark the end of the ritual.

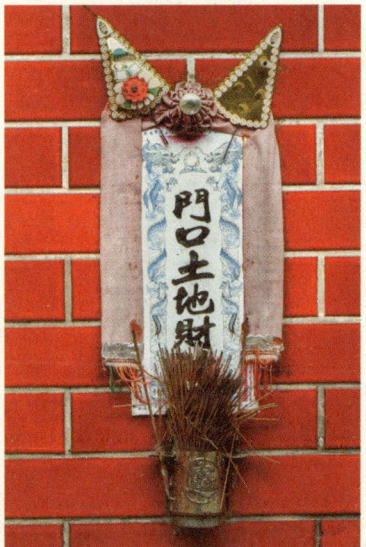

Many businesses set up small shrines which are dedicated to the local deities; the one pictured welcomes the Tu Di Gong (土地公) and the God of Wealth (Cai Shen 財神).

Back to the ceremony itself! Once a suitable date has been chosen, the business owner should pray to local deities and register their intention to start a new business with them. This step is similar to the part of the moving in ceremony where a new homeowner checks in with local deities. In Malaysia and Singapore, the practice of registering a new business with local deities is known as the Tu Di Gong (土地公) or Da Bo Gong (大伯公).

The day before a Business' Commencement ceremony is held, an office cleansing ritual should be carried out. Because a business can occupy far more floor space than a home, it may be impractical for a business owner to scatter beans and rice in every corner then sweep them away as they would in a home cleansing ceremony. Instead, they can take a handful of sticky rice, grind it into powder and mix it with water and salt. They can then spray the resulting mixture around their business and leave the lights on overnight instead.

During the opening ceremony itself, a business owner should offer the Three Offerings (*San Sheng* 三牲) which are pork, poultry and seafood. They should offer a pair of daikon radishes, too. Daikon radishes are known as the Chief of Vegetables (*Cai Tou* 菜頭) in China. Their Chinese name rhymes with the phrase "auspicious omen" (*Hao Cai Tou* 好彩頭) so they are considered auspicious.

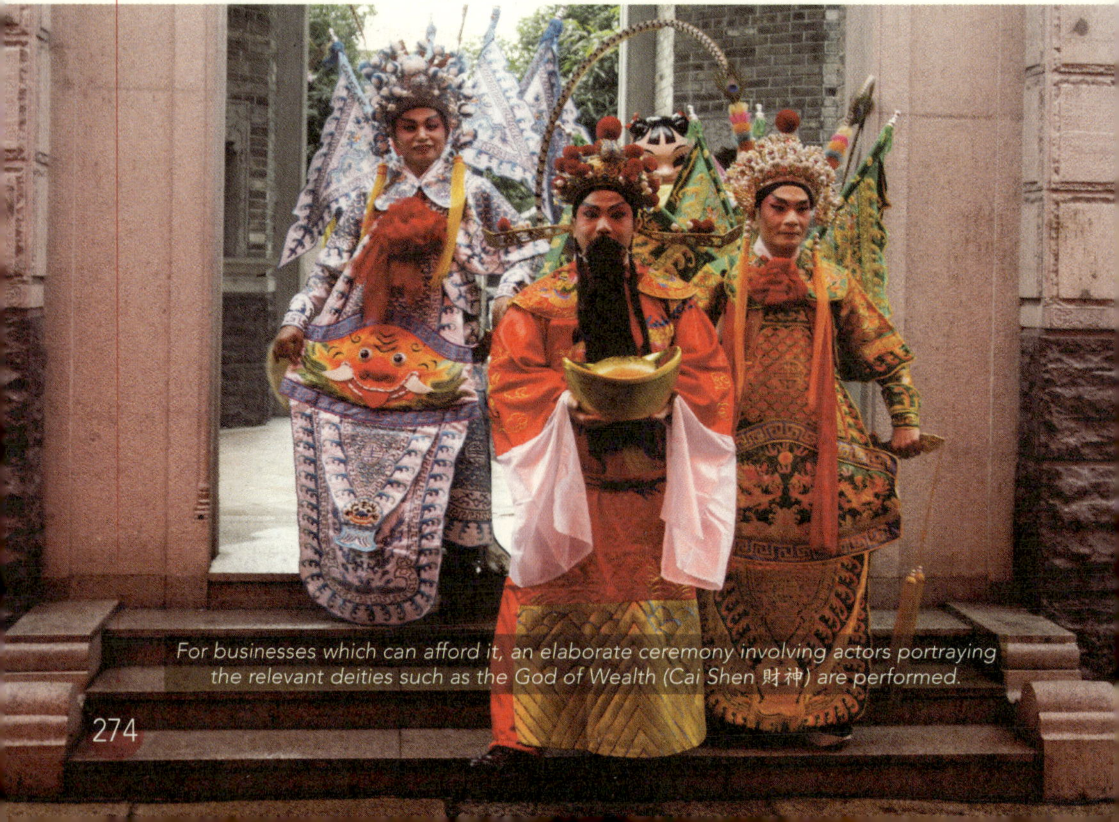

For businesses which can afford it, an elaborate ceremony involving actors portraying the relevant deities such as the God of Wealth (Cai Shen 財神) are performed.

All of the aforementioned items should be presented to the God of Wealth (*Cai Shen* 財神), the deity in charge of the economy. Chinese business owners routinely worship the God of Wealth in the hope that he will increase their profits.

When the auspicious hour is at hand, a business owner must open the front door of their establishment and shout "May the Door of Wealth open for me. May coins, jewellery and golden nuggets tumble into my business." (*Cai Men Cai Men Da Da Kai, Jin Yin Cai Bao Gun Jin Lai.* 財門財門大大開，金銀財寶滾進來。) Next, they should light up a string of firecrackers as safely possible and roll eight oranges through the door. These oranges represent the gold or wealth that the business owner seeks. After the firecrackers have gone off, the owner must collect the debris quickly. This symbolises the preservation of wealth and the speed at which a business owner does this is believed to influence the ease with which they will collect on debts owed.

At this point, employees may enter the premises and start working, although they must carry something related to money like their wallets as they do so. Some businesses offer their employees red envelopes with one unit of currency inside at this point, especially in China where the Yuan (元) is the currency used. The same word is used to refer to initial causes in some Chinese Metaphysical arguments. As such, a Yuan symbolises the entire world. This concept is captured in the saying "May everything be reinvigorated or reinvented in a new beginning." (*Yi Yuan Fu Shi, Wan Xiang Geng Xin.* 一元復始，萬象更新).

The Art of Date Selection (Ze Ri 擇日)

Date Selection (Ze Ri 擇日) is an important field of Chinese Metaphysics. For centuries, it has helped people make timely decisions and choose the most appropriate date for important events. Date Selection lets one select the most auspicious date based on the Chinese solar calendar associated with an activity. Date Selection can be help one plan a wedding, time renovations or choose when to launch a business among other things. This is possible because the same techniques that are used to select an auspicious date for personal events can be used for business events.

When it comes to matters of business, days that contain the Three Killings (San Sha 三殺) should be avoided and only days with auspicious stars should be chosen. Days where two of the 12 Chinese zodiac animals representing the Earthly Branches (Di Zhi 地支) clash with each other should be avoided, too. They are known as "clashing dates" and are inauspicious in general. Finally, days which have bad energy that could affect a person's "vibrations" should be avoided as well.

There are many resources online and offline which make Date Selection easy by listing what activities are advisable on any given day. To make the most of Date Selection and perform a comprehensive analysis, advanced techniques must be used. These are usually based on principles related to the 12 Day Officers (Shi Er Zhi Shen 十二值神), 28 Constellations (Nian Ba Xing Xiu 廿八星宿), Dong Gong Date Selection (Dong Gong Ze Ri 董公擇日) and Auxiliary Stars of the Day (Shen Sha 神煞). The two methods which are most commonly used are the Tong Shu 通書 and the art of Qi Men Dun Jia 奇門遁甲.

Tong Shu (通書), the Traditional Chinese Almanac

Tong Shu was first described in the Yellow Calendar (*Huang Li* 黃曆) which scholars believe was written by the Yellow Emperor (*Huang Di* 黃帝). This classic text was modified and updated over the centuries until it was locked down and given its current name during the Qin dynasty which lasted from 221 to 206 BC.

Feng Shui practitioners use Tong Shu to complement other Date Selection methods. It can help one choose the right date for business negotiations or other activities. Additionally, it provides a formula for converting the Chinese Lunar calendar into the western Gregorian calendar and vice versa.

More detailed versions of the Tong Shu forecast solar and lunar eclipses, the start of each season and predict the coldest and hottest days of the year. Some even provide complementary lessons on ethics and values in the form of stories. For those who want to keep things simple, the Tong Shu has special markings denoting the auspicious and inauspicious activities for each day. These are printed clearly, so even a beginner can use the Tong Shu without much difficulty.

If an individual finds that the date they originally scheduled a business activity on is inauspicious, the best course of action is to reschedule. Better yet, one should consult the Tong Shu when scheduling in the first place!

*Tong Shu (通書),
the Traditional Chinese Almanac*

Qi Men Dun Jia (奇門遁甲)

Qi Men Dun Jia is a Chinese Metaphysics forecasting and warfare tool which has existed for over 3,000 years. One can use it to optimize and enhance their own life and the lives of those around them. It can also be used to help one improve their career and business success, too.

Literally translated, Qi Men Dun Jia means "Mysterious Doors Escaping Technique". Unlike other methods, a Date Selection based on this system places more importance on time and location instead of the actual date. Where *Qi Men Dun Jia* is concerned, usage of the right formula will lead to the identification of the "golden moment". This refers to a specific hour in a day that, when combined with a specific direction, will result in success where a specific action is concerned. Because it is able to take more possibilities into consideration this way, it is seen as more sophisticated and multi-dimensional compared to other Date Selection methods.

Every Qi Men chart has eight boxes which each represents one direction and contains both a *Stem* (*Tian Gan* 天干) and a *Door* (*Men* 門) that will yield different results depending on how they are used. In Qi Men studies, the *Hour Stem* (*Shi Gan* 時干) represents the subject matter in question, and is usually known as the *Useful God* (*Yong Shen* 用神) and serves as the focus point of the reading. When it comes to a full-fledged Date Selection, it represents the end result instead.

For more information on Qi Men Dun Jia Date Selection, please refer to the Qi Men Dun Jia Date, Time and Activity Selection book.

Qi Men Dun Jia Strategic Execution

The Strategic Execution application of Qi Men refers to the practice of using Qi Men Dun Jia to either anticipate or engineer a desired outcome.

To understand which strategy one must employ for success, a person must use Qi Men Dun Jia to select the Chart that promises the most favourable outcome. The main focus is the Stem and Stem-related combinations in a Chart. By studying the Heaven and Earthly Stems in a Chart, one can predict the results of a given activity. For perspective, there are 10 Heavenly Stems and 10 Earthly Stems, making for 100 possible outcomes for any given activity. This means that Qi Men Dun Jia is a very specific and highly actionable business tool.

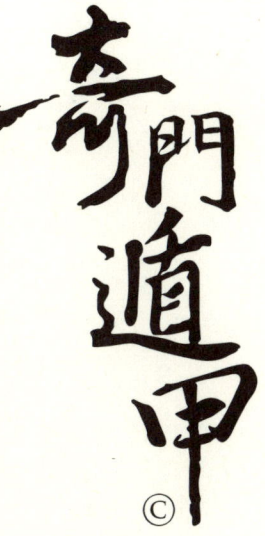

Qi Men Dun Jia

The Signboard

Signboards are an important way for businesses to advertise around the world but they have a special place in the annals of Chinese history.

In China, signboards have long served as a showcase for the art of calligraphy and they are an important consideration in Feng Shui. They are most often used by shops today. The shops of ancient China were the feudal equivalent of today's corporations. They were immensely powerful as they held a monopoly over everyday essential goods and materials. A shop owner with the right skills and luck could become rich and garner a lot of respect and power in their trade.

The shops of ancient China traditionally had mansion-like corporate headquarters and the signboard was part of their architecture. A set of complementary boards was used to create an aesthetically pleasing exterior (*Men Mian* 門面) for stores. A full signage set traditionally included a pair of signboards, decorations which reflect the shop's primary offering and a pair of couplets (*Dui Lian* 對聯).

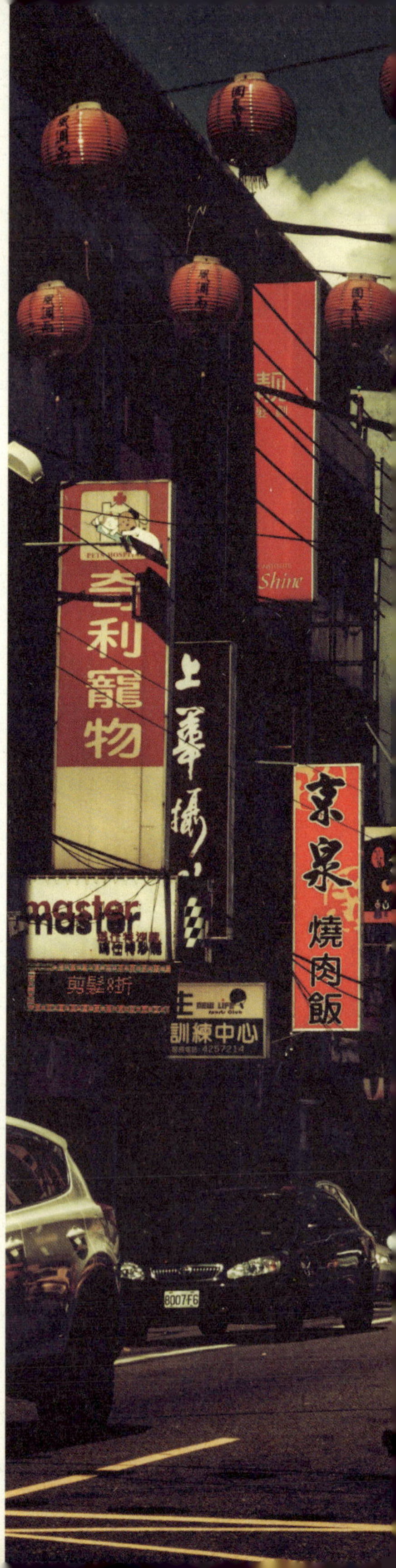

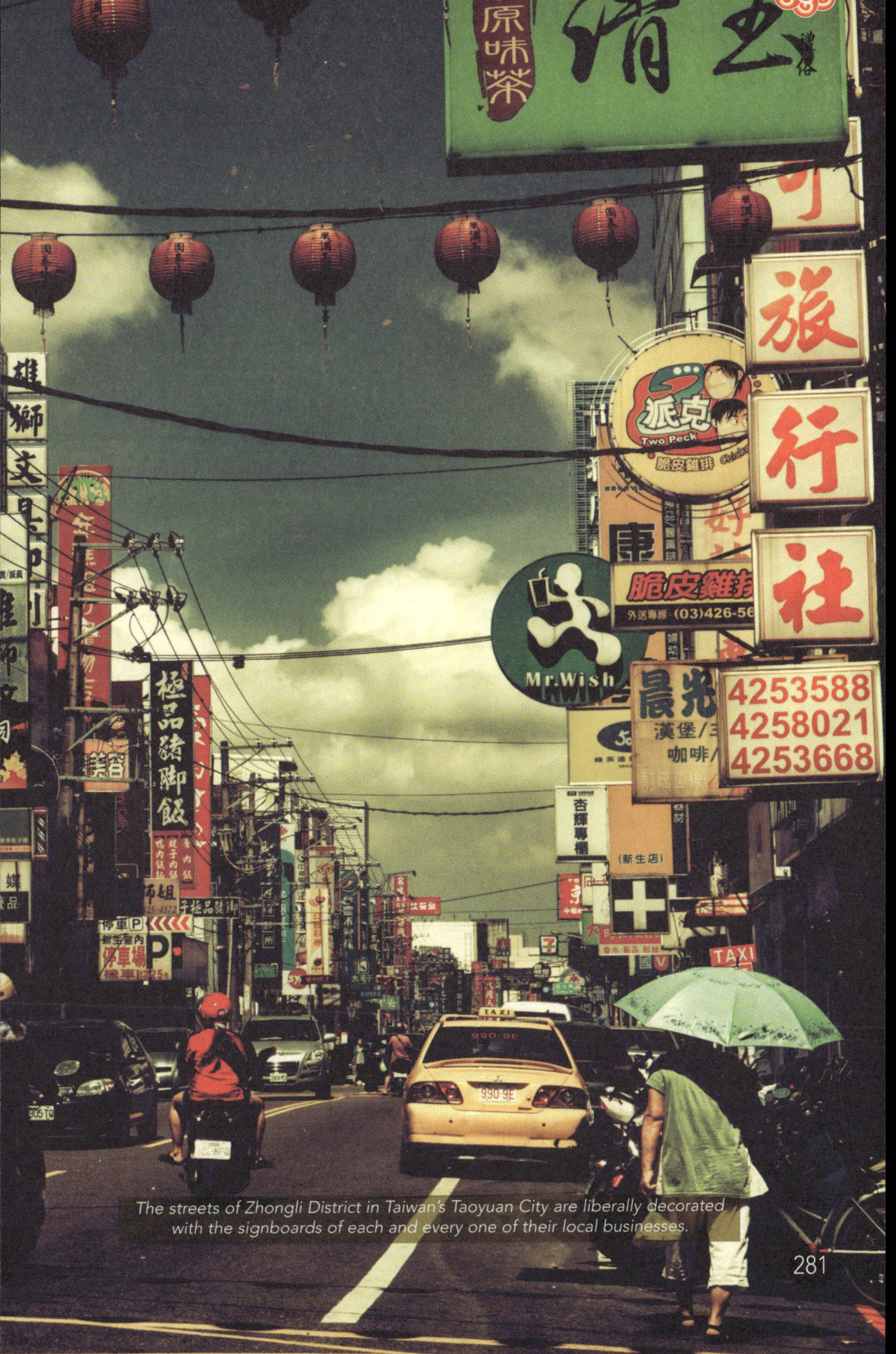
The streets of Zhongli District in Taiwan's Taoyuan City are liberally decorated with the signboards of each and every one of their local businesses.

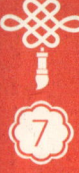

Signboard Details

Traditionally, Chinese shops have used horizontal signboards (*Bian E* 匾額) and vertical signboards (*Zhao Pai* 招牌) to attract customers. Horizontal signboards resemble those seen in the west and usually display the name of the shop, which may be the name of the family which runs the shop or a custom name. The Chinese name for vertical signboards, "*Zhao Pai*", means "invitation board". This is apt because they are used to "invite" potential customers inside by explaining what the business offers. They can be painted or engraved. Signboards which do not clearly and concisely explain what a business is for are considered unfit for their intended purpose.

By reading a shop's horizontal and vertical signboard, one learns a shop's full name. Three real life examples are Ho Yan Hor Herbal Tea (*He Ren Ke Liang Cha* 何人可涼茶), Fong Kei Patisserie (*Huang Ji Bing Jia* 晃記餅家) and Nanxiang Steamed Bun Restaurant (*Nan Xiang Man Tou Dian* 南翔饅頭店).

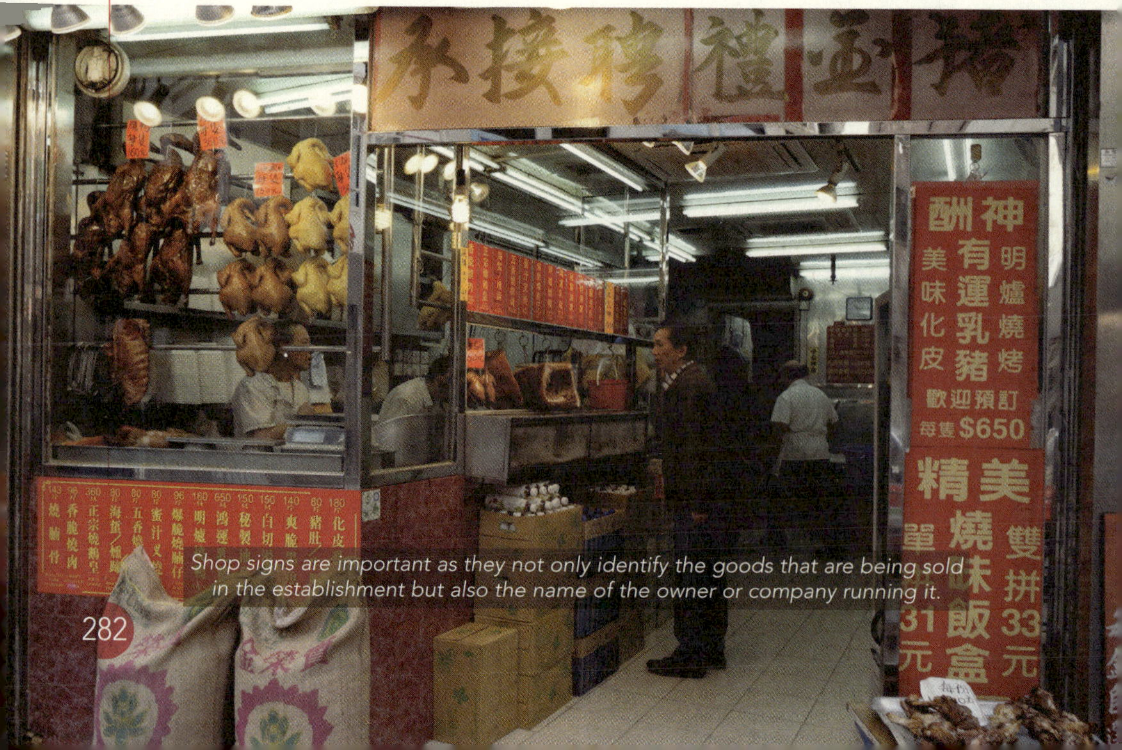

Shop signs are important as they not only identify the goods that are being sold in the establishment but also the name of the owner or company running it.

The quality of the material used for signboards and the quality of the calligraphy work on display reflected a shop's status. This stands to reason, since more profitable stores can afford more expensive wood and calligraphers when making their signboards and other stores must settle for cheaper alternatives.

The quality of calligraphy on a shop's horizontal signboard is particularly significant. Chinese business people place great importance on "relationships" (*Guan Xi* 關係). In theory, only a successful shop owner could afford to hire a skilled calligrapher for their signboard, and thus a well-made signboard meant that the business owner must have had a working relationship with a competent artist. In the past, only wealthy and powerful people would have had connections like this. A select few establishments in the past received the highest honour: their signboards were written by the Emperor of their time. One example is a restaurant in Beijing called *Du Yi Chu* (都一處) which claims that its signboard was written by Emperor Qian Long (*Qian Long Di* 乾隆帝) himself. Emperor Qian Long was a well-regarded calligrapher and respected leader, making the signboard an artistically and historically priceless object.

The most upmarket establishments used a different naming convention to regular stores. This had its basis in Chinese Metaphysics, as Date Selection was used to help owners open their shop on the most auspicious date. Well-informed owners chose highly poetic names drawing upon symbolic imagery and meaning, shunning more pragmatic naming conventions. Some used names that represented their hopes for their business. For example, a bank owner might call their establishment Sun Rising Unobstructed (*Ri Sheng Tong* 日昇通) with the hope that their bank and the economy would thrive.

The Decorations

Signboards are traditionally adorned with a decoration of some kind that helps advertise goods or services. The decoration is a symbolic representation of what the shop has to offer. Clothing shops using clothing-shaped signs, tobacconists hanging large smoking pipes outside their shop and funeral service providers displaying miniature caskets.

Sometimes, decorations only make sense in the context of Chinese culture. Liquor store owners used to hang a small hollow gourd beneath their signboards. They did this because hollow gourds were the favoured liquid containers for alcohol in ancient China. Note that vinegar and soy sauce stores also used hollow gourds as decoration because their wares were stored in the same way.

Some stores capitalize on the intricacies of the Chinese language to represent their goods. Pharmacies have been known to hang a pair of wooden fish referred to as Whole Fish (*Quan Yu* 全鱼) up. The Chinese name for Whole Fish is phonetically similar to the Chinese word for "cure" (*Quan Yu* 痊愈).

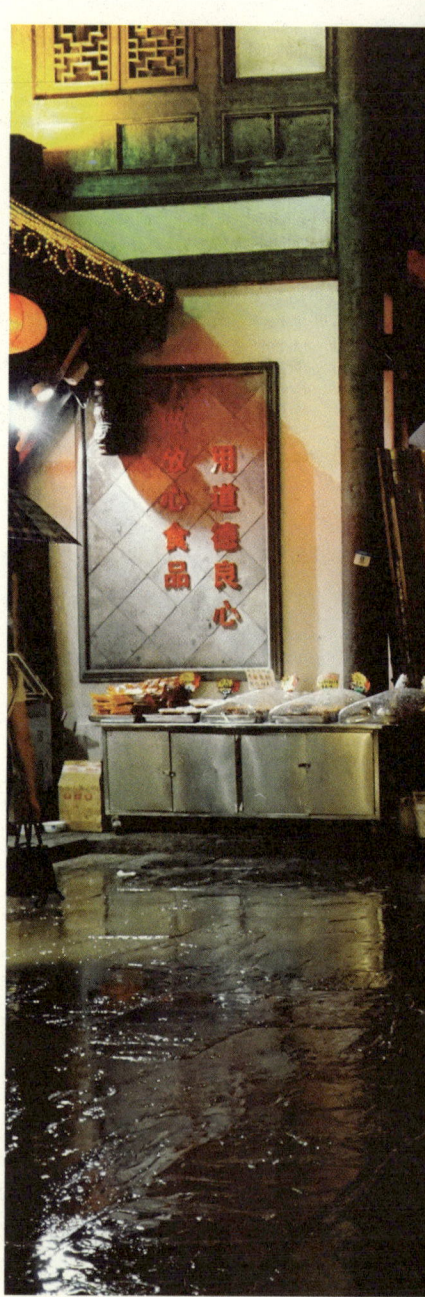

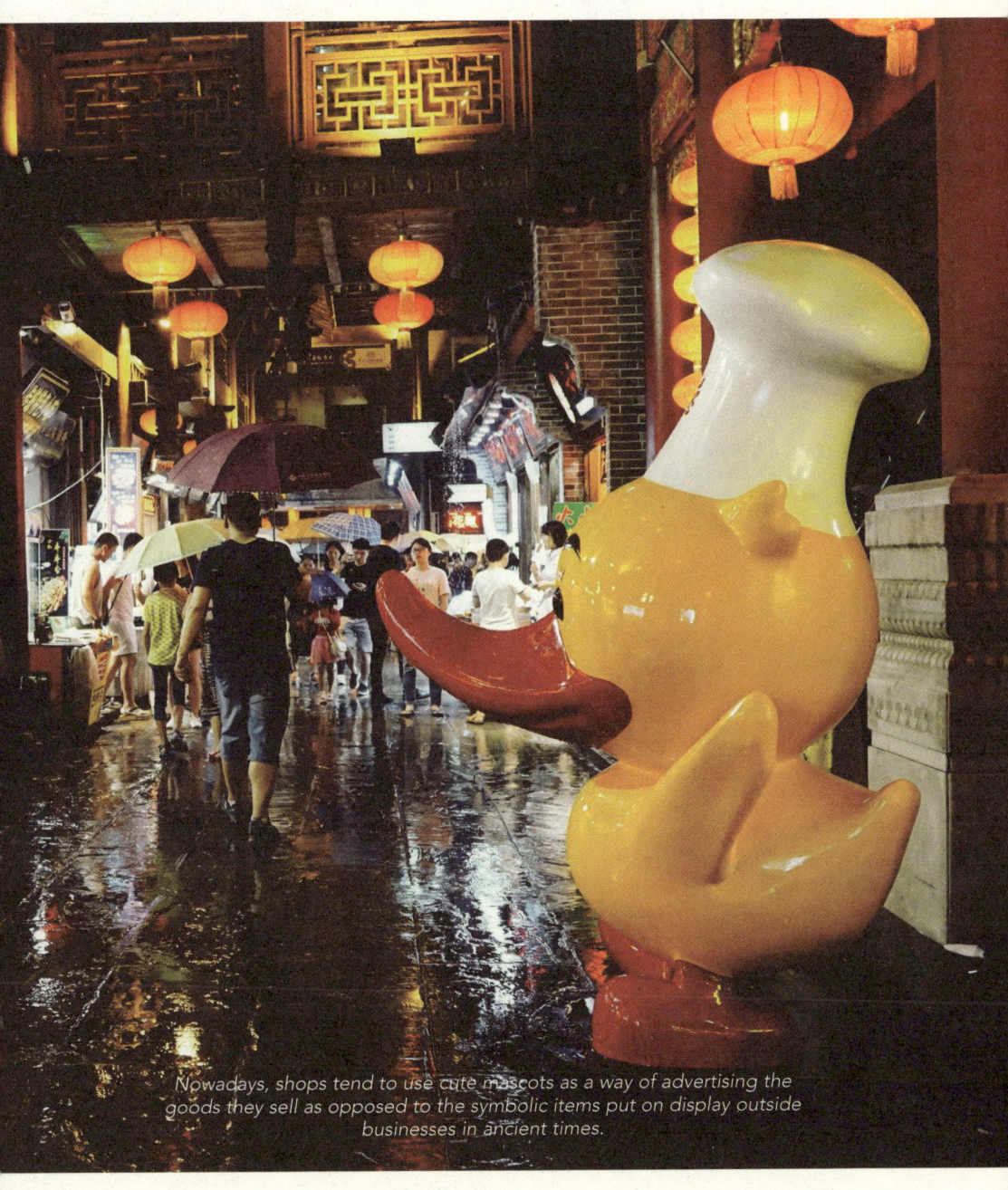

Nowadays, shops tend to use cute mascots as a way of advertising the goods they sell as opposed to the symbolic items put on display outside businesses in ancient times.

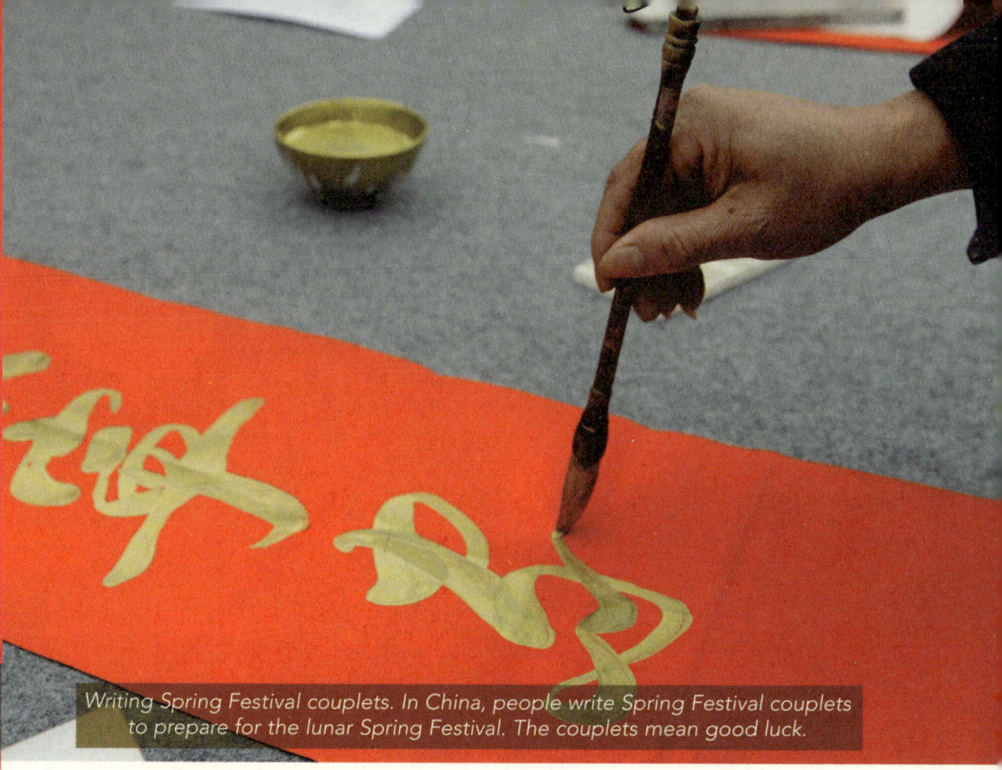

Writing Spring Festival couplets. In China, people write Spring Festival couplets to prepare for the lunar Spring Festival. The couplets mean good luck.

The Couplets (*Dui Lian* 對聯)

Couplets are another important element of Chinese shop signage. Couplets often accompany signboards and decorations. Unlike normal couplets which are written on red paper, they are usually carved into wooden plates and hung by the shop entrance. The design of these plates varies, depending on where they are intended to be placed. Those meant for posts or pillars are slightly curved to resemble roof tiles. They are hence called Tile Plates (*Wa Dui* 瓦對). Plates which are to be hung on flat surfaces are simply called Flat Plates (*Ping Dui* 平對).

Couplets often carry a philosophical message related to the business they advertise, but sometimes they carry bespoke messages. Couplet writers like to use word games, using the name of a shop as the first word of the couplet. This kind of couplet is called a Framed Couplet (*Qian Zi Lian* 嵌字聯).

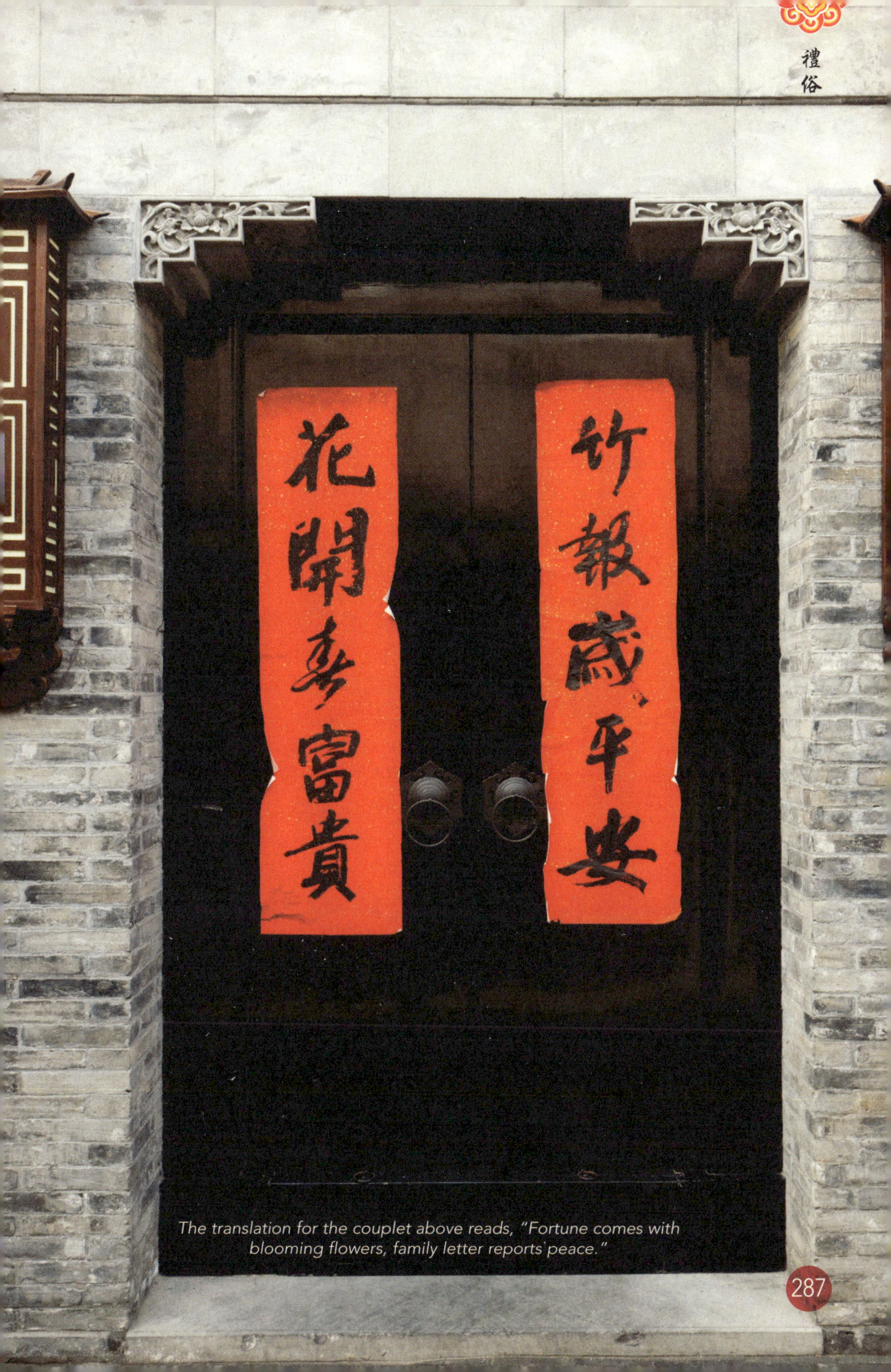

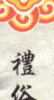
禮俗

The translation for the couplet above reads, "Fortune comes with blooming flowers, family letter reports peace."

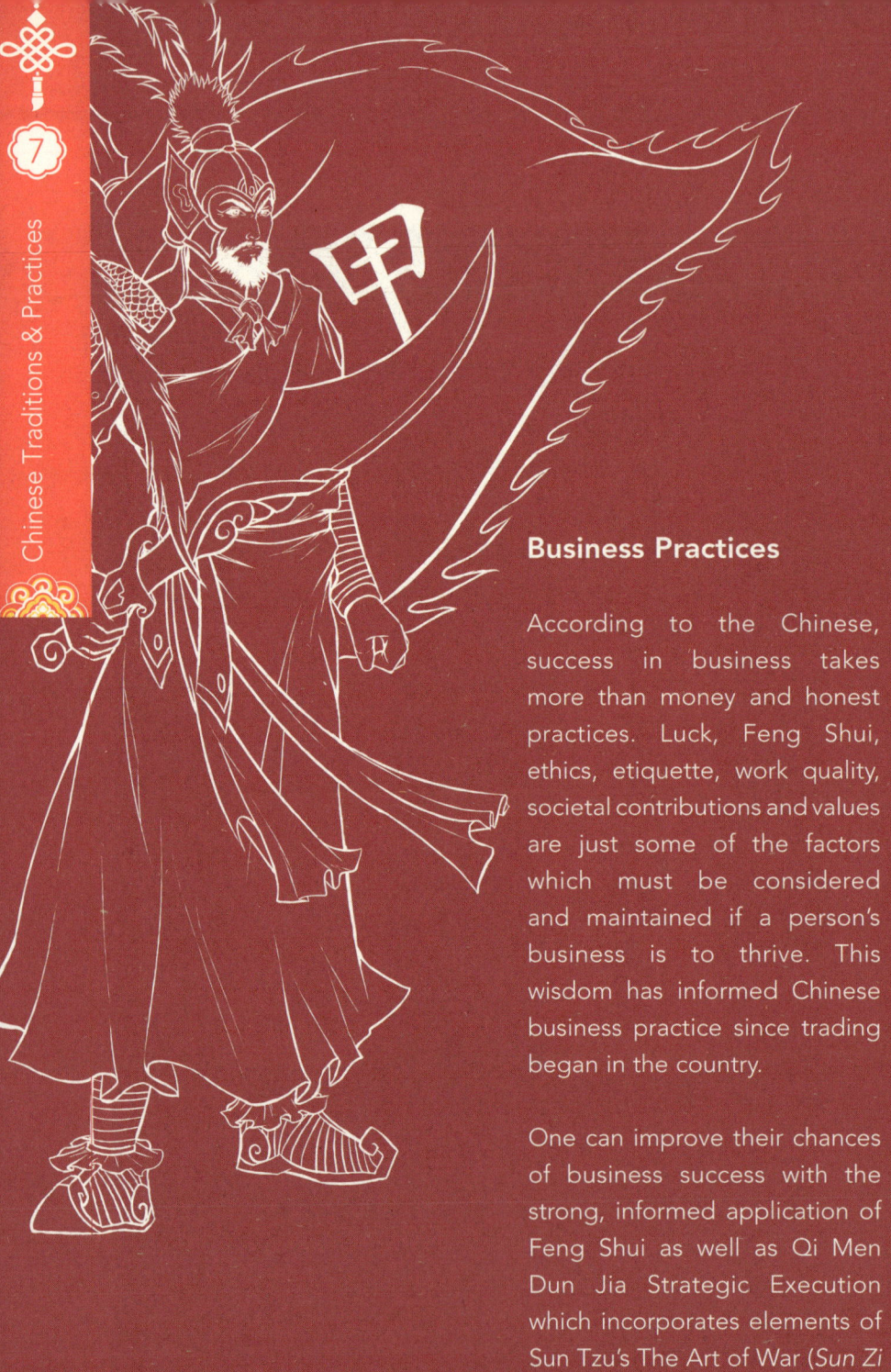

Business Practices

According to the Chinese, success in business takes more than money and honest practices. Luck, Feng Shui, ethics, etiquette, work quality, societal contributions and values are just some of the factors which must be considered and maintained if a person's business is to thrive. This wisdom has informed Chinese business practice since trading began in the country.

One can improve their chances of business success with the strong, informed application of Feng Shui as well as Qi Men Dun Jia Strategic Execution which incorporates elements of Sun Tzu's The Art of War (*Sun Zi Bing Fa* 孫子兵法).

Basic Etiquette

When doing business, etiquette is at least as important as it is in personal interactions and perhaps even more so. In China, strong business relationships are best built upon a foundation of mutual respect and good etiquette goes a long way towards creating it.

For starters, business people must not interfere with or cut into a conversation that their customer or client is having with someone else: it is seen as extremely rude. For the same reason, business people should never argue with their clients or customers, as this can permanently ruin their relationship.

Punctuality is a prized quality in the world of business. Arriving on time to one's appointments gives the impression of sincerity and shows that one respects their commitments and other people's time.

Chinese business people maintain a professional distance with their clients or customers. The greetings practised in many Western cultures are seen as over familiar in China, so a more restrained approach must be used. Clients and customers should not be treated like friends or family in Chinese business. This contrasts with American business practice where business people try to be as friendly as possible with their prospects.

Travelling

As trading caught on in ancient China it became necessary to link different parts of the country. First, existing infrastructure was improved to prioritise vehicles. Although maritime transport options existed, land-based travel was preferred as most cities and towns in China are separated by land.

Commoners used animal carts to move people and goods across long distances. Oxen were the favoured animals as horses were reserved for military use. As an aside, the number of horse carriages a kingdom had was a good proxy for their military might.

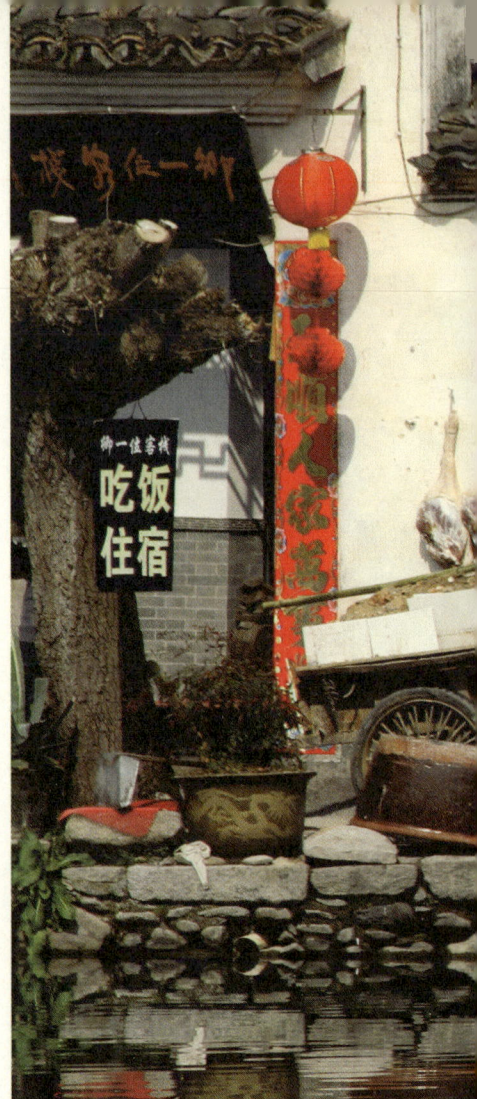

Animal Carts

The animal carts used in ancient China were constructed entirely out of wood. The first were built with functionality in mind. They had canopies to protect their passengers or cargo although carts carrying criminals or warriors lacked this feature. Many animal carts of the day were so small that passengers had no space to sit down, so they had to stand for the duration of their journey.

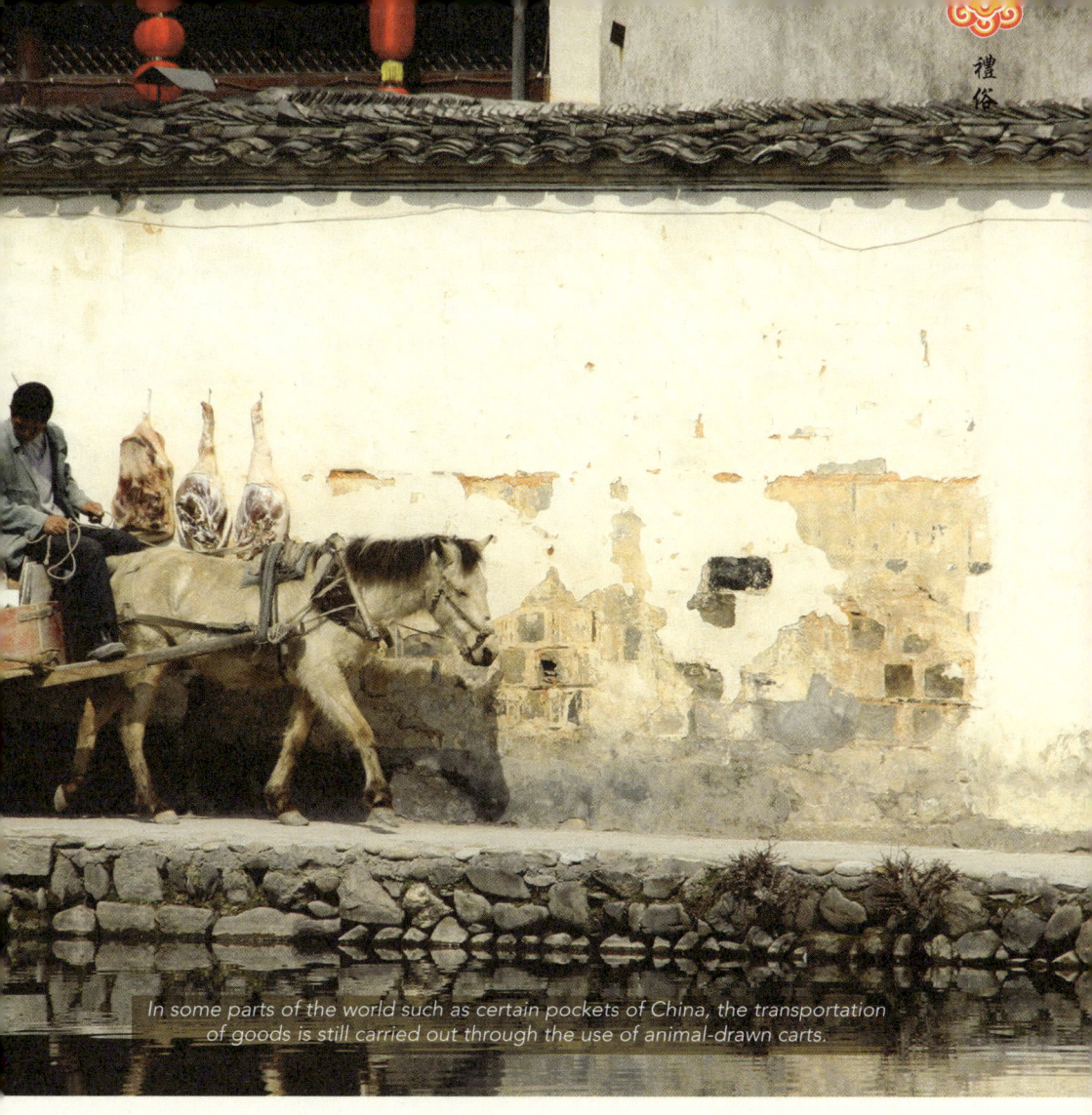

In some parts of the world such as certain pockets of China, the transportation of goods is still carried out through the use of animal-drawn carts.

The basic animal cart design was improved with the addition of seats, albeit only in carts used for transporting important individuals. Merchants and businessmen opted against such comforts so that they had more space for goods. The overall beauty of a cart was measured by the height of its canopy. Naturally, more rich and powerful people insisted on carts with taller canopies.

Restrictions

Whether a cart was used by a merchant carrying goods or a government official travelling to carry out their official duties, they were subject to the rules of the road. Most were created to ensure everyone's safety but some were based on superstitious beliefs of the time.

Cart drivers were discouraged from stopping at any funerals or burial ceremonies they encountered on their travels. To do so was believed to bring bad luck to the driver and their passengers. Cart drivers were also expected to give way to any bridal sedans they encountered. Blocking a sedan or bumping into it was believed to bring both parties bad luck. In both instances, these rules demonstrate simple respect for others.

A popular folk belief of the time claimed that evil spirits haunted the roadside, waiting to stop drivers and hitch a ride. A driver who picked them up would go on to have a miserable life. This folk tale was most likely based on real encounters with bandits who would hide by the side of the road to prey on unsuspecting road users.

In carts which had seats, social status dictated where people sat. The seat on the left side of a cart was reserved for respected members of society. The driver would sit in the middle with his attending to his right. Lone passengers were not to sit at the back of the cart, as it might appear that the driver was transporting a slave.

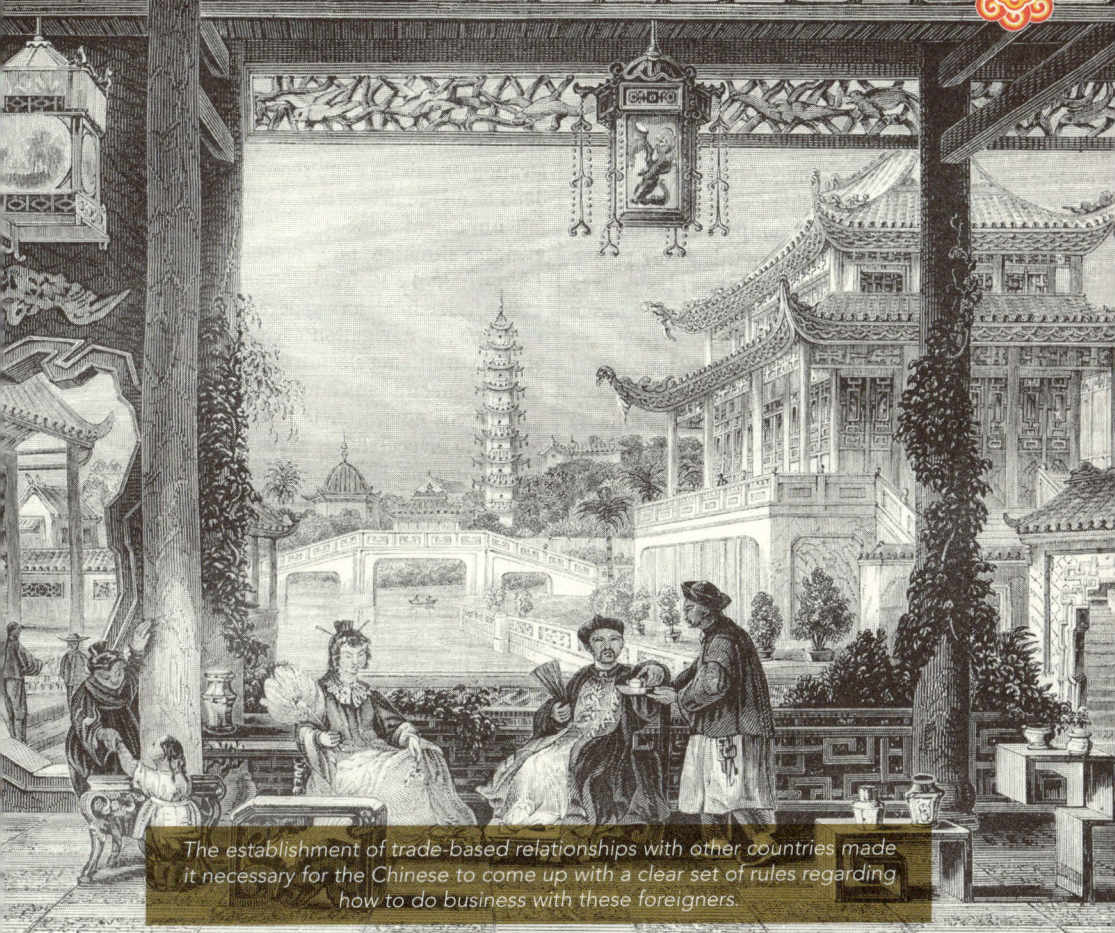

The establishment of trade-based relationships with other countries made it necessary for the Chinese to come up with a clear set of rules regarding how to do business with these foreigners.

Doing Business with Foreigners

The Chinese have a complex view of foreigners (*Wai Guo Ren* 外國人). Foreigners are often romanticised like oriental culture is in the west. In fact, the phrase "Wai Guo Ren" literally means "people from another country". If the country is not specified then this phrase is usually used to refer to a Caucasian. It is interchangeable with the phrase "people from the Western world"(*Xi Fang Ren* 西方人).

The attitude that the Chinese have towards foreigners is related to but not governed by the ancient concept of the Sino-Foreigner Dichotomy (*Hua Yi Zhi Bian* 華夷之辨). The rules that emerged from this concept gave birth to the concept of the Vicinity of Relations (*Qin Shu* 親疏). It, in turn, is the foundation for the concept of "relationships" (*Guan Xi* 關係) in business.

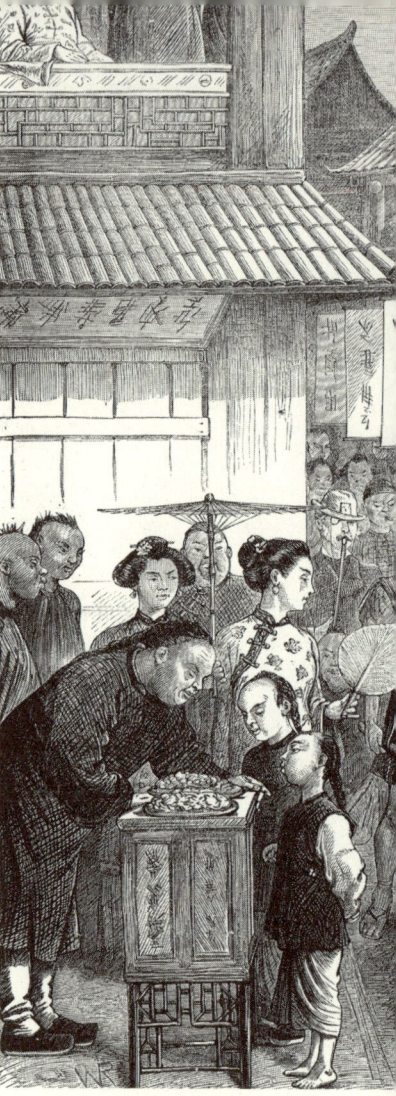

The Sino-Foreigner Dichotomy (*Hua Yi Zhi Bian* 華夷之辨)

Although it is no longer an effective tool for establishing relationships with foreigners, the Sino-Foreigner Dichotomy lives on in Chinese culture. It is based on a theory created by Confucius to help differentiate between the Chinese (*Hua* 華) and foreigners (*Yi* 夷).

The tool seems to place Chinese people above those of other cultures. This sense of superiority was based on the Chinese use of rites (*Li* 禮), which some believed made Chinese culture more civil and organised. Fortunately, because the distinction was based on culture instead of race, a person who was not born in China could still become a Chinese person for all intents and purposes by adopting Chinese values and customs. Confucius first proposed this theory in Section 14, Chapter 9 of the Analects (*Lun Yu* 論語), stating that:

"The Master wanted to go and stay with the Nine Tribes of the East [the foreigners]. Someone said, "They are unruly! Why do you want to do such a thing?" Confucius replied, "If a noble man dwells with them, how could they be unruly?"

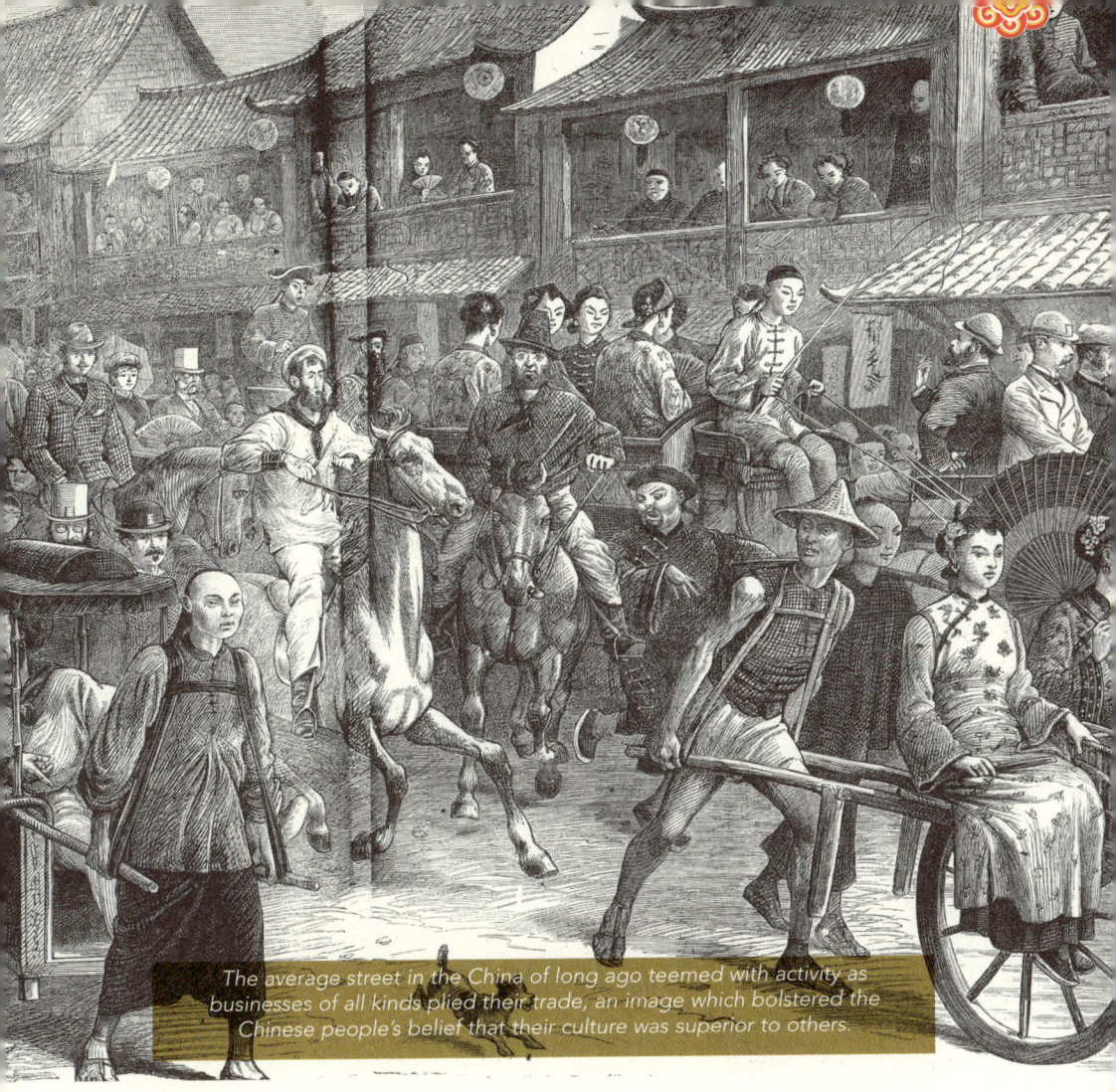

The average street in the China of long ago teemed with activity as businesses of all kinds plied their trade, an image which bolstered the Chinese people's belief that their culture was superior to others.

This Sino-centric attitude was the core of imperial China's diplomatic relationships with its neighbours. Some Asian countries adopted facets of it along with the Sino-Foreigner Dichotomy, including the prioritisation of collectivism, conservatism, organisational hierarchy, strict rules, etiquette and respect for the elderly.

When the Sino-Foreigner Dichotomy was abolished in the 19th century as colonialism swept the world, the Chinese were forced to abandon their notions of superiority. All the same, the idea that rules and lifestyle choices can be used to differentiate ethnic groups lives on.

The Sino-Foreign Relationship in the Business World

When doing business with foreigners, the Chinese usually go to lengths to speak the other party's language or adopt some of their cultural norms. They expect the same courtesy from foreign trade partners in exchange.

The "relationships" that Chinese business people develop with others have much in common with political connections in the Western world. Chinese business is characterised by connections that allows one to ask another for a favour based on their friendship, "face" (*Mian Zi* 面子) or expertise. Naturally, this goes both ways. If someone asks for a favour in the context of a "relationship", they are expected to return it in the future. A favour can be straightforward or a big ask, but the same expectations apply.

Favours can create conflict. A person might be approached by several associates all asking for the same favour. In this case, one must consider the status of those asking for help. In general, it is believed that political power trumps corporate or professional status. The needs of business associates trump personal ones in the name of collectivism. This hierarchy is based on a concept known as the Vicinity of Relationships (*Qin Shu* 親疏) which considers social distance. According to this concept, one can rank people in their social group based on the distance between them and their family.

The usual result of this sorting process is as follows:

Relationships	Vicinity	Priority
Family Member Mentor Emperor	Closest (*Qin* 親)	Highest
Close Friend	Closer (*Qin* 親)	High
Government Official People with the Same Ethnic Background	Far (*Shu* 疏)	High
Acquaintance	Further (*Shu* 疏)	Low
Foreigner Stranger People with Different Ethnic Background	Furthest (*Shu* 疏)	Lowest

As shown in the table above, a complete stranger bears no significance in a "relationship" network. This is not uncommon in Chinese business culture, where social groups are created in accordance with Confucian ethics as well as the Vicinity of Relationships. While this may seem to openly shun foreigners it is largely a private and informal system. A tactful Chinese business person should be frank with their foreign business associate about these customs and ideas and figure out a solution that pleases everyone and adheres to tradition.

Moving Forward, Looking Back

Over the centuries, many Chinese customs have been lost. Others have evolved to keep pace with changes in technology, religion and so on.

In the rush to embrace modernisation and Western culture, many Chinese customs have been diluted or fallen out of favour. A good example of this trend is the fact that Western style weddings are more popular than today's Chinese weddings.

Interestingly, Chinese people who migrate to other countries often bring their traditions with them, adapting them for the culture of their new home. This has led to new variation of old traditions and practices.

Recently there has been a shift towards reclaiming and reviving cultural traditions of the past. An increasing number of couples are now opting again for a traditional Chinese wedding – complete with customs that have not been practised in decades.

The Chinese government has taken steps to help preserve tradition. In January of 2017, it issued guidelines to help preserve and develop traditional culture, for the purpose of stimulating a "marked boost" in the international influence of Chinese culture by 2025. The guidelines are aimed at protecting physical representations of China's history like certain buildings and places as well as intangible parts of it like dialects, literature and music. It is my hope that this book will contribute to the effort to preserve old customs and spread awareness of their origins and true meaning. It is important that we not just keep our customs alive, but that we understand them – otherwise they will become empty, pointless and redundant.

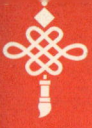

In my own life, I didn't see any value in traditions like the confinement period after my wife gave birth to our beautiful twin daughters. That changed when I did my research and learned about the reasons behind the confinement period. Learning about tradition allows one to see their true significance and benefits and discard those which are no longer relevant or appropriate. It is this kind of understanding and critical thinking that I want to promote with this book.

Once again, I want to clarify that some of the customs which supposedly have their basis in Feng Shui actually do not adhere to real classic Feng Shui principles and core concepts. I feel it is my duty to dispel misconceptions about the connection between Feng Shui and Chinese customs.

Ultimately, it is my wish that everyone will be able to value the richness of Chinese culture and understand the story until now. Furthermore, it is my hope that people will know which practices are still relevant and that they will be able to follow tradition properly and with purpose and fun!

JOEY YAP'S QI MEN DUN JIA
Reference Series

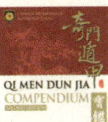 Qi Men Dun Jia **Compendium** Second edition

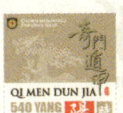 Qi Men Dun Jia **540 Yang Structure**

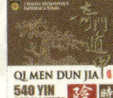 Qi Men Dun Jia **540 Yin Structure**

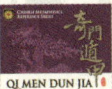 Qi Men Dun Jia **Year Charts**

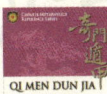 Qi Men Dun Jia **Month Charts**

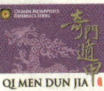 Qi Men Dun Jia **Day Charts**

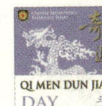 Qi Men Dun Jia **Day Charts** (San Yuan Method)

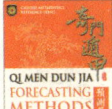 Qi Men Dun Jia **Forecasting Method** (Book 1)

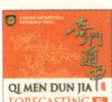 Qi Men Dun Jia **Forecasting Method** (Book 2)

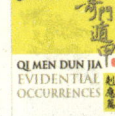 Qi Men Dun Jia **Evidential Occurrences**

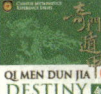 Qi Men Dun Jia **Destiny Analysis**

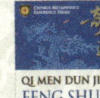 Qi Men Dun Jia **Feng Shui**

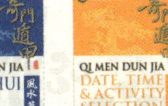 Qi Men Dun Jia **Date, Time & Activity Selection**

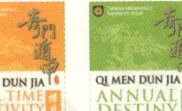 Qi Men Dun Jia **Annual Destiny Analysis**

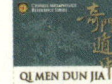 Qi Men Dun Jia **Strategic Executions**

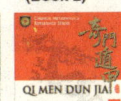 Qi Men Dun Jia **The 100 Formations**

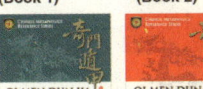 Qi Men Dun Jia **Sun Tzu Warcraft**

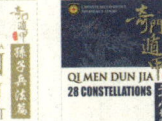 Qi Men Dun Jia **28 Constellations**

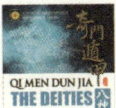 Qi Men Dun Jia **The Deities**

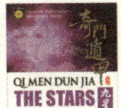 Qi Men Dun Jia **The Stars**

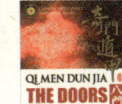 Qi Men Dun Jia **The Doors**

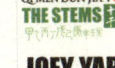 Qi Men Dun Jia **The Stems**

This is the most comprehensive reference series to Qi Men Dun Jia in the Chinese Metaphysics world. Exhaustively written for the purpose of facilitating studies and further research, this collection of reference texts and educational books aims to bridge the gap for students who want to learn, and the teachers who want to teach Qi Men.

These essential references provide practical guidance for all branches under the Qi Men Dun Jia studies including Destiny Analysis, Feng Shui, Strategic Executions and Forecasting method.

These books are available exclusively at:
store.joeyyap.com

Email: order@masteryacademy.com | +6(03) - 2284 8080

JOEY YAP's
QI MEN DUN JIA MASTERY PROGRAM

This is the world's most comprehensive training program on the subject of Qi Men Dun Jia. Joey Yap is the Qi Men Strategist for some of Asia's wealthiest tycoons. This program is modelled after Joey Yap's personal application methods, covering techniques and strategies he applies for his high net worth clients. There is a huge difference between studying the subject as a scholar and learning how to use it successfully as a Qi Men strategist. In this program, Joey Yap shares with you what he personally uses to transform his own life and the lives of million others. In other words, he shares with his students what actually works and not just what looks good in theory with no real practical value. This means that the program covers his personal trade secrets in using the art of Qi Men Dun Jia.

There are five unique programs, with each of them covering one specific application aspect of the Joey Yap's Qi Men Dun Jia system.

Joey Yap's training program focuses on getting results. Theories and formulas are provided in the course workbook so that valuable class time are not wasted dwelling on formulas. Each course comes with its own comprehensive 400-plus pages workbook. Taught once a year exclusively by Joey Yap, seats to these programs are extremely limited.

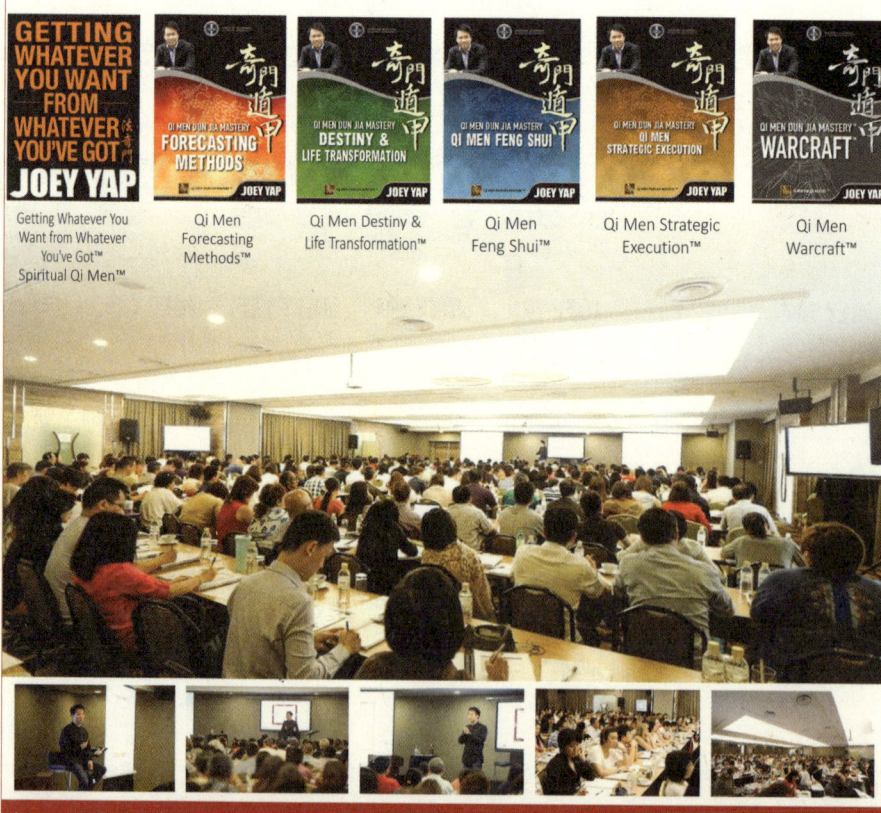

Getting Whatever You Want from Whatever You've Got™ Spiritual Qi Men™ | Qi Men Forecasting Methods™ | Qi Men Destiny & Life Transformation™ | Qi Men Feng Shui™ | Qi Men Strategic Execution™ | Qi Men Warcraft™

Call +6(03) 2284 8080 or
email courses@masteryacademy.com for enquiries

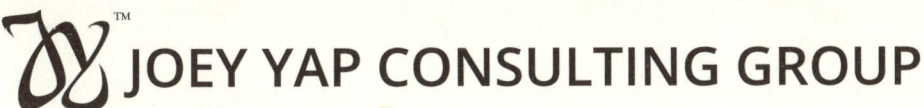

JOEY YAP CONSULTING GROUP

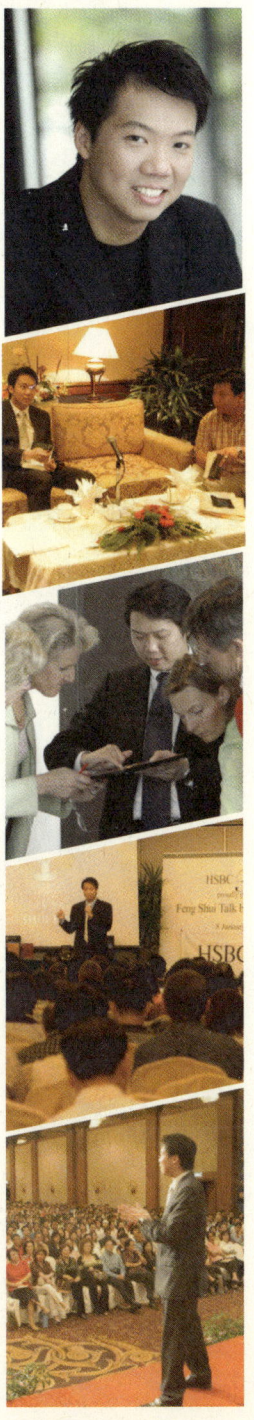

Pioneering Metaphysics-Centric Personal and Corporate Consultations

Founded in 2002, the Joey Yap Consulting Group is the pioneer in the provision of metaphysics-driven coaching and consultation services for professionals and individuals alike. Under the leadership of the renowned international Chinese Metaphysics consultant, author and trainer, Dato' Joey Yap, it has become a world-class specialised metaphysics consulting firm with a strong presence in four continents, meeting the metaphysics-centric needs of its A-list clientele, ranging from celebrities to multinational corporations.

The Group's core consultation practice areas include Feng Shui, BaZi and Qi Men Dun Jia, which are complemented by ancillary services such as Date Selection, Face Reading and Yi Jing. Its team of highly trained professional consultants, led by its Chief Consultant, Dato' Joey Yap, is well-equipped with unparalleled knowledge and experience to help clients achieve their ultimate potentials in various fields and specialisations. Given its credentials, the Group is certainly the firm of choice across the globe for metaphysics-related consultations.

The Peerless Industry Expert

Benchmarked against the standards of top international consulting firms, our consultants work closely with our clients to achieve the best possible outcomes. The possibilities are infinite as our expertise extends from consultations related to the forces of nature under the subject of Feng Shui, to those related to Destiny Analysis and effective strategising under BaZi and Qi Men Dun Jia respectively.

To date, we have consulted a great diversity of clients, ranging from corporate clients – from various industries such as real estate, finance and telecommunication, amongst others – to the hundreds of thousands of individuals in their key life aspects. Adopting up-to-date and pragmatic approaches, we provide comprehensive services while upholding the importance of clients' priorities and effective outcomes. Recognised as the epitome of Chinese Metaphysics, we possess significant testimonies from worldwide clients as a trusted Brand.

www.joeyyap.com | +6(03) - 2284 8080

Feng Shui Consultation

Residential Properties
- Initial Land/Property Assessment
- Residential Feng Shui Consultation
- Residential Land Selection
- End-to-End Residential Consultation

Commercial Properties
- Initial Land/Property Assessment
- Commercial Feng Shui Consultation
- Commercial Land Selection
- End-to-End Commercial Consultation

Property Developers
- End-to-End Consultation
- Post-Consultation Advisory Services
- Panel Feng Shui Consultant

Property Investors
- Your Personal Feng Shui Consultant
- Tailor-Made Packages

Memorial Parks & Burial Sites
- Yin House Feng Shui

BaZi Consultation

Personal Destiny Analysis
- Individual BaZi Analysis
- BaZi Analysis for Families

Strategic Analysis for Corporate Organizations
- BaZi Consultations for Corporations
- BaZi Analysis for Human Resource Management

Entrepreneurs and Business Owners
- BaZi Analysis for Entrepreneurs

Career Pursuits
- BaZi Career Analysis

Relationships
- Marriage and Compatibility Analysis
- Partnership Analysis

General Public
- Annual BaZi Forecast
- Your Personal BaZi Coach

Date Selection Consultation

- Marriage Date Selection
- Caesarean Birth Date Selection
- House-Moving Date Selection
- Renovation and Groundbreaking Dates
- Signing of Contracts
- Official Openings
- Product Launches

Qi Men Dun Jia Consultation

Strategic Execution
- Business and Investment Prospects

Forecasting
- Wealth and Life Pursuits
- People and Environmental Matters

Feng Shui
- Residential Properties
- Commercial Properties

Speaking Engagement

Many reputable organisations and institutions have worked closely with Joey Yap Consulting Group to build a synergistic business relationship by engaging our team of consultants, which are led by Joey Yap, as speakers at their corporate events.

We tailor our seminars and talks to suit the anticipated or pertinent group of audience. Be it department subsidiary, your clients or even the entire corporation, we aim to fit your requirements in delivering the intended message(s) across.

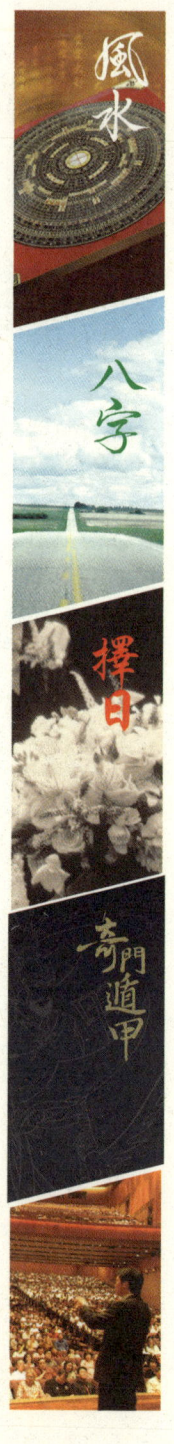

www.joeyyap.com | +6(03) - 2284 8080

CHINESE METAPHYSICS REFERENCE SERIES

The Chinese Metaphysics Reference Series is a collection of reference texts, source material, and educational textbooks to be used as supplementary guides by scholars, students, researchers, teachers and practitioners of Chinese Metaphysics.

These comprehensive and structured books provide fast, easy reference to aid in the study and practice of various Chinese Metaphysics subjects including Feng Shui, BaZi, Yi Jing, Zi Wei, Liu Ren, Ze Ri, Ta Yi, Qi Men Dun Jia and Mian Xiang.

The Chinese Metaphysics Compendium

At over 1,000 pages, the Chinese Metaphysics Compendium is a unique one-volume reference book that compiles ALL the formulas relating to Feng Shui, BaZi (Four Pillars of Destiny), Zi Wei (Purple Star Astrology), Yi Jing (I-Ching), Qi Men (Mystical Doorways), Ze Ri (Date Selection), Mian Xiang (Face Reading) and other sources of Chinese Metaphysics.

It is presented in the form of easy-to-read tables, diagrams and reference charts, all of which are compiled into one handy book. This first-of-its-kind compendium is presented in both English and its original Chinese language, so that none of the meanings and contexts of the technical terminologies are lost.

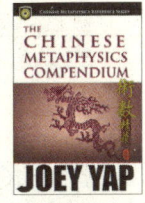

The only essential and comprehensive reference on Chinese Metaphysics, and an absolute must-have for all students, scholars, and practitioners of Chinese Metaphysics.

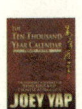 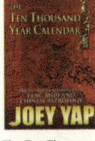 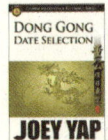 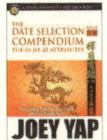 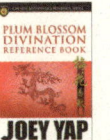 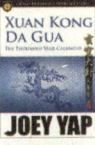 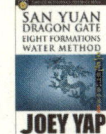

The Ten Thousand Year Calendar (Pocket Edition) | The Ten Thousand Year Calendar | Dong Gong Date Selection | The Date Selection Compendium | Plum Blossoms Divination Reference Book | Xuan Kong Da Gua Ten Thousand Year Calendar | San Yuan Dragon Gate Eight Formations Water Method

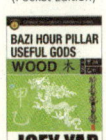 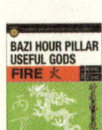 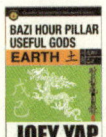 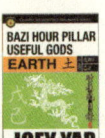 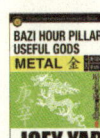 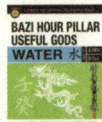 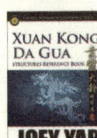 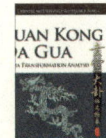

BaZi Hour Pillar Useful Gods - Wood | BaZi Hour Pillar Useful Gods - Fire | BaZi Hour Pillar Useful Gods - Earth | BaZi Hour Pillar Useful Gods - Metal | BaZi Hour Pillar Useful Gods - Water | Xuan Kong Da Gua Structures Reference Book | Xuan Kong Da Gua 64 Gua Transformation Analysis

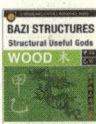 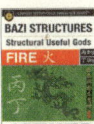 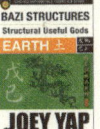 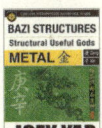 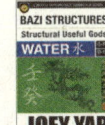 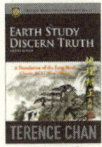 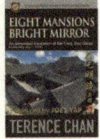

BaZi Structures and Structural Useful Gods - Wood | BaZi Structures and Structural Useful Gods - Fire | BaZi Structures and Structural Useful Gods - Earth | BaZi Structures and Structural Useful Gods - Metal | BaZi Structures and Structural Useful Gods - Water | Earth Study Discern Truth Second Edition | Eight Mansions Bright Mirror

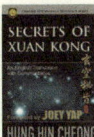 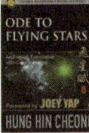 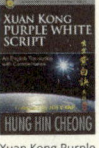 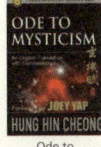 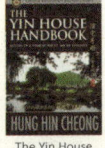 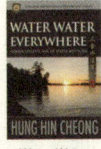 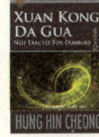

Secret of Xuan Kong | Ode to Flying Stars | Xuan Kong Purple White Script | Ode to Mysticism | The Yin House Handbook | Water Water Everywhere | Xuan Kong Da Gua Not Exactly For Dummies

www.masteryacademy.com | +6(03) - 2284 8080

SAN YUAN QI MEN XUAN KONG DA GUA
Reference Series

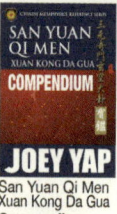 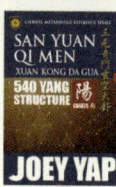 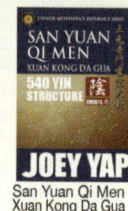 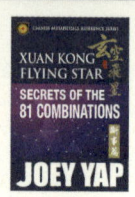

San Yuan Qi Men Xuan Kong Da Gua **Compendium** | San Yuan Qi Men Xuan Kong Da Gua **540 Yang Structure** | San Yuan Qi Men Xuan Kong Da Gua **540 Yin Structure** | Xuan Kong Flying Star **Secrets Of The 81 Combinations**

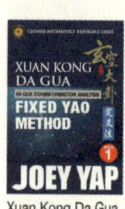 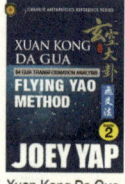 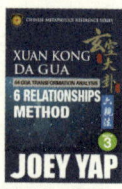 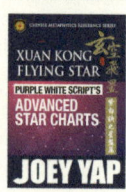

Xuan Kong Da Gua **Fixed Yao Method** | Xuan Kong Da Gua **Flying Yao Method** | Xuan Kong Da Gua **6 Relationships Method** | Xuan Kong Flying Star **Purple White Script's Advanced Star Charts**

The **San Yuan Qi Men Xuan Kong Da Gua Series** is written for the advanced learners in mind. Unlock the secrets to this highly exclusive art and seamlessly integrate both Qi Men Dun Jia and the Xuan Kong Da Gua 64 Hexagrams into one unified practice for effective applications.

This collection is an excellent companion for genuine enthusiasts, students and professional practitioners of the San Yuan Qi Men Xuan Kong Da Gua studies.

Xuan Kong Collection

Xuan Kong Flying Stars

This book is an essential introductory book to the subject of Xuan Kong Fei Xing, a well-known and popular system of Feng Shui. Learn 'tricks of the trade' and 'trade secrets' to enhance and maximise Qi in your home or office.

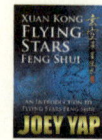

Xuan Kong Nine Life Star Series (Available in English & Chinese versions)

Joey Yap's Feng Shui Essentials - The Xuan Kong Nine Life Star Series of books comprises of nine individual titles that provide detailed information about each individual Life Star.

Based on the complex and highly-evolved Xuan Kong Feng Shui system, each book focuses on a particular Life Star and provides you with a detailed Feng Shui guide.

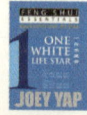 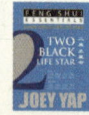 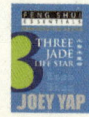 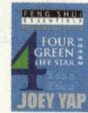 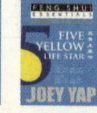 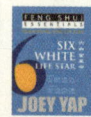 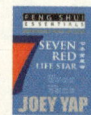 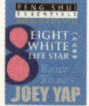 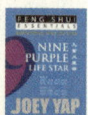

www.masteryacademy.com | +6(03) - 2284 8080

Joey Yap's BaZi Profiling System

Three Levels of BaZi Profiling (English & Chinese versions)

In BaZi Profiling, there are three levels that reflect three different stages of a person's personal nature and character structure.

Level 1 – The Day Master

The Day Master in a nutshell is the basic you. The inborn personality. It is your essential character. It answers the basic question "who am I". There are ten basic personality profiles – the ten Day Masters – each with its unique set of personality traits, likes and dislikes.

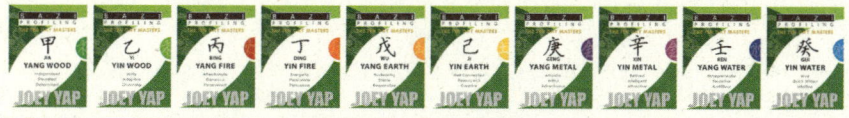

Level 2 – The Structure

The Structure is your behavior and attitude – in other words, it is about how you use your personality. It expands on the Day Master (Level 1). The structure reveals your natural tendencies in life – are you a controller, creator, supporter, thinker or connector? Each of the Ten Day Masters express themselves differently through the five Structures. Why do we do the things we do? Why do we like the things we like? The answers are in our BaZi Structure.

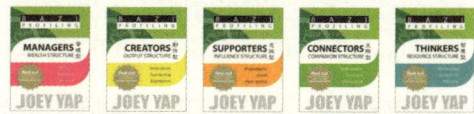

Level 3 – The Profile

The Profile depicts your role in your life. There are ten roles (Ten BaZi Profiles) related to us. As to each to his or her own - the roles we play are different from one another and it is unique to each Profile.

What success means to you, for instance, differs from your friends – this is similar to your sense of achievement or whatever you think of your purpose in life is.

Through the BaZi Profile, you will learn the deeper level of your personality. It helps you become aware of your personal strengths and works as a trigger for you to make all the positive changes to be a better version of you.

Keep in mind, only through awareness that you will be able to maximise your natural talents, abilities and skills. Only then, ultimately, you will get to enter into what we refer as 'flow' of life – a state where you have the powerful force to naturally succeed in life.

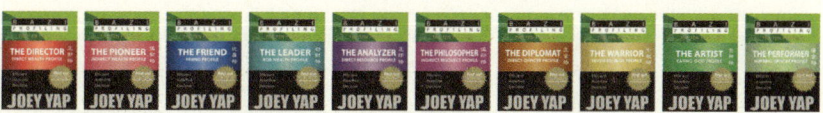

w w w . B a Z i p r o f i l i n g . c o m

THE BaZi 60 PILLARS SERIES

The BaZi 60 Pillars Series is a collection of ten volumes focusing on each of the Pillars or Jia Zi in BaZi Astrology. Learn how to see BaZi Chart in a new light through the Pictorial Method of BaZi analysis and elevate your proficiency in BaZi studies through this new understanding. Joey Yap's 60 Pillars Life Analysis Method is a refined and enhanced technique that is based on the fundamentals set by the true masters of olden times, and modified to fit to the sophistication of current times.

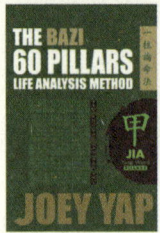 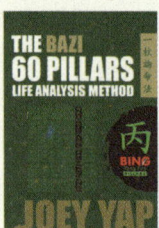 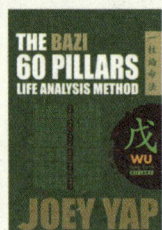 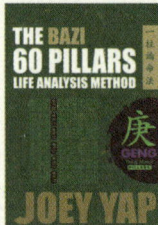 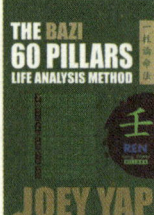
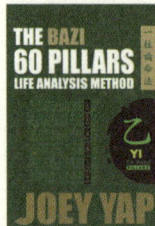 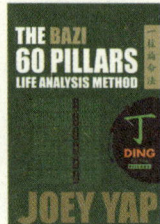 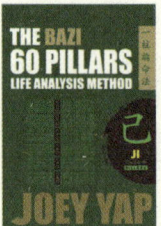 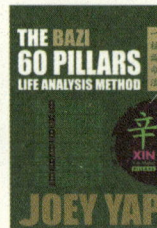 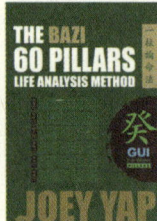

BaZi Collection

With these books, leading Chinese Astrology Master Trainer Joey Yap makes it easy to learn how to unlock your Destiny through your BaZi. BaZi or Four Pillars of Destiny is an ancient Chinese science which enables individuals to understand their personality, hidden talents and abilities, as well as their luck cycle - by examining the information contained within their birth data.

Understand and learn more about this accurate ancient science with this BaZi Collection.

 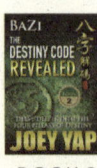 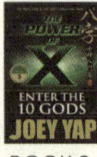 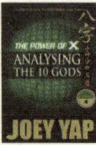 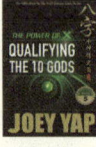 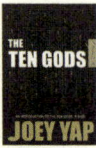

BOOK 1   BOOK 2   BOOK 3   BOOK 4   BOOK 5   The 10 Gods

(Available in English & Chinese)

www.masteryacademy.com | +6(03) - 2284 8080

Feng Shui Collection

Design Your Legacy

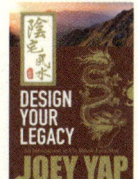

Design Your Legacy is Joey Yap's first book on the profound subject of Yin House Feng Shui, which is the study Feng Shui for burials and tombs. Although it is still pretty much a hidden practice that is largely unexplored by modern literature, the significance of Yin House Feng Shui has permeated through the centuries – from the creation of the imperial lineage of emperors in ancient times to the iconic leaders who founded modern China.

This book unveils the true essence of Yin House Feng Shui with its significant applications that are unlike the myths and superstition which have for years, overshadowed the genuine practice itself. Discover how Yin House Feng Shui – the true precursor to all modern Feng Shui practice, can be used to safeguard the future of your descendants and create a lasting legacy.

Must-Haves for Property Analysis!

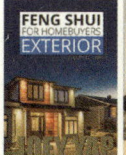 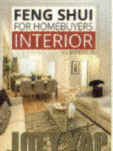 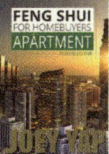

For homeowners, those looking to build their own home or even investors who are looking to apply Feng Shui to their homes, these series of books provides valuable information from the classical Feng Shui therioes and applications.

In his trademark straight-to-the-point manner, Joey shares with you the Feng Shui do's and dont's when it comes to finding a property with favorable Feng Shui, which is condusive for home living.

Stories and Lessons on Feng Shui Series

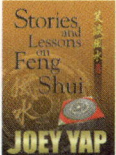 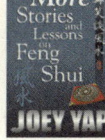 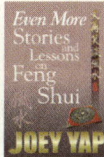

(Available in English & Chinese)

All in all, this series is a delightful chronicle of Joey's articles, thoughts and vast experience - as a professional Feng Shui consultant and instructor - that have been purposely refined, edited and expanded upon to make for a light-hearted, interesting yet educational read. And with Feng Shui, BaZi, Mian Xiang and Yi Jing all thrown into this one dish, there's something for everyone.

More Titles under Joey Yap Books

Pure Feng Shui

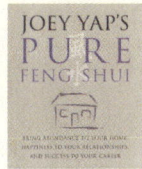

Pure Feng Shui is Joey Yap's debut with an international publisher, CICO Books. It is a refreshing and elegant look at the intricacies of Classical Feng Shui - now compiled in a useful manner for modern day readers. This book is a comprehensive introduction to all the important precepts and techniques of Feng Shui practices.

Your Aquarium Here

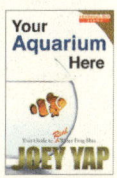

This book is the first in Fengshuilogy Series, which is a series of matter-of-fact and useful Feng Shui books designed for the person who wants to do a fuss-free Feng Shui.

www.masteryacademy.com | +6(03) - 2284 8080

More Titles under Joey Yap Books

Walking the Dragons

Compiled in one book for the first time from Joey Yap's Feng Shui Mastery Excursion Series, the book highlights China's extensive, vibrant history with astute observations on the Feng Shui of important sites and places. Learn the landform formations of Yin Houses (tombs and burial places), as well as mountains, temples, castles and villages.

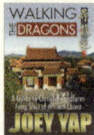

Walking the Dragons : Taiwan Excursion

A Guide to Classical Landform Feng Shui of Taiwan

From China to Tibet, Joey Yap turns his analytical eye towards Taiwan in this extensive Walking the Dragons series. Combined with beautiful images and detailed information about an island once known as Formosa, or "Beautiful Island" in Portuguese, this compelling series of essays highlights the colourful history and wonders of Taiwan. It also provides readers with fascinating insights into the living science of Feng Shui.

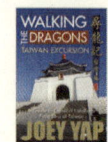

The Art of Date Selection: Personal Date Selection (Available in English & Chinese)

With the Art of Date Selection: Personal Date Selection, you can learn simple, practical methods to select not just good dates, but personalised good dates as well. Whether it is a personal activity such as a marriage or professional endeavour, such as launching a business - signing a contract or even acquiring assets, this book will show you how to pick the good dates and tailor them to suit the activity in question, and to avoid the negative ones too!

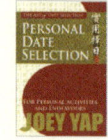

Your Head Here

Your Head Here is the first book by Sherwin Ng. She is an accomplished student of Joey Yap, and an experienced Feng Shui consultant and instructor with Joey Yap Consulting Group and Mastery Academy respectively. It is the second book under the Fengshuilogy series, which focuses on Bedroom Feng Shui, a specific topic dedicated to optimum bed location and placement.

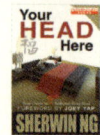

If the Shoe Fits

This book is for those who want to make the effort to enhance their relationship.

In her debut release, Jessie Lee humbly shares with you the classical BaZi method of the Ten Day Masters and the combination of a new profiling system developed by Joey Yap, to understand and deal with the people around you.

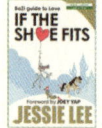

Being Happy and Successful at Work and in your Career

Have you ever wondered why some of us are so successful in our careers while others are dragging their feet to work or switching from one job to another? Janet Yung hopes to answer this question by helping others through the knowledge and application of BaZi and Chinese Astrology. In her debut release, she shares with the readers the right way of using BaZi to understand themselves: their inborn talents, motivations, skills, and passions, to find their own place in the path of professional development.

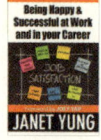

Being Happy & Successful - Managing Yourself & Others

Manage Your Talent & Have Effective Relationships at the Workplace

While many strive for efficiency in the workplace, it is vital to know how to utilize your talents. In this book, Janet Yung will take you further on how to use the BaZi profiling system as a tool to assess your personality and understanding your approach to the job. From ways in communicating with your colleagues to understanding your boss, you will be astounded by what this ancient system can reveal about you and the people in your life. Tips and guidance will also be given in this book so that you will make better decisions for your next step in advancing in your career.

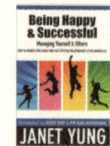

The BaZi Road to Success

The BaZi Road to Success explains your journey in life through a chart that is obtained just from looking at the date you were born and its connection with key BaZi elements.

Your Day Pillar, Hour Pillar, Luck Pillar and Annual Pillar all come together to paint a BaZi chart that churns out a combination of different elements, which the book helps interpret. From relationships, career advice, future plans and possibility of wealth accumulation - this book covers it all!

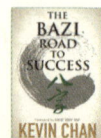

www.masteryacademy.com | +6(03) - 2284 8080

Face Reading Collection

The Chinese Art of Face Reading: The Book of Moles

The Book of Moles by Joey Yap delves into the inner meanings of moles and what they reveal about the personality and destiny of an individual. Complemented by fascinating illustrations and Joey Yap's easy-to-understand commentaries and guides, this book takes a deeper focus into a Face Reading subject, which can be used for everyday decisions – from personal relationships to professional dealings and many others.

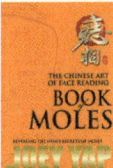

Discover Face Reading (Available in English & Chinese)

This is a comprehensive book on all areas of Face Reading, covering some of the most important facial features, including the forehead, mouth, ears and even philtrum above your lips. This book will help you analyse not just your Destiny but also help you achieve your full potential and achieve life fulfillment.

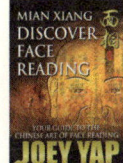

Joey Yap's Art of Face Reading

The Art of Face Reading is Joey Yap's second effort with CICO Books, and it takes a lighter, more practical approach to Face Reading. This book does not focus on the individual features as it does on reading the entire face. It is about identifying common personality types and characters.

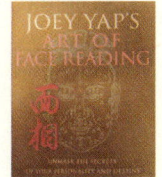

Faces of Fortune 2

We don't need to go far to look for entrepreneurs with the X-Factor. Malaysia produces some of the best entrepreneurs in the world. In this book, we will tell you the rags-to-riches stories of 9 ordinary people who has no special privileges, and how they made it on their own.

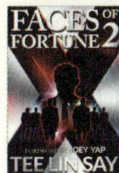

Easy Guide on Face Reading (Available in English & Chinese)

The Face Reading Essentials series of books comprises of five individual books on the key features of the face – the Eyes, the Eyebrows, the Ears, the Nose, and the Mouth. Each book provides a detailed illustration and a simple yet descriptive explanation on the individual types of the features.

The books are equally useful and effective for beginners, enthusiasts and those who are curious. The series is designed to enable people who are new to Face Reading to make the most out of first impressions and learn to apply Face Reading skills to understand the personality and character of their friends, family, co-workers and business associates.

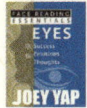 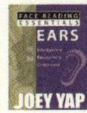 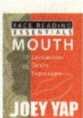 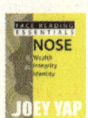 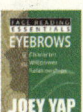 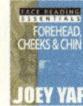 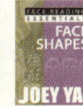 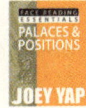 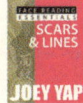 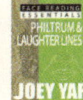

2021 Annual Releases

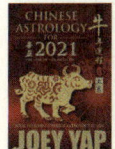 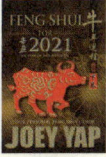 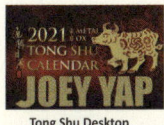 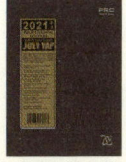 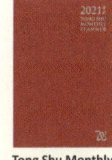 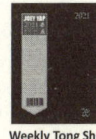

Chinese Astrology for 2021 | Feng Shui for 2021 | Tong Shu Desktop Calendar 2021 | Professional Tong Shu Diary 2021 | Tong Shu Monthly Planner 2021 | Weekly Tong Shu Diary 2021

www.masteryacademy.com | +6(03) - 2284 8080

Cultural Series

Discover the True Significance of the Ancient Art of Lion Dance

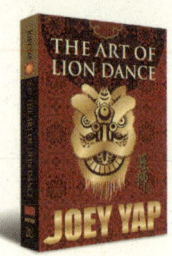

The Lion has long been a symbol of power and strength. That powerful symbol has evolved into an incredible display of a mixture of martial arts and ritualism that is the Lion Dance. Throughout ancient and modern times, the Lion Dance has stamped itself as a popular part of culture, but is there a meaning lost behind this magnificent spectacle?

The Art of Lion Dance written by the world's number one man in Chinese Metaphysics, Dato' Joey Yap, explains the history and origins of the art and its connection to Qi Men Dun Jia. By creating that bridge with Qi Men, the Lion Dance is able to ritualise any type of ceremony, celebrations and mourning alike.

The book is the perfect companion to the modern interpretation of the art as it reveals the significance behind each part of the Lion costume, as well as rituals that are put in place to bring the costume and its spectacle to life.

Chinese Traditions & Practices

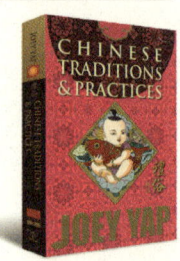

China has a long, rich history spanning centuries. As Chinese culture has evolved over the centuries, so have the country's many customs and traditions. Today, there's a Chinese custom for just about every important event in a person's life – from cradle to the grave.

Although many China's customs have survived to the present day, some have been all but forgotten: rendered obsolete by modern day technology. This book explores the history of Chinese traditions and cultural practices, their purpose, and the differences between the traditions of the past and their modern incarnations.

If you are a westerner or less informed about Chinese culture, you may find this book particularly useful, especially when it comes to doing business with the Chinese – whether it be in China itself or some other country with a considerable Chinese population. If anything, it will allow you to have a better casual understanding of the culture and traditions of your Chinese friends or acquaintances. An understanding of Chinese traditions leads to a more informed, richer appreciation of Chinese culture and China itself.

Educational Tools and Software

Joey Yap's Feng Shui Template Set

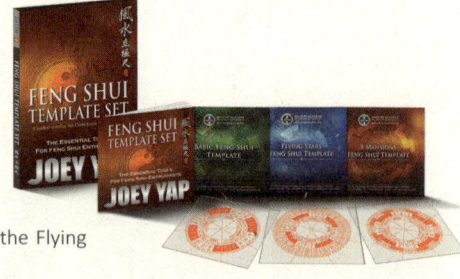

Directions are the cornerstone of any successful Feng Shui audit or application. The Joey Yap Feng Shui Template Set is a set of three templates to simplify the process of taking directions and determining locations and positions, whether it is for a building, a house, or an open area such as a plot of land - all of it done with just a floor plan or area map.

The Set comprises three basic templates: The Basic Feng Shui Template, Eight Mansions Feng Shui Template, and the Flying Stars Feng Shui Template.

Mini Feng Shui Compass

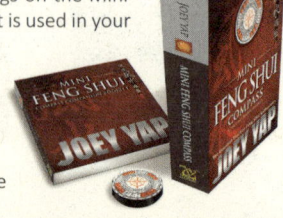

The Mini Feng Shui Compass is a self-aligning compass that is not only light at 100gms but also built sturdily to ensure it will be convenient to use anywhere. The rings on the Mini Feng Shui Compass are bilingual and incorporate the 24 Mountain Rings that is used in your traditional Luo Pan.

The comprehensive booklet included with this, will guide you in applying the 24 Mountain Directions on your Mini Feng Shui Compass effectively and the Eight Mansions Feng Shui to locate the most auspicious locations within your home, office and surroundings. You can also use the Mini Feng Shui Compass when measuring the direction of your property for the purpose of applying Flying Stars Feng Shui.

MASTERY ACADEMY
OF CHINESE METAPHYSICS

Your **Preferred** Choice to the Art & Science of Classical Chinese Metaphysics Studies

Bringing **innovative** techniques and **creative** teaching methods to an ancient study.

Mastery Academy of Chinese Metaphysics was established by Joey Yap to play the role of disseminating this Eastern knowledge to the modern world with the belief that this valuable knowledge should be accessible to everyone and everywhere.

Its goal is to enrich people's lives through accurate, professional teaching and practice of Chinese Metaphysics knowledge globally. It is the first academic institution of its kind in the world to adopt the tradition of Western institutions of higher learning - where students are encouraged to explore, question and challenge themselves, as well as to respect different fields and branches of studies. This is done together with the appreciation and respect of classical ideas and applications that have stood the test of time.

The Art and Science of Chinese Metaphysics – be it Feng Shui, BaZi (Astrology), Qi Men Dun Jia, Mian Xiang (Face Reading), ZeRi (Date Selection) or Yi Jing – is no longer a field shrouded with mystery and superstition. In light of new technology, fresher interpretations and innovative methods, as well as modern teaching tools like the Internet, interactive learning, e-learning and distance learning, anyone from virtually any corner of the globe, who is keen to master these disciplines can do so with ease and confidence under the guidance and support of the Academy.

It has indeed proven to be a centre of educational excellence for thousands of students from over thirty countries across the world; many of whom have moved on to practice classical Chinese Metaphysics professionally in their home countries.

At the Academy, we believe in enriching people's lives by empowering their destinies through the disciplines of Chinese Metaphysics. Learning is not an option - it is a way of life!

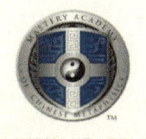

MALAYSIA
19-3, The Boulevard, Mid Valley City, 59200 Kuala Lumpur, Malaysia
Tel : +6(03)-2284 8080 | Fax : +6(03)-2284 1218
Email : info@masteryacademy.com
Website : www.masteryacademy.com

Australia, Austria, Canada, China, Croatia, Cyprus, Czech Republic, Denmark, France, Germany, Greece, Hungary, India, Italy, Kazakhstan, Malaysia, Netherlands (Holland), New Zealand, Philippines, Poland, Russian Federation, Singapore, Slovenia, South Africa, Switzerland, Turkey, United States of America, Ukraine, United Kingdom

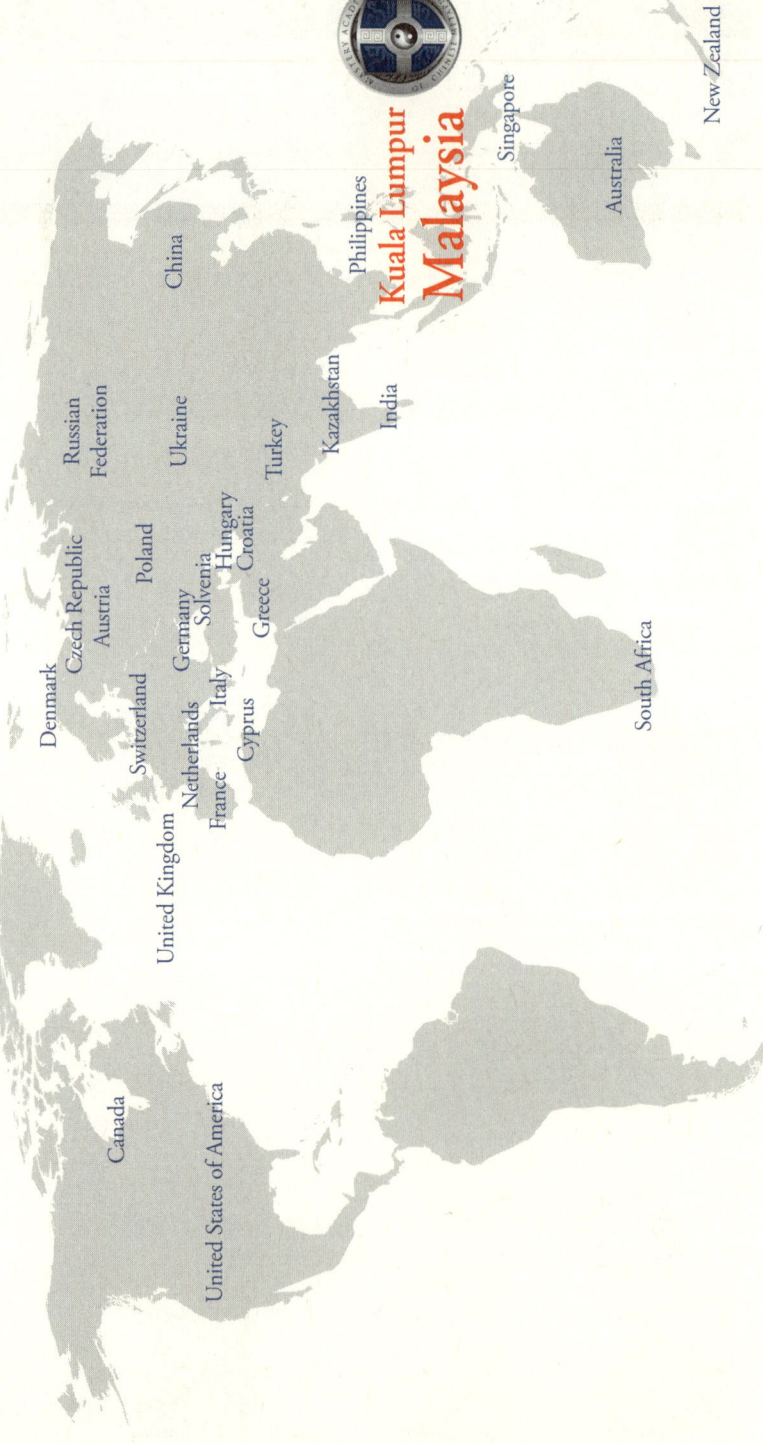

Feng Shui Mastery™
LIVE COURSES (MODULES ONE TO FOUR)

This an ideal program for those who wants to achieve mastery in Feng Shui from the comfort of their homes. This comprehensive program covers the foundation up to the advanced practitioner levels, touching upon the important theories from various classical Feng Shui systems including Ba Zhai, San Yuan, San He and Xuan Kong.

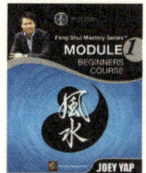 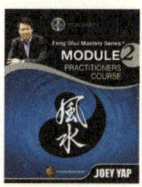 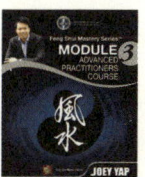 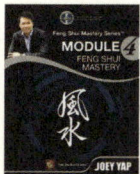

Module One: Beginners Course

Module Two: Practitioners Course

Module Three: Advanced Practitioners Course

Module Four: Master Course

BaZi Mastery™
LIVE COURSES (MODULES ONE TO FOUR)

This lesson-based program brings a thorough introduction to BaZi and guides the student step-by-step, all the way to the professional practitioner level. From the theories to the practical, BaZi students along with serious Feng Shui practitioners, can master its application with accuracy and confidence.

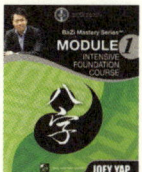 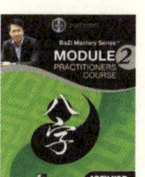 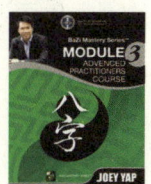 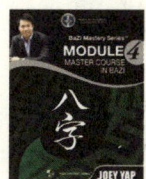

Module One: Intensive Foundation Course

Module Two: Practitioners Course

Module Three: Advanced Practitioners Course

Module Four: Master Course in BaZi

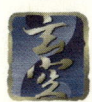
Xuan Kong Mastery™
LIVE COURSES (MODULES ONE TO THREE)
* Advanced Courses For Master Practitioners

Xuan Kong is a sophisticated branch of Feng Shui, replete with many techniques and formulae, which encompass numerology, symbology and the science of the Ba Gua, along with the mathematics of time. This program is ideal for practitioners looking to bring their practice to a more in-depth level.

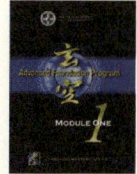 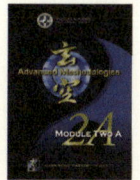 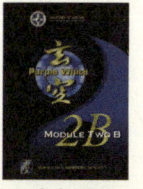 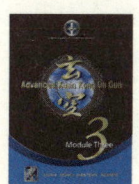

Module One: Advanced Foundation Course

Module Two A: Advanced Xuan Kong Methodologies

Module Two B: Purple White

Module Three: Advanced Xuan Kong Da Gua

www.masteryacademy.com | +6(03) - 2284 8080

Mian Xiang Mastery™
LIVE COURSES (MODULES ONE AND TWO)

This program comprises of two modules, each carefully developed to allow students to familiarise with the fundamentals of Mian Xiang or Face Reading and the intricacies of its theories and principles. With lessons guided by video lectures, presentations and notes, students are able to understand and practice Mian Xiang with greater depth.

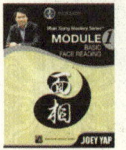

Module One:
Basic Face Reading

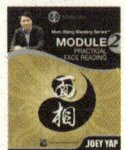

Module Two:
Practical Face Reading

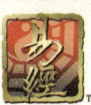

Yi Jing Mastery™
LIVE COURSES (MODULES ONE AND TWO)

Whether you are a casual or serious Yi Jing enthusiast, this lesson-based program contains two modules that brings students deeper into the Chinese science of divination. The lessons will guide students on the mastery of its sophisticated formulas and calculations to derive answers to questions we pose.

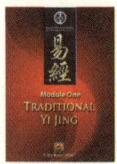

Module One:
Traditional Yi Jing

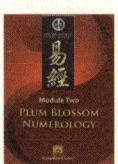

Module Two:
Plum Blossom Numerology

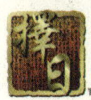

Ze Ri Mastery™
LIVE COURSES (MODULES ONE AND TWO)

In two modules, students will undergo a thorough instruction on the fundamentals of ZeRi or Date Selection. The comprehensive program covers Date Selection for both Personal and Feng Shui purposes to Xuan Kong Da Gua Date Selection.

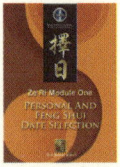

Module One:
Personal and Feng Shui Date Selection

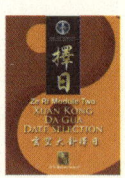

Module Two:
Xuan Kong Da Gua Date Selection

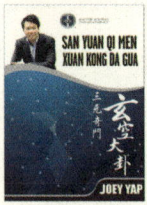

Joey Yap's
San Yuan Qi Men Xuan Kong Da Gua™

This is an advanced level program which can be summed up as the Integral Vision of San Yuan studies – an integration of the ancient potent discipline of Qi Men Dun Jia and the highly popular Xuan Kong 64 Hexagrams. Often regarded as two independent systems, San Yuan Qi Men and San Yuan Xuan Kong Da Gua can trace their origins to the same source and were actually used together in ancient times by great Chinese sages.

This method enables practitioners to harness the Qi of time and space, and predict the outcomes through a highly-detailed analysis of landforms, places and sites.

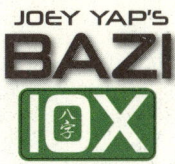

BaZi 10X

Emphasising on the practical aspects of BaZi, this programme is rich with numerous applications and techniques pertaining to the pursuit of wealth, health, relationship and career, all of which constitute the formula of success. This programme is designed for all levels of practitioners and is supplemented with innovative learning materials to enable easy learning. Discover the different layers of BaZi from a brand new perspective with BaZi 10X.

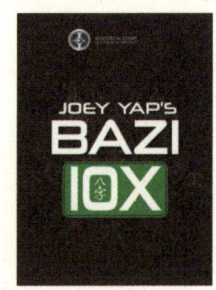

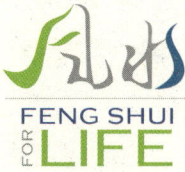

Feng Shui for Life

This is an entry-level five-day course designed for the Feng Shui beginner to learn the application of practical Feng Shui in day-to-day living. Lessons include quick tips on analysing the BaZi chart, simple Feng Shui solutions for the home, basic Date Selection, useful Face Reading techniques and practical Water formulas. A great introduction course on Chinese Metaphysics studies for beginners.

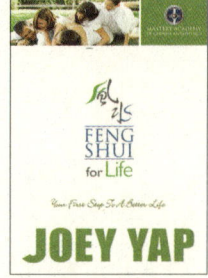

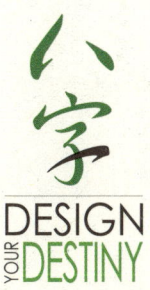

Joey Yap's Design Your Destiny

This is a three-day life transformation program designed to inspire awareness and action for you to create a better quality of life. It introduces the DRT™ (Decision Referential Technology) method, which utilises the BaZi Personality Profiling system to determine the right version of you, and serves as a tool to help you make better decisions and achieve a better life in the least resistant way possible, based on your Personality Profile Type.

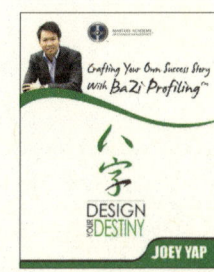

Millionaire Feng Shui Secrets Programme

This program is geared towards maximising your financial goals and dreams through the use of Feng Shui. Focusing mainly on the execution of Wealth Feng Shui techniques such as Luo Shu sectors and more, it is perfect for boosting careers, businesses and investment opportunities.

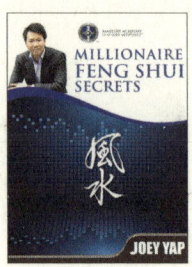

Grow Rich With BaZi Programme

This comprehensive programme covers the foundation of BaZi studies and presents information from the career, wealth and business standpoint. This course is ideal for those who want to maximise their wealth potential and live the life they deserve. Knowledge gained in this course will be used as driving factors to encourage personal development towards a better future.

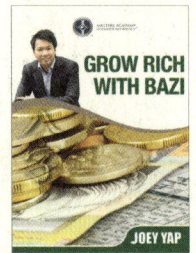

Walk the Mountains!
Learn Feng Shui in a Practical and Hands-on Program

 Feng Shui Mastery Excursion™

Learn landform (Luan Tou) Feng Shui by walking the mountains and chasing the Dragon's vein in China. This program takes the students in a study tour to examine notable Feng Shui landmarks, mountains, hills, valleys, ancient palaces, famous mansions, houses and tombs in China. The excursion is a practical hands-on course where students are shown to perform readings using the formulas they have learnt and to recognise and read Feng Shui Landform (Luan Tou) formations.

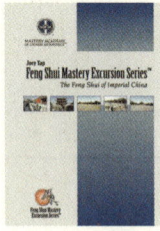

Read about the China Excursion here:
http://www.fengshuiexcursion.com

Mastery Academy courses are conducted around the world. Find out when will Joey Yap be in your area by visiting

www.masteryacademy.com

or call our offices at **+6(03)-2284 8080**.